Chalkis Aitolias III

Chalkis Aitolias III

The Emporion. Fortification systems at Aghia Triada and the Late Classical and Hellenistic habitation in AREA III. The fortifications at Pangali

Edited by

Søren Dietz and Lazaros Kolonas

Monographs of the Danish Institute at Athens,
Volume 7.3

Chalkis Aitolias III

Monographs of the Danish Institute at Athens. Volume 7.3

Typeset and printed by Narayana Press, Denmark
Cover design by Erik Hallager
Cover illustration: The valley of Aghia Triada
– the Gulf and Peleponnese in the background.
From the diary of Kaj Strand Petersen.
Printed in Denmark 2016

ISBN 978 87 7124 997 2
ISSN 1397 1433

AARHUS UNIVERSITY PRESS
Langelandsgade 177
DK-8200 Aarhus N
www.unipress.dk

Gazelle Book Services Ltd.
White Cross Mills, Hightown
Lancaster LA1 4XS
England
www.gazellebooks.com

ISD
70 Enterprise Drive
Bristol, CT 06010
USA
www.isdistribution.com

The publication was sponsored by
Consul General Gösta Enboms Foundation

MIX
Paper from responsible sources
FSC® C010651

Contents

General Introduction

Søren Dietz and Lazaros Kolonas

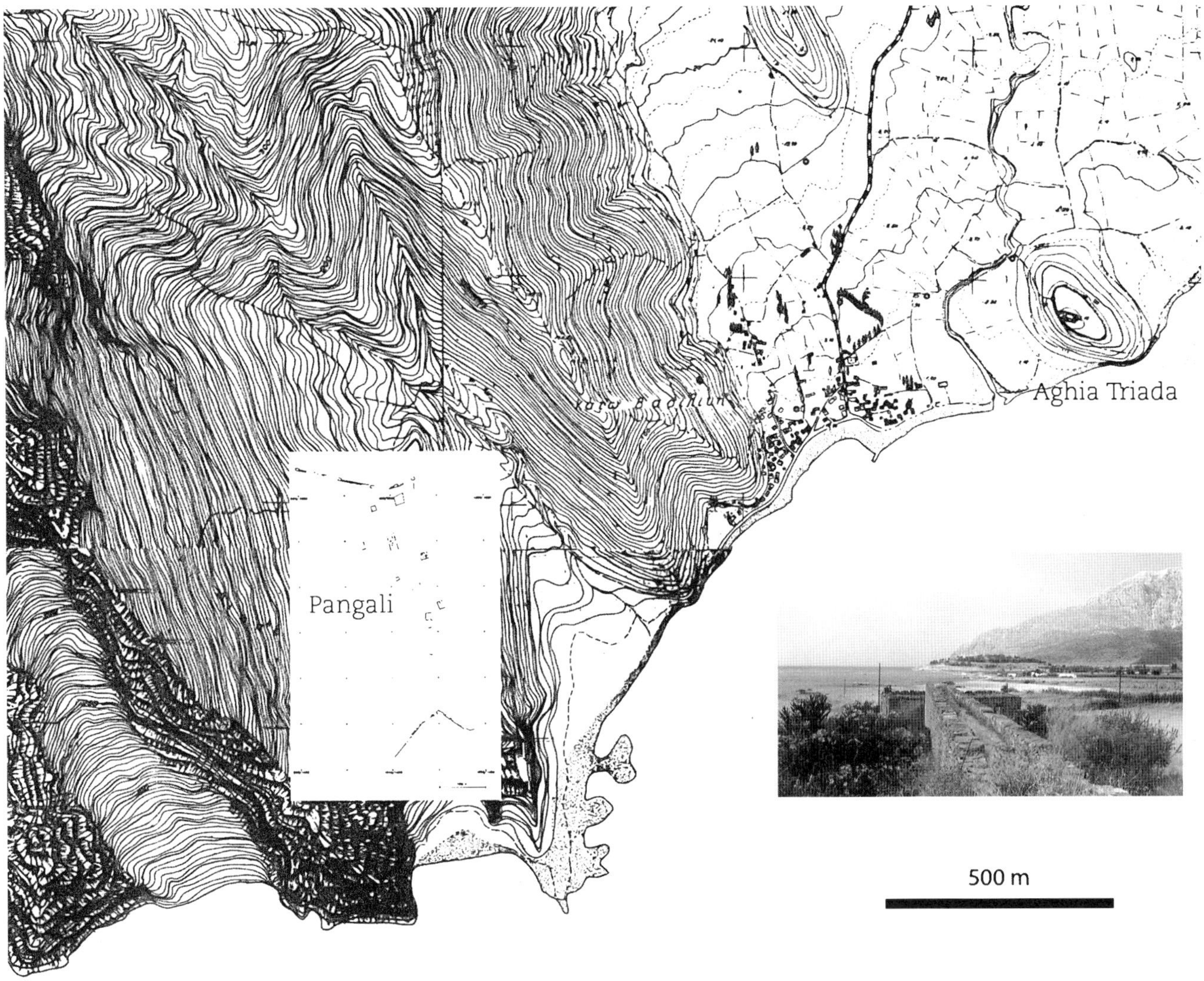

Fig. 1 *Chalkis Aitolias. The area around Kato Vasiliki with the mound of Aghia Triada and the Pangali terrace. Photo showing the hill of Aghia Triada in the middle distance, seen from East. The mountain of Varassova is in the background with the site of Pangali invisible on the lower ridge behind Aghia Triada. (Map after Hellenic Military Geographical Service).*

The present volume is the third and final report of the Danish/Greek archaeological field work in Chalkis Aitolias near the present-day village of Kato Vasiliki, between Mesolonghi and Naupaktos on the south coast of Aitolia.[1] Excavations were implemented at

1 The name "Chalkis Aitolias" was suggested by Professor Richard Tomlinson of Birmingham. For Chalkis in ancient written sources and modern travel accounts see Sanne Houby-Nielsen in *FPR*, 238-254. The Prehistoric Periods on Aghia Triada and Pangali are treated in *Chalkis Aitolias I: The Prehistoric Periods* (2006). Søren Dietz & Ioannis Moschos (eds.), while the important and extensive Archaic habitation is treated by Sanne Houby-Nielsen in *Chalkis Aitolias II* (forthcoming).

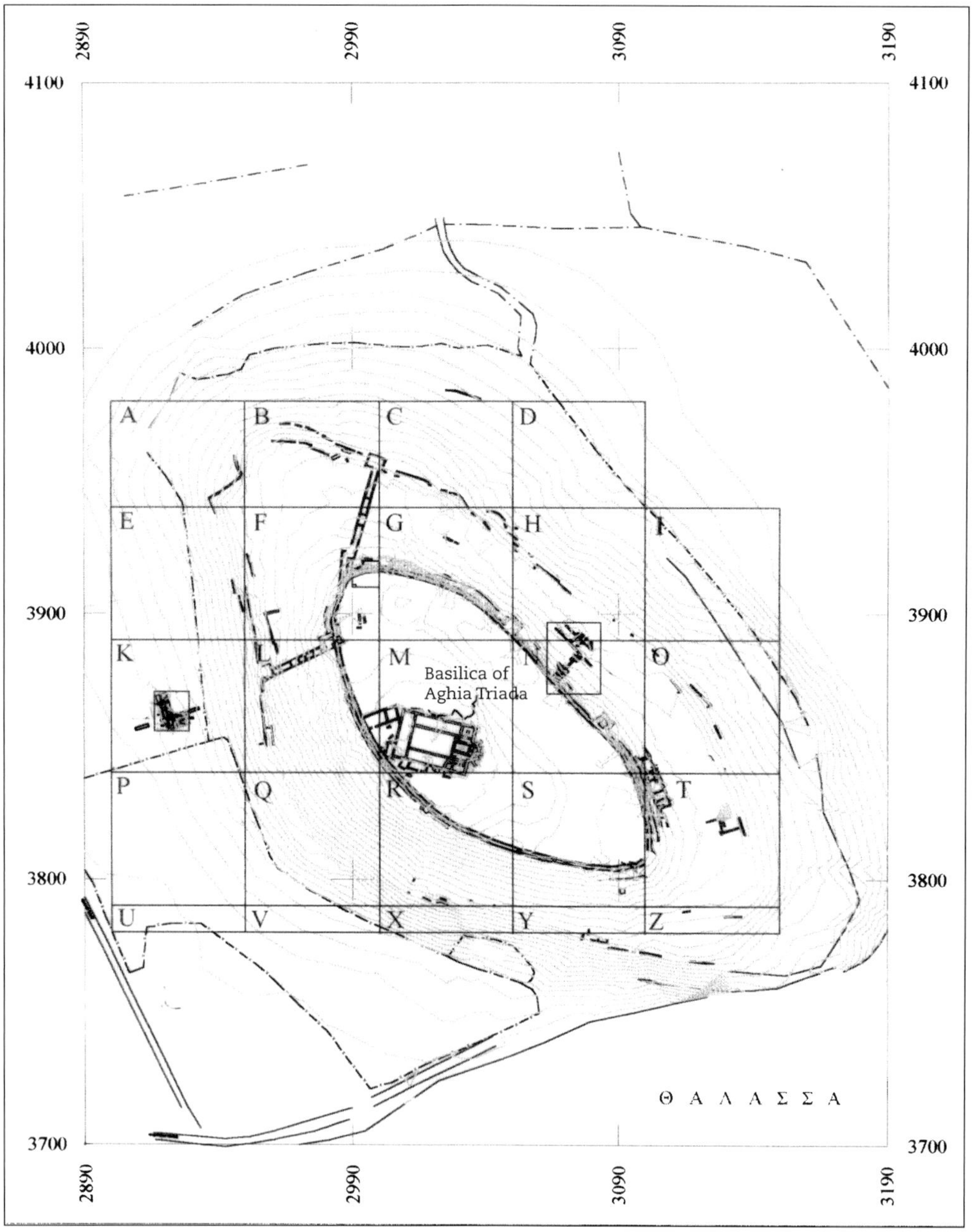

Fig. 2. *Aghia Triada and its surroundings, showing its division into 50 × 50 m squares identified by letters A-Z which were used in trench names, and also the larger topographic grid (1999 status). (Note that this excavation grid does not follow the topografic grit system).*

Aghia Triada from the end of June to the end of July in seven campaigns from 1995 to 2001. It is the opinion of the editors that the main site of Chalkis mentioned by Thucydides, Strabon and others[2] should be identified as the hill of Aghia Triada to the east of Kato Vasiliki, not at Pangali c. 2 km to the west on the lower slope of Mt Varassova, as suggested by some previous scholars.[3] We have not been able to substantiate the idea forwarded by the late Professor Paliouras that a stadium was situated on the Eastern side of the Aghia Triada mound.[4]

Chalkis Aitolias III focuses on the dating, construction and re-construction of the considerable terrace-and fortification walls on Aghia Triada and the extensive excavations of the Late Classical and early Hellenistic workshops and storerooms on the north-east side of the mound. The possibility, in 2014, of conducting ge-

2 See Houby-Nielsen in *FPR*.

3 K. Rhomaios promoted the idea already in 1916. See also *Paliouras* 2004.

4 2004, 414 et al.

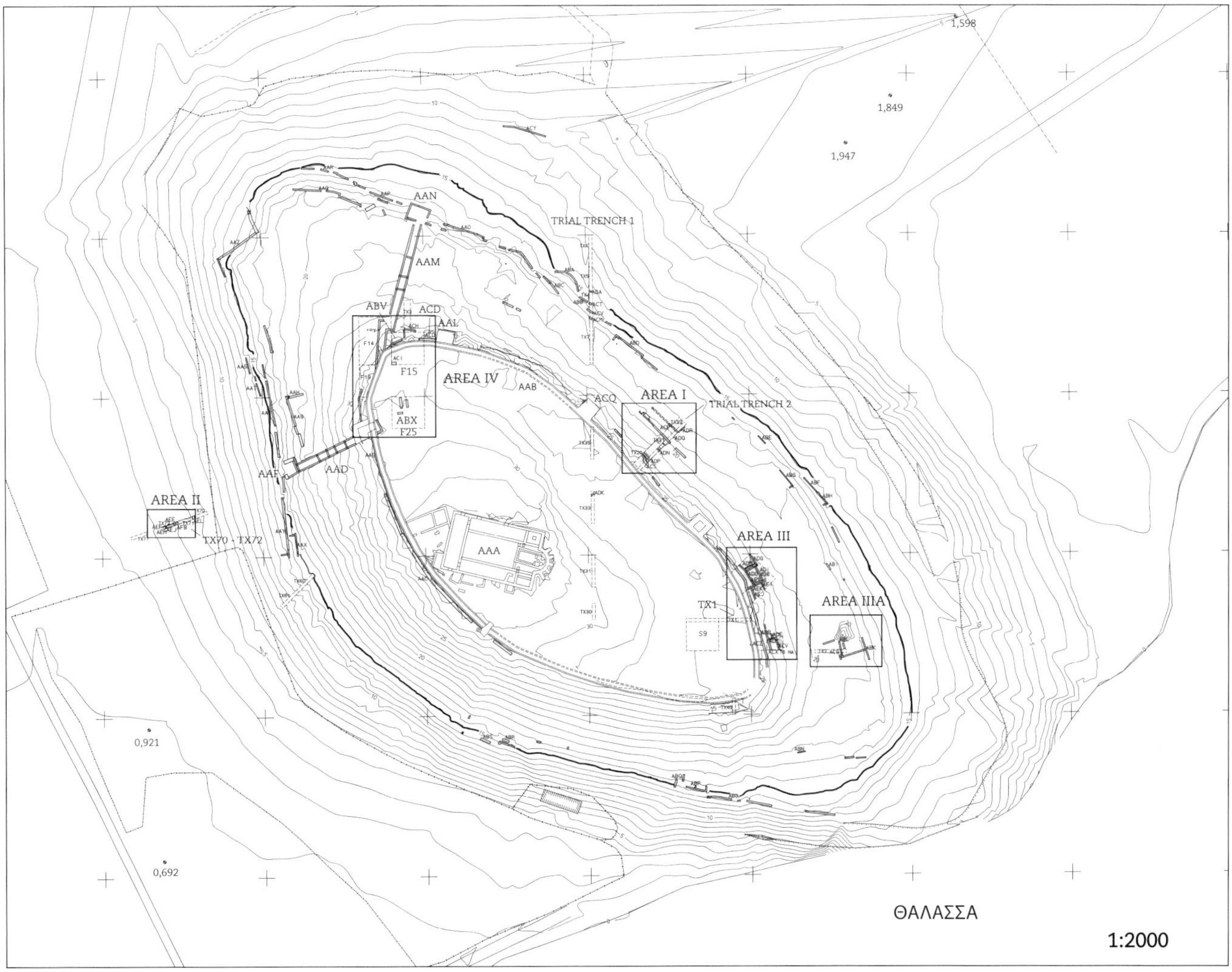

Fig. 3. *The mound of Aghia Triada with areas excavated (only the most important trial trenches are indicated) (1998 campaign status)(15 m contour emphasized).*

omagnetic surveys in the flat, alluvial area between the Aghia Triada mound and the village of Kato Vasiliki, increased our understanding of the topography and function of the ancient Emporion of Chalkis Aitolias from the Early Archaic period to the end of habitation around 200 BC.

The Late Classical fortifications on Pangali are well-preserved and were well-known from the late 19th century. The walls, studied and drawn by the architect Mette Mouritzen, are included in this volume (Chapter D).

Terminology (The terminology is described in *Chalkis Aitolias* I, 35-36)

Grids

The mound of Aghia Triada and its surroundings was divided into 50 × 50 m. squares identified by capital letters from A to Z. Trench numbers begin with the square number in which the trench is located, followed by a running number. This system is depicted on Fig. 2.[5] However, a more extensive topographical grid is also widely used to identify locations across the area. This metric grid has its origin (zero point) c. 1.5 km SW of Pangali, and the figures are shown where possible along the edges of the main site plans (as on Fig. 3).

5 See also *Chalkis Aitolias I*, fig. 7.

Areas[6]

The areas within which the main excavations were conducted are indicated on Fig. 3 as Areas I-IV. AREA I: half way along the NE side of the Byzantine wall, was excavated during the campaigns of 1997-2000 (including trial trenches and trenches N26 to N28) (SRP, 235-238 and *TRP* 175-182). AREA II: some 50 m SW of the W end of the Byzantine circuit, was excavated 1998-2001 (*SPR*, 235-238 and TPR 182-188. See also *Chalkis Aitolias* II passim). AREA III: at the S end of the NE side of the Byzantine wall was excavated in 1997-98 (*SPR* 241-247) and 1999 to 2000 (A full report on the excavations in AREA III is presented below, chapter C). AREA IIIA: to the E of AREA III was a restricted sounding was out in 1996. AREA IV at the NW end of the Byzantine circuit was excavated in 1996 (*FPR* 282 ff and below p 55).

Trial trenches

In addition a series of trial trenches were dug in order to investigate the use of the area in Antiquity.[7] These are identified by Tx followed by a running number. However, where a series of trial trenches were dug along one line, they are commonly identified by a linking name. Thus TRIAL TRENCH 1 Is the common name for the series of 1 meter wide trial trenches Tx 4-7 and Tx 30-35. It measures 120 metres from north to south, and was excavated in the 1997-1998 campaigns (although not all sections were excavated).[8] TRIAL TRENCH 2 consists of various trial trenches (Tx 20-22 and Tx 41-43) placed perpendicular to the Byzantine wall in AREA I[9] were Excavated in campaigns 1997-1998 with a further three (Tx 91-93) opened in 1999-2000. TRIAL TRENCH Tx 1 is a 1 metre wide trench excavated behind the Byzantine wall in AREA III.[10] The section and the material excavated in Tx 1 are studied below (p 103). Tx 70-72 excavated in 1998 West of Aghia Triada.[11]

Find numbers consist of the last two digits of the relevant year, followed by a running number.

Note:

'Grid north. The north arrows on Figs 13 and 21 show that grid north on the Chalkis topographical grid is c. 4° west of magnetic north. Since true north (or geographical north) is 2-3° west of magnetic north in Greece (magnetic north varies with place and year), this implies that Chalkis grid north is 1-2° west of true north, coinciding more or less closely with north according to the Greek national co-ordinate system EGSA 87 (c. 1.8° west of true north). (Note. For magnetic variation see the text on the map of Πάρνηθα *Parnitha*, Athens. The angle between true north and EGSA 87 north was measured on grid line 290000E on the map Ευρυτανικά βουνά, *Mountains of Evritania* (scale 1:50.000). Anavasi, Topo50 map 2.4/2.5, Athens, 2009. However, it has not been possible to check the orientation of the Chalkis grid precisely, and topographical work associated with the magnetic survey in 2014 suggests that there may be an angle of about 1.5° (E or W?) between the two systems (see below, ch. A2).'

Acknowledgement

The editors are greatly indebted to the Consul General Gösta Enboms Foundation who sponsored the excavations at Aghia Triada and Pangali and the publication of the present volume. In addition we are most grateful to Elizabeth Bollen who revised the English text and made many useful suggestions and to Jim Coulton who contributed with many constructive ideas.

Athens, July 2016
Søren Dietz and Lazaros Kolonas

6 *Chalkis Aitolias I*, 35.
7 The more important main trenches and trial trenches are depicted on Fig. 3. The trial trenches are described in *SPR*, 232 ff.
8 *FPR* 232 ff.
9 See below and FPR 235 ff.
10 *SRP* 285-286, section 3830 N, Fig. 24.
11 *SPR* 238-240.

Abbreviations

General abbreviations:

m.a.s.: metres above sea level
Measurements
m – metre/metres
cm – centimeter
g – gramme
D – diameter
H – height
L – length
Th – Thickness
W – Width
We – Weight

Pottery types
FW = Fine ware
PW = Plain ware
CPW = Cooking pot ware
CW = Coarse ware

Periods
GE: Geometric
AR: Archaic
CL: Classic
HL: Hellenistic
RO: Roman

Excavation terms

Str: Stratum
Tr: Trench

Bibliography

Bibliographical Abbreviations:

(For periodicals we follow abbreviations used by the *American Journal of Archaeology*)

PDIA
Proceedings of the Danish Institute at Athens

KALYDON 2011
Dietz, S. & M. Stavropoulou-Gatsi (eds.)
Kalydon in Aitolia I. Reports and Studies. Danish/Greek Field Work 2001-2005
Kalydon in Aitolia II. Catalogues. Danish/Greek Field Work 2001-2005

Chalkis Aitolias I
Dietz, S. & I. Moschos (eds.) 2006
Chalkis Aitolias I. The Prehistoric Periods.

Chalkis Aitolias II
Houby-Nielsen, S. (forthcoming)
Chalkis Aitolias II. The Archaic Period (S. Dietz ed.)

FPR
Dietz, S., L. Kolonas, I. Moschos and Houby-Nielsen, S. "Surveys and Excavations in Chalkis, Aetolias, 1995-1996. First preliminary report", *PDIA* II (1998), 232-317.

SPR
Dietz, S., S. Houby-Nielsen, L. Kolonas, I. Moschos, 'Greek-Danish Excavations at Aetolian Chalkis 1997-1998. Second Preliminary Report', *PDIA* III (2000), 219-289.

TPR
Dietz, S., L. Kolonas, S. Houby-Nielsen, I. Moschos and J. Eiring, 'Greek-Danish Excavations at Aetolian Chalkis 1999-2001. Third Preliminary Report', *PDIA* IV (2002), 167-259.

The Athenian Agora: *The Athenian Agora: Results of excavations conducted by the American School of Classical Studies*, Princeton.

Corinth: Results of Excavations conducted by the American School of Classical Studies at Athens. Princeton.

Β' ΕλλΚερ 1990
Β' Επιστημονική Συνάντηση για την Ελληνιστική Κεραμική, Athens.

Γ' ΕλλΚερ 1994
Γ' Επιστημονική Συνάντηση για την Ελληνιστική Κεραμική, Athens.

Δ' ΕλλΚερ 1997
Δ' Επιστημονική Συνάντηση για την Ελληνιστική Κεραμική, Athens.

Ε' ΕλλΚερ 2000
Ε' Επιστημονική Συνάντηση για την Ελληνιστική Κεραμική, Athens.

ΕλλΚερ Θεσσαλία 2000
Ελληνιστική Κεραμική από τη Θεσσαλία, Volos.

ΣΤ' ΕλλΚερ 2004
ΣΤ' Επιστημονική Συνάντηση για την Ελληνιστική Κεραμική, Athens.

Ζ' ΕλλΚερ (forthcoming)
Ζ' Επιστημονική Συνάντηση για την Ελληνιστική Κεραμική, Athens.

Bibliography

Adam, J.P. 1982
L'architecture militaire grecque, Paris.

Adam Veleni, P., P. Georgaki and H. Zografou 2004
"Σκύφοι και πινάκα από την αρχαία αγορά Θεσσαλονίκης", ΣΤ' ΕλλΚερ 2004, 185-192.

Adrimi-Sismani, B. 2000
"Ταφικά σύνολα από το Δυτικό νεκροταφείο των Φθιωτίδων Θηβών", *ΕλλΚερ Θεσσαλία 2000*, Volos, 133-146.

Alexandropoulou, A. 2002
Gnathia- und Westabhangkeramik. Eine vergleichende Betrachtung, Münster.

Alexopoulou, G. 1999
"Ναύπακτος 1994", *ΑΔελτ* 49 B1, 1994, 243-244.

Amouretti, M.-C. et J.-P. Brun (eds.) 1993
La production du vin et de l'huile en Méditerranée = Oil and Wine Production in the Mediterranean Area, Athènes.

Ancient Macedonia 1988
Ancient Macedonia. Greek Ministry of Culture, Athens.

Anderson-Stojanović, V.R. 1993
"A Well in the Rachi Settlement at Isthmia", *Hesperia* 62, 257-302.

Anderson-Stojanović, V.R. 1996
"The University of Chicago Excavations in the Rachi Settlement at Isthmia, 1989", *Hesperia* 65, 57-98.

Anderson-Stojanović, V.R. 1997
"A Third Century B.C. Deposit from the South Slope Cistern in the Rachi Settlement at Isthmia", *Δ' ΕλλΚερ 1997*, 13-19.

Anderson-Stojanović, V. 2000
"Corinthian West Slope Pottery from Isthmia", *E' ΕλλΚερ 2000*, 381-385.

Anderson-Stojanović, V. R. 2004
"Dinner at the Isthmus: Hellenistic Cooking Ware from the Rachi Settlement at Isthmia", ΣΤ' ΕλλΚερ 2004, 623-630.

Andreiomenou, A.K. 1994
"Το νεκροταφείο της Ακραίφιας", *ΠΑΕ* 1991, 131-145.

Andreou, I. 2004
"Πρώιμη ελληνιστική κεραμική από το νεκροταφείο της Δουρούτης", ΣΤ' ΕλλΚερ 2004, 557-568.

Andreou I. & H. Andreou 1997
"Ελληνιστικά κεραμικά σύνολα από το δυτικό νεκροταφείο της Αμβρακίας", *Δ' ΕλλΚερ 1997*, 79-92.

Antonetti, C. (ed.) 2010
Lo spazio ionico e le comunità della Grecia nord-occidentale. Territorio, società, instituzioni, Pisa.

Baatz, D. 1994
"Die Handmühlen." In: *Das Wreck der antike Schiffsfund von Madia*. (eds.) Hellenkemper Salies G., H.-H. von Prittwitz und Gaffron, and G. Bauchhents, 97-103, Köln.

Bangsgaard, P., 2006a: "The Animal Bones from Pangali". In: *Chalkis Aitolias I*, 162-170.

Bangsgaard, P., 2006b: "The Faunal Remains from the Bronze Age deposits at Aghia Triada". In: *Chalkis Aitolias I*, 63.

Bangsgaard, P. 2006c
"The Animal Bones from Aghia Triada". *Chalkis Aitolias I*, 178-194.

Baziotopoulou-Valavani, E. 1994
"Άπό τήν ελληνιστική κεραμική της αιτωλικής Καλλιπόλεως", *Γ' ΕλλΚερ* 1994, 46-55.

Bean G.E. and Cook, J.N. 1955
"The Halicarnassian Peninsula", *BSA* 50, 122 ff.

Behr, D. 1988
"Neue Ergebnisse zur pergamenischen Westabhungkeramik", *IstMitt 38, 97-178.*

Benton, S. 1938
"Excavations in Ithaca, III", *BSA* 39, 1-51.

Boggess, E.M. 1970
"A Hellenistic Pithos from Corinth", *Hesperia* 39, 73-78.

Bollen, E.A. 2002
"A West Slope Bowl in Sydney: Trans-Aegean Relations of Hellenistic Pottery Production", *Mediterranean Archaeology* 15, 95-108.

Bollen, E.A. 2011
"West Slope pottery: some observations on comparative sequences", in: *Z' ΕλλΚερ (forthcoming).*

Bollen, E.A. 2013
"Western Greece and West Slope Pottery: a Reversible Lid from Chalkis Aitlias," in N. Fenn and C. Römer-Strehl (eds.), *Networks in the Hellenistic World. According to the Pottery in the Eastern Mediterranean and Beyond.* BAR International Series, S2539, Oxford. 41-45

Bommeljé S. 1988
"Aeolis in Aetolia. Thuc. 3.102.5 and the origins of the Aetolian *ethnos*", *Historia* 37, 297-316.

Braun, K. 1970
"Der Dipylon-Brunnen B1: Die Funde", *AM* 85, 129-269.

Braun, K., T.E. Haevernick 1981
Das Kabirenheiligtum bei Theben IV. Bemalte Keramik und Glas aus dem Kabirenheiligtum bei Theben, Berlin.

Broneer, O. 1977
Isthmia III. Terracotta Lamps, Princeton.

Bruneau, P. 1976
'La céramique des tombes hellénistiques'. In: Vatin, C., P. Bruneau, C. Rolley, T. Hackens (eds.): *Médéon de Phocide V.Tombes hellénistiques, objets de metal-monnaies,* Paris, 33-93.

Cahill, N. 2002
Household and City Organization at Olynthus, New Haven.

Camilli, A. 1999
Ampullae. Balsamari ceramici di età ellenistica e romana, Rome.

Camps-Fabrer, H. 1953
L'olivier et l'huile dans l'Afrique romaine, Alger.

Catling, R.W.V. 1996
"The Archaic and Classical Pottery". In: Cavanagh et al., *Continuity and Change in a Greek Rural Landscape; The Laconia Survey II, BSA* suppl. Vol. 27, 33-89.

Charitonides, S. 1981
"Ανασκαφή παρά τον Άγιον Δημήτριον τον Λουμπαρδιάρην εν Αθήναις", *AE* 1979, 161-187.

Cullen, T. & D.R. Keller 1990
"The Greek Pithos Through Time: multiple functions and diverse imagery", W.D. Kingery (ed.), *The Changing Roles of Ceramics in Society: 26,000 B.P to the Present, Ceramics and Civilization* vol. 5, 183-209.

Davidson, G.R. 1942
"A Hellenistic Deposit at Corinth", *Hesperia* 11, 10-12.

Davidson, G.R. 1952
Corinth XII, The Minor Objects. Princeton.

Dietz, S., 2005
"En Helligdom for Kalydons Bygudinde". *Carlsbergfondets Årsskrift.* 148-163.

Dietz, S. & P. Bangsgaard, (forthcoming)
The Kastria/Pangali group and the beginning of the Chalcolithic in Southern Greece. In the Conference volume "Communities in Transition: The Circum-Aegean Later Neolithic Stages (ca. 5000/4800-3200/3000 BC)".

Dietz, S & I. Kolonas, 1998
Surveys and excavations in Chalkis, Aetolias 1995-1996. *FPR.*

Deonna, W. 1938
Exploration archéologique de Délos faite par l'Ecole franaçaise d'Atenes XVIII, *Le Mobilier dèlien*, Paris.

Drachmann, A.G. 1932
Ancient Oil Mills and Presses, København.

Drougou, S. 1991
"Τα πήλινα κτερίσματα του Μακεδονικού τάφου στην Πλατεία Συντριβανίου Θεσσαλονίκης. Μικρή συμβολή στην πρώιμη ελληνιστική κεραμική", *AE* 1988, 71-93.

Drougou, S.T. and I. Touratsoglou 1980
Ελληνιστικοί Λαξευτοί Τάφοι Βέροιας (*ΑΔελτ Suppl.* 28). Athens.

Drougou, S. & I. Touratsoglou 1991
"Hellenistische Keramik aus Makedonien: chronogische Indizien", *AntK* 34, 13-27.

Ducrey, P., I. Metzger and K. Reber 1993
Eretria: Ausgrabungen und Forschungen VIII. Le quartier de la maison aux mosaïques. Lausanne.

Dunbabin, T.J. (ed.) 1962
Perachora: The Sanctuaries of Hera Akraia and Limenia II. *Pottery, Ivories, Scarabs and Other Objects from the Votive Deposits of Hera Limenia,* Oxford.

Dyggve, E., F. Poulsen and K. Rhomaios 1934
Das Heroon von Kalydon. Copenhagen.

Dyggve, E. and R. Eggers 1939
Der altchristliche Friedhof Marusinac (Forschungen i Salone, dritter Band), Wien.

Edwards, G.R. 1975
Corinth VII, iii. Corinthian Hellenistic Pottery. Princeton.

Eggebrecht, A., F. Prendi, M. Korkuti, N. Ceka & G. Kohl *et. al.* 1988
Albanien Schätze aus dem Land der Skipetaren. Mainz.

Eiring, J. 2001
Hellenistic Knossos: The Pottery, PhD. Thesis, University of Sydney.

Eiring, J. 2004
"Death in Aetolia. The Hellenistic Graves at Chalkis," *PDIA* IV, 93-166.

Ergon 1965
"Ηπειρος", *Έργον 1965*, 51-64.

Foxhall, L. 2007
Olive Cultivation in Ancient Greece: Seeking the Ancient Economy, Oxford.

Frankel, R. 1999
Wine and Oil Production in Antiquity in Israel and Other Mediterranean Countries, JOT/ASOR Monograph 10. Sheffield.

Frankel, R. 2003
"The Olynthus Mill, its Origin, and Diffusion: Typology and Distribution", *AJA* 107, 1-21.

Frederiksen, R. 2011
Greek City Walls of the Archaic Period 900-480 BC, Oxford.

Freitag, K. 1999
Der Golf von Korinth. Historisch-topograpische Untersuchungen von der Archaik bis in das 1. Jh.v.Chr. München.

Funke, P. 1987
"Zur Datierung befestigter Stadtanlagen in Aitolien. Historisch-Philologische Anmerkungen zu einem Wechelverhältnis zwischen Siedlungsstruktur und Politischer Organisation" *BOREAS* 10, 87-96.

Funke, P. 1997
"Polisgenese und Urbanisierung in Aitolien im 5. und 4. Jh.v.Chr., *CPCActs* 4, 145-188.

Furtwängler, A.E. 1990
"Demetrias. Ein Produktionsort "attischer" Keramik?", *B' ΕλλΚερ 1990*, 49-53.

Gassner, V. 1997
Forschungen in Ephesos XII/i/I. *Das Südtor der Tetragonos-Agora. Keramik und Kleinfunde,* Vienna.

Gejvall, N-G., 1969
Lerna a preclassical site in the Argolid vol. I, *The Fauna*, Princeton.

Giese, J. 2010
"Bautechnische Beobachtungen am nördlichen und nordwestlichen Mauerabschnitt in Messene". In: Lorentzen J., F. Pirson, P. Schneider und U. Wulf-Rheidt (eds.): *Aktuelle Forschungen zur Konstruktion, Funktion und Semantikantiker Stadtbefestigungen (BYZAS)*, Istanbul.

Gravani, K. 1986
"Die Keramik von Kassope. Ein vorläufiger Überblick". In: Hoepfner W. and E.L. Schwandner (eds.), *Haus und Stadt im klassischen Griechenland*, Munich, 123-134.

Green, J.R. 1979
"Ears of Corn and Other Offerings". In: Cambitoglou A. (ed.), *Studies in Honour of Arthur Dale Trendall*, Sydney, 81-90.

Grønne, C. 2000
"Roof Tiles from Hagia Triada", *SPR*, 257-258.

Hadjisavvas, S. 1992
Olive oil processing in Cyprus: from the Bronze Age to the Byzantine period, Nicosia.

Hansen, M.H. 2006
"Emporion: A Study in the Use and Meaning of the term in Archaic and Classical Greece", Tsetskhladze Gocha R. (ed.), *Greek Colonization: An Account of Greek Colonies and Other Settlements Overseas* I, (*Mnemosyne suppl.* 193), Leiden, 1-39.

Hansen, M.H. & T. Heine Nielsen (eds.) 2004
An Inventory of Archaic and Classical Poleis. An Investigation Conducted by the Copenhagen Polis Centre for the Danish National Research Foundation, Oxford.

Haselberger, U.L.A. 1978
"Zum Paläopyrgos von Naoussa auf Paros", *AA*, 345 ff.

Hayes, J. W. 1975
Roman and Pre-Roman Glass in the Royal Ontario Museum. A Catalogue, Toronto.

Heimberg, U. 1982
Das Kabirenheiligtum bei Theben III. *Die Keramik des Kabirions*, Berlin.

Hjohlman, J. 2005
"Pyrgouthi in the Late Antiquity". In: Hjohlman, J., A. Penttinen & B. Wells (eds.): *Pyrgouthi, a Rural Site in the Berbati Valley from the Early Iron Age to Late Antiquity, ActaAth 52,* 127-266.

Howland, R.H. 1958
The Athenian Agora IV. Greek Lamps and Their Survivals, Princeton.

Houby-Nielsen, S., I. Moschos and M. Gazis 2000
"Excavations on the Hill of Haghia Triada", *SPR*, 229-249.

Isler, H.P. & T.E. Kalpaxis 1978
Samos IV. Das archaische Nordtor und seine Umgebung im Heraion von Samos, Bonn.

Johnson, F.P. 1953
"An Owl Skyphos". In: Mylonas G.E. & D. Raymond (eds.) *Studies Presented to David Moore Robinson II*, 1953, 96-105.

Johnson, F.P. 1955
"A Note on Owl Skyphoi', *AJA* 59, 119-124.

Jones, J.E. 1974
"Δύο αττικα αγροτικα οικαι", *AAA 7*, 293 ff.

Jones, J.E., A.J. Graham and L.H. Sackett L.H. 1962
"The Dema House in Attica", *BSA* 57, 75 ff.

Kaninia, E. 1998
"Χρυσά στεφάνια από τη νεκρόπολη της αρχαίας Ρόδου', *ΑΔελτ* 49-50 A, 1994-1995, 97-130.

Karapanagiotou, A.B. 2000
'Σπάρτη', *ΑΔελτ* 50, 1995, 133-140.

Karlsson, L. 1992
Fortification Towers and Masonry Techniques in the Hegemony of Syracuse, 405-211 B.C. Stockholm.

Kaponis, N. Ch. 2013
"Akarnania: A Byzantine Landscape and its Study". In: Lang F., P. Funke, L. Kolonas, E.-L. Schwandner and D. Maschek (eds.): *Interdisziplinäre Forschungen in Akarnanien*, Bonn.

Kastler, R. 2000
"Die Keramik der Südhalle von Elis und die Problematik der regionalen Keramikchronologie der Region Elis", *E' ΕλλΚερ 2000*, 403-416.

Knigge, U. & W. Kovacsovics 1981
"Kerameikos Tätigkeitsbericht 1979", *AA*, 385-396.

Koehler, C.G. 1982
"Amphoras on Amphoras", *Hesperia* 51, 1982, 284-292.

Kotitsa, Z. 1996
Hellenistische Tonpyxiden. Untersuchung zweier hellenistischer Typen einer Keramikform, Mainz.

Kotitsa, Z. 2004
'Πρώιμη κεραμική και πινάκια από κλειστά ταφικά σύνολα της αρχαίας Πύδνας', ΣΤ' ΕλλΚερ 2004, 193-206.

Kreeb, M. 1988
"Zur typologischen Einordnung eines Bauerhaft klassischer Zeit auf Naxos", Praktika tou XII. *Diethnous Synedriou Klassikes Archaiologia* IV, 108 ff.

Krautheimer, R. 1986
Early Christian and Byzantine Architecture (Pelican), New Haven and London.

Kuhn, G. 2008
"Zur Funktion rinnenförmiger Löcher in Brüstungen und Fensterwänden griechischer Wehrbauten", *AthMitt* 123, 341-380.

Künzl, S. 2004
"Eine kleinasiatische Werkstattgruppe von Formschüsseln zur Herstellung von megarischen Bechern", *ΣΤ' ΕλλΚερ 2004Σ*, 737-738.

Lang, F. 1996
Archaische Siedlungen in Griechenland, Berlin.

Lang F., P. Funke, L. Kolonas, E--L. Schwandner, D. Maschek (eds.) 2013
Interdisziplinäre Forschungen in Akarnanien (*Akarnanien-Forschungen 1*), Bonn.

Lambrinoudakis, V., J. Boardman and C. Vafopoulou Richardson (eds.), 1984 (1986)
"Ancient farmhouses on Mount Aipos", In: Boardman J. and C. Vafopoulou Richardson (eds.) *Chios. A Conference at the Homereion in Chios,* 295 ff.

Langridge-Noti, E. 2002
"First Preliminary Report on the Pottery of the Classical through Roman period", Crouwel J.H. et al. "Geraki, an Acropolis site in Lakonia", *Pharos* X, 52-68.

Lauter, H. 1980
"Zu Heimstätten und Guteshäusern im klassischen Attika". In: Lauter H. (ed.) *Forschungen und Funde. Festschrift B. Neutsch,* 279 ff.

Lawall, M. 2004
"Amphoras without Stamps: Chronologies and Typologies from the Athenian Agora", ΣΤ' ΕλλΚερ 2004, 445-454.

Lawrence, A.W. 1979
Greek Aims in Fortification, Oxford.

Lawrence, A.W. 1983
Greek Architecture (Revised with additions by R.A. Tomlinson), New Haven and London.

Lemoine, X., Melinda A. Z., K. J. Bishop and S. J. Rufolo, 2014
"A New System for Computing Dentition-Based Age Profiles in Sus Scrofa", *JAS, 179-193.*

Lohmann, H. 1993
Atene. Forschungen zur Siedlungs-und Wirtschaftsstrukturen des klassischen Attika, Köln.

Mancz, E. A. 1989
An Examination of changing Patterns of Animal-Husbandry of the Late Bronze Age and Dark Ages of Nichoria in the Southwestern Peloponnese. Unpublished Thesis, University of Minnesota.

Mayer, J. J., J. M. Novak & I. Lehr Brisbin Jr., 1998
"Evaluation of molar size as a basis for distinguishing wild boar from dom. Swine: employing the present to decipher the past". In. Nelson S.M. (ed.): *Ancestors for the Pigs: Pigs in Prehistory. MASCAP 15,* 39-53.

Mettos, A. and I. Karfakis, 1991
Geological Map of Greece 1:50.000. Evinokhorion Sheet. Institute of Geology and Mineral Exploration.

Metzger, I.R. 1969
Eretria: Ausgrabungen und Forschungen II. Die hellenistische Keramik in Eretria, Bern.

McPhee, I. 1997
"Stemless Bell-Kraters from Ancient Corinth", *Hesperia* 66, 99-145.

Metzger, I.R. 1973
"Piraeus-Zisterne", *ΑΔελτ* 26, 1971, 41-94.

Metzger, I.R. 1984
'Ein frühhellenistisches Keramikdepot in Eretria', *ΑΔελτ* 33A, 1978, 198-239.

Milojčić,V. and D. Theocharis 1976
Demetrias I, (Beiträge zur ur- und frühgeschichtlichen Archäologie des Mittelmeer – Kulturraumes 12), Bonn.

Mitsopoulos-Leon, V. 1971-72
"Zur Keramik aus Aigeira", *ÖJh Grabungen,* 17-32.

Mitsopoulos-Leon, V. 1991
Forschungen in Ephesos IX, 2/2. *Die Basilika am Staatsmarkt in Ephesos. Kleinfunde, I. Teil Keramik hellenistischer und römischer Zeit,* Vienna.

Monaco, M.C. & M.Ch. Monaco, 2000
"Un deposito di ceramiche tardoclassiche ed ellenistiche del Cabirio di Lemno. Analisi delle forme II: ceramica acroma e da cucina", E' ΕλλΚερ 2000, 153-160.

Moore, M.B. 1997
"Athenian Red-Figured and White-Ground Pottery", *The Athenian Agora* XXX, Princeton.

Morel, J.-P. 1981
Céramique campanienne: Les formes, BEFAR 244, Rome.

Morel, J.-P. 1990
"L'apport des fouilles de Carthage a la chronologie des céramiques hellénistiques", *B' ΕλλΚερ 1990,* 17-30.

Morris, S.P. 2009/10
"Prehistoric Torone: A Bronze Age Emporion in the Northern Aegean. Preliminary report on the Lekythos excavations 1986 and 1988-1990". *Mediterranean Archaeology 22*/23, 2009/10, 1-68.

Moschos, I. 2000
'The Cemetery of Ancient Chalkis. Recent Rescue Excavation', *SPR,* 291-300.

Müth, S. 2010
"Fortifikationskunst und Repräsentation an der Stadtmauer von Messene". In: Lorentzen L., F. Pirson, P. Schneider und U. Wulf-Rheidt (eds.): *Aktuelle Forschungen zur Konstruktion, Funktion und Semantik antiker Stadtbefestigungen. (Byzas 10).* Istanbul, 57-84.

Müth, S. 2014
"The historical Context of the City of Messene. Preconditions, Written Sources, Success Balance and Social Impacts". *PDIA* VII, 105-122.

Müth, S. & U. Ruppe (forthcoming)
Regional begrenzte Phänomene. In: Müth S., P. Schneider, M. Schnelle and P. de Staebler (eds.), *Ancient For-*

tifications A compendium of theory and practice, Fokus Fortifikation Studies no. 1, Oxford.

Mylanos, D., 2005
"The Animal Bones from Pyrgouthi in the Berbati Valley". In: Hjohlman J., A. Penttinen & B. Wells (eds.). *Pyrgouthi, a Rural Site in the Berbati Valley from the Early Iron Age Late Antiquity. ActaAth* LII, 301-308.

Nicodemus, A., 2008
"The Mammal and Reptile Remains, 1973-77". In: Taylor W.D.& R. Janko (eds.): *Ayios Stephanos, Excavations at a Bronze Age and Medieval Settlement in Southern Laconia*. The British School in Athens, Supplementary vol. no. 44, 506-513.

Noack, F. 1916
"Befestigte griechiche Städte in Aetolien und Akarnanien", *AA* XXXI, 215-239.

Nowicka, M. 1975
Les maisons à tour dans le monde grec, Warsaw.

Ober, J. 1992
"Towards a typology of Greek Artillery Towers: The First and Second Generations (c. 375-275 B.C.)". In: Van de Maele S. and J.H. Fossey (eds.) *Fortificationes Antiquae*, Amsterdam, 147-169.

Odigos tis Ekthesis Thessaloniki 1986
Οδηγός της Έκθεσης. "Θεσσαλονική από τα Προϊστορικά μέχρι τα Χριστιανικά Χρόνια", Athens, 102-121.

Paliouras, A. 2004
Βυζαντινή Αιτωλοακαρνανία. Σύμβολη στη Βυζαντινή και μεταβυζαντινή Μνημειακή τεχνή, Agrinio.

Papakonstantinou, M.-F. 1997
"Ελληνιστική κεραμική από τη Λαμία", *Δ' ΕλλΚερ 1997*, 50-58.

Papapostolou, I.A. 1977
"Αρχαιότητες και μνημεία Αιτολίας-Ακαρνανίας. Καλυδών', *ΑΔελτ* 27 B2, 1972, 434.

Patsiada, B. 1989
'Κεραμική του τύπου της "Δυτικής Κλιτύος" από τη Ρόδο', *ΑΔελτ* 38, 1983, 105-210.

Paton, W.R. and H.J.L. Myres 1896
"Karian Sites and Inscriptions", *JHS* 16, 188 ff.

Payne, S., 1973: Kill-off Patterns in Sheep and Goats: The Mandibles from Asvan Kale. *AnatSt 23*, 281-303.

Pecirka J. 1973
"Homestead Farms in Classical and Hellenistical Hellas". In: Finley M. (ed.) *Problémes de la terre en Grèce ancienne*, 113 ff.

Pemberton, E. 1989
Corinth XVIII, I. The Sanctuary of Demeter and Kore: The Greek Pottery.

Poggesi, G., S. Savona, M.Ch. Monaco and M.C. Monaco 1997
"Un deposito di ceramiche tardoclassiche ed ellenistiche del Cabirio di Lemno: Analisi delle forme", *Δ' ΕλλΚερ 1997*, 220-231.

Portale, E.-C. 2000
"Ceramica comune e da fuoco da contesti della metà del II secolo a.C. a Festòs. La c.d. "officina del figulo" e i vani adiacenti", *E' ΕλλΚερ 2000*, 75-86.

Portelanos, A. K. 1998
Οι αρχαίες Αιτωλικές οχυρώσεις, vol. A-E. Unpublished PhD thesis, University of Crete, Athens.

Prummel, W., 2003
"Animal Remains from the Hellenistic Town of New Halos in the Almiros Plain, Thessaly". In: *Zooarchaeology in Greece: Recent Advances*, British School at Athens Studies vol. 9, 153-159.

Radt, W. 1970
"Siedlungen und Bauten auf der Halbinsel von Halikarnassos unter besonderer Berücksichtung der archaischen Epoche, *IstMitt 3. Beiheft,* 145 ff.

Radt, W. 2000
"Ein sigillata-rotes Thymiaterion mit Ritzdekor im Westabhang-Nachfolgestil aus Pergamon", *RCRF* Acta 3, 123-28.

Reber, K. 1998
Eretria: Ausgrabungen und Forschungen X. Die klassischen und hellenistischen Wohnhäuser im Westquartier, Lausanne.

Robinson, D.M. & J.W. Graham 1938
Excavations at Olynthus. Part VIII. The Hellenistic House: A Study of the Houses found at Olynthus with a Detailed Account of those Excavated in 1931 and 1934, Baltimore.

Romaios, K. 1916
"Χαλκίς", *AD* 2.

Romano, I.B. 1994
"A Hellenistic Deposit from Corinth: Evidence for Interim Period Activity (146-44B.C.)", *Hesperia* 63, 57-104.

Rotroff, S.I. 1996
The Missing Krater and the Hellenistic Symposium: Drinking in the Age of Alexander the Great (Broadhead Classical Lecture no. 7, University of Canterbury). Christchurch.

Rotroff, S.I. 1997
The Athenian Agora XXIX. *Hellenistic Pottery: Athenian and Imported Wheelmade Table Ware and Related Material.* Princeton.

Rotroff, S.I. 2002
"West Slope in the East" In: Blondé F., P. Ballet, J.-F. Salles, *Céramiques hellénistiques et romaines. Productions et diffusion en Méditerranée orientale (Chypre, Égypte et côte syro-palestinienne)*, 97-115.

Rotroff, S.I. 2004
"Coarse Wares at the Athenian Agora", ΣΤ' *ΕλλΚερ* 2004, 455-460.

Rotroff, S.I. 2006
"The Introduction of the Moldmade Bowl Revisited: Tracking a Hellenistic Innovation", *Hesperia* 75, 357-378.

Rotroff, S. & J.H. Oakley 1992
Debris from a Public Dining Place in the Athenian Agora, (*Hesperia* Suppl. 25), Princeton.

Roy, J. 2014
"Emplekton technique in Fortification at Ithome/Messene, Megalopolis, and Mantinea". *PDIA* VII, 123-131.

Runnels, C.N. 1981
A Diachronic Study and Economic Analysis of Millstones from the Argolid, Greece. Ph.D. diss. Indiana University.

Runnels, C.N. 1985
'Trade and Demand for Millstones in Southern Greece in the Neolithic and the Early Bronze Age', *Prehistoric production and exchange: the Aegean and Eastern Mediterranean,* eds. A.B. Knapp & T. Stech, Los Angeles 1985, 30-43.

Sabetai, V. 2004
"Μελαμβαφής και ύστερη ερυθρόμορφη κεραμική από νεκροταφεία της Βοιωτίας", ΣΤ' *ΕλλΚερ* 2004, 461-472.

Sanders, G.D.R. 1999
"A Late Roman Bath at Corinth: Excavations in the Panayia Field, 1995 -1996", *Hesperia* 68, 441- 480.

Schack, M. 1997
"Beiträge zur Topographie Akarnaniens in klassischer und hellenistischer Zeit". *Studien zur Geschichte Nordwest Griechenlands* Bd. 2, Würzburg.

Schäfer, J. 1968
Hellenistische Keramik aus Pergamon. Pergamenische Forschungen II, Berlin.

Schauenberg, K. 1988
"Eulen aus Athen und Unteritalian", *JDI* 103, 67-85.

Schmid, S. 2000
"A Group of Early Hellenistic Pottery from a Well in Eretria", *E' ΕλλΚερ 2000*, 361-372.

Schöne, A. 1991
"Die Sandfüllung im Bau Y". In: Knigge U., A. Rügler, A. Schöne, B. von Freytag and B. Löringhoff, "Die Ausgrabungen im Kerameikos 1988/89", *AA*, 378-380.

Schöne-Denkinger, A. 1994
"Eine frûhhellenistische Einfullschicht im Bau Y/ Kerameikos - zur Datierung der jûngsten Funde', *Γ' ΕλλΚερ* 1994, 35-38.

Schwandner, E.L. 1977
"Die Böotische Hafenstadt Siphae". *AA* 1977, 513-551.

Schwertheim, U. 2010
"Monumentale Hoftore in Messene". In: Lorentzen J., F. Pirson, P. Schneider und U. Wulf-Rheidt (eds.): *Aktuelle Forschungen zur Konstruktion, Funktion und Semantik antiker Stadtbefestigungen. (Byzas 10).* Istanbul, 97-106.

Semantone-Bournia, E. 1982-84
"Αρχαίες εγκαταστάσεις στό Απος", *Archaiognosia* 3, 195 ff.

Sigalos, E. 2004
Housing in Medieval and Post-Medieval Greece (*Archaeopress BAR* S1291).

Sismanides, K. 1990
'Ποτίδαια. Θέση Μύλος', *ΑΔελτ* 40 B, 1985, 237-238.

Sloan, R. E. & M. A. Duncan, 1978
"Zooarchaeology of Nichoria". In: Rapp G. Jr. and S.E. Aschenbrenner (eds.). *Excavations at Nichoria in Southwest Greece, vol. I Site, Environs, and Techniques.* Minneapolis, 60-77.

Smekalova, T.N., 2011
"Magnetic surveys in Kalydon", *KALYDON 2011*, 47-58.

Smekalova, T. N., O. Voss, and S. L. Smekalov, 2008
Magnetic Surveying in Archaeology, Wormanium (Denmark).

Snyder, L. M. & W. E. Klippel, 2003
"From Lerna to Kastro: Further Thoughts on Dogs as Food in Ancient Greece". In: Kotjabopoulou E. et al (eds.): *Zooarchaeology in Greece, recent advances.* British School at Athens Studies 9, 221-231.

Sokolicek A. 2009
Diateichismata. Zu dem Phänomen inneren Befestigungsmauern im griechischen Städtebau. ÖAI Ergänzungshefte 11, Wien.

Sokolovska, V. 1986
Isar-Marvinci and the Vardar Valley in Ancient Times, Skopje (in Russian).

Sparkes, B.A. and L. Talcott 1970
The Athenian Agora XII. Black and Plain Pottery of the 6th, 5th and 4th Centuries BC, Princeton.

Stillwell, A.N. and J. L. Benson 1984
Corinth XV iii. *The Potters' Quarter: The Pottery.*

Strand Petersen, K. 2006
"Shellfish in the strategraphical contexts of Final Neolithic and Bronze Age supplemented by ^{14}C dating", *Chalkis Aitolias I,* 171-177.

Themelis, P. 1982
"Ανασκαφή Ερέτριας", *ΠΑΕ* 1980, 78-102.

Themelis, P.G. & I.P. Touratsoglou 1997
Οι Τάφοι του Δερβενίου (*ΑΔελτ*, Suppl. 59), Athens.

Thompson, H. A. 1934
"Two Centuries of Hellenistic Pottery", *Hesperia* 3, 311-480.

Thompson, H.A. & R.L. Scranton 1943
"Stoas and City Walls on the Pnyx", *Hesperia* 12, 269-383.

Tolstikov, V. & D. Zhuravlev 2004
'Hellenistic Pottery from Two Cisterns on the Acropolis of Panticapaeum', ΣΤ' ΕλλΚερ 2004, 269-276

Townsend, R.F. 1995
The Athenian Agora XXVII. *The East Side of the Agora: The Remains beneath the Stoa of Attalos,* Princeton.

Typaldou-Fakiris, C. 2004
Villes fortifiées de Phocide et la IIIe guerre sacrée 356-346 av. J.-C. (Publ. de l'université de Provence).

Vdovichenko, I. 2004
'Pottery from the Hellenistic House in Kerkinitida', ΣΤ' ΕλλΚερ 2004, 759-764.

Vickers, M., O. Impey and J. Allan, 1986
From Silver to Ceramic. Oxford.

Vierneisel, K. 1964
"Die Ausgrabungen im Kerameikos: Die Grabung in der Nekropole, 1962", *AA* [JdI 79], 420-467.

Vogeikoff, N. 1993
Hellenistic Pottery from the South Slope of the Akropolis, dissertation Bryn Mawr College.

Wacker, Chr. 1999a
Palairos. Eine historische Landeskunde der Halbinsel Plagia in Akarnanien. Studien zur Geschichte Nordwest-Griechenlands, BD. 3. (Oberhummer Gesellschaft V). München.

Wacker, Chr. 1999b
Kakavoula. A rural site at Northwestakarnanien, Acheloos. Schriften der Oberhummer Gesellschaft e.V, I,1. München, 18 ff.

Walter, H., W. Felten & R. Smetana-Scherrer 1982
Alt Ägina II,1. *Spätklassische und hellenistiche Keramik,* Mainz, 56-89.

Watzinger, C. 1901
"Vasenfunde aus Athen", *AM* 26, 50-102.

Weinberg, G.D. and E. M. Stern 2009
The Athenian Agora XXXIV. Vessel Glass.

Wells, B. 1992
Agriculture in Ancient Greece. Sthlm.

William-Thorpe, O. 1988
"Provenancing and Archaeology of Roman Millstones from Sardinia (Italy)". *OJA* 8, 89-117.

William-Thorpe, O. and R.S. Thorpe 1990
"Millstone Provenancing Used in Tracing the Route of a Fourth-Century B.C. Greek Merchant Ship". *Archaeometry* 32, 115-137.

Winter, F.E. 1971
Greek Fortifications. London.

Wolters, P., G. Bruns 1940
Das Kabirenheiligtum bei Theben I. Berlin.

Young, J.H. 1956
"Studies in South Attica". *Hesperia* 25, 122 ff.

Zafeiropoulou, F. 1979
"Αιτωλοακαρνανία. Θυρρείον", *ΑΔελτ* 29 B2, 1973-74, 539-542.

Zaytsev, Y. 2004
"The Ceramic Complex of Scythian Neapolis (Crimea, Northern Black Sea)", ΣΤ' ΕλλΚερ 2004, 751-758.

Zeder, M. A. 2006
"Reconciling Rates of Long Bone Fusion and Tooth Eruption and Wear in Sheep (*Ovis aries*) and Goat (*Capra hircus*)". In: Rucillo D. (ed.): *Recent Advances in Ageing and Sexing Animal Bone*, Oxford, 87-118.

THE MOUND OF AGHIA TRIADA

A. SCIENTIFIC ANALYSIS AND GENERAL TOPOGRAPHY

A.1 Geological investigations in the area of Aghia Triada*

Kaj Strand Petersen (†)

The Bay of Kato Vasiliki

The small fishing village of Kato Vasiliki c. 12 km from Antirio is situated on the Bay of Patras on the western side of a delta which was formed between the mountains Varassova (914 m) and Klokova (1037 m). The small Bay of Kato Vasiliki is very shallow even at a distance of 1-2 km from the shore and in the eastern part of the Bay of Patras, the depth never exceeds 80 m. Accordingly, during the periods of low sea level during the last glaciation most of the Bay of Kato Vasiliki was land.

The karstic limestone and the site af Aghia Triada

According to the Geological Map of Greece[12], the high crest of Varassova in the West running NNW-SSE consists of strongly karstic limestone with marine gastropods and bivalves, and dates from the Upper Cretaceous period (Cenomanian – Senonian). Following the Upper Cretaceous limestone, one passes through younger limestone beds from the Paleocene – Middle Eocene period into cohesive conglomerates, shales and sandstones, again of Upper Eocene date belonging to the Flysch. The hill of Aghia Triada, also visible on the Geological Map of Greece, forms a small 'island' in the delta, consisting of conglomerates alternating with thin layers of sandstone and shale. These layers constitute the youngest part of the Tertiary sequence, more than 1000 m thick, overlying the Mesozoic limestone.[13] To the East of Aghia Triada, Flysch series are visible in a low ridge (287 m), and further towards the East the limestone of Palaeocene – Middle Eocene age reappears overlying the upper Cretaceous limestone in Mt. Klokova.

The geological character of the valley of Kato Vasiliki was found to be a syncline. Thus, the older sediments visible along the lower flanks of the Varassova and Klokova mountains lie beneath the delta at varying depth depending on the dip of the synclinal axis.

The changing face of the landscape around Aghia Triada

The strongly karstic limestone from the Upper Cretaceous period, described above, forms one of the most conspicuous geological features of the valley of Kato Vasiliki. Moreover, it is characterized by a multitude of caves which are of archaeological and historical interest. Caves of this kind were often used for habitation in the Paleolithic period, and in more recent times the caves of the Varassova were inhabited by monks. It was therefore important to obtain a fuller picture of the karstic limestone in the area. For this reason, strike and dips were measured of the strata in four areas covering the delta northwards towards Gavrolimni and the slopes of Varasova and Klokova (hatched areas marked A-D in Fig. 4). As appears from Fig. 4, 81 strike and dips were measured resulting in an orientation best-fit-great-circle 162/76 (dip/direction) which gives a fold axis orientation 342/14. The

* This article is identical with the one published in *SPR*, 269-276 with a few alterations and supplementary information (SD).

12 Mettos & Karfakis, 1991.

13 Mettos & Karfakis, 1991.

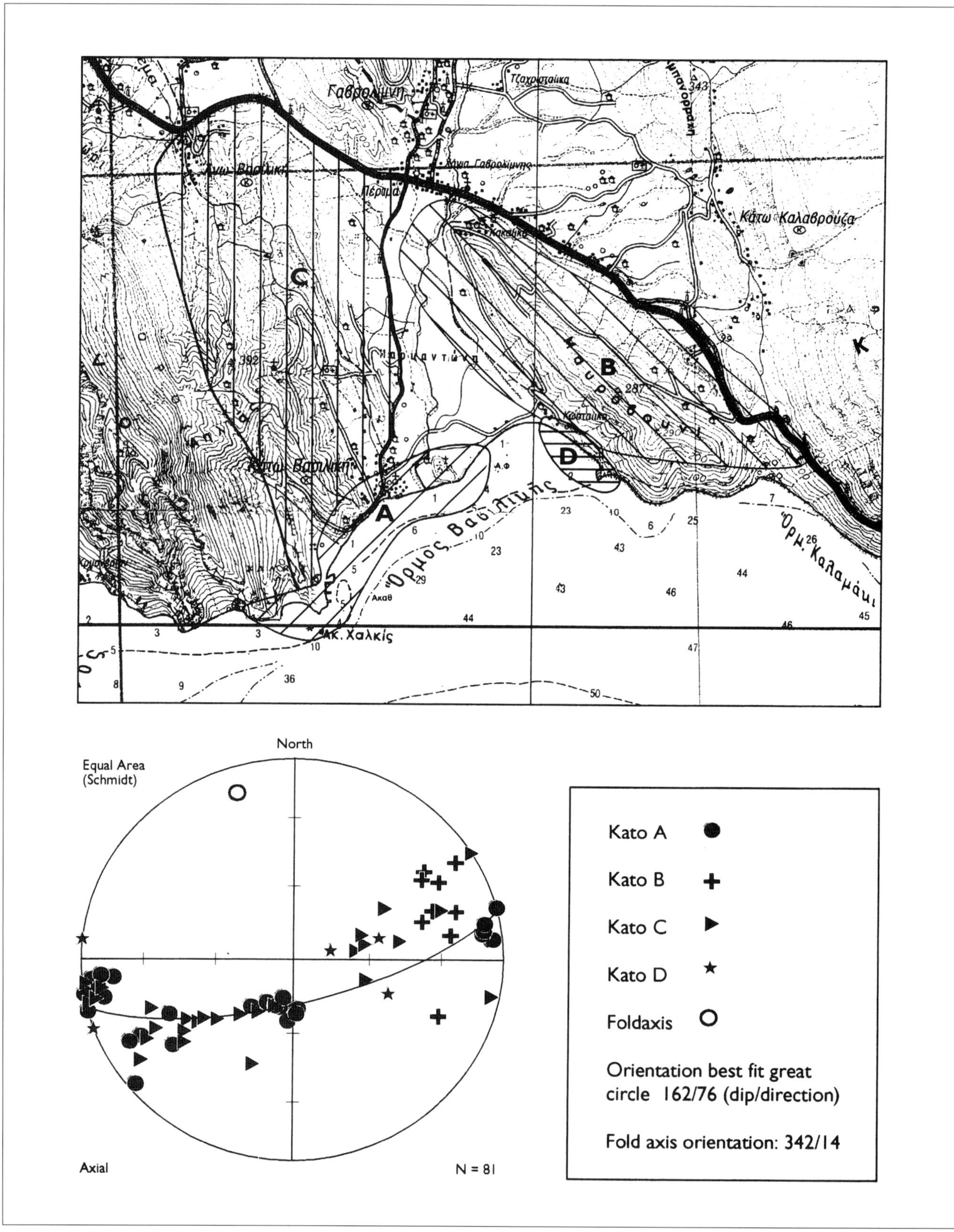

Fig. 4 *Structural analysis of the region around Kato Vasiliki showing the best-fit-great-circle and fold axis orientation.*

Fig. 5 *Sketch drawn from the hill of Aghia Triada towards the east showing a crescent shaped island in the sea which was revealed to be part of the Flysch.*

crest zone of the fold can then be estimated to dip 14° towards North-North-West. This observation is highly important for our understanding of the profound ways in which the landscape around the hill of Aghia Triada has changed during the last approximately 25.000 years. The structural analysis implies that during the Late Weichselian period, when the sea level was around 120 m below the present sea level, karstic limestone formed part of a vast landscape which extended far to the South of the Aghia Triada hill into what is today the Bay of Kato Vasiliki. Thus, karstic limestone might appear less than two km from the coast at the hill of Aghia Triada in a South-South-East direction at a depth of approx. 50 m.

A small crescent shaped island which is visible in the sea close to the coast on the eastern side of the Aghia Triada hill must also have formed part of this landscape (Fig 5). This island was first considered to be a beach ridge, but was revealed to be part of the Flysch. It might be the trace in the horizontal plane of the syncline dipping North-North-West.

Marine deposits

Marine deposits were not located on the eastern side of the hill of Aghia Triada, but only on the western side. Here marine strata were found in three places proving the existence of a small Bay. These marine sediments were characterized by molluscs such as *Conus, Bittium* and *Gibbula* which facilitated AMS-datings of the sediments. According to the datings so far obtained by this method, the small bay existed in 3310-2930 BC (AAR-4348) and in 1750-1630 BC (AAR-4347) (see note below).[14]

Diet of the people in ancient Chalkis

A considerable quantity of molluscs were found during the excavations on the hill af Aghia Triada which gives a valuable insight into the diet of the people who once lived here. So far, as many as 25 marine species have

14 The radiocarbon dates were published by Jan Heinemeier in *Chalkis Aitolias I*, 196-198.

Fig. 6 *Cerastoderma glaucum (Poiret, 1789).*

been identified, all of which no doubt once served as an important food-supply. To judge by its frequency, *Cerastoderma glaucum* (Poiret,1789) was by far the most popular (Fig. 6) and among the gastropods the *Cerithium vulgatum* (Bruguiere, 1792) (Fig. 7). In addition, ten terrestrial gastropods were recorded. Of these, only the *Helix pomatia* (L., 175) is likely to have been eaten. The fragments of shellfish that were found, *Pinna nobilis* L., 1758 (Fig. 8) and the large predatory gastropod *Tonna galea* (L.,1758) (Fig. 9), both spectacular molluscs, are both still to be found on the sandy sea floor along the coast of Aghia Triada. The ^{14}C dates point to the Bronze Age: 1890-1740 BC (AAR-4586), 1740-1620 BC (AAR-4588), and 1520-1430 BC (AAR-4587). In other words they stem from a period in which the area Southwest of the mound formed a small bay.

Rise of sea level

Most of the molluscs have a habitat of sandy shores like those found off the hill of Aghia Triada today. It is therefore also interesting that epifauna elements can be found on the solid rock of the hill of Aghia Triada, as well as to the East of this site. Thus, heavy bio-erosion occurs on outcrops of limestone to the West of the hill and the forming of such notches is a well-known effect of bio-erosion. Of particular interest are the exposures in the western part of the bay of Kato Vasiliki immediately below the site of Pangali. In this area it appears that from a depth of around 2 m below the present sea level the limestone has been substantially bio-eroded as seen on Fig. 10. This might show a constant rise of sea level up to the present position. However, the former levels have not been dated.

Summary

Up until now the geological studies including records of recent and sub-fossil molluscs have depicted the geological setting of the strongly karstic limestone with the potential of Paleolithic settlements in caves as found in caves in the Marseilles area below present day sea level. The demonstration of the existence of a former bay West of the site of Aghia Triada allows us to suggest a possible place for anchorage. Moreover an overlap of the dates from the marine deposits of the former bay and the dates of the shellfish from the excavation – both falling within the Helladic period – was demonstrated.[15] The progradation of the delta seems *to* indicate rising sea level, and the studies of bio-erosion from under the water (no traces were observed above sea level) may support the idea of rising

15 See *Chalkis Aitolias I* for a more detailed study of the ancient diet of the site.

Fig. 7 *Cerithium vulgatum (Bruguiére, 1792).*

Fig. 8 *Prima nobilis (L., 1758).*

Fig. 9 *Tonna galea (L., 1758).*

sea level in the last part of the Holocene. So far no age can be established for the older sea level.

Note

Core samples were taken in the area of the former bay by Kaj Strand Petersen who planned to publish a more extensive report of the geological features in the Aitolian coastland in the present volume. Kaj's death in 2011 prevented him in finishing this work – it was, for personal and professional reasons, a great loss for all of us. We are greatly indebted to Kaj's wife Ella Hoch, who handed over all the material from his work in Greece to the expedition.

Fig. 10 *Underwater photo off the site at Pangali showing the substantial bioerosion up to present day sea level.*

Kaj's papers recorded the following information about the core samples. The two radiocarbon dates derive from core sample D, which was positioned at the coordinate: N: 3713/E: 2880 at the level 0.18 m.a.s., very close to the present day coastline of the Gulf of Patras (the test point D is shown on the map Fig. 21. below (just outside the frame)). The tests were taken at the following levels[16]:

AAR-4347: 3.10-3.60 m: 1750-1630 BC
AAR-4348: 4.30-4.50 m: 3310-2930 BC

As the molluscs were living at the bottom of the bay, the depth of the sea floor must have been 4-4.5 metres below the present surface in the EHI period. This is well-attested on the Eastern terrace of Aghia Triada, where remains dating to the transition to the Mycenaean Age were found about 3-3.5 metres below the present surface.

SD

16 For ^{14}C dating compare also *Chalkis Aitolias I*, 196-198.

A.2 A magnetic exploration of Chalkis Aitolias

Tatiana Smekalova and Bruce Bevan

The goals of this survey

Magnetic surveys are frequently carried out in order to provide some guidance to an archaeological excavation that will follow; no excavations are planned to follow this magnetic survey. Instead, a major goal of this survey was to extrapolate archaeological features from the excavations that have already been completed. This will allow better knowledge of the extent of these and similar features in unexcavated areas.

Features and structures that have been excavated before a geophysical survey can provide excellent information about the depth, size, and character of what is underground; this information can aid the interpretation of a magnetic map. However, magnetic maps that are measured over open excavations generally reveal little about the detectability of those formerly-buried features (since much soil has been removed). Still, those excavations can suggest where similar features might remain buried nearby. The interpretation of the magnetic survey can then be aided by the excavations, and the geophysical survey can also add new archaeological information. At Chalkis Aitolias the geomagnetic survey was moderately successful in achieving this aim.

A second goal of the magnetic survey was an exploration for features along the shoreline of the former bay on the western side of Aghia Triada. A small area near this shore has been tested by excavation, but much remains unknown. Large areas were mapped with the magnetometer around the ancient shore and bay. Little of importance was revealed in the northern area, for there was too much modern junk in that area. However, the southern bay appears to be dense with shoreline features that are probably ancient.

A third goal of the project was to reveal the foundations of ancient buildings near the Classical-Byzantine wall on the inner side of the eastern terrace but this found little success. It appears that few buildings were detected, although there were certainly many in the area of survey. This failure may have been caused by several factors: a greater thickness of soil over the foundations there, an irregular layer of stone rubble on top of the foundations, and also the invisibility of some foundation stone to a magnetic survey. The small area that was available for survey along the steep slope may also have contributed.

THE SITE

The archaeological site of Chalkis Aitolias is centered on a 30-m tall hill called Aghia Triada. This hill has an area of 2-3 ha and it borders the sea on the northern side of the bay of Patras; the city of Patras is directly South.

A satellite overview of the site is shown in Fig. 11; white lines mark the perimeters of this magnetic survey. The village of Kato Vasiliki is just to the West (left), across a small river.

Studies by a team of Greek and Danish archaeologists[17] in the years between 1995 and 2001 have revealed that Chalkis had significant occupation between the Neolithic, the Bronze Age and Byzantine times. However, the foundation stones of a Byzantine church now dominate the top of the hill; it is possible that earlier architectural stone from the hilltop now forms a talus slope on the sides of the hill. This rock rubble is particularly apparent on the eastern side of the hill.

Almost the entire eastern terrace was explored with a magnetic survey, along a 25-m wide band defined by the Archaic/Classical-Byzantine fortification walls

17 *FRP, SPR, TPR* and *Chalkis Aitolias I.*

Fig. 11 *The site of Chalkis. The wooded oval of the hill of Aghia Triada is centered in this Google Earth photograph, taken on 17 June 2012. A 200-m scale is shown and north is toward the top. A registration error (georeferencing) of several meters in this satellite image has not been corrected.*

on the westerly side and an abrupt drop on the East side. The topographic relief in this area was about 6 m, with the steepest slope near the fortification wall. The ground surface was covered by grass, weeds, and bushes that were 1-1.5 m tall. Woody bushes were particularly difficult to pass through, while loose stones that were invisible in the vegetation made walking hazardous on the slopes. Two fallen trees prevented access to small areas. This eastern terrace had the benefit of beautiful views of the sea and surrounding mountains. Much of the soil that was excavated from this area ten years ago was placed at the southeastern edge of the terrace, and outside the area of this magnetic survey.

A larger area was explored on the western side of the hill. A geological study completed by Kaj Strand Pederson (1998)[18] confirmed what ancient authors had suggested: There was a deep bay and probably a harbour in ancient times. The magnetic survey was undertaken in this area in order to search for the ancient shoreline and its architectural features. This survey was carried out in two areas that were separated by a wall of dense bushes; see Fig. 12.

The tall grass in the northern area had been cut and collected for livestock before the start of this survey; the grass that remained was about 20 cm tall and this allowed an easy survey. An olive orchard is found on the side, and there are two terraces there, with step heights of 0.5 and 1.5 m. Except for those terrace steps, the surface is almost flat.

Many modern iron features are found around the perimeter of this survey area. There are several fences with iron posts and wires. There two huts for pumping irrigation water on the North side, and discarded irrigation pipes are also found there. Sheets of corrugated iron cover the archaeological excavations at the southeastern corner of the area of survey. While some iron trash is found near the olive trees on the East, the western region, near the river, is much cleaner, although a reinforcing wall along the river (and perhaps buildings across the river) contribute to magnetic interference there.

The survey of the southern shoreline was much less affected by modern iron. This area had been covered by natural reeds 2 m heigh; these were cut and left in place in order to allow access to the area. The area of cutting was limited on the East (uphill) by stones on the surface that would have damaged the cutter; on the West, the cutting had to stop where the soil became soft and swampy. The relief of the area along the southern shoreline is only about 2 m.

In addition to the magnetic survey of the former western bay, two soil cores were taken there in order to investigate the sediments that now fill the ancient harbour. A split-spoon corer, manufactured by Eijkelkap

18 Of the Geological Survey of Denmark (*GEUS*). See Chapter A.1.

Fig. 12 *The areas of survey on the western side of Aghia Triada. Reeds formerly covered the light area in front this area is adjacent to the sea. The larger area to the right locates the survey of the northern shoreline. The town of Kato Vasiliki and mount Varassova are in the background.*

Agrisearch Equipment, was used for these tests; this corer had been left at the site by Kaj Petersen after his work two decades earlier. The coring tool had a diameter of 3 cm and a length of about 1 m. Extension rods allowed cores to be made to depths of 4.5 m (in the northern area) and 6.9 m (in the southern area); these coring locations are marked with filled green circles in Fig. 13.

The sediments from these cores have been saved for later study, but a brief qualitative description is given here. In the upper 1.5 m, the soil was dry and hard, grading from mostly silt to mostly clay at a greater depth. Below a depth of about 1.5 m (approximately sea level at both locations), the sediments were wet, with strata of sand and soft mud. The water in the sediments was not apparently saline. Essentially no gravel was found and only one small sherd; there were no shells. Bedrock was not encountered in either location. However, an extrapolation of the slope of the hill near the southern coring suggests that bedrock could be less than a meter below the bottom of the coring. The sediments in the deeper part of the southern coring (nearest the sea) appeared to be sandier than in the northern coring.

The magnetic susceptibility of these sediments was measured in a search for invisible stratification. However, the readings were surprisingly uniform and they usually ranged between only 2 and 3 ppt (this quantity is described shortly). It was hoped that these readings would allow sediment depths to be interpreted in the magnetic maps, but this was not possible, for the sediments are only slightly more magnetic than bedrock.

The archaeological base map of the entire site of Chalkis is shown as a background to Figure 13; this map was prepared by Charalambos Marinopoulos and Poul Erik Skovgaard in 1995, with later additions. Fig. 13 includes the magnetic maps of five separate geophysical grids, each with different orientations; this allowed an efficient mapping of the moderately complex areas. The coordinates in the geophysical maps of a dozen features that are located in this archaeological map (plus another) have enabled the alignment of these magnetic maps with the archaeological base map to an error of less than 0.5 m. This alignment has

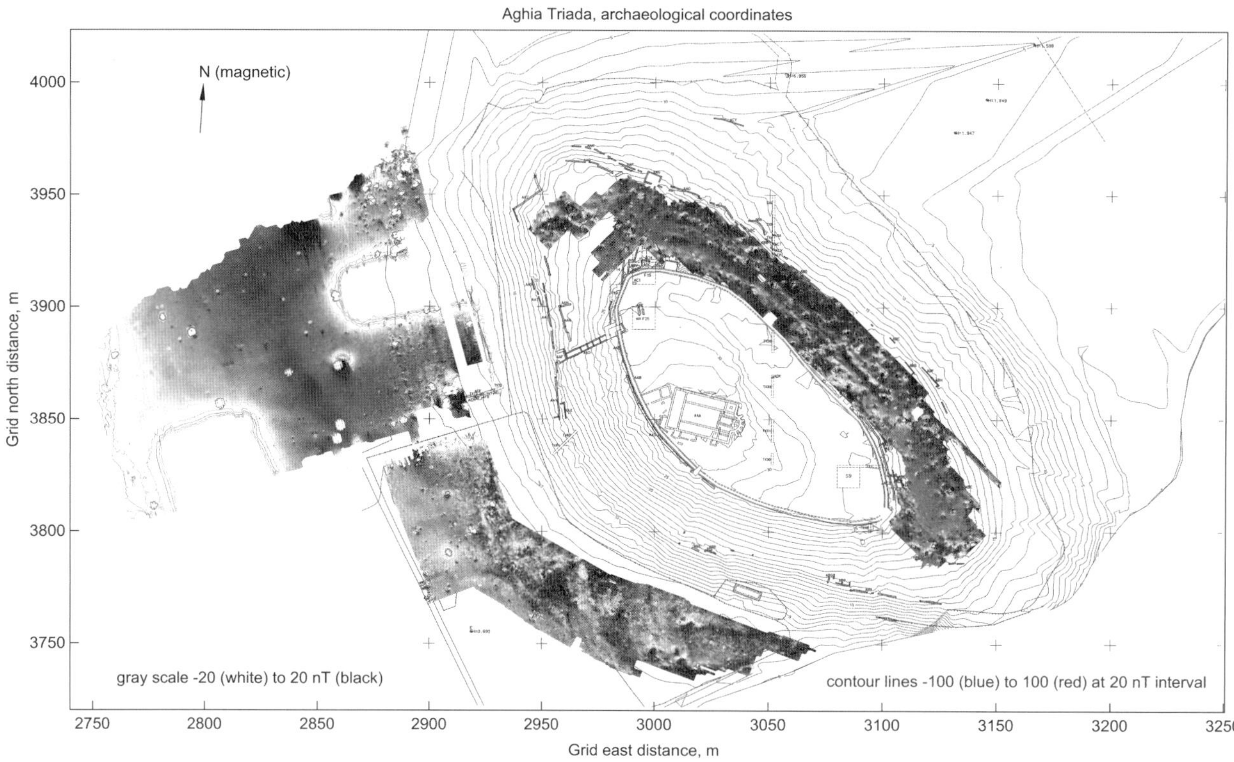

Fig. 13 *All of the magnetic maps are plotted here on an archaeological base map. Areas with high magnetic readings are dark gray or black, and supplemented with contour lines that are red or yellow; magnetic objects such as concentrations of sherds or iron are likely at these locations. Magnetic lows are indicated with light gray or white tones, along with contour lines that are green or blue.Concentrations of stone may be at these places.*

allowed the magnetic maps to be compared with the findings of the earlier archaeological excavations.

Additionally, the exact locations of nine points in the magnetic grids were determined with a precise GPS receiver. These measurements, by George Lolos (Survey Engineering), will allow the magnetic survey to be relocated with the greatest accuracy in the future. Furthermore, the GPS coordinate of one point in the archaeological grid was also measured. This point is on the northern side of the hill. Its coordinate is as follows: In the archaeological grid, it is at E2993.13 N3918.01 m; the GPS location of this point in the Greek coordinate system EGSA 87 is E292,846.70 N4,247,477.71 m. While the orientation of the archaeological grid relative to the GPS grid cannot be determined for certain, there appears to be an angle of about 1.2 degrees between the two coordinate systems.

The magnetic characteristics of the site

The soil at many archaeological sites in Greece is more magnetic than the native stone. It is this magnetic contrast that allows the detection of stone foundations that are buried in the soil. At Chalkis, however, it appears that this magnetic contrast was not as marked or certain as usual.

The magnetic character of many objects was tested during this survey; Fig. 14 shows the findings. As always, ceramic objects are the most magnetic (only metallic iron is more magnetic). Limestone is less magnetic than any other material at this site; the magnetic contrast between limestone and soil is particularly good. Sandstone is frequently as weak in its magnetism as limestone; however, some sandstone at this site is about as magnetic as the soil. This is unfortunate.

While some wall foundations at Chalkis were built with blocks of limestone, most were constructed of sandstone. Fig. 14 suggests that perhaps half of these

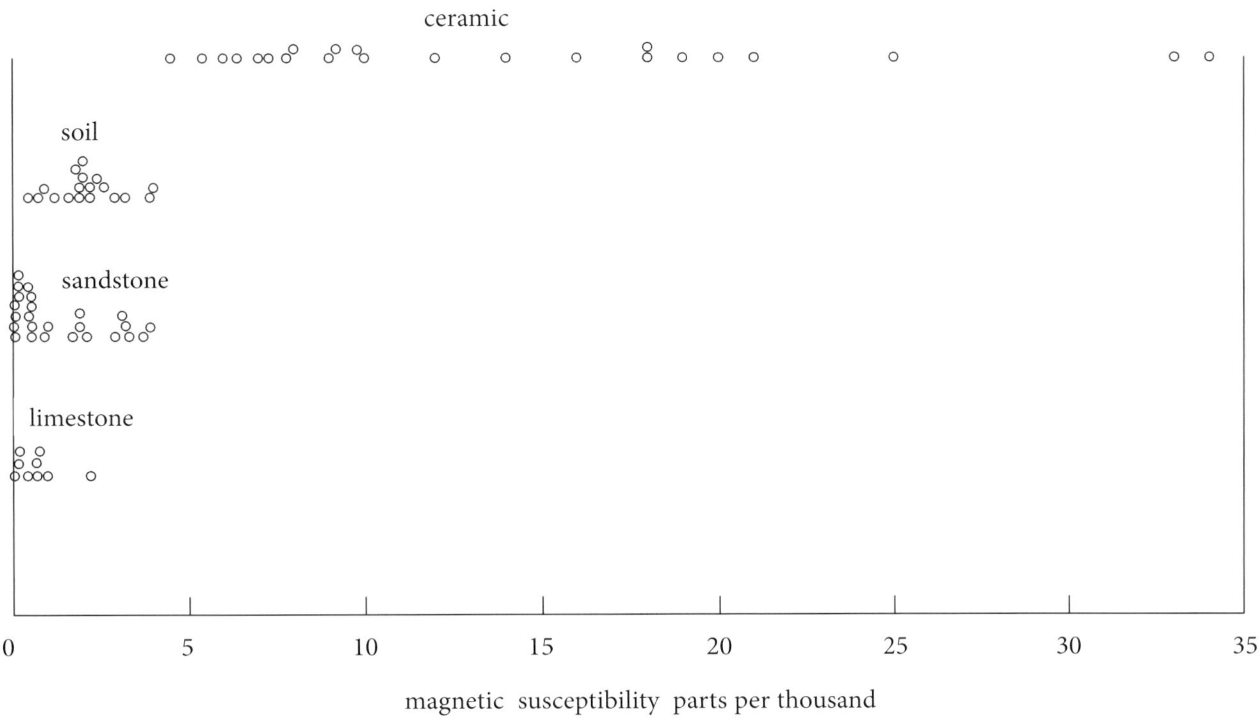

Fig. 14 *The magnetic character of ceramic, soil, and stone from Chalkis. The horizontal scale is magnetic susceptibility; magnetic materials are on the right, while relatively non-magnetic samples are plotted to the left. This magnetic parameter is a pure number and therefore has no unit name. However, it is called "parts per thousand" here (ppt), and the full values in the SI system of units can be determined by dividing the numbers by 1000. Each small circle marks the measurement of one sample.*

sandstone blocks were invisible to this magnetic survey; this is because the magnetic susceptibility of these blocks is about the same as the susceptibility of the soil.

Sandstone can be composed entirely of quartz grains; it is then almost nonmagnetic, and easily detectable. However, if some grains of volcanic stone or magnetite are included with the quartz sand, that sandstone can be moderately magnetic and difficult to find.

The magnetic contrast between ceramic and soil is excellent. It is likely that the features that were detected most distinctly by this survey are accumulations of ceramic.

There are two components or sources to the magnetism of ceramic. One component is magnetic susceptibility, as described above; this quantifies how magnetic the ceramic becomes in the Earth's magnetic field. Secondly, ceramic can also be a permanent magnet; this magnetic effect can be much stronger than the effect of susceptibility.

Magnetic measurements were made on one large fragment of a roof tile from Chalkis; these tests revealed that the permanent magnetism of the tile was about 40 times the magnetism caused by its susceptibility. This strong effect of permanent magnetism is most apparent at kilns and burned buildings. Most of the permanent magnetism of a cluster or concentration of ceramic sherds is lost because of the random orientation of the North and South magnetic poles within sherds of ceramic; this cancels much of the effect of permanent magnetization.

The earlier excavations at Chalkis unearthed large numbers of roof tiles, and most of these had little archaeological importance. At the request of the Sixth Ephorate of Antiquities in Patras, these unwanted tiles were buried along the outer perimeter of the eastern terrace, at locations where no archaeological features were encountered. The pits were about 1.5 m in diameter and they could be deeper than 1 m. Calculations indicate that these tile-containing pits can cause magnetic anomalies of 50-300 nT; about 40 % of the amplitude of each anomaly is caused by susceptibility and about 60 % by permanent magnetism. The effect of permanent magnetism is strong enough that the magnetic lows found near these pits can be expected at almost any angle from the main magnetic high.

Many anomalies like these were revealed along the outer edge of the eastern terrace; most of these are probably caused by pits containing excavated ceramic.

The magnetic survey

Two magnetometers were used in this survey. A Canadian company, Gem Systems, manufactured these magnetometers; the two instruments have a model number of GSM-19WG. These apply the Overhauser principle to their magnetic measurement, which allows precise readings while using little electrical power. One of them, shown on Fig. 20 is the moving or mapping magnetometer. The second one remained fixed at one location during each day's survey and recorded natural changes in the Earth's magnetic field. The readings of this second magnetometer later corrected the temporal changes in the magnetic maps that were created by the first.

Both instruments measured the total flux density of the Earth's magnetic field. The unit of measurement is the nanotesla, abbreviated nT. A typical reading of the magnetic field was about 45,812.37 nT; a change of 5 nT was found to be significant, and some archaeological features caused changes, or anomalies, of over 200 nT.[19]

The magnetic sensor was held at a height of about 0.25 m above the ground surface wherever possible; dense vegetation could require that it be lifted somewhat. Within each area of survey, measurements were recorded while traversing in a single direction; these lines of traverse were spaced by 0.5 m.

Along each traverse, measurements were usually made at time intervals of 0.2 s; while the spacing between readings varied, it was typically about 0.2 m. The traverses were located with guide ropes having painted bands at intervals of 2 m along their length; electronic markers were put in the streams of data to indicate these 2-m intervals along each traverse. The maximum length of each line of measurement was about 50 m.

The procedure above was applied to the areas West of Aghia Triada hill; dense brush and grass on the eastern terrace of the hill required a different procedure. In that area, the magnetic sensor could not be pulled through the vegetation (which was 1-1.5 m tall); instead, separate magnetic readings were made at 0.5-m intervals along lines. This allowed the magnetic sensor to be lifted over a bush, and then pushed down into it at the correct location. While this slowed the survey, it did allow good readings.

This geophysical survey was completed between June 10 and July 5, 2014. Tatiana Smekalova directed the survey and made the magnetic measurements, while Bruce Bevan assisted by setting up survey grids and moving guide ropes. Tatiana Smekalova prepared the initial magnetic maps from this survey, and most of the final maps; Bruce Bevan wrote the majority of this report. Both worked on the analysis of the magnetic anomalies.

The weather during the fieldwork was somewhat cooler than usual for the time of year; essentially no rain fell during the period. On June 25, there was an earthquake whose epicenter was only about 3 km distant. It was detected as a loud boom and an abrupt shaking of the earth for a second. While earthquakes can sometimes cause magnetic effects, none were detected by the magnetometers.

Interpretation of the magnetic maps

The magnetic maps from the separate areas of survey are combined in Fig. 13. The findings in the three areas will be described separately.

Interpretation of the eastern terrace

The magnetic map of this area is enlarged as Fig. 15. The patterns in the map reveal arcs that are parallel with the fortification wall, which is at the southwest-

19 For a general review of magnetic surveys, see the publication of Smekalova, Voss, and Smekalov (2008).

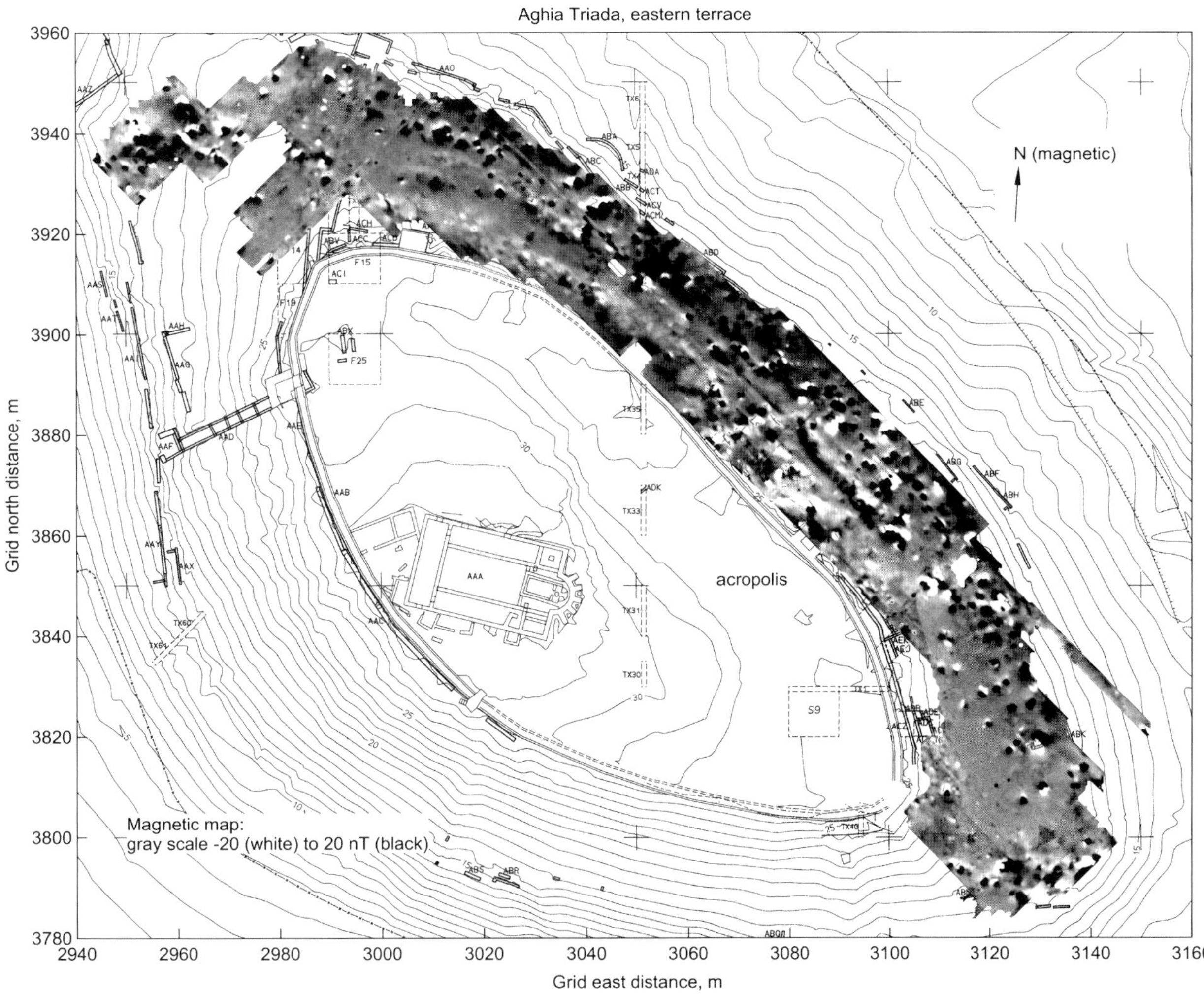

Fig. 15 *The magnetic map of the site overlaid on the archaeological map of the eastern terrace. White or light gray colors in this map show where the magnetic field was low; masses of stone could be buried in those areas. Black or dark gray colors indicate high magnetic field; there may be concentrations of roof tiles or other sherds in these areas.*

ern edge of the magnetic map. These arcing bands could locate either lines of buildings or roads that encircle the hill.

The most distinct band is 50 m long and it is centered at E3080 N3883; this feature is marked with an orange line and the label R2 in the interpretation shown in Fig. 15 and Fig. 16 (with just the interpretation). An analysis of the southern half of this feature suggests that the anomaly could be caused by a layer of magnetic material that is 2 m wide and found at a depth between 0.5 and 1.0 m underground. The interpretation indicates a high susceptibility for the layer (10 ppt) and this suggests that it could contain large amounts of clay tiles or sherds.

An excavation that was earlier made to the centre found a buried road that was constructed of discarded coarseware sherds; these sherds were found between a depth of about 0.5 and 1 m. This excavation is marked with red lines in Fig. 16; the letters *ACP* and *ADQ* are placed at E3075 N3888 where that road was revealed between two stone walls that extend toward the northwest. It is almost certain that the magnetic anomaly at R2 is caused by that road; while the excavated road was 4 m wide, the southern part of the road is interpreted to be only half that width. This road fill was not revealed to the north or south of the R2 span.

However, the magnetic survey suggests that a stone-based road goes to the Northwest from the

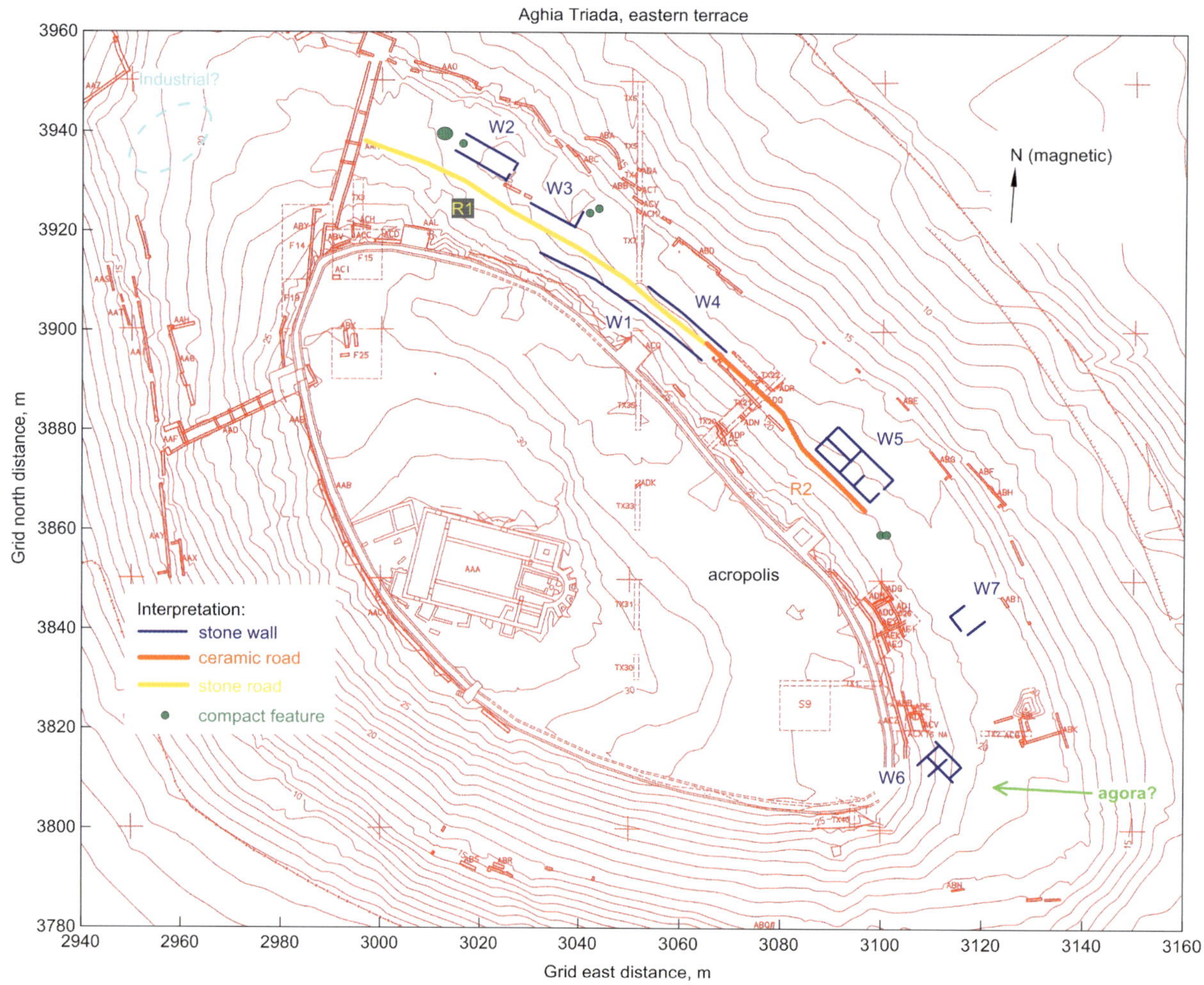

Fig. 16 *An interpretation of the magnetic map that was measured on the eastern terrace. This version allows an easy comparison with the archaeological base map that is printed red here. The archaeological map here does not include the results of the later excavations at the site in 2001; this map may indicate findings as they were in 1996–1999.*

ceramic-based road, R2. This band is marked with a yellow line and the text R1 in Fig. 16; this feature is centered near E3034 N3920 and it has a length of about 80 m. There is probably a greater density of stone in the soil along that span, and a road may have a base of stone, rather than ceramic.

The magnetic map of Fig. 15 also shows additional linear bands where the magnetic field was low; these bands are narrower and shorter than that at road R1, and they are marked with blue in the interpretations. The stone of buried wall foundations may cause these bands. There are several clusters of these possible walls, and they are labeled with the letter W followed by a number. It is possible that wall segments W1 and W4 locate extensions of walls that were revealed in an excavation to the South. Segments W2 and W3 are aligned with a possible terrace wall that was visible at the surface; this is located in the archaeological base map at E3028 N3928. The groups of possible walls at W5 and W7 are aligned with road segment R2, but the walls at W6 are not oriented with the findings of wall foundations that were revealed in nearby excavations in AREA III and IIIa.

None of these interpretations of walls is certain, but, they are based on successful interpretations at dozens of other sites with similar anomalies. There are several causes for the uncertainty in the interpretation of walls here: Only some of the stones in these foundations can be detected with this magnetic survey; this causes the ideally-simple magnetic patterns to be broken into irregular shapes. There is also a layer of stone rubble that covers much of the eastern terrace; this rubble was revealed in the excavations that were made earlier here. An irregular thickness or concentration of this rubble creates complex patterns that can obscure the linear patterns of the walls that are sought. This rubble is thought to have been stone that was discarded from the Acropolis, perhaps in Byzantine times.

The rubble is particularly thick close to the fortification wall on the southwestern side of the area of survey; this rubble appears to have hidden the wall foundations that were sought next to that fortification. The wall cluster at W6 (Fig. 16) is close to the fortification wall, but the rubble may be a thinner layer there because of the lower slope and greater distance from the Acropolis.

The magnetic map of the eastern terrace (Fig. 15) shows many anomalies that are rather circular on the outer half (northeastern side) of the terrace. While some of these anomalies may have an archaeological importance, almost all of them are probably just pits that have been filled with excavated roof tiles. The spatial size and amplitude of these anomalies agree with this interpretation. Those anomalies, which are most likely not caused by excavated tiles, are marked with dark green ovals in Fig. 16. Near the northwestern corner of the map, around E2957 N3938, there is a cluster of strong anomalies that may be caused by ancient industrial features, such as kilns. This area is outlined with a light blue dashed line.

The magnetic map of the terrace found many areas where the magnetic field was unusually high or unusually low. However, near the southeastern end of the terrace, a region was found that had few anomalies; this is located in Fig. 16 with a green arrow. It is possible that there might have been an agora at this location.

Interpretation of the northern harbour

Fig. 17 is the magnetic map of the northern harbour or shore, along with its interpretation (red lines and text).

The eastern side of this map (to the right of the grid line W140) reveals dozens of small-area anomalies near A2 and A4. Almost all of these are probably caused by modern metal trash that is buried there;

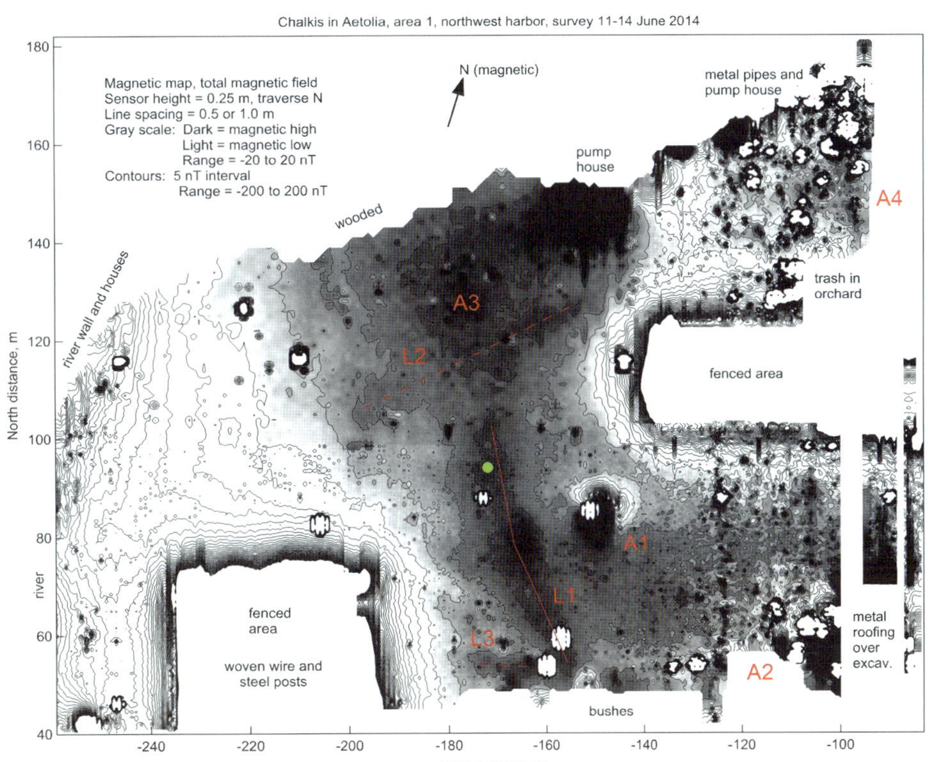

Fig. 17 A magnetic map of the northwestern side of Aghia Triada. Dense areas of parallel contour lines reveal the proximity of modern iron; fences caused most of these patterns. The coordinates at the edge of this map are those of this magnetic survey.

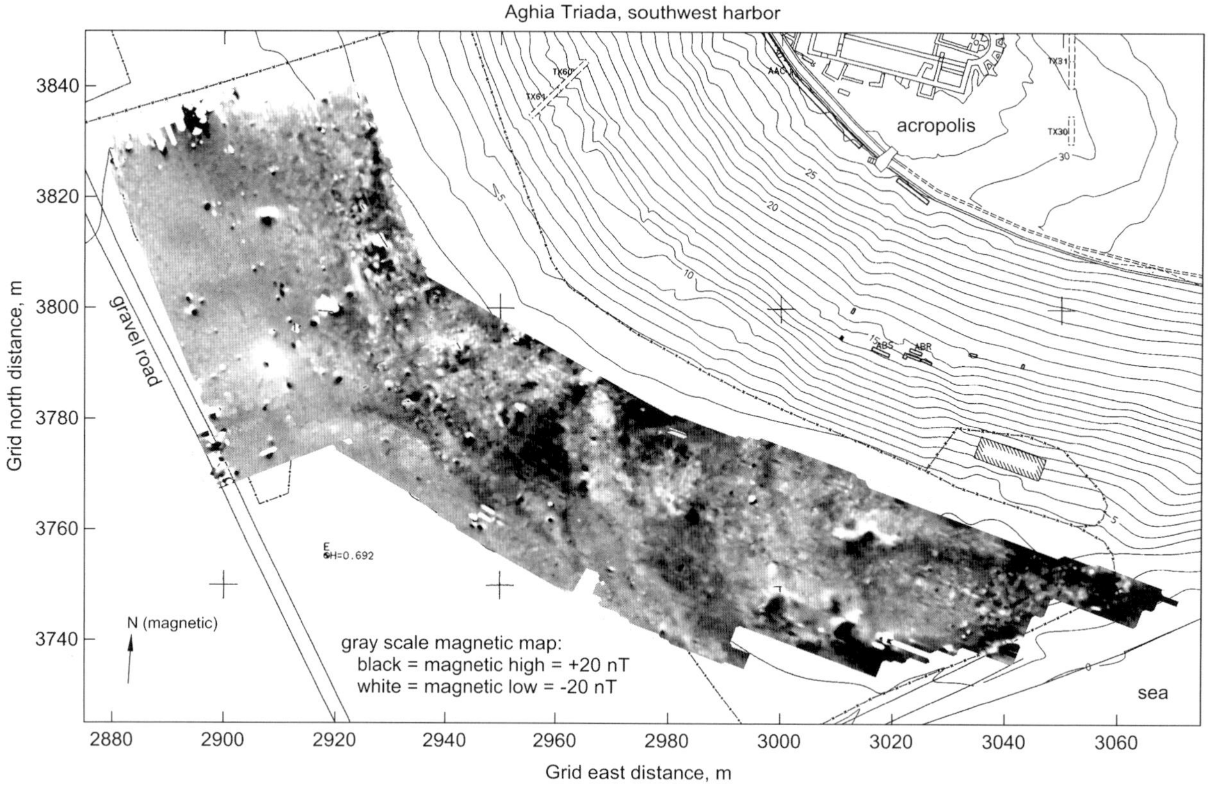

Fig. 18 *A magnetic map of the area on the southwestern side of Aghia Triada. Dark tones indicate magnetic areas where there may be concentrations of ceramic, such as sherds or roof tiles. Light tones may locate concentrations of stone in the soil.*

this is the area of an olive orchard. No archaeological interpretation of the magnetic map is possible here.

A very strong and isolated magnetic anomaly is seen at A1 (W-149 N86); this very likely has a modern origin. An analysis of this anomaly indicates that its source is at a depth of 1-2 m. Several small anomalies are located around A3, but no pattern to them is seen there, and this area was probably part of the open bay before sediments filled it. A soil coring at the location of the green circle in Fig. 17 found soft sediments to a depth of 4.4 m.

Several linear magnetic anomalies have been revealed and these are marked with the letter L. Feature L1 appeared to be quite interesting at first, but it may just be caused by the steel fences to the East and West. The contour lines show that these fences were detected for a distance of more than 30 m. While the effect of these fences can be reduced in the magnetic map by data processing (window smoothing and low-pass filtering), that processing does not add any definite information and it does create artificial patterns.

The two remaining linear magnetic highs are not as distinct, but they are at least not caused by fences. These are marked L2 and L3 in Fig. 17. While these magnetic anomalies could locate archaeological features, such as deepened channels in a harbour, there is no further evidence for this interpretation.

Interpretation of the southern harbour

The magnetic map of the southern harbour is plotted here as Fig. 18. The many strong-amplitude and small-area magnetic anomalies that were found in the northern harbour are almost missing here. This is probably because the area has not been farmed and there have never been any orchards here. There was once a pig sty nearby (the rectangle near the right side of the map), but that building is no longer there.

The magnetic map shows an area of moderately weak and small-area anomalies close to the hill. At a

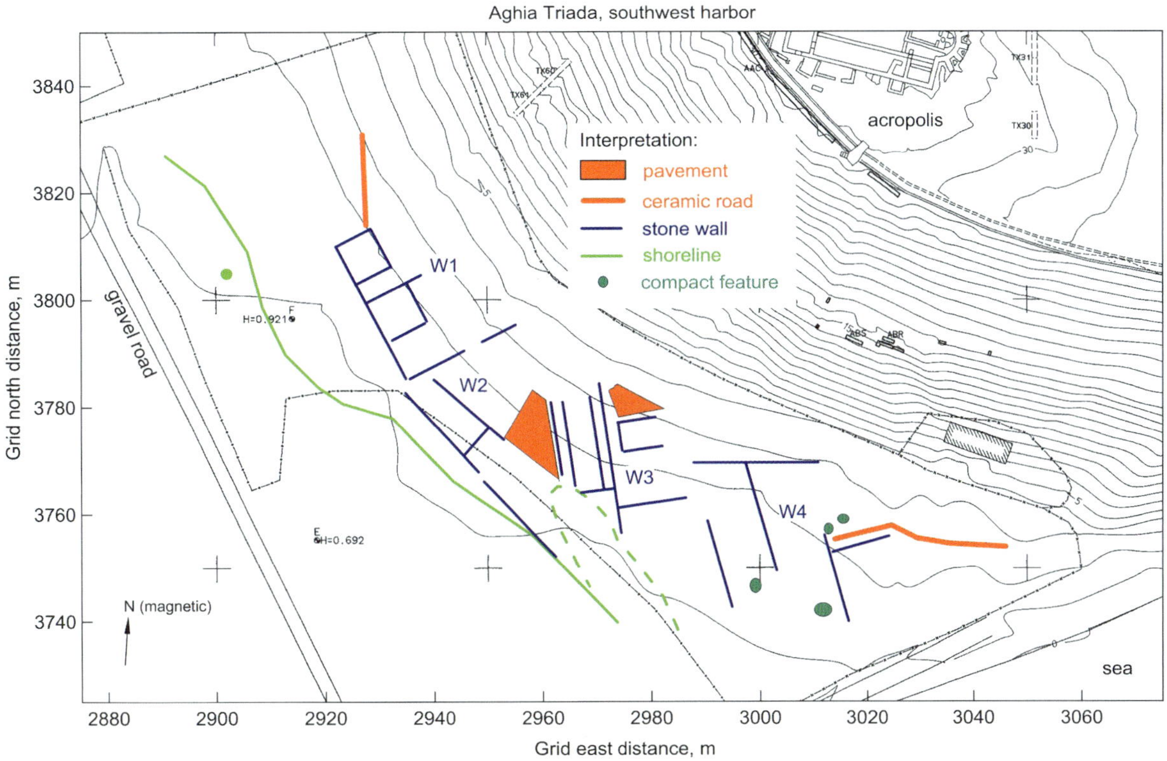

Fig. 19 *An interpretation of the magnetic map of the southwestern shoreline around Aghia Triada. The surface slopes up to the acropolis where part of the foundation of the Byzantine church is seen. The interval between elevation lines in the contour map is 1 m.*

greater distance, these anomalies disappear abruptly. It is reasonable to suppose that this change, which is marked with a green line in Figs. 18 and 19, indicates the shoreline of the former Bay.

There is an interesting indentation in this line near E2970 that is 10 m wide. A broken green line locates this feature, and its boundary is dashed because it is less certain. It is possible that this feature might locate a dredged area where boats could approach the shore more closely.

Major magnetic anomalies are near this indentation in the shoreline. Magnetic areas to the East and West are shown as orange polygons; these anomalies could be caused by concentrations of ceramic or magnetic stone that have been discarded along the shore in order to make a good foundation for a pavement. Perhaps ballast (stabilizing loads in the bottom of boats) has been dumped in this area also.

Two orange lines in Fig. 19 could delineate ceramic-based roads, like the one that was traced on the eastern terrace. Also like the eastern terrace, a number of possible buried wall foundations of stone have been delineated. These are marked with blue lines; clusters of these are labeled W1 through W4.

Four strong anomalies at the eastern edge of the magnetic map are marked with dark green ovals in Fig. 19. It is possible that these patterns could be caused by kilns that were next to the shore. One of these anomalies, near the lower right side of the map (at E3011 N3742), was analyzed and the depth of this feature could be about 0.6 m.

Conclusions

The most interesting findings of this survey were along the southern shoreline of the former bay. The unusual magnetic patterns in this area do suggest shore facilities, such as docks and storage areas.

It could be valuable to extend that part of the magnetic survey farther inland in order to detect additional buildings slightly uphill from the shore. The dense bushes in that area would need to be cut (probably with hand machinery) to allow access for the magnetometer.

While it is likely that a sherd-packed road was traced along the eastern terrace, the results of the magnetic survey in this area were poorer than was wished. The layer of stone rubble that overlies the architectural features probably caused the major difficulty for the survey here. This stone rubble was encountered in the earlier archaeological excavations, and it was thought that this rubble had been removed from the Acropolis at some earlier time.

This layer of stone rubble harmed the magnetic survey in two ways. First, it buried the architectural walls that were sought to a greater depth underground; this greater depth decreased the amplitude of the magnetic anomalies of the stone foundations. Second, the thickness of the rubble is probably irregular; each area of thicker or thinner stone rubble creates its own magnetic pattern that will tend to mask the linear anomalies of foundations.

The magnetic survey of the eastern terrace would have been easier, and the results could have been more certain, if this survey had been done after the area was cleared of brush before the excavations in the 1990's.

While unrelated to the results of this magnetic survey, the ancient access way to the eastern terrace and the Acropolis is still unknown; there must have been roads in ancient times, but these cannot now be identified. For many years, a road has run up the eastern end of the mound to allow cars to get up to the eastern terrace. It is not impossible that this modern road follows the ancient road. There is a hint of a road on the western side of the hill also, but the brush there is too dense to allow exploration. These suggestions of ancient roads could be further investigated in the future.

Acknowledgements

This magnetic survey was commissioned and directed by Søren Dietz (Danish Institute at Athens). His earlier success with magnetic surveys at the nearby site of Kalydon encouraged him to employ the same methods to answer some archaeological questions at Chalkis. He kindly provided our local transportation and lodging in Greece, and he shared his detailed knowledge of Chalkis in order to aid our understanding of the magnetic anomalies that we found. We enjoyed his cooking and companionship during our field survey, as he prepared his own reports of the site.

The Danish Institute in Athens furnished us with pleasant lodging during our two trips to the city; Søren Handberg coordinated our stay there in July 2014.

Fig. 20 *The magnetometer that was used for this survey. The sensor is within the white cylinder that Tatiana is holding close to the surface of the ground. She carries a control console in front of her, and this records the measurements. This instrument measures the strength of the Earth's magnetic field, but not its direction; this can be compared to a magnetic compass, which indicates only direction, and not strength. The mountain of Varassova is in the background.*

A.3 Changing space and habitation pattern

Søren Dietz

Introduction

The general lay-out of the habitation on the Aghia Triada mound and the western side of the mound is shown on Fig. 21 where information from excavations, registration of architectural remains visible on the surface and the results of the geomagnetic surveys are shown. The plain, between the foot of the mound and the small river, which today marks the eastern border of the village of Kato Vasiliki, is practically level (Fig. 22) defining approximately the limit of the small bay shown by the geological and geophysical survey to have existed in Antiquity. The area east of Aghia Triada, where marine sediments were not detected by the geological examinations, was flat land as it is today, with a shallow layer of soil covering the bedrock.

The habitation on the mound is restricted to the Acropolis, where only a few traces of ancient habitation are preserved, and the northeastern and northwestern terrace from the 17 m contour line towards the Acropolis (emphasized on Fig. 21). Foundation walls on the southern part of the hill, follow the 14-15 m contour lines between the level area and the steep slope towards the sea and the bay.

The foundations, built of sandstone ashlars of various size that line the northeastern and northwestern terraces, were probably terrace walls and prevented the buildings on the terrace from sliding down. The fact, however, that the constructions join the towers of the late Classical fortification walls might indicate that they had defensive functions as well.

The habitation on the Eastern Terrace

Almost in the middle of the eastern terrace is a road (in the following we call this road the *terrace-road*), excavated in AREA I from 1997 onwards and in subsequent seasons. In the lower strata quite a quantity of EH and MH sherds were found. The road is shown to have functioned from the early Archaic period until early Classical times, when the former sherd packing, consisting of several well defined layers, was replaced by a slab stone pavement. Around 9 m of this road was excavated, measuring 3.5 m in width in Classical times.[20] The geomagnetic survey indicates that the *terrace-road* was "clay-packed" from AREA I to the southeast, while it was stone paved from this area to the Late Classical defense wall to the Northwest. The road could have been around 130 m long measured from the late Classical wall (1st quarter of 4th century BC) to just before the workshops and store buildings, excavated in AREA III, at which point the road terminates.

The first defense wall, was built in late Archaic, in the late 6th (-480 BC) century BC (see below). It defined the Acropolis as a specific space separated from the habitation zone on the terrace and the harbour area west of the hill. Habitation on the mound, however, started much earlier with a few traces of use already in the mid 4th Mill., the Final Neolithic/Chalcolithic period, succeeded by a well-defined EHI deposit sealed between the Archaic fortification/terrace-wall and the Byzantine fortification, excavated in AREA I. Evidence for habitation during the transitional period MH/LH and late Mycenaean was rather abundant on the mound, but was not found in sealed contexts.[21] The first more substantial habitation with preserved architecture derives from the early Archaic period (7th century), and is situated on the East side

20 For the Prehistoric remains see *Chalkis Aitolias I*, 83 ff. The road is described in TPR, 176-179. Also Houby-Nielsen in *Chalkis Aitolias II*.

21 In contrast to the harbour area, *AREA II* (*Chalkis Aitolias I*, 38 ff.).

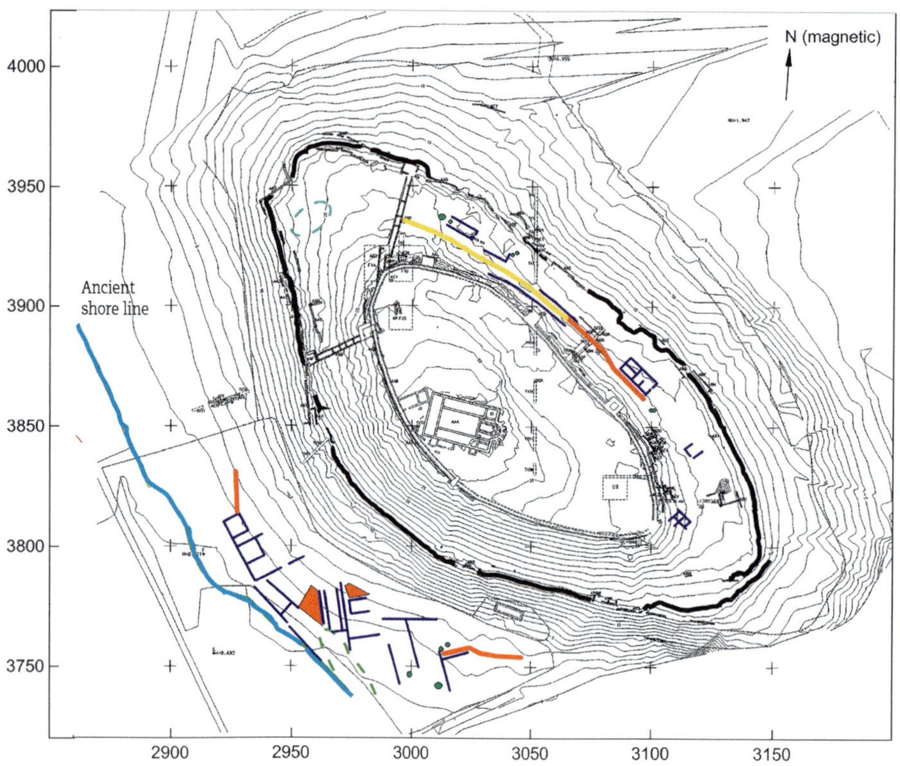

Fig. 21 *Aghia Triada. Interpretation map with information from excavations, measurements of surface structures and geomagnetic explorations are shown on the same plan. The 15 and 17 m contour line are emphasized. Note that the deviation of the arrowhead of the North point is caused by the fact that archaeological grit system differs about 1, 2 degrees from the GPS measurements in 2014 (see chapter A.2).*

of the *terrace-road* (*ANA/AFL*) in AREA I.[22] On the other side of the road, towards the Acropolis, smaller parts of a seemingly substantial building dated to the Classical period were partly excavated.[23]

There are considerable differences between the habitations along the *terrace-road* in AREA I, and the buildings excavated in AREA III.[24] The buildings along the road are larger, differently constructed, with quite a different plan and without tiles used for roofing. That the road didn't continue further South East is indicated by the fact that houses in AREA III are founded directly on bedrock and no traces of a road was found in front of these rooms. On the other hand this doesn't mean that buildings were not erected further south; thus the rather large unexcavated building in AREA IIIA was surely built in Archaic times (see below). Buildings in AREA III are small workshops and storerooms built in the late 4th and early 3rd century BC with mud brick walls on stone foundations and heavy tile-roofs. The buildings along the road in AREA I are older than the workshop/storerooms in AREA III.

We suggest that a systematic local production of laconian tile, in the Aitolian coastland, started in the late 4th/early 3rd century when tiles were produced in large quantities, as indicated by the roofs and the stack of stored tiles in the rooms in AREA III. A more advanced stage of industrial standardized tile production in the coastal region is attested in the Peristyle building in the Lower Town of Kalydon, which dates from very late in the third century BC, where several factories are identified by their stamps.[25] An earlier stage of this production is found on Pangali, where buildings from the second quarter of the third century used tiles of Laconian and (less frequently) Corinthian type (Chapter E below).

22 *TPR*, 179 ff and Houby-Nielsen in *Chalkis Aitolias II*.

23 *TPR*, 180 ff. But not dated, as is recorded there "or early 3rd century BC".

24 See below Chapter C.

25 *Kalydon* 2011, Chapter 11.0 p. 579 ff.

Fig. 22 *Aghia Triada. Vertical photo of the area between the village of Kato Vasiliki (left) and the mound of Aghia Triada (right). North is up, the golf of Patras to the South! The excavation in AREA II is seen as a white spot in the olive grove in the northern corner, right (photo by Rune Frederiksen and Søren Handberg July, 2014).*

In summary – the first division of functional, social and religious (?) space on the mound was created when the fortification wall was constructed around the Acropolis plateau in the late 6th century BC. Probably at the same time (or perhaps more gradually) the terrace/defense system on the 17 m contour line was built, creating a defined habitation zone between the Acropolis wall and the 17 m line. At this time there was free access from the eastern terrace to the north western corner where the entrance to the Acropolis most likely was placed (see also below p 64). In the first half of the 4th century, the fortification of the Acropolis was considerably augmented and two substantial fortification walls were erected around the NW plateau (see below p 64), thus blocking the communication between the Eastern terrace and the Acropolis. Later in the 4th century, the workshops/ storerooms in the Southern part of the Eastern terrace were erected. Perhaps the empty space in the south-eastern corner of the plateau was now used as an Agora – with access up the slope to the East – in contrast to the more ancient pathway up the North West slope from the harbour.

The buildings on the East- and Northwest Terrace

The houses along the *terrace-road* (ANA/AFL) on the terrace East and Northwest of the Acropolis were long, rectangular buildings, divided into two or more, narrow rooms at one end by a wall, and placed parallel to the contour lines along the road (Fig. 21)

In AREA I a smaller part of such a house (house *AXA* on Fig. 23) has been excavated (Figs. 23-24).[26] The building is situated along the above mentioned terrace-road, the building separated from the road by a stone block wall.[27] The wall *ACP* is constructed with a low foundation of small, 15 to 20 cm rectangular stones supporting a row of stone blocks measuring 40-70 cm to almost 1 m in length and up to 40 cm high. The lower foundation was uncovered for a length of approximately 23 m while only about 8 m of the upper row of stone blocks was preserved. This construction is not appropriate for supporting a house wall and perhaps indicates the border of the road. In contrast, the SE wall of the building (*ANB*) was made of substantial sandstone blocks founded on bedrock and preserved in up to 4 courses to around 1.5 m high.[28] If our reconstruction of the building Fig. 23 is correct, the building was around 7.5 m wide.[29] The foundations are between 60 and 70 cm wide except for the central wall, *ADN*, which measures about 1 m – perhaps as a result of reconstruction. If the dimensions of the building are similar to the rectangular building on the other side of the road – indicated by the geomagnetic survey – the length could have been around 12-17 m – that is a building of around 90-120 m² (see below). The rather substantial foundations might indicate the existence of an upper floor. The lack of tiles means that the roof was built of lighter material for instance thatch – a material readily available in the harbour area. Probably the roof was a ridged roof – the total span was 7.5 meter divided by the wall (approximately) in the middle.[30] The building and the wall *ACP* were probably constructed at the earliest in the 5th century BC.[31]

The rectangular building (W5 on Fig. 16) drawn on the geomagnetic survey map measures 15 × 7 m or 105 m². Another rectangular building W2 on Fig. 16), found closer to the late Classical fortification wall is narrower, measuring around 12 × 4 m or approximately 50 m². If a column is placed in the western opening, as indicated on the plan, we might have a construction similar to the well-known Prostas house type (but no cross wall separating the porch).[32] Finally it seems possible that the foundation uncovered by cleaning in the NW sector[33] with a preserved length of 17 m and a preserved width of 5 m is a long rectangular building of the same type. This building could thus have been more than 100 m² (only 85 m² preserved), as the long

26 *TPR*, 180 ff.

27 *ACP* on Fig. 23. See also *TPR*, 177, fig. 4.

28 *TPR*, 181, Fig. 7.

29 Not "long" as indicated in *TPR*, 181.

30 Compare the Attic Deme house, *BSA* 57, 1968 and Schack 1997, Wacker 1997.

31 And not "perhaps not until the 4th/3rd century ..." *TPR*, 180-181. This suggestion was based on the dating of the foundation *ADP* which is, however, later than the rectangular house.

32 Drerup 1967, et al.

33 *AAH/AAG* see also Figs.3 and 39.

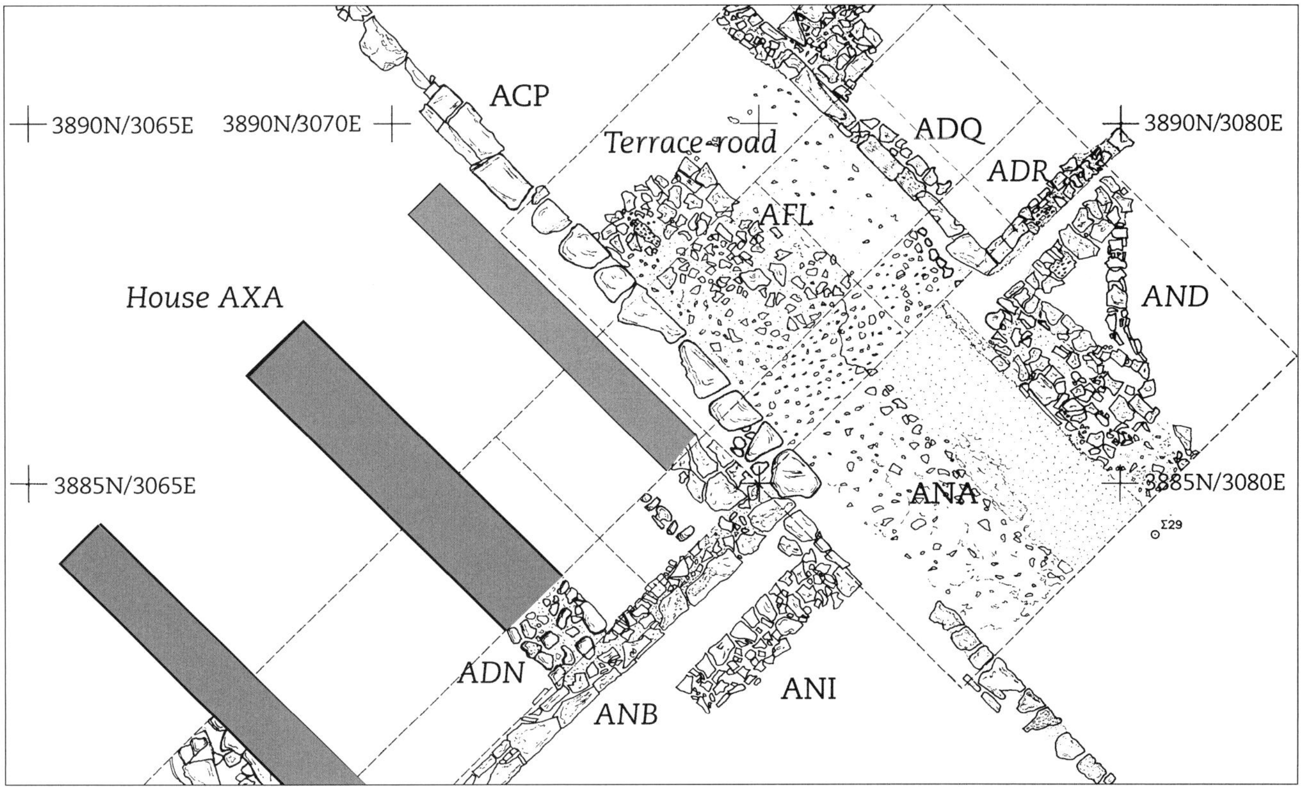

Fig. 23 *Architecture in AREA I. The structure AFL/ANA is the terrace-road attested by excavation and the geophysical exploration. The grey bars are reconstructions.*

Fig. 24 *Aghia Triada, the Eastern terrace AREA I. In the foreground is seen the terrace-road AFL/ ANA in front of the stone wall ACP.*

building in AREA I.

We conclude that in Prehistoric times and through to the Archaic period the terrace and the Acropolis formed one large open (unwalled) space. After the construction of the fortification wall in the late 6th century, the access to the Acropolis was restricted to the NW corner. Long rectangular buildings were built on the terrace after the Archaic period but before the early 4th century, when the large fortification walls were built. Perhaps the flat NW corner of the terrace served as an Agora and industrial zone for the small society, and provided access to the harbour from the northwest. After the construction of the 4th century fortifications, the East Terrace was isolated from the North West corner which still had access to the harbour and an entrance to the Acropolis. On the East terrace the workshops and store buildings were constructed (in AREA III) and a new access was created from the East, up the slope perhaps to a possible Agora (?) shown on Fig. 16 on the flattish area, E of W6.

The harbour area

In the harbour area, the shoreline of the small bay was traced by the geomagnetic survey (chapter A2 and Fig. 19). Excavations were conducted between the 3 m and the 5 m contour lines in a rectangular trench 14 × 4 m and a smaller trench further east.[34] In the large trench (AREA II) which in part extended down to 3 m below the present surface, deposits of MHIII/LHIA, LHIB and LHIIIC were excavated. Above these a series of Archaic building horizons were recorded, dating from the early 7th century BC to late 6th/early 5th century.[35] After the last Archaic settlement, habitation ceased, but in early Hellenistic times the area (east of the Archaic habitation) was turned into a cemetery for "well-to-do inhabitants"[36] – the cemetery is contemporary with the workshops/storerooms at the Eastern terrace AREA III. The Archaic houses are placed approximately 30 m from the ancient shoreline. In the different phases of the Archaic settlement, the lay-out of the rooms changed considerably but it is evident, as pointed out by Houby-Nielsen, that at least in the later periods of the habitation the southern complex of the trench formed a small part of a larger house extending towards the west and the shore and probably towards the south. Evidence suggests the house was occupied mainly by textile production.[37] Around the excavation in AREA II there was too much magnetic "noise" for the geomagnetic survey to reveal further structures (see chapter A.2).

Some 40 m to the south, the geomagnetic survey revealed traces which could be interpreted as a large building placed 15-17 m from the shore (W1 on Fig. 19). The design is square/rectangular with one side measuring 27 m, the other preserved 23 m – a surprisingly large building measuring more than 600 m^2 with inner partitions. A road links AREA II with this building. Among other patterns drawn by the geomagnetic survey are two small squares and in between them, a narrow track approximately 5 m wide between a 6-8 m wide section seaward. It is tempting to interpret the narrow building as a ship shed. There were evidently more rather large buildings in the area, possible for harbour facilities or for various industries.

Settlement size, density of population, social and economic status

Habitation is found primarily on the terraces NW and NE of the Acropolis, and large buildings are placed on the flat land between the ancient shoreline of the bay and the foot of the mound. On the terraces, habitation only sporadically extended below the 17 m contour-line. A rough estimatien indicates the size of the settlement on the terraces as around 1.2 ha. On the Acropolis the entire space is around 0.7 ha and if we estimate that the shallow land along the shoreline of the bay was in use for habitation from the sea coastline to the 4000 m line N (Fig. 21), the entire inhabited area makes up some 3.7 ha or 4 ha at the most.

Commercial production of textiles seems to have taken place at the site – not only in the Archaic period

34 *TPR*, 182 ff. *Chalkis Aitolias I.*

35 See Sanne Houby-Nielsen in *Chalkis Aitolias II* (forthcoming).

36 Eiring cit. in *PDAI*, 93-166.

37 *Chalkis Aitolias II.*

but also in Hellenistic times.[38] One of the buildings on the coast (in AREA II), partly excavated, is suggrested to have been dedicated to production of woven materials. Other buildings along the shoreline might have had other functions, related to the harbour administration. Textile production is not only attested along the shoreline but also abundantly on the upper terraces (more than 400 loom-weights are registered from the site).

The small society first flourished during Archaic times from the 7th century onwards. Archaic buildings were found in the central part of the NE terrace and in AREA IV where late Archaic buildings were constructed against the Late Archaic/Classical fortification wall. The most intensive habitation in Archaic times was probably in the area along the bay – but it is difficult to estimate the size from the restricted excavations carried out and the difficulties encountered during the geomagnetic surveys.[39] The Acropolis was in use in Archaic times more than in the Hellenistic period, but the evidence doesn't suggest intensive use. Perhaps it remained a refuge for use in troubled times.

Communication with the surrounding world was intensive, as shown by the pottery, and the small society evidently participated in the busy trade along the Corinthian Gulf.[40] In Classical times a series of rather large, elongated houses framed the long terrace-road, but the road itself was constructed in the Archaic period. The chronology is not well established and the function of the houses is not clear – farmhouses might be a possibility?

During the turbulent years of the second quarter of the 4th century BC, when the coastland was "liberated" from the Achaeans by the Boeotian troops under Epaminondas, large engineering works were initiated in order to improve the defense systems. Two large, double-faced limestone walls including three substantial towers were built around the NW corner, the old fortification walls were re-enforced and a new and strong defensive refuge, much bigger than Aghia Triada, was built at Pangali on the east slopes of Varassova. On the southern end of the eastern terrace at Aghia Triada, finds in a series of workshops and store rooms evidence that the textile production was still performed in the late 4th to early 3rd century; production for domestic use for sure but probably also of importance for the commercial actitivities of the community. In addition, a systematic tile-production was initiated, and grain was ground on imported millstones. Cattle, pigs, sheep and goats supplemented with shellfish and bread, (?) made up the staple food of the people who inhabited the workshops and store rooms (se Chapter E.2). Along the shoreline, behind the earlier Archaic building, well-built cist graves constructed of large sandstone slabs contained skeletons with grave goods indicating that they were important members of the society. As before, trade flourished – the harbour evidently still functioned, for among the coins found were examples from as far away as Punic Carthage in North Africa in the Western Mediterranean.

Conclusion

From this brief survey it should be clear, that the fortified settlement (see chapter B) of Chalkis Aitolias was a low density habitation. There is no indication of a planned habitation zone where inhabitants lived close together. A generous estimation would be 100 to 150 inhabitants per ha or between 400 and 600 inhabitants in all – perhaps around 600 inhabitants in Archaic and less, around 400, in Late Classical/Early Hellenistic times.[41] In Hansen & Nielsen 2004, 382, Chalkis is classified as a polis – evidently on the basis of Thucydides "... a Corinthian dependency, though probably not a colony settled by the Corinthians". After the Amphictionic war (356-346 BC) the settlement became a dependant of Athens.[42] In the written sources there is no doubt about the strategic importance of Chalkis – but as demonstrated above, the small settlement could hardly have been a polis – no town planning, the fortification restricted to the Acropolis, no politi-

38 *Paliouras* mentions a find of 200 loom-weights from the Byzantine habitation. *Paliouras* 2004,215.

39 See Ch. A.2.

40 For Archaic Chalkis see Houby-Nielsen in *Chalkis II.*

41 In *Kalydon* which is clearly a Polis we estimated 200 inhabitants/ha and the entire population to be around 5000 inhabitants (*Kalydon* 2011, 79).

42 Hansen & Nielsen cit.

cal and no religious architecture. Sanctuaries are not found and whatever traces of shrines there are, point rather to private cults.[43] That no inscriptions were found might be coincidental.[44]

Rather than a Polis, the fortified site of Aghia Triada should be classified as an Emporion, a broad term, used in antiquity either for a dependant settlement, sometimes even included in the town plan of a polis, or a more independent social structure.[45] The status of Chalkis Aitolias is discussed in Klaus Freitag (1999) Peter Funke (1987 and 1997) and Sebastian Bommeljé (et al. 1987, 112). In this connection we use the term Emporion in the broad sense of the word: a trading station or, more specifically[46] "a port-of-trade".

It has been suggested that Chalkis was the harbour of Kalydon. Even though there must have been connections with the closest large town in the area it is more probable that Kalydon's primary harbour was located at today's Kryoneri where Varassova meets the sea on the Western side of the mountain.[47] There are no genuine poleis behind Aghia Triada and we would suggest that Chalkis first of all functioned as a local trade centre with good harbour facilities and an economy dependent on trade, textile industry, tile production (in Hellenistic times) and the preparation of agricultural products relying on supplies from the fertile hinterland. The textile production must have demanded considerable amounts of both wool and linen. The dye was probably based on the marine shell Hexaplus Trunculus.[48] At Kalydon, the East-Gate and the main section of the exterior curtains a were probably constructed in the late 4th century, contemporary with the workshops in AREA III, at a time when the small harbour town of Chalkis saw a considerable economic activity and a certain prosperity among some of its inhabitants. At the end of the century, before 200 BC, Chalkis was abandoned, while Kalydon saw a veritable building boom with the erection of the Peristyle building in the Lower Town a prestigious building constructed inside the reinforced defense systems on the Acropolis along and a new gate protected by impressive towers. The building activities in the Aitolian coastland were considerable in the later 3rd century – in 230 BC for instance, the strong fortified town of New Pleuron was founded – replacing an older site lower down the slope. Why the population left Chalkis at this time is difficult to say. Perhaps the small bay and the harbour became silted up, or perhaps it became evident that it was not, after all, possible to defend the small town despite the improvements of the early 4th century. Whatever happened, the small mound was not used again until 700 years later at the time of Justinian, when a strong new fortification wall was constructed around a large basilica dedicated to the Aghia Triada.

43 The isolated early 4th century, painted, raking sima (F97-7) found during cleaning of the Byzantine corner tower *ACR* could, but does not necessarily, derive from a public or a semi-public structure on the Acropolis (*SPR*, 231-232, Fig. 7).

44 The information that a coin in the British Museum indicates that coins were struck in Chalkis has not been confirmed. Kenneth Sheedy personal information.

45 On the many different aspects of the meaning of the word Emporion, see Hansen 2006, 1-39.

46 Karl Polanyi, cited Hansen 2006.

47 *Kalydon* 2011, 43.

48 See Houby-Nielsen in *Chalkis Aitolias II* and Strand Petersen above.

B. FORTIFICATION SYSTEMS – ARCHAIC TO BYZANTINE

B.1 The Archaic/Classical and Hellenistic fortification and terrace walls and the excavations in AREA IV

Søren Dietz

The Acropolis

The Acropolis terrace is a level plateau of around 7000 m^2, situated between 26 and 33 m.a.s. with the three-aisled basilica (*AAA*) placed right on the top in the southwestern part of the plateau (Figs. 3 and 25). The northern and eastern part of the plateau is more or less level, situated between 26 and 28 m.a.s. The surface of the Acropolis is heavily eroded and consists mainly of conglomerate and sandstone with the original surface soil found mainly as dump slipped down from the higher levels towards east and southeast against the Byzantine fortification wall. The only architectural remains (except for the early Byzantine basilica with associated buildings) found during the campaigns were the foundations in the southern part of excavation section IV, trench F25 (*ABX*) situated directly on the bedrock (Fig. 25).

Excavations in AREA IV

General stratigraphy and chronology. In the northwestern corner of the Aghia Triada Acropolis (AREA IV), a series of trenches were opened in 1996 in order to examine the relations between the inside and the

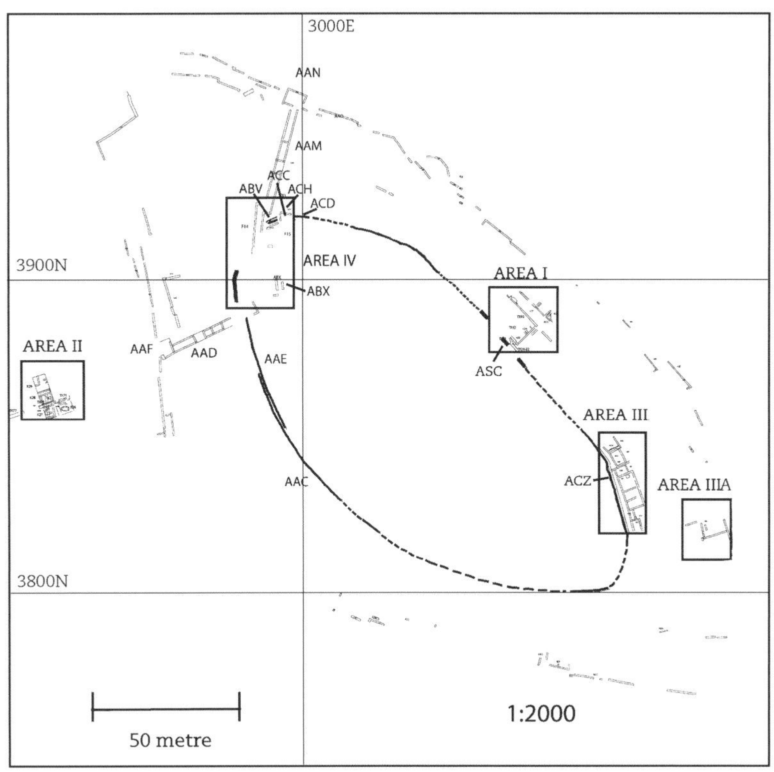

Fig. 25 *Aghia Triada shows the Archaic, Classical and Hellenistic architectural features with the main excavations indicated. The Archaic, Classical and Hellenistic fortification/terrace wall around the Acropolis are emphasized (compare Fig. 3) and partly reconstructed (stippled lines) (2000-2001 state). 1:2000.*

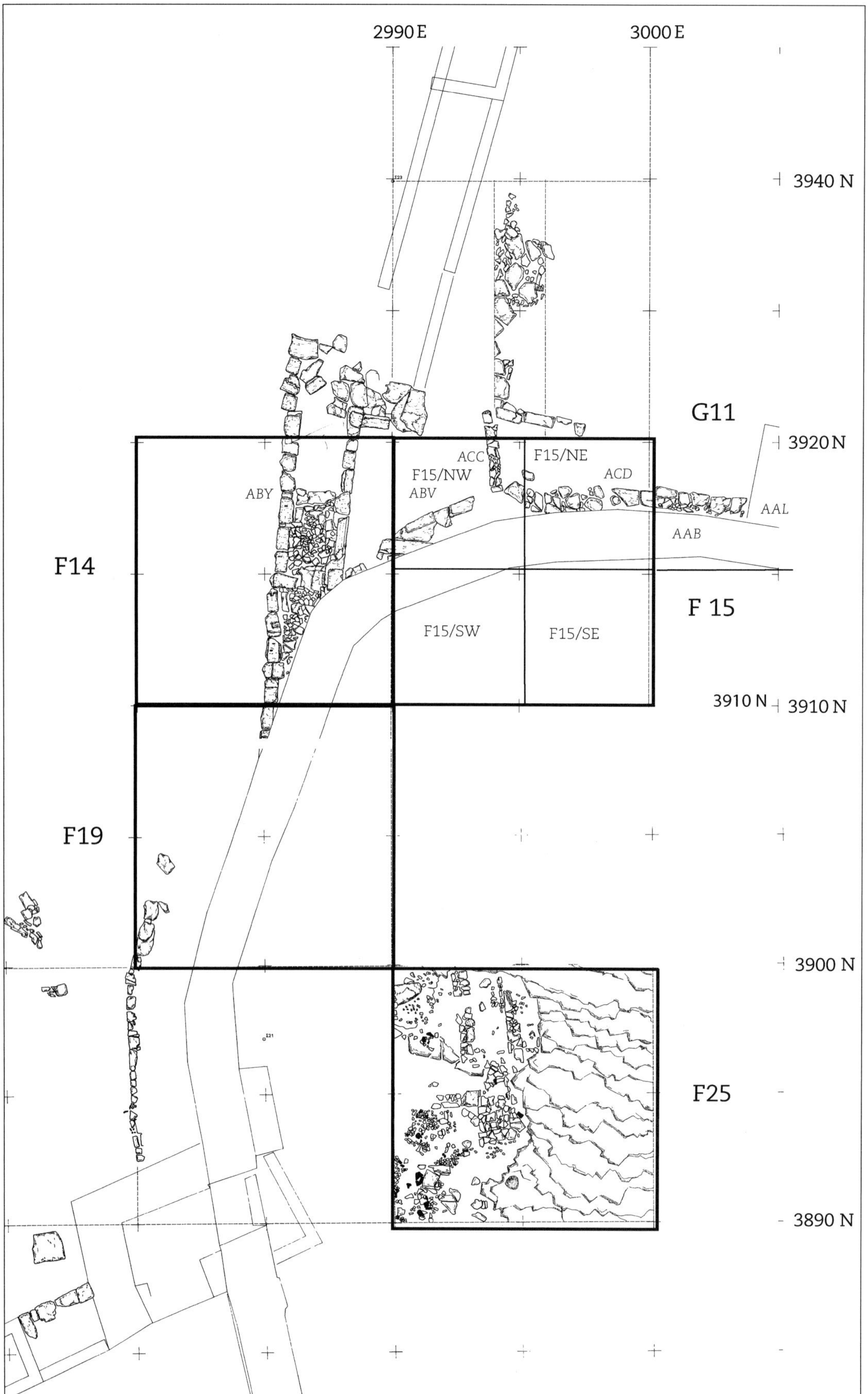

Fig. 26 *Excavations in AREA IV. Trench and – structure numbers.*

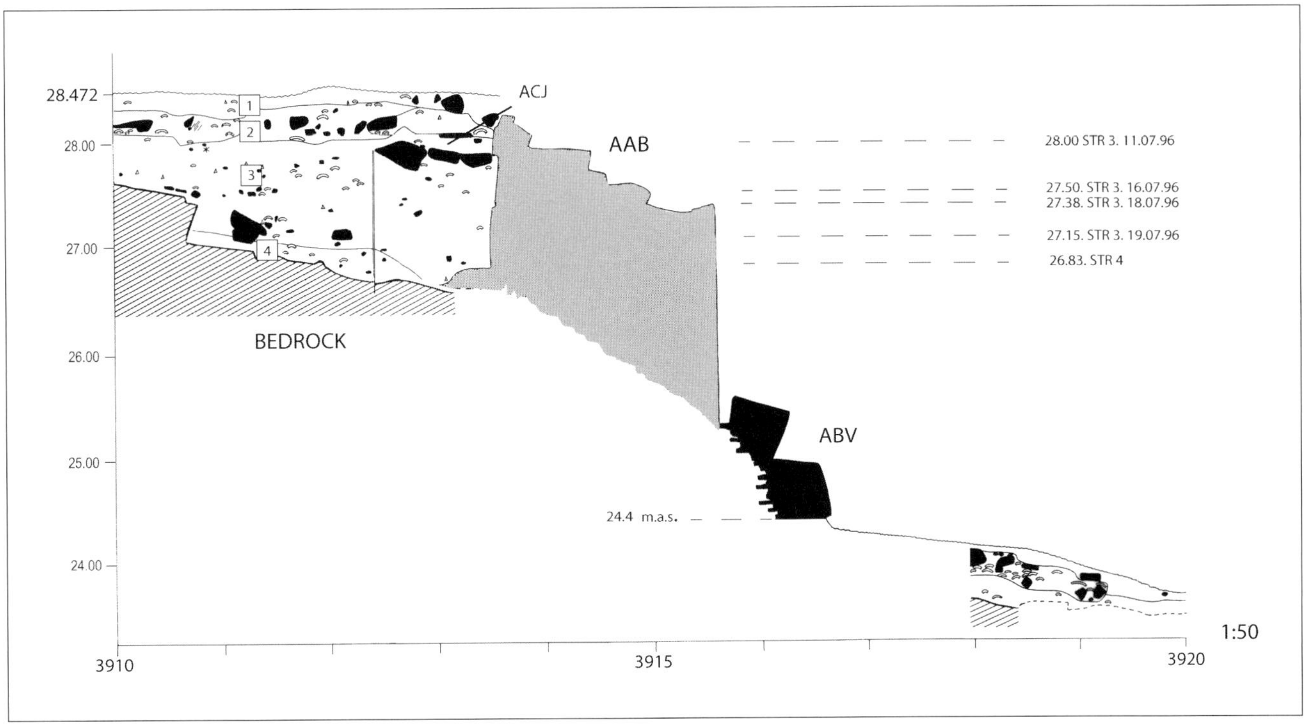

Fig. 27 *Section F16E (along the gridline 2990 E) showing the relation between the Byzantine fortification wall and the Archaic/Classical terrace-fortification wall. Excavation dates are shown to the right.*

outside of the Byzantine fortification wall – i.e. the Acropolis and the terrace below the wall. Trenches F14, 15, 19 and 25 and G11 are seen on Fig. 26.

Excavation in trench F15, south (SW and SE)

The excavation in trench F15, south (SW and SE) is briefly described in *FPR*, 282-283. Of special importance is the excavation to bedrock in the wide trench along the west side of F15, east of the N-S grid line 2990E:

F15/3-4[49]

The section (Fig. 27) is an elaboration of the section shown in F*PR*, Fig. *2*. We have added a division of stratum 3 as described in the diary. Stratum 3 appeared rather homogeneous during the excavation, the strata, however, were excavated in horizontal layers and measurements of the level taken every day. The more important of these dates and the "day-levels" are written on the right side on Fig. 27. More than 2000 sherds were found during the excavation of STR 3 and 4.

Chronology. First of all it should be pointed out that the material excavated in the 2 m wide trench east of grid line 2990E in trench F15/SW is a fill deposit deriving from higher up the mound, either slipping down the slope or intentionally placed in order to create a level surface near the wall. Fig. 28.

In the two uppermost horizons of STR 3 (11.07.96 and 12.07.96) the Archaic and Byzantine periods clearly dominate, but with a considerable amount of Hellenistic sherds from 12.07.96. Around level 27.50 m.a.s. the Byzantine material vanishes (with only 2 and 1 from 15.07.96 and 16.07.96) and further down neither

49 The Byzantine material from the trench F15, STR 1-2 and upper 3, is treated in some details in chapter B.3.

	Preh.	Neo	FN	EH I	MH	LH	Arch.	Class.	Hell.	Byz.	Med.	Undiagn.
11.07.96							55 + 22?			67		44
12.07.96							37	1	37	29		133
15.07.96	15 BA			1		1	123			2		94
16.07.96							113			1		
17.07.96							243					
19.07.96	21			11	3		48					81
22.07.96				1	11	8	130					85
23.07.96	11	13		3	3+4?	14	22					111
24.07.96	35+11?	7		1	9	6	5					182
25.07.96	8	6			2	4						
F15/3 SW	5		1			21	95					
F15/4 general		1?		12		28	19					
Total:	85+11?	26+1?	1	29	28+4?	82	975+22?	1	37	99		730

Fig. 28 *Statistical evaluation of pottery material excavated in strata 3 and 4 of the 2 m wide trench along the West-side of F15.*

Byzantine nor Hellenistic was registered. It is remarkable that this level corresponds to the 0.85 m deep cavity in the bedrock beginning 2.9 metres from the Byzantine wall. We conclude that there are two different fillings present – one at level 27.50 m deposited in around 500 BC, and an upper filling corresponding to the habitation level of the Byzantine fortification wall.

Prehistoric coarse ware is present almost everywhere at the mound at Aghia Triada, but only in a few instances in an undisturbed context.[50] A series of sherds, especially from the lower levels have been classified as Neolithic. The presence of Neolithic material has been recognized previously but a clear definition of a Neolithic phase was not possible. A C^{14} dating from the early EHI layer on the Eastern Terrace indicates the presence of Final Neolithic intrusions (3.700 BC) in the EHI horizon.[51] In contrast to the Neolithic, the EHI is relatively well understood from the deposits on the Eastern Terrace.[52] Grey Minyan, Yellow Minyan and Matt painted ware groups are typical for the Middle Helladic material from the lower fill in trench F15/SW – probably all from the MHIII&LHI transition. The majority of the material from the later LH periods is dated within the LHIIIC late/Submycenaen horizon with a few probably to be dated within the LHIIIB. This corresponds to the general picture of the later LH presence on the plain West of the mound.[53] On Fig. 29 we depict some selected sherds from F15/4. These sherds are dated between EHI to LHIIIC late/Submycenean.

With more than 50 % of the total sherd material found in the trench – or more than 70 % of the diagnostic sherds – the Archaic pottery makes up by far the most significant element in the deposits – undoubtedly indicating that habitation on the Acropolis

50 See in general *Chalkis Aitolias I.*

51 *Chalkis Aitolias I,* 48.

52 *Chalkis Aitolias I,* 38 ff.

53 *Chalkis Aitolias I,* 55 ff.

Fig. 29 *Sherds from trench F15 stratum 4.*
1-3: EHI coarse ware. Fabric no. 3 so-called "terrazzo ware" (Chalkis Aitolias I, 78, Fig. 26, no. 98).
4: White on burnished dark – MH.
5: Mycenaean.
6: LHIIIC.
7: SM kalathos.
8: PG.
9: Archaic.

was most extensive during Archaic times.[54] Quite an amount of Archaic material from the trench was published in FPR.[55]

Conclusion

The fortification wall must have been erected before the deposition of the fill – if not, the soil would have flowed down the steep slope. Below level 27.50 m.a.s. the fill does not contain sherd material later than the 6th century BC indicating that this must be the lowest possible surface for the Archaic habitation at the Acropolis, and that the 6th century BC indicates a terminus post quem for the erection of the wall which is thus without doubt originally Archaic – and probably late 6th century BC. This conclusion is supported by the dating of the fill in trial trench Tx1 behind rooms X-XI in the row houses in AREA III (see below).

54 See Sanne Houby-Nielsen in *Chalkis Aitolias II.*
55 S. Dietz in *FPR*, 287 ff where stratum 3 is not separated into layers, however, and later on re-considered by Sanne Houby-Nielsen in *Chalkis Aitolias II.*

The fortification wall

The ancient fortification and terrace wall, *ABV, ACD, ASC* etc. runs outside and parallel to the Byzantine fortification *AAB* (Fig. 25). The wall was originally around 320 m long, of which traces of two thirds or some 210 m are still visible. In no place is the wall totally preserved and many repairs and reconstructions were performed during the long period when the wall defined and protected the Acropolis. The wall was in use from Archaic times to the end of the Early Hellenistic period around 200 BC – for slightly more than 300 years. The most systematic and comprehensive destruction took place when the Byzantine fortification was constructed in the 6th century AD (see below). Many stone blocks from the old wall were re-used in the early Medieval fortification where it is still to be seen.

The relation between the Byzantine fortification *AAB* and the Archaic/Classical terrace wall, *ABV* etc. (Fig. 30), is seen in *AREA IV*, section 2990 E (Figs. 26 and 27). The wall is placed close to the Byzantine fortification in this area and undoubtedly rested on bedrock as seen on the section 10 m further east at grid

Fig. 30 *The fortification/terrace wall ABV in AREA IV. Stone blocks from this wall and from the Late Classical wall AAM were reused in the Byzantine wall behind.*

line 3000 m E (Fig. 31).[56] The wall *ABV* is an isodomic construction, built with rectangular sandstone blocks, the longest measuring 1.0 (L) x 0.5 × 0.5 metres. Further east, the wall is called *ACD* (Figs. 26 and 31) and is less well preserved. It serves in addition as the back wall of an Archaic/Early Classical building. As *ABV* the base rests on bedrock at level 24.4 m.a.s.[57] The larger blocks of *ACD* measure 1.0 × 0.25 × 0.50 m and are thus considerably lower than the ashlars of *ABV*. It remains a question as to whether this foundation is part of the terrace wall.[58]

56 *FRP*, 286, Fig. 23

57 FPR, 286, Fig. 23.

58 FPR, 284, Fig. 18.

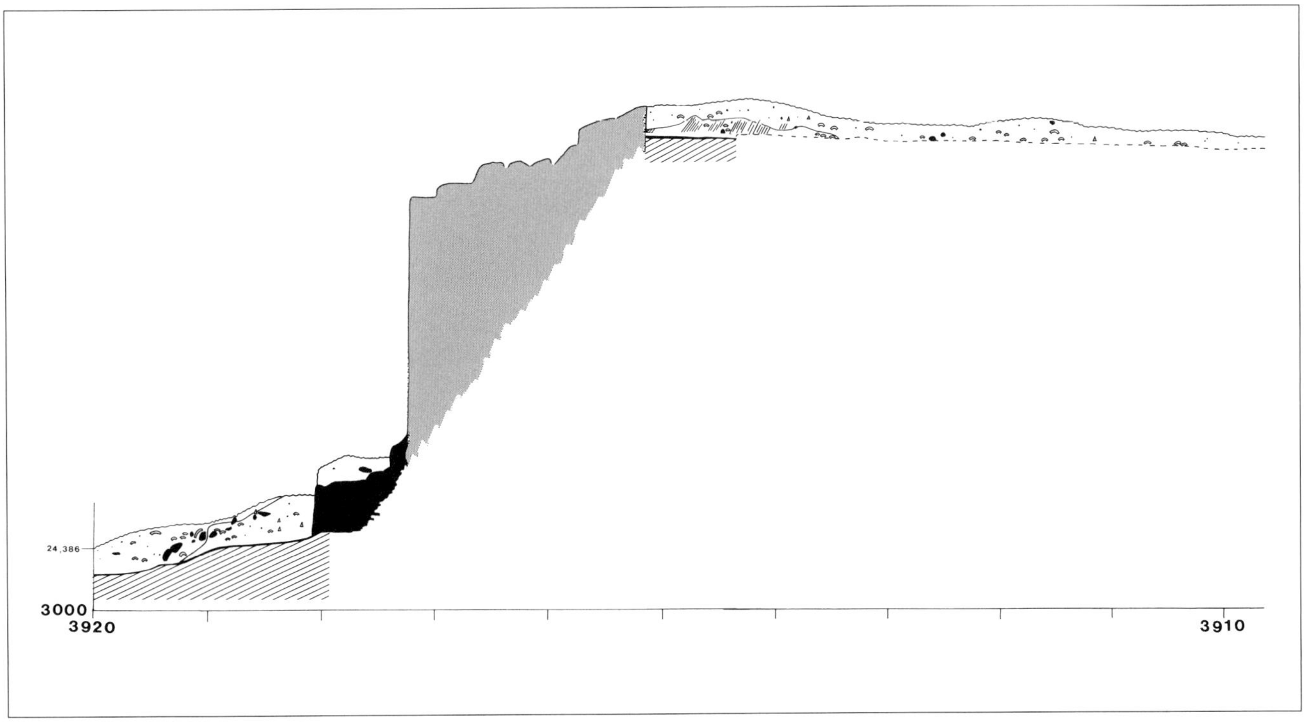

Fig. 31 *AREA IV, NW corner of the Acropolis of Aghia Triada. Section 3000 m East (=N15E).*

Fig. 32 *The Archaic/Classical fortification/terrace wall in AREA III/room IV.*

A longer section of the terrace wall is preserved between the two northeastern towers of the Byzantine fortification, *AAL* and *ACQ*, on the northeast side of the Acropolis (Plan Fig. 3 and 25). Only the lowest course is preserved, placed on the "shelf" 24.5 to 25.0 m.a.s. (See the contours on the map Fig. 3) between 2 and 2.5 metres outside the Byzantine fortification.

In AREA I, the terrace wall is registered as *ACS*, placed slightly more than three metres from the plinth of the Byzantine fortification.[59] Approximately 3.5 m of the wall length was uncovered. The wall is preserved up to one m height, the width measuring up to 0.85 m.

59 TPR, 176, Figs. 2 and 3 and *Chalkis Aitolias I*, 71, Fig. 21. Also Fig. 23 and 24 above.

Fig. 33 *Remains of the Archaic/Classical fortification wall AAC.*

Three courses are visible of which the lowest is badly defined, but clearly projects forwards beyond the upper courses. The second course is dominated by one large sandstone block, 0.33 × 0.80 × 1.0 m, while the uppermost course is composed of rather flat stones; 0.85 × 0.30. The wall is placed at a lower level than the earlier walls in AREA IV, founded at approximately 21.50 m.a.s. One further fragment of the wall was found between the Byzantine tower *ACQ* and AREA I (Approximately 2.7 m. from the Byzantine fortification) and another one further Southeast (See plan Fig. 3).

In AREA III, longer section of the fortification wall (*ACZ*) were uncovered. The best preserved part is the back wall *ACZ* in room IV – behind the courtyard room I and room II (below p 85 and Figs 25-27 and 30-33). On Fig. 32 we depict a drawing of this wall which is placed in a natural cut/depression approximately 2 m. from the Byzantine wall in the bedrock right in the line of the terrace wall. The massive wall is constructed with large rectangular stone blocks of various sizes in a more or less isodomic/pseudo-isodomic pattern (with several repairs). The largest piece is placed in the bottom course on the bedrock and measures 1.20 × 0.35 m – the width of the wall varies between 0.65 and 0.80 m. The wall is founded on bedrock, level 21.80 m.a.s. The lower courses are clearly protruding to give the wall a stronger plinth[60]. Six courses are preserved, up to 1.80 m.

Further SSE, near the sea, the line of the fortification wall continues in one or more courses placed on bedrock, around level 23.0 m.a.s., at a distance of approximately 1 m from the Byzantine wall. An especially well preserved section is found above room VIII in the houses (see plan and Fig. 57). The fragment consists of three courses with the first two (H.

60 As often seen on fortification walls, see Frederiksen 2011, 57 citing Lang 2006 (Siedlungen), 26 and Lawrence, Aims, 344.

approximately 0.40 m), lower than the upper course (approximately 0.85 m), thus rather pseudo-isodomic in character as is the back wall in room IV.

Finally a rather substantial section of wall *ACZ* was uncovered behind room XV in the houses (Fig. 57). Three courses of almost equal height, flat rectangular ashlars, around 0.25 m. high and up to 1.20 m. long were laid in isodomic order. The southernmost ashlar in the trench T6NA is square with sides approximately 0.85 m. (Fig. 65). The width might be around 0.85 m (?). The wall rests on bedrock at a level of 23.0 m.a.s., upper level approximately 23.75 ma.s.l.

What remains of the wall (*AAE* on Fig. 3) on the western side of the mound, towards the ancient harbour is simply a row of ashlars (two courses preserved) resting on bedrock. Ground level approximately 28 m.a.s. (Fig. 33).[61] A reconstruction of the Late Classical terrace wall is suggested for AREA III (see below Fig 69).

Summary

As has been attested, a wall (of stone) was erected towards the end of the Archaic period, at the late 6th century BC. Fragments of the wall can still be seen at around two-thirds of the circumference of the Acropolis, in most cases rather rudimentary survivals, but in other cases preserved to a considerable hight. In most cases the better preserved parts are additions built after Archaic times. The dating is thus first of all depending of the two sections 2990 m E (W side of F15)(Fig. 27) and the EW line 3830N (the northern trench wall of Tx1)(Fig. 67) which clearly indicate that the soil fill from the Acropolis were retained by a wall which could be dated to the end of the Archaic period. We suggest that this wall was built, primarily for reasons of defence of the considerable Archaic society at and around the hill of Aghia Triada, but that it, in addition, functioned as a terrace wall preventing the sparse soil (and habitation constructions?) to flow down the steep slopes of the Acropolis hill.

61 The wall is built of sandstone blocks and is not of the late Classical limestone phase as indicated by *Paliouras*, 2004, 411, Fig. 8

B.2 The Late Classical/Early Hellenistic fortification system

Søren Dietz

Introduction

In the 4th century BC, the Archaic/Classical fortification wall was supplemented by a more substantial system of fortifications in the northern and northwestern part of the terrace surrounding the Acropolis. The walls extend from the old fortification curtain towards the flat area to the North, ABY, AAM and AAN and down the slope to the West, AAD and AAF (and Fig. 34 to Fig. 36). Of the northern extension, AAM, only the foundation, consisting of plain rectangular blocks, is preserved, while ABY continuing to the South after an angular break, is better preserved – interrupted, however, by the construction of the Byzantine fortification system. Structures AAD and AAF are likewise only preserved at their lower level.[62]

The curtains are double faced, dry-stone walls constructed with quarry faced rectangular or square limestone blocks shaped to fit each other, often with oblique joints. The widths of the walls vary between 2.60 and 2.75 m (Fig. 35). The space between the two faces is divided into compartments by cross walls running from face to face and binding the two faces together. The distance between the cross walls varies between 3 m to more than 10 m.[63] The limestone was quarried from the east side of Varassova probably just above Pangali (also Chapter D).

Construction – Re-construction

The Late Classical wall system was destroyed, at the latest, when the Byzantine fortification was constructed in the 6th century AD and a considerable amount of the old limestone blocks were re-used in the Byzantine constructions (see Fig. 37).[64] The well-prepared blocks are carefully fitted with each other with stepped joints (Fig. 38). Sizes vary, the larger blocks measure up to: 1.15 (L) x 0.50 (H) x 0.50 (W) m or 1.00 (L) x 0.60 (H) x 0.50 (W) m and 1.00 (L) x 0.72 (H) x 0.50 (W) m (the last one Fig. 38, upper right). The width of the wall/blocks in the outer (western) curtain ABY is almost precisely 0.50 m.

The curtain might have been around 6 m high as the better preserved walls of Pangali and Kalydon suggest.[65] Two towers are placed at the termination of the walls, *ANN* to the north of *AMM*, measuring approximately 6.6 m (E-W) x 5.6 m (N-S) and *AFF* to the west of *ADD* measuring approximately 5.9 m (n-S) x 4.4 m (E-W). In addition we suggest the angular structure *AXB* at the upper end of *ADD* inside the Byzantine entrance building (see below chapter B.3) was another, smaller tower of a estimated size 4 × 4 m.[66] The protrusion created by the slightly different alignment of *AAM* and *ABY* was probably intended to create a salient angle in the defense system.

A study of the contours on Figs. 3 and 34 makes it clear that the northeastern part of the terrace below the Acropolis is the most easily accessible spot from which to enter the Acropolis itself and it therefore seems logical to concentrate the efforts to strengthen the defense system at this point. The terrace slopes upwards only slightly, as it does on the main part of the eastern terrace, but in addition the bedrock creates a relatively easy access to the top.

As has been shown, the Byzantine fortification wall

62 Foundations *AAN, AAM, AAD* and *AAF* were cleaned and drawn – but not "excavated". Only the better preserved wall ABY was partly excavated in trench F14 (see below.

63 For this type of wall construction see *Kalydon* 2011, 67.

64 See also *Paliouras* 2004, 410, Fig. 7.

65 Chapter D below and *Kalydon* 2011, 75.

66 See also *Paliouras* 2004, 411 for the existence of a Late Classical tower. *Portelanos* 1998, "fig. 4".

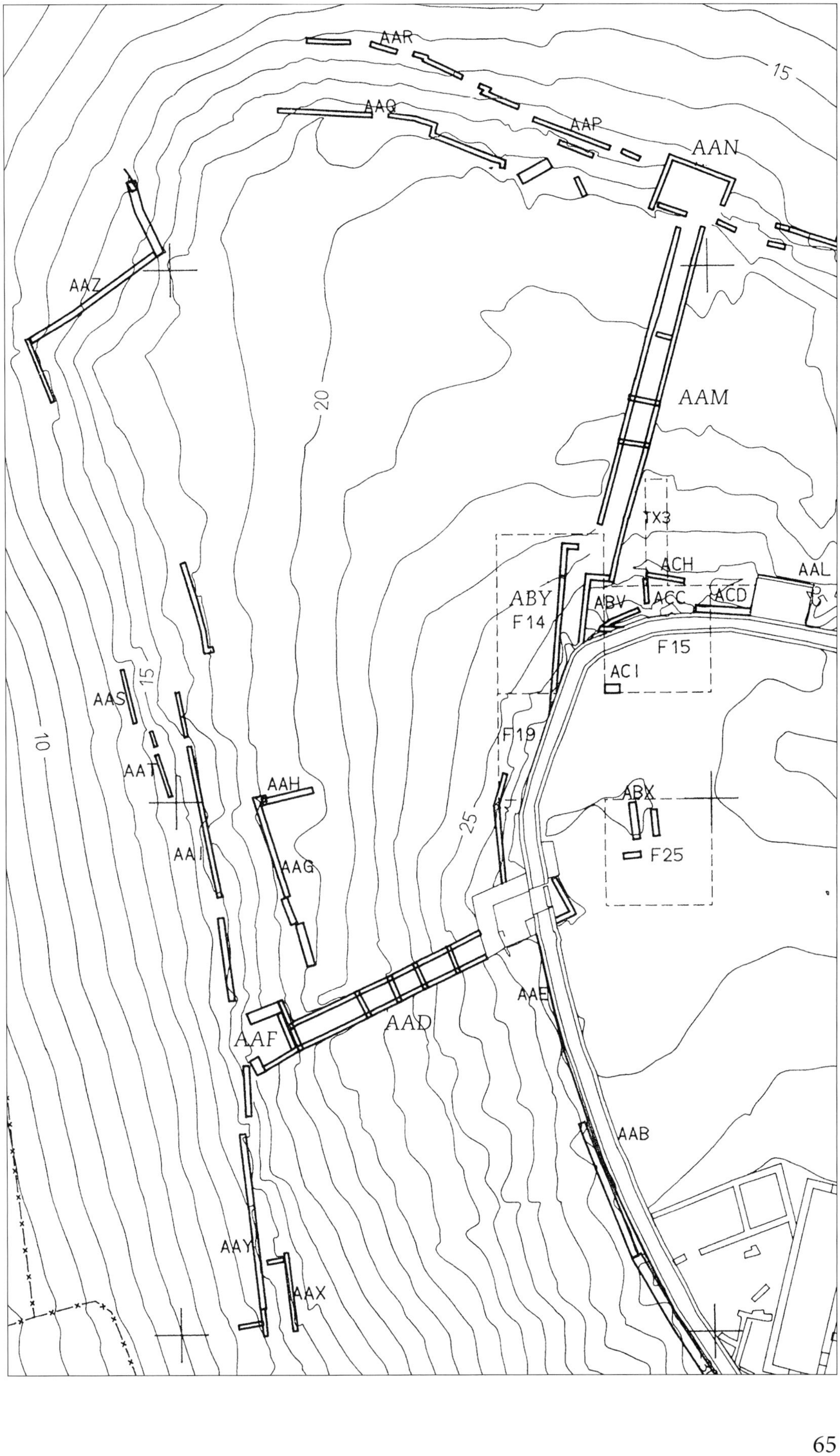

Fig. 34 *The Northwest corner of Aghia Triada with the late Classical reinforcement fortification walls: ABY, AAM, AAN, AAD and AAF.*

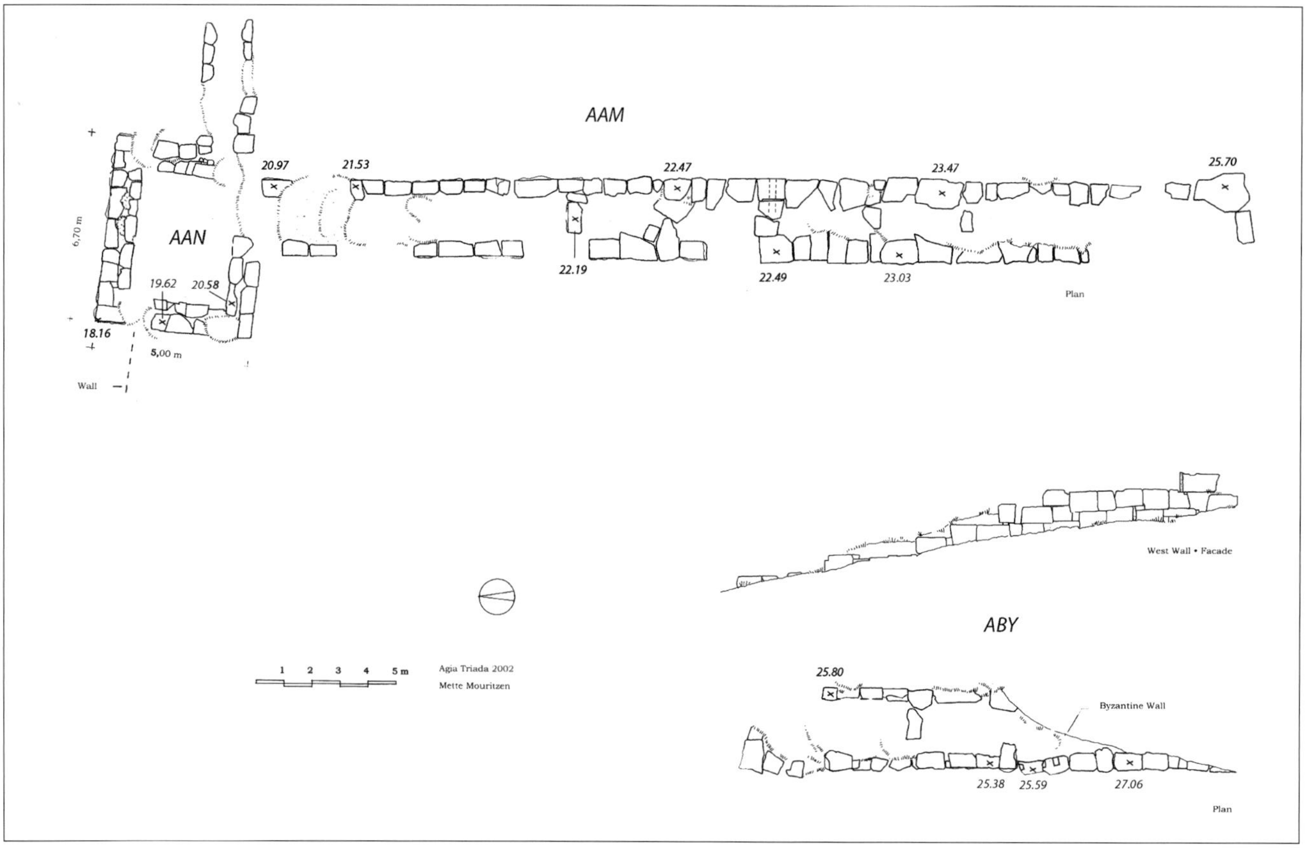

Fig. 35 *The Late Classical (limestone) northwest fortifications AAM and ABY (Drawn by Mette Mouritzen) 1:200.*

(*AAB*) was constructed inside the Archaic/Classical/Hellenistic wall system (chapter B1) – the only exception is the NW corner, where the Byzantine wall was actually built on top of and outside the Late Classical addition, which evidently replaced the more ancient walls at this spot. The more or less level space is defined by the limestone curtains and towers and by the terrace walls. Portelanos 1998 suggests that fortification walls at the 17 m contour line were attached east and west of tower ANN[67] where the wall west of the tower is considered to be "probable". We have not been able to substantiate this theory. Although the terrace walls *AAP,AAR, AAQ* and *AAI* might have had a defensive function framing the level space approximately 4.500 m² in the NW corner – a space which could have functioned as a market place, probably approached from the northwest, northeast of the building *AAZ*.[68]

As for the entrance to the Acropolis we would suggest that the gate was situated between the tower (*AXB*) above wall *ADD* and the prolongation of wall *ABY*. Access is straight if not easy (Fig. 39), and there does not seem to be any other possibility. In Byzantine times the entrance was in the same position, but the gate was oriented to the south – and the access made even more difficult. The sandstone foundation *AXC* (on Fig. 39) in front of the entrance might indicate the passage to the pre-Byzantine gateway.

Dating

Excavation in trench F14/ABY. The area with two cross walls between the two faces of *ABY* was partly excavated (Fig. 40).[69] Byzantine and Archaic sherds were found in the surface layer. The packing between the two wall faces consisted of rather large stones,

67 See also reconstruction (Portelanos "fig. 5").

68 *AAZ* and *AAH/AAG* are parts of buildings.

69 *FPR*, Figs. 16 and 19, b.

Fig. 36 *The late Classical fortification wall AAD from East. In the background is seen the Northern part of the "harbour area".*

Fig. 37 *The wall ABY from West. In the Byzantine wall behind, lime stones from the late Classical construction are re-used.*

Fig. 38 *Detail of the construction of the western course of the wall ABY. Note the "angular cuts".*

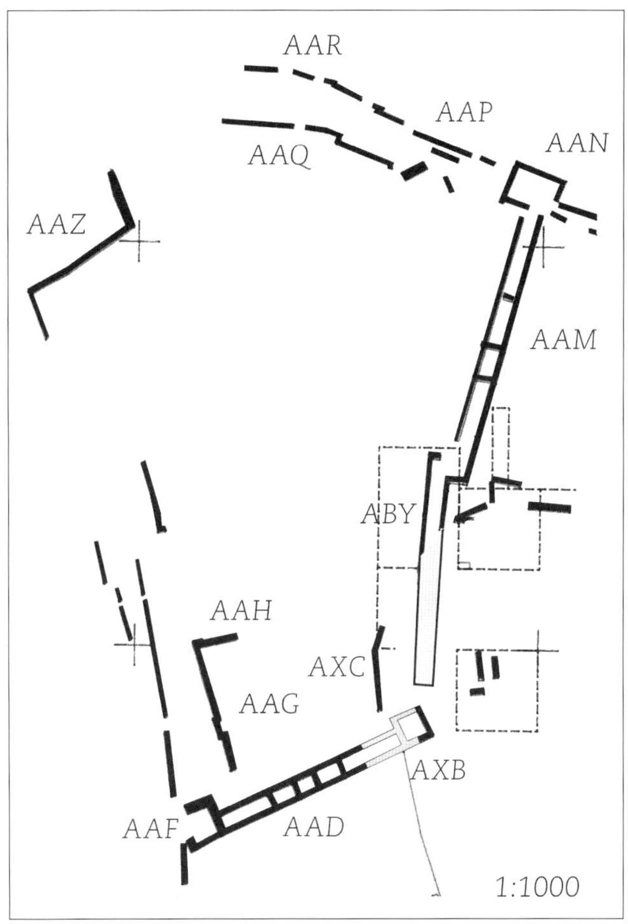

Fig. 39 *Suggested reconstruction of the northeast quarter. Black indicates existing structures, grey are reconstruction suggestions.*

Fig. 40 *ABY from South. The curtains are double faced, dry stone walls constructed by square, quarry faced limestone blocks. In the background is seen the wall AAM.*

some of them broken stone blocks and pebbles and rubble in yellowish, hard packed clay. This layer, called F14/2a was stratified below the blocks in the eastern row and below the mortar packed layer in the Byzantine wall *AAB*. Layer F14/2a rested on bedrock.

Sherd material from f14/2a.

Fine tempered:
- Plain (local ware reddish fabric): 74
- Plain black glazed (and with reddish-brown paint): 56
- Plain with white fabric and surface (sometimes with reddish- brown paint) ("Corinthian"): 26
- One plate with concentric incised circles: D. 8 cm.

Coarse ware: 17
- Medium tempered: 32

All listed sherds are Archaic.

Conclusion

A clear Archaic context without mixture (could derive from cleaning of the habitation level in G11). This context evidently points (not surprisingly) to the Late Archaic period as a terminus ante quem for the construction of the curtain and, as no Hellenistic material is at hand – before the Hellenistic period. A typological examination of the construction supports this dating.

Limestone for construction is only used during a short period of the habitation in Chalkis Aitolias. Both before and after the substantial constructions in the 4th century BC, sandstone was the preferred building material – probably because it is much easier to prepare. The limestone blocks are prepared more or less as the blocks used for the Pangali fortifications and the dimensions at the two sites are close to each other. The technique of stepped courses is used in Pangali as well as at Aghia Triada, where it is even more prevalent. The double faced walls in the Aghia Triada curtains correspond to the eastern section of the Pangali north wall (*PAA*), while the construction, with blocks of many different sizes meeting in "stepped joints" without any attempt to create an isodomic impression, looks much more like the southern wall (*PAN*) at Pangali (Plan X). It is important, however, to emphasize that there are no trapezoidal blocks used in Aghia Triada, while this feature is very typical for the Pangali fortifications.

In spite of the differences between Pangali and the NW additions at Aghia Triada we consider it most likely that the two systems are more or less contemporary and that they are constructed during the first half of the 4th century BC in connection with the "liberation" of the Aitolian coastland from the Achaians by the Boeotians, and that these construction are part of a substantial program initiated by Epaminondas in order to improve the fortification system at a time when mechanized siege craft developed dramatically.[70]

70 See below Chapter D for Pangali.

B.3 Some comments on the Early Christian and Byzantine churches and fortification system

Søren Dietz

Introduction

The mound of Aghia Triada was excavated by Professor A. Paliouras of the University of Ioannina from 1982 to 1991, the excavations and surveys mainly concentrating on the Early Christian and Byzantine remains.[71] Even though the Danish/Greek excavations 1995 to 2001 mainly concentrated on the pre-Byzantine periods we find if important to comment briefly on the Early Christian and Byzantine occupation of the mound which radically changed the character of the ancient habitation. The succeeding comments thus refer to Paliouras's treatment in general, supplemented with data and reflections supplied by the results of the Danish/Greek excavations 1995 to 2001 – and are not to be considered an excavation report as such.

Fig. 41 shows the Basilica and the surrounding fortification wall as measured in 1995 (part of the fortification was covered by heavy scrub and could not be included on the plan). The Basilica was only preserved to the foundations and is heavily restored. It measures in the present state 34.0 m. (L) x 18.5 m. (W) or around 630 m^2. The orientation is E-W – slightly turned NW-SE. The naos with two narrow aisles and an 8 metres wide nave is a tri-part transept type construction – cross-transept and quatrefoil plans were revived in the early 6th century AD in NE Greece and the eastern Balkans. The semi-circular apse, articulated and strengthened on the outside by five buttresses, is closely related to, and the same age as, the Basilica A at Nikopolis.[72] An early construction of the type is found in Salona-Marusinac, Anastasius Basilica from 426 AD.[73] The bad preservation of the monument makes it difficult to clarify details in the plan. It is, however, evident that there must have been a central entrance from the narthex to the nave[74] and the transept wings must have communicated with the centre bay through a wide arch – neither to be detected today. Most likely a doorway led from the Western courtyard into the narthex.[75] The buildings between the fortification wall and the narthex with different orientations might be older than the naos itself as one of the walls was evidently cut by the fortification.

The small 10th century naos was built into the apse of the ancient Basilica. Neither this building was well preserved. Terracotta-bricks or tiles were not used in the construction as in other contemporary buildings.[76]

The upper plateau with the 6th century Basilica was surrounded by a substantial ovoid fortification wall (Figs. 41) – approximately 360 meter long – protecting an area of approximately 6.500 m^2 – which, except on the Northern side – was placed just inside the Archaic/ Classical/ Hellenistic fortification system.

The wall, called *AAB,* is constructed of un-dressed or slightly prepared, square sandstone, much smaller than the stones/ashlars used for the earlier fortification wall. Stones are usually placed in irregular courses, alternating between courses of large stones and narrower stone slabs – creating a pseudo-isodomic appearence. In the northern part of the fortification the sandstone wall is supplemented by large limestone ashlars removed from the late Classical fortification

71 *Paliouras* 2004, 408-420 with bibliographical references note 1.

72 *Paliouras* 2004, 411. See also Krautheimer 1986, 130-31, and fig. 87.

73 Krautheimer 1986, 180 and Fig. 143 and Dyggve and Eggers 1939, passim, Fig. 23 and Tafel 1.

74 Not seen today but reconstructed by *Paliouras* 2004, Fig. 4.

75 *Paliouras* 2004, as seen on the reconstruction Fig. 28.

76 As for instance Aghios Dimitrios, Varassovas. *Paliouras* 2004, Fig. 191.

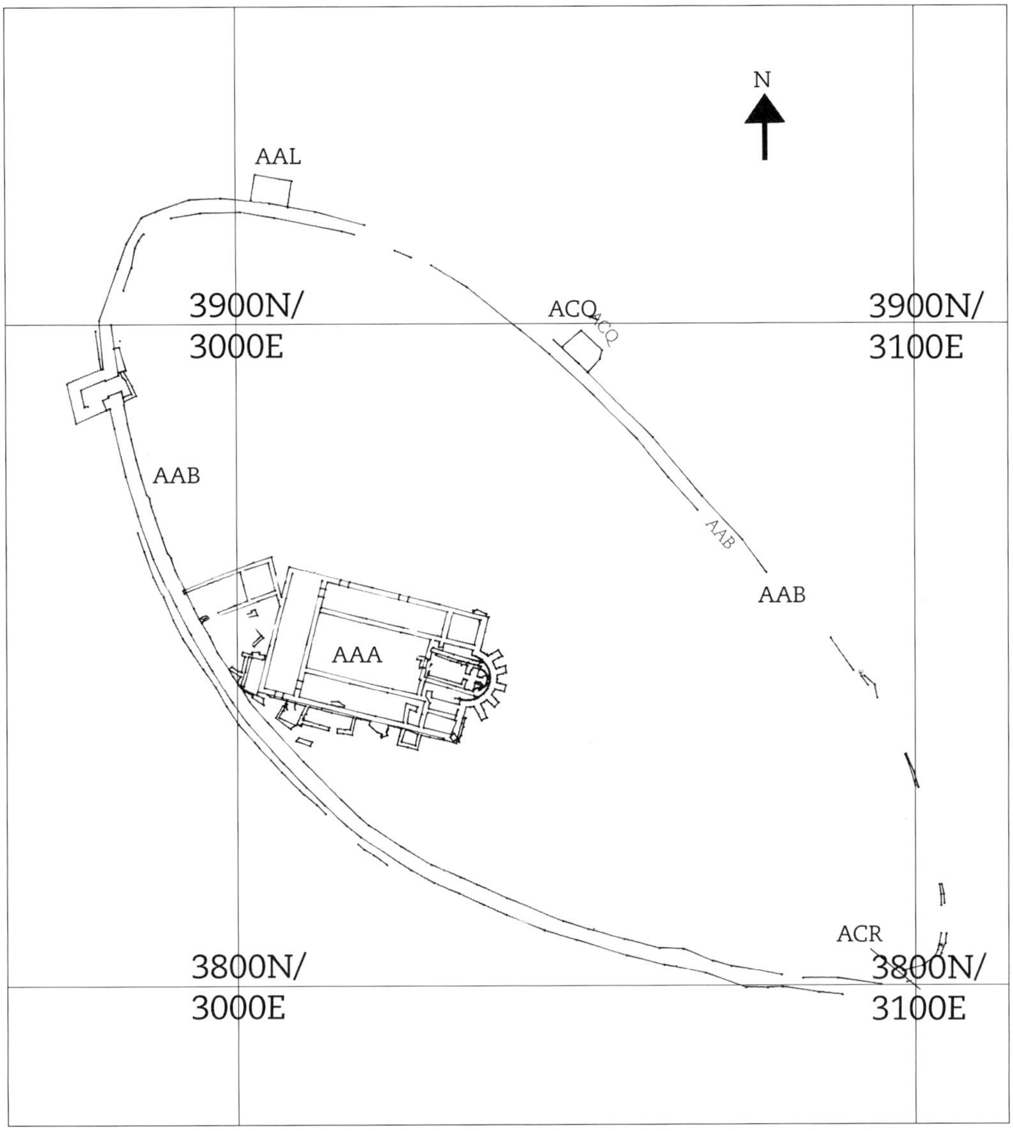

Fig. 41 *The Basilica and the surrounding fortification wall as measured in 1995 (Poul Erik Skovgaard).*

walls.[77] The stones are fixed with mortar, the inner face of the curtain (towards the Acropolis) is smooth – while the outer face is rougher (probably because the mortar between the stones was eroded away). The wall is double-faced, 1.90 to 2.00 m wide. The inner- and outer faces of the wall measure 0.50 m – 0.60 m. The smoother or slightly worked faces of the blocks are turned outwards, while the inner faces remain un-worked. The material from the fill between the walls was not registered. There is no evidence that terracotta-bricks or tiles were used in the construction.

Three towers and a gatehouse were found integrated in the wall and were undoubtedly built at the same time as the wall itself. The tower *AAL* (Fig. 3) measures: 5.30 m. (W) x 3.60 m. (D). *ACQ* measures: 4.70/90 m. (W) x 3.50 m. (D). One further and more substantial tower (*ACR*) (Fig. 3)(the tower is seen on Fig. 6 in *FPR*) was placed in the Eastern end of the fortification.[78] The gatehouse on the Western part of the mound above the late Classical wall *AAD,* and built on top of the late Classical tower, evidently opens towards the steep slope on the Southern side of the mound.[79]

77 Figs. 30 and 37. Sections of the wall are seen on Figs. 27 and 31. Also *Paliouras* 2004, Fig. 7.

78 *Paliouras* 2004, Fig. 24 and *SPR,* Fig. 6.

79 A reconstruction is suggested in *Paliouras* 2004, Fig. 18.

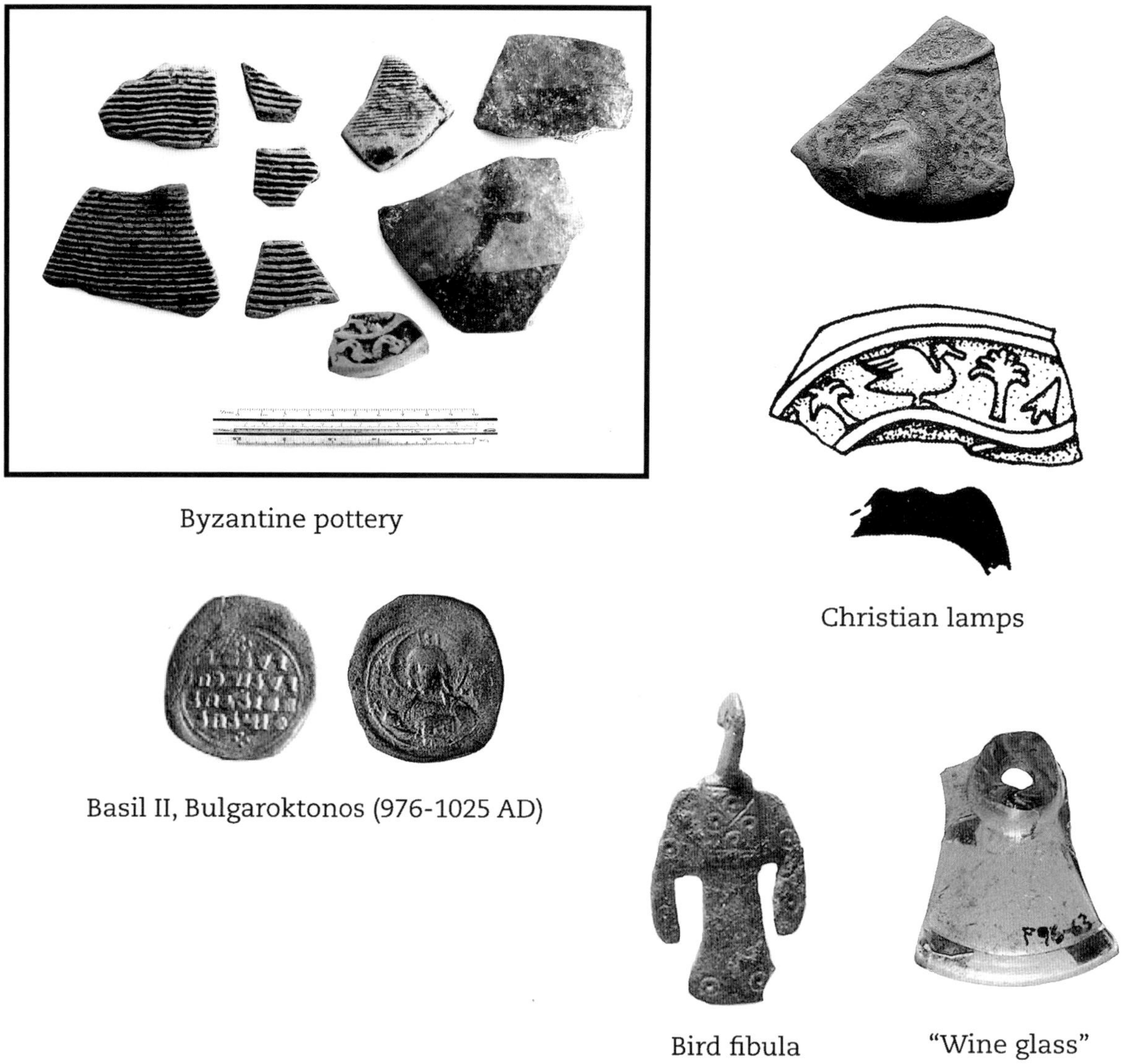

Fig. 42 *Various Byzantine artifacts from the Acropolis (not to scale).*

Evidence for dating

Neither habitation buildings nor closed contexts of objects were found from the Early Christian/Byzantine periods during the campaigns 1995-2001. Material from the period was, however, found in mixed contexts on the Acropolis. A selection (Fig. 42) supplements dating information given by Paliouras 2004.

Catalogue:

- F98-4006. Coin. O27/1/09.07.98. *SPR*, 197 and 213 no. 94 (Fig. p. 206)). Constantinople, Justin II + Sophia 568/9 AD
- F96-11. Coin (Fig. 42). F15/1. Unpublished. Compare Dumbarton Oaks Catalogue, 21 Fig. 39: Basil II, Bulgaroktonos: 976-1025 AD. Compare Paliouras 2004, Fig. 29. a. 11 coins of same type from a hoard at Agia Triada.
- F96-32. Bird fibula (bronze) (Fig. 42). F25/2. FPR Fig. 32, 11.
- F96-63. Stem of "Wine glass" (Fig. 42). S9/1. Hayes 1975, 109, no. 407. Dating: 5th or early 6th century A.D.
- Christian lamps *(480-520 AD)*

1. F15/2/NW (Fig. 42). FRP, Fig. 27, no. 23.
2. F15/3/07.07.96 (Fig. 42).
3. F15/2/SW (Fig. 42).

Selected Pottery: Only a selection of pottery is presented here.

Conclusion

The large Basilica *AAA* was built in the early 6th century AD. The dating is primarily based on the close relationship with Basilica A in Nikopolis but the type as such is earlier. At the same time it seems that the fortification wall was constructed, probably as part of the vast building-programme initiated by Justinian and lasting until the turn of the century.[80] Procopius informs us that as a result of the programme, many new fortifications were erected and older fortifications were repaired in Albania and Epirus; and it is most likely, that the Aghia Triada defense system should be seen in the light of the same large movement. To be sure – no direct archaeological evidence can support this dating.[81] Paliouras considers the complex to be the seat of a Bishop – probably the most important ecclesiastical site between Mesolonghi and Naupaktos.[82]

Another and more difficult question is when the Basilica and fortification ceased to function – and why? A considerable destruction horizon was detected during the excavations in the 80's and it is reasonable to believe that raiding barbarians (the so called "Slavic invasion?") caused the demolition sometime between the 6th and the 10th century. At any rate, as a huge amount of architectural members derive from what seems to be a systematic plundering of Aghia Triada – both the late Classical constructions and the early Christian. The Basilica went out of use before the great recovery (the "Byzantine Renovation") in the 9th to 10/11th century.[83] It is possible, of course, that the fortification was preserved even if the church was destroyed. The large limestone ashlars re-used in the neighboring 10th century church probably derive directly from the late Classical wall system.

The recovering of Christianity in the 9th to 11th century, the so-called "Middle Byzantine Renaissance", was caused by the growing importance of the monasticisms. In Aghia Triada a small naos was built into the apse of the great Basilica with a slightly different longitudinal axis from the old building. As no habitations are found it is difficult to say if a monastery had replaced the old Basilica, but in the neighborhood we have at least three monasteries from the 10th century – early 11th: Aghios Nikolaos on the south side of Mount Varassova[84]; Aghios Dimitrios on the east side of Varassova[85]; and the monastery on Panaxiotissa Gavrolimnis around 1 km N of Gavrolimni.[86] A vast number of loom-weights (200) indicate that the textile industry was quite as important at Aghia Triada in the 10th century, as it was in Antiquity.[87] The objects found during the excavation, in general support the dating of the use of the area in the period between the 6th and the 10th century AD.

80 Krautheimer 1986, 258 ff.

81 *Paliouras* 2004, 412 and note 13.

82 *Paliouras* 2004, 411.As for the "Byzantine landscape" in Acarnania see Kaponis 2013, 87-106.

83 *Paliouras* 2004, 415, Figs. 19 and 25/26/27.

84 *Paliouras* 2004, 421- 432.

85 *Paliouras* 2004, 178-180.

86 *Paliouras* 2004, 183-185.

87 *Paliouras* 2004, 415 and fig. 21. For Antiquity see *Chalkis Aitolias II* passim and this volume.

C. THE CLASSICAL AND HELLENISTIC ROW-HOUSES IN AREA III

C.1 General Stratigraphy

Søren Dietz and Elizabeth Bollen

Introduction

The series of rooms excavated in *AREA III*, sit just below the Archaic/Classical fortification wall that surrounds the Acropolis (Figs. 43-44).[88] Coupled with the graves excavated on the other side of the Acropolis,[89] they provide evidence of the late Classical/ early Hellenistic occupation. Excavation in this area occurred in the June-July seasons of 1997, 1998, 1999 and 2000 and in an additional October season in 2000. Eight rooms were excavated, running from north to south and covering an area of 400 square metres. Zones in front of and behind these rooms were also excavated. The material found in the rooms and adjacent zones is discussed in chapter C.4.[90]

There is a certain level of homogeneity in the stratigraphy found within the rooms. The first levels excavated are filled with rubble, including large stones deriving mainly from the collapse of the Byzantine fortification wall *AAB*. These strata contain a mix of ceramics, dating mainly from the Archaic to the Hellenistic period, though including some Prehistoric sherds.This material can be interpreted as displaced from the Acropolis that rises above. Below this a strata is found that includes a large number of Laconian tiles. In many of the trenches this is a distinct tile layer. The position and preservation of the tiles, indicates that they represent the collapse of roofs in the area.[91]

Beneath this tile layer, is a level that is rich in finds, both ceramic and of other objects (including coins).[92] Near complete ceramics of fine, plain, cooking and coarse wares were excavated. This level is clearly the pre-destruction and latest use phase of the room. In some rooms the layers were dug to bedrock. When the strata name is identified cross-joins might suggest a continuation of the use phase down to bedrock. The finds from below the tile layer date the latest and major (?) period of use of the rooms from the late fourth to the late 3rd century. Occupation did not continue much beyond the fourth quarter of the third (the absence of mouldmade vessels, which are widely traded throughout the Greek world from the late 3rd century, are the clearest indicator of this).[93] Room I differs slightly from this description, given the lack of a distinct tile layer across the room, though a number of tile pieces were excavated. The main exception to this summary of levels is room VIII, in which a large quantity of Archaic, probably cultic, material is located which indicates a different use phase and pattern, though the tile collapse in the room is common with those in the other rooms.

The zones outside the rooms fall into three different groups: III, IX, and XII lie open outside the rooms. They carry material that is mixed in date, but includes Hellenistic sherds, all of which tend to be worn and are distinctly less well preserved than the material within the rooms. It seems likely that these zones served as a pathway in front of the houses. Zones VI and XIII are also to the East of the rooms but are both partially sheltered by walls on three sides. This sheltered nature indicates the potential for different functions for

88 Preliminary report of the rooms: Houby-Nielsen, Moschos & Gazis, 2000, p. 229-249; esp. p. 241-249.
89 Graves: Moschos 2000, 291-301; Eiring 2004, 93-166.
90 Note that the roman numerals ascribed to the rooms and zones are not the same as numbers used in the *SPR* produced when the area was only partly excavated. Houby-Nielsen, Moschos & Gazis, 2000, fig. 28.
91 For discussion of the tiles from this area see Grønne 2000, p. 257-258 and Chapter C.4 below.
92 Reports on the coins, see *SPR & TPR*.
93 See Rotroff 2006, pp. 357-378, for discussion of the date of the introduction of mouldmade relief bowls and the time lag between their production, dispersal and appearance in the archaeological record.

the zones, and the finds associate the zones with the interior spaces. Zones IV and VII are different again, occurring between the rooms and the fortification wall to the west. They are both narrow, walled zones.

In **summary**, there is evidence of both food storage and preparation, along with drinking and dining, mixed with some cultic elements (particularly strong in the Archaic levels of VIII, but also evident in II). The loom weights allow for a small industry but also domestic weaving. The number of coins found, particularly in V and II, suggests commercial transactions in the area. Perhaps we must be content to accept a broad range of activities within these rooms; well suited to a small trading post, with a partially itinerant population.

GENERAL STRATIGRAPHY (FIG. 43)

TRENCH O26. The trench is the northernmost in the series of trenches in AREA III. The irregular trench measures slightly less than 70 m². The NW side is

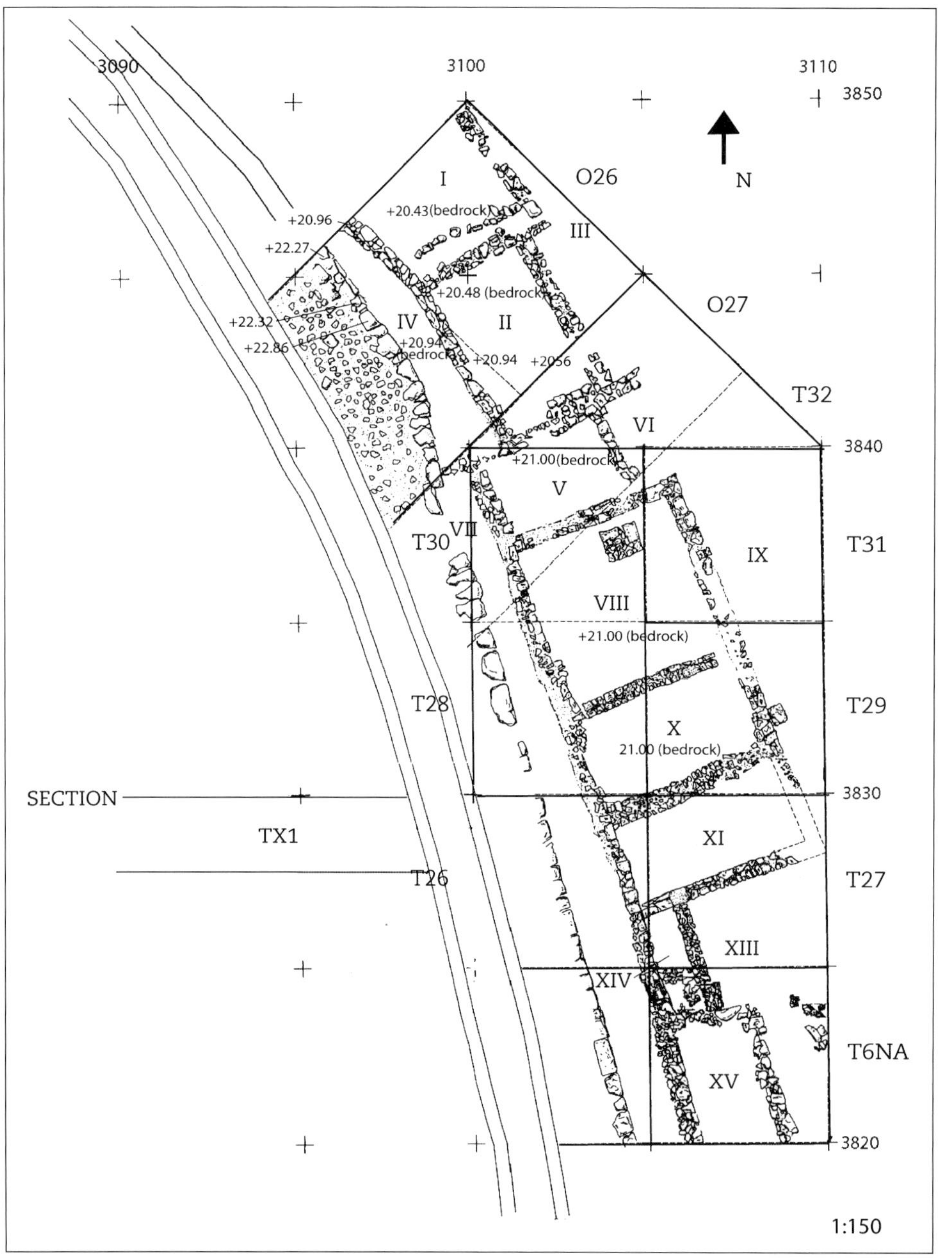

Fig. 43 *Plan of AREA III with trench numbers and room/zone numbers indicated. 1:200.*

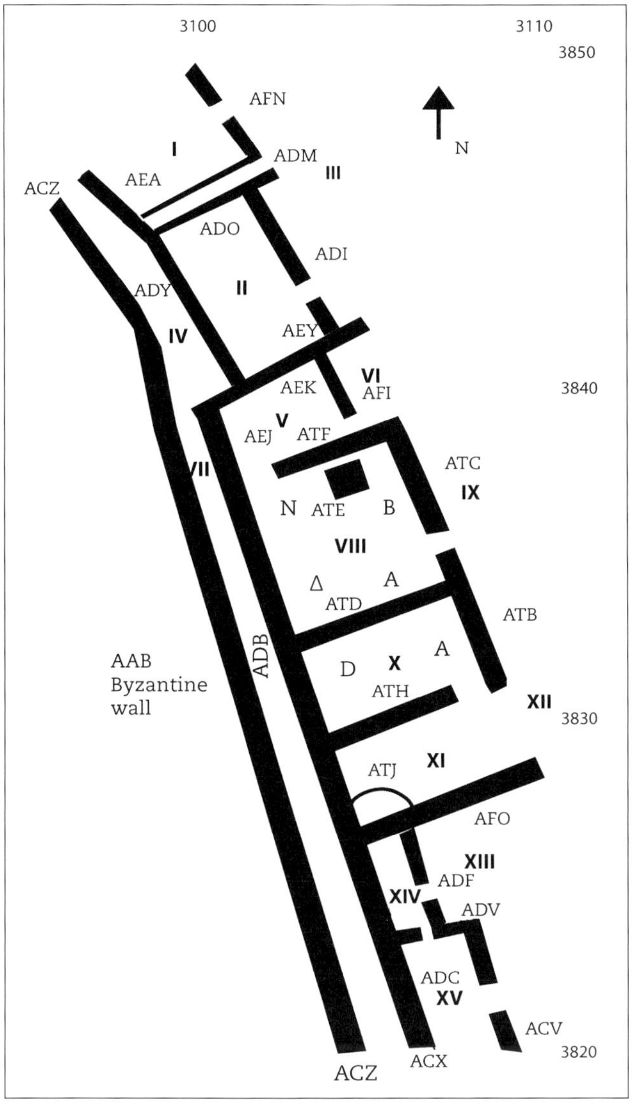

Fig. 44 *Plan of AREA III with indication of room/zone numbers and wall identifiers. 1:200.*

7.0 m long, the South western line of the trench is limited by the Byzantine fortification wall *AAB*. In the lower levels, AREA I in trench O26 was called O26BD to distinguish it from room II. Fig. 44

Room I (Fig. 45)
Walls *AFN, ADO, AEA* (*/ADY*) and the northern baulk define room I. There is a passage way through wall *AFN* leading out to AREA III. The drain *ADM* runs along the North side of the wall *ADO.*

The room as located under several deposits of rubble (strata 1 and 2). The many large stones had tumbled from the partially collapsed terrace wall *ACZ* above, and the Byzantine fortification wall, *AAB*. Tiles were plentiful in the upper deposits of the trench, though did not appear as a distinct layer.

Olive brown (2.5Y 4/3-4/4) hard packed soil with many pieces of tile. Three iron nails (F97-3001, 3002 and 3003), loom weights (F97-3004, 3009, 3011, 3014, 3015, 3022-3025, 3031 and 3044 (not EB)), flint, pottery, architectural fragments (?) (F97-3006, 3030 and 3035), pithos fragments and some fragments of mortar (F97-3017-3018), stucco and a bronze coin (F97-3026).

O26BD/3 F98-1113-1149 (coins, loom weights, iron and lead)(including finds from the drain *ADM*) (F98-1044 to 1972 are tiles. F98-1074 is a coin).

F98-1113 was interpreted as a crucible indicating that smelting of metals was performed in the courtyard (Fig. 46). F98-1122 is the rim of a large pithos (Fig. 47)

O26BD/3a (Finds on surface of STR3a): shells, 16 "polished" bone fragments (F97-3041), loom weight and pottery. 6 coins: F98-1108, 1116 and 3040, a large jar (in *ADM*) and a standing laconian tile (F97-3043) (in *ADM).* Two iron nails (F98-1075-1076).

ADM is a drain cut in the bedrock along the North side of wall *ADO* in AREA I (Fig. 48). Tiles were found during the excavation of the channel and provided *O26BD/2*probably a cover to the drain*:* Tile deposit *AEA*-1, *ADM*-1 (tile deposit in drain), F97-3049 ("a pipe"). Other concentrations of tile and sherds found in *ADM* are called *AEU*, *AET* and AES

Structure *AFG (*Fig. 49a and b) is a large, well-preserved Corinthian tile (*AFG-1*) covered by three stone slabs placed North of the drain *ADM*.

The deposit *AEV* is placed in a depression in the bedrock near wall *AEA* (clearly seen on Fig. 48) and west of the structure *AFG* (near but not in the drain *ADM*) (described as a black layer in O26BD/3). Dark yellowish brown (10YR 3/4) soil changing to very dark (10YR 3/2) near the two chytrae F98-1117 (Catalogue no. 27?) and F98-1118 (catalogue nos. 26). The deposit

Fig. 45 *Trench O26 after removal of strata 1 and 2. Behind the wall defining the rooms/zones, is seen the Archaic/Classical/Hellenistic terrace/fortification wall and further in the background the Byzantine fortification wall, AAB. From East.*

is characterized by having many well preserved vessels (cooking ware, plain and fine ware).

Lower level of the deposit *AEV*: 20.43-20.53 a.s.l.

Room II (Fig. 45)

O26/2 Loom weights: F97-3034, 3037 and 3042. In the bottom of STR 2, the entire area was covered by a substantial level of fallen Laconian tiles mixed with flat stones, *ADG*.

An unfinished marble lamp (*ADO*-1) was found close to the wall *ADO* in stratum 2 (see *SPR*, 247, Fig. 36 and Fig. 50).

Bottom level of Str 2 in room II, between *ADI* and *ADY*: average 20.43-20.75 m.a.s.

Room II, stratum 3 (lower level) is the habitation/floor level in room II:

O26/3 North western corner of room II (Fig. 51 a+b): LEVELS: 20.54-20.88 m.a.s. In the uppermost pass of STR 3, a long series of tiles (F98-1044 to 1072) were registered.

In the lower level (just above bedrock), dark yellowish brown (10YR 4/4) soil with tiles and almost complete vessels were found. Pieces of mud bricks

Fig. 46 *Crucible or melting pit in room I. Hard burned soil/clay structure including many tiles/sherds. The burnt clay is light red (2.5YR 7/6). The ring around the centre is built up by pieces of Laconian tile. L. 46 cm. W. 31 cm. H. 13 cm.*

Fig. 47 *Rim of pithos. Biscuit: Light red (2.5YR 7/6). Medium-coarse tempered fabric. Many white inclusions. Surface: perhaps black painted? D 58 cm (on outside).*

Fig. 48 *The drain ADM cutting through the wall ADY into zone IV. In the background the Archaic/Classical/Hellenistic terrace/fortification wall ACZ. From East.*

and lots of charcoal. Finds: F98-1006-1037. (see *SPR*, 245-246 and figs. 36-37): lead handle (F98-1007. Lamp (F98-1010. Catalogue no. 60), iron nail (F98-1011), bronze nail (F98-1012), bronze coins (F98-1016, 1017, 1024 and 1025), silver coins (F98-1018 and 1020), various bronze-and iron fragments, pottery and animal bones. In the area East of *AEP* (-see below) another series of finds were recorded: F98-1079 to 1097: loom weights (F98-1079, 1081 (2 pieces) and 1089), coins (F98-1080, 1087,1088, 1094, and 1095), iron nail (F98-1082 and 1096), various iron fragments (F98-1083, 1084 and 1093), iron plates (F98-1090, 1091 and 1096) and lead.

Level of structure *AEP* in the North western corner of room II: 20.60-20.85 metre a.s.l. Upper stratum 3 excavated close to *ADI*: coin (F97-3040).

O26/3 2nd pass is a pit cut in the rock (*AEO*) in the southwestern corner of room II (seen on Figs. 52-53), with finds F98-2187 to 2189: Olive brown (2.5YR 4/4) soil with pebbles – but fewer stones and tiles than Str 2. The soil in the pit was the same as in O26/3 but with patches of dark soil and large pebbles (4-5 cm D). The soil of *AEO* continues below the foundation *ADY* and (possibly) below *AED* (with Classical and Archaic material).

The bottom level of *AEO* is 20.38 metre a.s.l., top level is 20.81 metre a.s.l. The pit is thus around 0.40 m deep.

O26/3 4th pass (excavated close to wall *ADI*)(with Classical and Archaic pottery and no Hellenistic).

Finds in the southwest corner of room II/3: 2 loom weights (F99-3071 and 3075 [Catalogue 78]), 4 coins (F99-3072, 3073, 3074 and 3076), lead, iron and bronze.

Clay packing *AED* – dark yellowish brown (10YR 3/4) to very dark greyish brown (10YR 3/2). *AED* is placed between trenches O26 and O27 – a coin

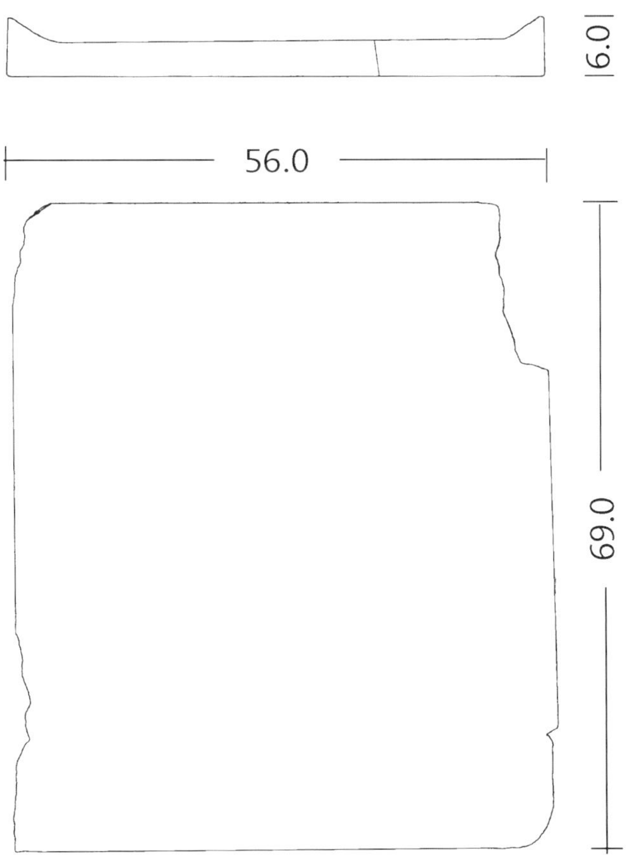

Fig. 49a + b *The large, well-preserved Corinthian tile (AFG-1) placed north of the drain ADM (Bag no. 2288/ F98-1153/O26NW/AFG1). Biscuit: Pale yellow (5Y 8/3) coarse tempered black/brown inclusions. Surface: idem, smoothed. Description: Corinthian tile. The rims of the two sides are turned upwards. L. 69, 00 cm. W.: 56, 00 cm. Th. (at rim): 5, 60 cm. Th. (middle): 4, 02 cm. Comments: Imported.*

Fig. 50 *Unfinished marble lamp ADO-1 from Room II Str 2.*

Fig. 51a *Floor level, stratum 3 in room II, Northwest corner seen from the east with walls ADO and ADY to the right and the Archaic/Classical/Hellenistic fortification/terrace wall in the background. From East.*

Fig. 51b *Detail of floor level in room II Seen from East.*

Fig. 52 *Drawing of room II stratum 3 with structure numbers and finds.*

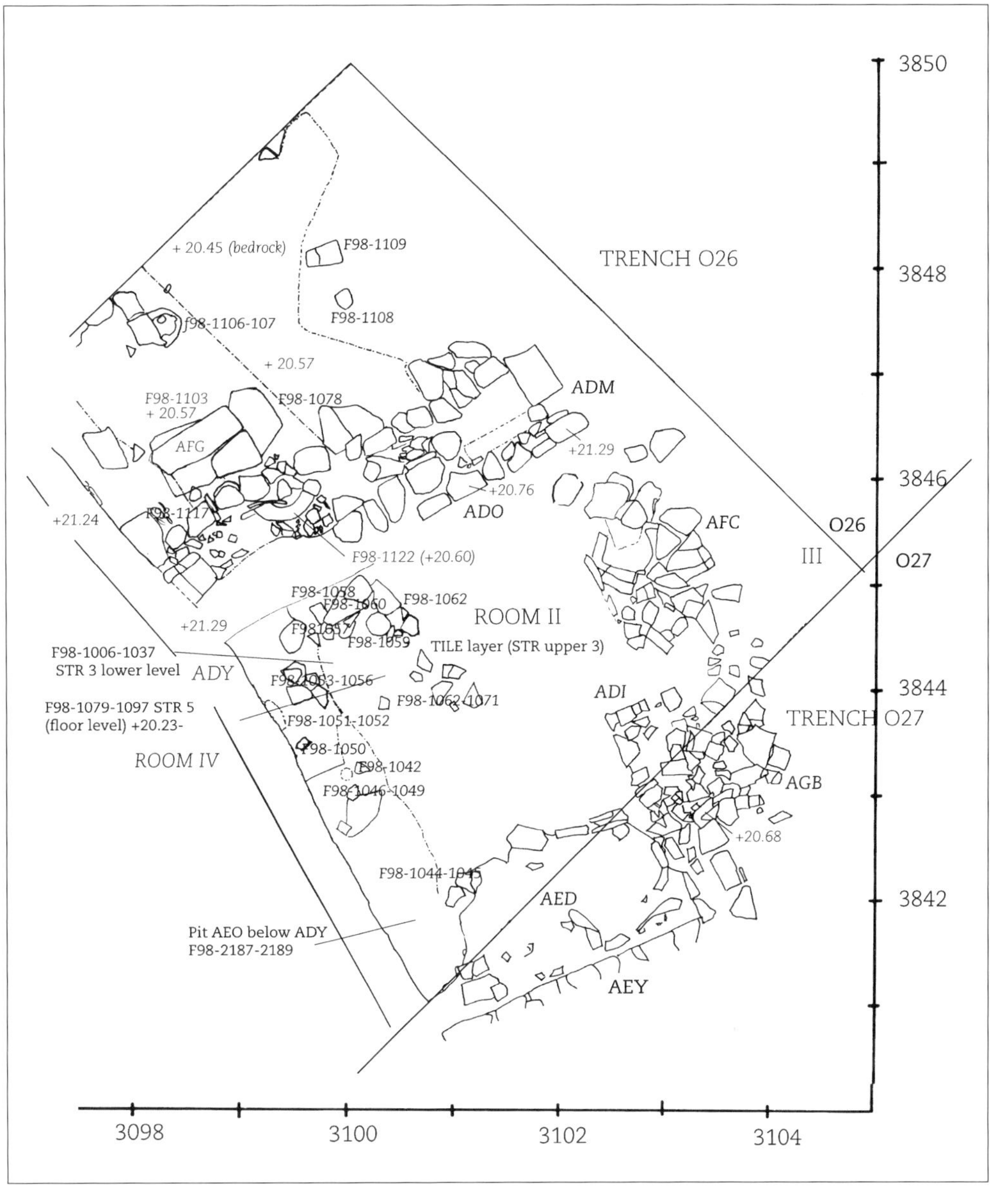

(F99-3088), iron and animal bones. A shallow pit below *AED* was cut into the bedrock contained "a mix of pottery from different periods"

O27/3 3 coins, loom weights and Archaic/Mycenaean pottery and Corinthian tiles, loom weights, bronze coin, lead, iron and bronze.

Average level of bedrock in room II: 20.46-20.56 metre a.s.l.

Zone III

O26/3 – Lots of tile structures (*AFC, AFD* and *AFE*), large pithos (F98-2124-2125), coins (F98-1133, 1135, 1138 and 1139), marine shells, pottery and iron nails. Pit in zone III is called *AGD* (2.5Y 5/6) light olive brown with some tiles, pottery, animal bones and a loom weight (F99-3083. Catalogue no. 141).

Room IV (Fig. 54).

Between *AAB* and *ACZ*, Str 1-2: Tiles, Laconian and some Corinthian (?)

O26/2 Olive brown (2.5Y 4/4) soil with tiles and pottery.

O26/3 Olive brown (2.5Y 4/4) sandy soil with many broken tiles and pottery. Fragment of a metope (?)

O26/4 Layer below the uppermost tile layer. Olive brown (2.5Y 4/4) crumbly soil with large-medium

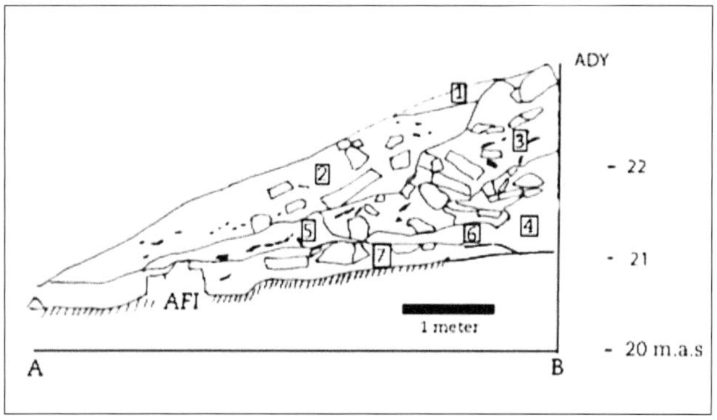

Fig. 53 *Section of SE side of trench O26 (O26SE) – line between trenches 26 and 27.*

1. *Surface*
2. *Pebble/stone layer – loose soil (2.5YR 4/4) olive brown, small shells, sherds, tiles.*
3. *Same but harder.*
4. *Stone spill – stones from wall AEJ.*
5. *"Red" tile layer.*
6. *Black layer below tile layer – olive brown (2.5YR 5/3).*
7. *Layer rich in finds – floor level.*

Fig. 54 *Room IV stratum 3 from N. The fortification/ terrace wall ACZ to the right, to the left wall ADY.*

sized stones and lots of tiles (probably the same layer as Str3).

O26/5 Top level: 21.25 m. The soil in SW corner is darker, dark yellowish brown

(10YR 4/4). Bedrock with a grooved channel in the middle. In room I and room IV, *ADY* is standing on soil not stones.

The level of bedrock is sloping from 20.84 in the southern part to 20.55 towards North.

Room V (Fig. 55)

Excavated in trench O27 (The trench measures: W (NE): 4.0 m; L (NW): 10.3 m; L (SE): 12.1 m.

O27/1 2nd pass/surface of STR 2: Olive brown (2.5Y 4/4) crumbly soil. Loom weights (F98-4007, 4010 and 4011) and a coin (F99-4008) – one fragment of a sima (F98-4009), tiles and pottery, bronze handle (F98-4012), bronze nail (F98-4013) and lots of charcoal.

O27/2 Olive brown (2.5Y 4/4) crumbly soil with many stones, many tiles and pottery. A sima fragment (F98-4016), a flat, round stone (for grinding?) (F98-4015), pithos (F98-4018), iron slags (?), some glass (F98-4021) and mortar.

O27/3 Structure *AER*, reddish-brown (7.5YR 4/4) soil East of *AEK* Structure *AEZ* is a huge tile layer South of *AEK* – Str3

Str 3, 2nd pass. Excavation below the tile layer *AEZ* (area near *AFI*)) (Fig. 56) "Lower stratum 3", light olive brown (2.5YR 5/4) with many finds (F99-3004-3082): pottery, iron, glass, loom weights, bronze and iron, animal bones, charcoal and 32 coins spread around the floor, especially along *AFI* (F99- 3004, 3005, 3007, 3008, 3009, 3014, 3018, 3019, 3021, 3025, 3028, 3031, 3031, 3032, 3033, 3036, 3037, 3039, 3041, 3044, 3045,

Fig. 55 *Room V with tile layer AEZ. In front wall AFI. To the right walls AFY and AEK. From East.*

3047, 3048, 3049, 3050, 3052, 3054, 3070, 3072, 3073, 3074, 3076). 2 fish hooks. All found in the same level 20.90 a.s.l.(+/-). Str 3/2nd pass: 20.76-20.97 m.a.s.

Str 3/3rd pass – the soil is the same as above (2nd pass) – light olive brown (2.5Y 5/4), but not nearly as many finds as in the 2nd pass and only one coin (F99-3056). More loom weights than in 3, 2nd pass (F99-3057 (Cat. no. 130), 3060, 3062 (Cat. no. 132), 3064 (Cat. no. 131), 3067 (Cat. no. 133) and 3069), iron nail and some finer pottery.

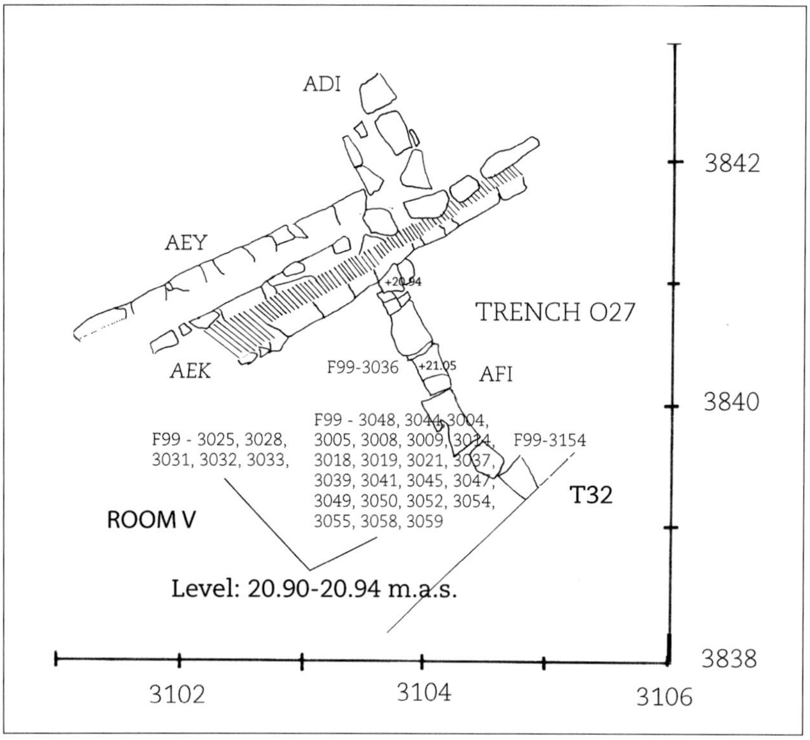

Fig. 56 *Room V, Str 3, 2nd pass, area near AFI. "Excavation below the tile layer AEZ".*

AEZ (upper 3) – heavy packing of tiles, especially close to the *AEJ*, very few sherds. "Homogeneous" layer with "clean" soil, light olive brown (2.5Y 5/4) – towards the bottom the soil becomes more dark, very dark greyish brown (2.5Y 3/2) – the fallen roof.

Zone VI

T31/4 (corner between *ATC* and *AFI*). Quite a lot of potsherds. Iron nail (F00-1134), astragalus (F00-1135 and 1139). Bronze coin (F00-1136). Loom weights (F00-1137 and 1138 (Cat. no. 197)).

Zone VII

Str 2a related to the fill of the zone post-destruction level 2b, the hard-packed zone, to be the phase of use of the rooms below.

THE AREA BETWEEN *AAB* AND *ACZ*: *O27/2* Olive brown (2.5Y 4/3) somewhat clayish soil. Loom weight (F98-4001), pottery (especially in Str 2b, slightly darker than 2a – see also O26).

THE AREA BETWEEN *ACZ* AND *AEJ*: *O27/1* Sandy surface with stones, tiles, pottery and some mortar. Bronze coin (F98-4006) – bottom Str1.

TRENCHES T28, T 29, T30 AND T31: STRATA 1-3 (Fig. 57):

Str 1

T28/1 Brown (10YR 5/3), loose surface soil with medium sized stones, pottery and tiles. 4 loom weights. Small pieces of bronze. Further down, light olive brown (2.5Y 5/3) soil with many tiles and pottery, especially close to the Archaic/ Classical terrace wall.

T29/1 Surface soil, very dark greyish brown (10YR 3/2) loose surface soil with small stones, some pottery and tiles. In the eastern part of the trench, with brown (10YR 5/3) soil a tile packing *ATA*. Few sherds. The "complete tile in T29/1 is called F00-1001 "below Str 1" (see Catalogue below Chapter C.1.4 (in AREA X)). The western part of the trench contains more tiles and sherds than the eastern part. Two loom weights.

T30/1 Brown (7.5YR 4/3) surface soil with many sherds. Two loom weights (F00-1003 and 1004). More tiles in Str 1 in T30 than in the same level in T31.

T 31/1 – Dark greyish brown (10YR 4/2) to brown (10YR 5/3) surface soil with few stones and a little pottery and tiles. A loom weight. Piece of bronze (F00-1006), bronze coin (F00-1007), iron nail (F00-1008) + iron (F00-1009).

Fig. 57 *Trenches T28, T 29, T30 and T31 from the east.*

Str 2

T28/2 Brown (10YR 5/3) clayish soil with quite a lot of tiles and sherds.

T29/2 (level below the tile structure *ATA* – later on zone IX). Light yellowish brown (2.5Y 6/3) soil. Bronze coins (F00-1015 and 1016). Charcoal was found below the tile structure.

T30/2 Brown (10YR 5/3) loosely packed surface soil with lots of tile and a few sherds. Loom weight (F00-1017). "Platform" *ATE*. Layers of tiles in the western part.

T31/2 With many finds in the level below the tile layer *ATA* in T29/1 (rooom IX below). A piece of iron, a loom weight, an astragal, a bronze coin (F00-1010) and bronze tweezers (F00-1011). No tile layers in T31 East.

T32/2 Light olive brown (2.5Y 5/3) soil. Piece of lead, loom weight (F00-1014).

Str 3

T28/3 Light yellowish brown (2.5Y 6/4) soil. Loom weight (F00-1025), bronze coin (bag 4149) and column krater (F00-1023. Catalogue no. 200). Tile layer *ACG.*

T29/3 Two loom weights (F00-1021 and 1022).

T30/3 ATI (wattle and daub – reddish yellow (5YR 6/8) (F00-1024). Tile structure *ATG* continues South of *ATE* – the structure lies below Str3.

T31/3 Light olive brown (2.5Y 5/3) dry soil. A foundation, iron nail (F00-1018), bronze fragment, a bronze bottom, iron slag.

Room VIII (NB. The area N of *ATD* and W of *ATC* is called T30 = Room VIII) (Fig. 58).

Strata 1 to 3 are excavated across the room proper and it is only after the removal of these strata and the tile

Fig. 58 *Room VIII from NW.*

layer *ATG* and the deposit *ATI* (with wattle and daub), which represent the destruction of the room, that the Room VIII was excavated as a distinct unit. With the removal of the tile layer *ATG*, which appears even below stratum 3,[94] the area is redefined so that room VIII is excavated as one unit. The trench lines which quarter the room were kept and the area is excavated in quadrants, identified by the compass points B, N, A, D. After the division T31 refers to the zone outside the room, our IX (for T28 and T29 see room V and zone VIII, below) (Fig. 59).

T30/4 Yellowish brown (10YR 5/4) and dark yellowish brown (10YR 4/4) soil.

ATI contained the following finds: iron slag, 3 bronze coins (F00-1034, 1035 and 1036) + pottery

T30/5 Bronze coins (F00-1039, 1042, 1043, 1045 and 1046) + bronze hook, a bronze pin (F00-1040), lead, loom weights (Bag nos. 4582 and 4592).

EXCAVATIONS IN SQUARES T30/A, N, D AND B STRATA /7 AND /8.

A number of structures occur in level 7. *ATV* is found within stratum 7 and rests on bedrock. It consists of about 23 stones laid horizontally on the bedrock and covers 1.20-1.50 m. The stones are approximately 10 cm. in height. It is a paved area set to the west and abutting platform *ATE* (Fig. 60) a small section is pre-

94 Corresponds to "stratum 2" in trenches =O26/27. Obs! Two kiln wedges, 147 and 148.

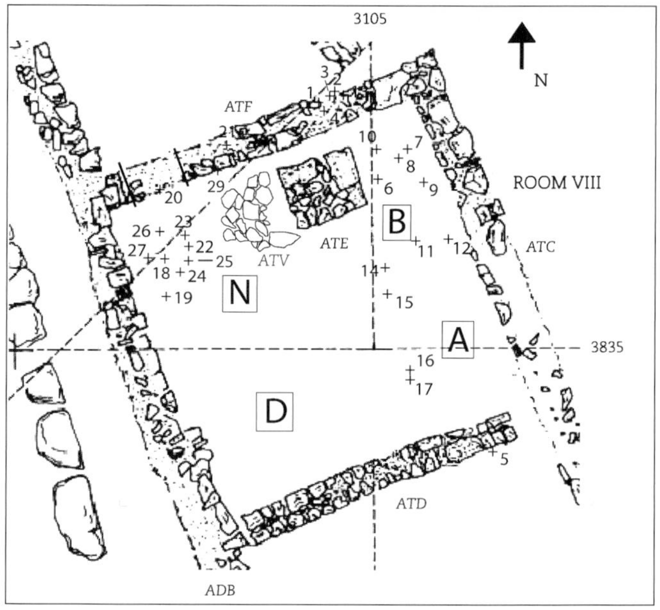

Fig. 59 *Room VIII (T30) finds from strata /4 and /5. Captions:*
1. *F00-1034: coin*
2. *F00-1035: coin*
3. *F00-1036: coin*
4. *F00-1037: pottery*
5. *F00-1038: charcoal*
6. *F00-1039: coin*
7. *F00-1040: bronze pin*
8. *F00-1041: lead*
9. *F00-1042:coin*
10. *F00-1043: coin*
11. *F00-1044: bronze hook*
12 *F00-1045: coin*
13. *F00-1046: coin*
14. *F00-1047: miniature vessel*
15. *F00-1048: miniature vessel*
16. *F00-1049: miniature vessel*
17. *F00-1050: bronze nail*
18. *F00-1052: lead*
19. *F00-1052: oyster shell*
20. *F00-1053: loom weight*
21. *F00-1054: bronze needle*
22. *F00-1055: miniature vessel*
23. *F00-1056: coin*
24. *F00-1057: fine ware vessel*
25. *F00-1058: lead*
26. *F00-1059: coin*
27. *F00-1060: lead*
28. *F00-1061: bronze sheet*
29. *F00-1062: coin*

Fig. 60 *The altar ATE in room VIII. From East.*

served wrapping around the southern side of *ATE*. The large stone *ATY* sits in the corner of *ATD* and *ADB*, it covers an area of 0.7 × 0.8 m. and stands 5 cm. high. It rests on stratum 8, though on the southern edge a second stone and then bedrock is visible beneath.[95]

A pit in stratum 7 *ATT* was 30 cm. in diameter and dug to bedrock. Located in quadrant N it was positioned close to wall *ADB*. The deposit was textured, a little as mudbrick, and was reddish-yellow in colour. A second pit, *ATU*, was empty.

T30B/7 Bronze fragment (F00-1092), loom weights (F00-1094 and 1097 (Cat. nos. 178 and 179), terracotta bead (F00-1095) and coin (F00-1096).

T30N/7: Coins (F00-1101, 1102, 1108 and 1120), astragalus (F00-1104, lead mask (F00-1106) and bronze nail (F00-1127).

T30D/7 Coins (F00-1107 and 1115), loom weights (F00-1105, 1112 and 1116), iron nail (F00-1111), iron fragments (F00-1109), lead fragments (F00-1113 and 1114) and astragalus (F00-1110).

T30D/8 Lead fragment (F00-1118), loom weights (F00-1121 and 1129 Cat. no. 190 and 191), astragalus (F00-1119), iron nails (F00-1122 and 1125), coins (F00-1123 and 1124), fine ware vessel (F00-1026) and terracotta knob (F00-1128).

T30A/7 Coins (F00-1093 and 1100), bronze fragments (F00-1098 and 1103) and an iron nail (F00-1099).

A substantial groove was cut in the bedrock, running from the platform *ATE* to the foundation *ATD* (Fig. 58).

Zone IX

T29/4 The stratum below tile layer *ATA* (Fig. 57) (ATA is placed outside room X=zone IX) is called 4: Charcoal (F00-1028), bronze coin (F00-1032), fragment of bronze. Bronze coins (F00-1034, 1035 and 1036). The

95 *T31/4* (=-/7 in room VIII). Bronze fragments (F00-1131, 1132 and 1133).

Fig. 61 *Room X from East. In the foreground a large ashlar in front of wall ATB. Room XI to the left.*

complete tile piece F00-1001 is the upper part of *ATA*. Below the tile layer *ATA* a large stone block is placed close to the foundation *ATB* (Fig. 61).

Room X

Room X (Figs. 61-62) lies between rooms VIII and XI. It is walled by *ADB, ATH, ATD* and *ATB* which extends from *ATH* across half the width of the room. The room is located in trenches T28 and T29 with the southwest corner crossing into trench T27. In stratum 4 the area South of *ATD* (V) is excavated as T28 and distinguished from that to the North of *ATD* and to the area East of *ATB*.

Fig. 57 shows Str 3, the tile layer *ATG* (room VIII), *ACG* (room X and XI) and the tile concentration *ATA* in front of room X with the preserved Laconian tile F00-1001.

Under the tile layer (Str 3) the area South of *ATD* was referred to as T28=room X

EXCAVATIONS BELOW THE TILE LAYER *ACG* (*ATG*):

T28/4 a good quantity of charcoal (F00-1038) and tiles – yellowish brown (10YR 5/4) soil. Bottom level of T28/4: 20,99 to 21,27 m a.s.l.

T29/5 Bronze coins (F00-1140, 1142 and 1143), lead (F00-1141), bronze fragment (F00-1143) and a loom weight (F00-1144 Cat. no. 241).

T28/5 Pyramidal bronze object (F00.1063), coin (F00-1064)

At 17/10, 2000 Room X (=T28) divided in three parts, T28N (=T26), T28D (=T28) and T28A (=T29).

T28D/5 A bronze ring (F00-1068), stucco (F00-4206), fine ware vase (F00-4373), two loom weights (F00-1069 and 1070 Cat. nos. 207 and 208) and bronze (F00-1073).

T28N Pit *ATK*.

T28A/6 The area by the foundation *ATB* has very many potsherds and loom weights (F00-1071 (Cat. no. 228), 1075, 1076 (225), 1077 (Cat. no. 229) and 1080 (227)), a coin (F00-1072), lead (F00-1074), iron nail (F00-1078). A group of ceramics was found East of the channel *ATM*. There are five post holes in T28: *ATN, ATO, ATP, ATQ and ATR*. (see above). *ATP* is situated in pit *ATK*. Stratum 6 is characterised by a layer of finds within a dark grey to olive-brown soil. The soil extends across the room, though in the southwest corner is cut by the large pit *ATK (*Fig. *62)*. One of the postholes, *ATP* was located within the pit.

In total, five postholes were identified in T28. These postholes form an irregular rectangle with the fifth set out in front. Only one, *ATN*, contains ceramic finds,

Fig. 62 *Room XI seen from room X. In the foreground wall ATH. The silo ATJ is seen in the corner between wall AFO in the background. In the foreground right the circular structure ATJ (silo for grain?). An olive press is seen in front to the left and a grinding stone North of wall AFO to the right the olive press to the left. Wall ADB to the right. The pit ATK in room X is seen in the foreground.*

these are scrappy but include glazed wares and a Prehistoric sherd. An iron nail is also found in *ATN* as is a stone; the stone is a standard find in the other, otherwise empty, post holes.

The drain *ATM* runs along the base of wall *ATD* (See Fig. 61). This structure is located within stratum 6 and rests on bedrock. It measures 2.8 m (L). Six terracotta slabs form the floor of the drain, while stones provide the southern border of the drain, the northern provided by wall *ATD*. Three stones were placed across the drain and effectively blocked it. The drain is not preserved along the length of wall *ATD*.

TRENCHES T26, T27 AND T29:

T26/1 Light olive brown (2.5Y 6/3) surface soil with many medium sized stones and some pottery.

T26/2 Yellowish brown (10YR 5/4) more clayish than Str1 with smaller stones, a few tiles and pottery, animal bones. A stone packing is supporting the foundation wall *ADB* from behind (W) – black glazed pottery. Lots of tiles (one big piece is Corinthian), fragments of iron – a fish hook (Bag no. 2951).

Bottom level:Str2: 22.55-22.70 m.a.s.

T26/3 (21.07.99) – Stone and tile structure *AGC* – *AFT*, a loom weight (F99-1014).

T27/1 Surface soil with lots of stones, pieces of tiles and some pottery. One loom weight.

T27/2 Light brown (10YR 4/4) loosely packed soil with big stones fallen from *ADB*), more tile fragments than in Str 1, pottery. Fragments of a lamp and loom weight (F99-1021).

Fig. 63 *Room XI strata /5 to /6. Tiles and pottery in the floor level.*

Top level: 22.28-23.70 m.a.s.

T27/3 dark brown (10YR 4/3) soil with some pebbles, few tiles and pottery, an(F99-1006), terracotta relief (?) (F99-1007). Structure *AFO* (a foundation) in Str3.

Top soil level: 20.89-22.35 m.a.s.

T27/3B Terracotta figurine (F99-1007) was found in 3B.

T27B/4 Dark yellowish brown (10YR 4/4) with tiles, pottery and animal bones. Structure *AGC* (both in T26 and T27) with many tiles in large pieces. The structure continues below stone packing *AFQ*. Bronze coin in *AGC* (F99-1015).

Room XI
Excavated in trenches T26, T27 and T29.

Room XI lies between room X and AREA XIII/room XIV. There is no wall preserved on the eastern front of the room, leaving the possibility that it was a three-sided shelter, rather than a room proper.

T27B/4 and *T26/3* contain two structures; the stone packing *AFQ* and tile layer *AGC* which are both part of the destruction level of the house. *AGC* is the tile spill as in room X, crossing the foundation wall *ATH* and spanning the area from *AFO* to *ATD*. A Coin in *T27B/4*, F99-1015.

Below Str 3/4, the levels of the room is united and excavated as T27B (=T27 North of *AFO*). By stratum 5 the term T27B is used for all of room XI.

Strata 5 and 6 (Fig. 62)

ATJ is a stone construction that forms a quarter of a circle in the corner between walls *ADB* and *AFO*. It rests on bedrock in Str 6 and consists of six big stones and two smaller ones. There are two courses of stones preserved in the western section of the structure, where it stands at approximately 0.37 m above the bedrock. The one course that is preserved throughout the structure is at 0.17 m. Two postholes are also recorded within *ATJ*, they are situated close to wall *ADB*.

T27B/6 (Fig. 63) Loose soil with many tiles. Not many sherds and a few shells. Fragments of a bronze coin. On the North side of *AFO* a grinding stone, 50 × 50 cm. was situated (see below chapter F2). An olive press (lower left on Fig. 63 (see below chapter E2)), a mortar (?), a bronze coin (F00-1065). Lead (F00-1066), bronze (F00-1067) and amphoras (F00-1089 (Cat. no. 262) and 1090).

T27B/7 (Str 7 corresponds to T29/5 and T31/4). Iron nail (F00-1081), spindle whorl (F00-1083), loom weight (F00-1084), an almost complete vessel (F00-1085) and lead (F00-1087).

T27A/7 A small bowl and a coin.

Zone XIII
AREA XIII is located to the South of wall *AFO* and the East of wall *ADF*. A door threshold in *ADF* leads from zone XIII into room XIV.

Zone XIII is first excavated in trench T6NA, when it is distinguished by a 'd' (e.g. T6NA/2d).[96] The northern regions of this are located in T27 and defined by an 'N' (*T27N/3* – though this also includes a part of

96 **266**, a catalogued West Slope fragment is from /2d.

Fig. 64 *The tile deposit ATX (In trench T6NA). The tiles are named F0050 to 0054) below the tile layer ADZ in room XIV as seen from room XV (South). Wall AFO in the background.*

room XIV).[97] Following *T27N/3* is T27N/4d. No stratum 5d is identified in T27N to equate the stratum 5d in T6NA. The soil is loosely packed, very dry and coloured a dark greyish brown.

There are some tiles in this area of the trench, including those associated with the wall *ADF*. The tiles are not as numerous however, as those in rooms XIV and XV, where *ADZ* provides a thick cover (See below).

T27N/3 Loom weight (with an Ω)(F99-1008 Cat. no. 284), a square terracotta box (F99-1009).

T27N/4d (AREA XIII) – dark greyish brown (2.5Y 4/2) loose soil. One loom weight (F99-1016 Cat. no. 273) and a bone astragalus (F99-1021).

Bronze coin (F99-1035) + structure *AGH* – light olive brown (2.5Y 5/4).

97 Only the stamped loom weight, **284**, is catalogued from T27N/3, AREA III.

Room XIV

Room XIV is a small narrow area walled by ADB, AFO, ADF and ADV. *ADC* is a short wall that runs perpendicular to wall ADB, a gap is left between the end of ADC and the wall ADF which runs parallel to ADB. Two threshold blocks were located within this room in stratum 5. One indicates a doorway between room XIV to AREA XIII. The second fills the gap between ADC and ADF. Excavation of this room was accomplished first in 1997 in the trench T6NA and then continued in 1999 within T27N. In both trenches 'e' is used to distinguish the room, i.e. T6NA/5e.

Room XIV was covered by the tile deposit ADZ. This tile deposit covered both room XIV and XV and a few tiles spilled into AREA XIII. In the excavation of T6NA the removal of ADZ can be associated with room XV (see below) while that of T27 saw the removal of the structure within room XIV Remains of a second tile deposit, this time in the fourth stratum,

ATX, is considerably smaller than *ADZ*.

T27/3N is primarily the remaining part of room XIV = ADZ.

T27N/3 Loom weight (F99-1008) and a square box in clay F99-1010) and some bronze.

T27N/4 In room XIV *ADZ* in this layer.

The remaining part of *ADZ* is excavated in TR 27. *ADZ* and *AFP* are tiles from a roof (*ADZ*: light olive brown (2.5Y 5/4) soil.

ADZ in the northern part of room XIV, standing tiles are called T0050 – T0054 (*ATX*) (Fig. 64).

Finds in *ADZ* (F97-2050-2071): Amphora, tiles, pithos, pottery and metals (square plate F97-2066), animal teeth (F97-2069). Clear floor level. The tiles in *ADZ* are resting on a layer of charcoal and almost occupied the entire room.

NB. tile number *ADZ*-105 found below *ADZ*-62 and directly on bedrock is an Archaic Corinthian type of tile.[98]

T27N/5e 1 pass Loom weights F99-1034 (Cat. no. 298), 1037 (Cat. no. 300), 1038 (Cat. no. 299) and 1039), lots of charcoal, a coin (F99-1035) and a fine ware bowl (F99-1029 Cat. no. 250)).

T27N/5e (layer below the tile deposit) is the area W of foundation *ADF* = Room XIV – iron nails (F99-1017, 1026, 1027 and 1033), a bronze spatula (F99-1018) (actually in T6NA), a lump of lead (F99-1019), bronze coins (F98-11 and 15 (silver), 19 and F99-1020), charcoal, an iron knife (F99-1023) (partly on wall *ADF*), fish hook (?) (F98-14), iron nails and iron fragments (F98-16, 20, 21, 24 and 26) and a bronze fragment.

TRENCH T6NA:

The trench measures 5 × 5 metres N-S/E-W and an addition of 2.5 metres towards W including the terrace wall.

Surface levels in the trench: NW: 22.36 m, NE: 20.78 m, SW: 23.18 and SE: 21.17 m.

T6NA/1 Grey-black loose, gravely soil.

T6NA/2 Yellowish grey soil mixed with small stones (excavation around *ACV*) and lots of pottery. A coin (F97-2003) was found between hard packed soil between stones in Str2 (?). A loom weight, F97-2004. Animal bones. Stones are covering the bottom of Str 2.

T6NA/3 (below stones in Str2). Yellowish grey but darker than Str2 – no sizeable stones in this layer.

Room XV (Fig. 65)

Room XV is located within trench T6NA, excavated in 1999. In its lower levels, it is distinguished from other zones in the trench by 'b' after the stratum (i.e. T6NA/5b)

The upper levels, strata 1-4 are post-destruction deposits and contain a mix of worn fragments of Archaic, Classical and Hellenistic date. Occasional fragments are well preserved, as the kantharos body fragment Catalogue no. 301, lamp fragment no. 302 and the saucer no. 303.

The tile layer *ADZ* covers the area below stratum 4 (*ADZ* spills into room XIV, see above). It contains a number of complete or near complete Laconian tiles amongst olive brown soil that is less compacted than the deposits above. During the excavation of this deposit, a number of ceramics were excavated, occurring within, but more often beneath, the tiles and there are some cross joins between the ADZ material and that found within stratum 5b below.

T6NA/2b Lots of tiles found between stones. Coin from southern part of trench (F97-2006 (niv. 22.28). F97-2007 is a broken millstone (see Chapter E.2). Further down the stones get larger and the tile fragments bigger (between level. 22.16 and 22.09). Cross-wall *ADC*. Larger tile fragments mixed up with stones covered the area between walls *ACV* and *ACX*.

T6NA/3b (Stratum 3 between *ACV* and *ACX* = room XV, is called 3b). Larger tile fragments mixed up with stones covered the area between the walls. Almost no stones, tiles and pottery absent. Fish hook (F97-2008)(close to *ADB*).

T6NA/3c (3c is the stratum above bedrock in room XV). F97-2005.

T6NA/4b Light yellowish brown to light olive brown (2.5YR 6/4-5/4) soil with medium to large stones, tiles and pottery – further down slightly darker (2.5YR 4/4). Pottery in Str 4b (F97-2014 Cat. no. 303). Str 4b lower level: 21.34 and 21.48.

T6NA/5b Light olive brown (2.5YR 5/4) with few stones, mainly in NW corner, few tile fragments,

98 Grønne 2000, 258 – combination tile.

Fig. 65 *Room XV from East. In the background the Archaic/Classical/Hellenistic fortification/terrace wall. Byzantine fortification wall AAB in the background.*

mainly in southern end but fragments of pottery (from several complete vessels – (for West slope pottery see *SPR* Fig. 32). Many finds: F97-2021-2034, flint and charcoal. Levels of finds: 21.39 m and 21.47 m (NB. floor level inside *ACV* – see also *ADZ* below). Tile spill in the northern part of AREA XIII (East of *ADF* – structure finds of *ADV* (tile spill *ADZ*). F97-2037 is a fish hook. Other finds from level of Str 5b: (F97-2038-2043 + 2044-2052), coin (F97-2044) and pottery, amphora (F97-2050. Catalogue no. 207) and charcoal.

Further finds from floor level in 5b (now called 6b): (F97-2072-2089, F98-27-39), sherds, coins (F97-2073, 2076 and 2077 and F98-29, 32 and 36), iron nails (F98-30, 33, 34 and 38), bronze fragments (F98-35) metals, shells, terracotta fragments, a fish hook (F98-37) charcoal, animal bones.

T6NA/5b, 3rd pass (room XV, North part): (F98-5001-5004) coin (F98-5001), iron nail (F98-5002) astragal (F98-5004) and a lead weight (F98-2004).

Zone in front of room XV (E of foundation ACV)

Str 2d Light olive brown (2.5YR 5/4) soil with few larger stones, little pottery but large to very large tiles especially in the eastern part of the trench at a distance from foundation *ACV*.

Str 3d doorway in *ADF*.

Str 4d not many finds.

AEM: tile layer in front of room XV. Coin (F98-5005) (outside room XIV), lead repair (F98-5006) and coin F98-5010.

Str 5d stratum below the tile spill *AEM*

C.2 The Architecture of AREA III. Construction and Reconstruction

Søren Dietz

The natural setting

The Archaic fortification wall is based on a level shelf around 1.4 m outside the Byzantine wall at a level of approximately 23.0 m.a.s. and we suppose that the wall went up to at least the level of the flat terrace behind the wall, between 27 and 28 m.a.s. If it should function as a fortification wall there must have been a parapet of approximately 1.2 m and the entire height of the wall should be at least 3.7 m high or 5.7 m above the floor level in the workshops (21.0 m.a.s.).

The fortication wall at the same time functioned as a terrace wall.

Description (Fig. 44)

Room I. The wall *AEA* (Figs. 45 and 48) is constructed from large rectangular sandstone blocks interrupted by square or almost square blocks. In order to create level surfaces tiny flat slabs are filled in. Towards the wall *ADO* separating AREA I from room II, a square opening (*AFK*) measuring approximately 0.75 m (H) x 0.60 m (W), bridged by a large, rectangular stone block (L. app. 0.75 m) connects room IV west of the area with the drain *ADM*. The construction of wall *AEA* is more related to the terrace wall *ACZ* than to its continuation to the South (ADY), on the western side of room II, which is more narrow, less regular and constructed with smaller slabs (see also Fig. 51a). The wall *AEA* is based on bedrock, but part of it was founded on soil, resulting in a lowering of the wall.

Around 0.70 m from the wall *AEA is* a large limestone slab (note that limestone is very rare in this part of the mound), *AFG* placed on top of (but separated by a layer of soil) a well preserved Corinthian pan tile which rests on bedrock (Fig. 49 a-b) at level 20.47-20.51 m.a.s. or the same level as bottom of the black soil *AEV* in the space between *AFG* and *AEA*.

ADM is a drain cut in the bedrock running from the square opening (*AFK*) to the line of stones *AFN* towards the "street". Vertically placed slabs lined the southeastern wall of the drain towards the wall *ADO* and room II. A grinding stone (F98-1143) was found amoung the slabs. To the North, the drain was framed by an irregular line of flat stones. The drain seems to have been covered by Laconian tiles of which several are found in a broken condition. Towards the "street" the drain was bridged by a sandstone slab still *in situ* in the stone line *AFN*. When the drain ceased to function it seems to have been used as a dump filled up with pieces of tiles and broken pottery (mainly coarse ware).

The drain was cut in the bedrock approximately 0.40 m below floor level.

Room II is a rectangular, narrow room measuring 4.50 m x 3.35 m or around 15 m^2. The wall *ADO* is a well-defined construction separating room II from room I and the drain *ADM*. It is preserved to a height of around 0.10 m near the "road" up to 0.82 m where it joins *ADY* and where five courses are preserved. The stones in the wall are rather small (10-20 cm in height). The width is 0.50 m. The wall is founded on bedrock.

The wall *ADY* continues the wall *AEA* from room I but is constructed by smaller stones in a more random order (Fig. 51a). The stones are flat rectangular or, in between, square sandstones of which 7 courses are preserved in the northern end, 9 courses in the southern where the height is 0.90 m. A large flat slab (0.80 × 0.20 m) is placed at the northern end where *ADY* joins the drain. *ADY* is narrower than the prolongation in AREA I (Fig. 52) with the width approximately 0.40 m in two more or less parallel rows. The wall is founded on bedrock, but on soil on top of the pit *AEO* and is supported by soil in some cases on the west side (towards room IV).

To the South, *ADY* joins the wall *AEK* in a right angle. The wall *ADY* is preserved in 2-5 courses, best preserved towards West (H. 0.20 m. East end and 1.00 m. at west end). It is built up by two parallel rows of large, well cut flat stones measuring 0.20 m. to 0.40 m. in length, partly by smaller natural stones. Width of wall, 0.40 m to 0.50 m. A clay concentration on top of the wall could derive from a mud brick superstructure. The smaller and less well defined wall structure, AEY is considered to be a later addition.

ADI is a 0.50 m wide, rather light foundation/socle in one course, constructed by two rows of stone. The line towards the "road" is made by 0.20-0.30 m wide, 0.10-0.20 m height rectangular cut stones. The construction is more substantial in the southern part where two courses are preserved creating one side of a door opening.

The clay packing *AED might* be from a mud brick superstructure (?) while the pit *AEO* cut in the bedrock probably derives from earlier phases of use of the area. The bedrock slopes rather considerably from South to North and a clay floor was constructed in order to level the floor (Fig. 45). Stratum 3 is a rich early Hellenistic habitation level.

Zone III in front of AREA I and room II towards East, is defined by the light foundations AFN/*ADI* and the eastern prolongation of the walls *ADO* and *AEK*, creating an anteroom with antae projecting at least 0.80 m from the eastern wall of room II. A tile spill in the area indicates that the ante was covered by a tile roof.

Room IV is the narrow, irregular space defined by the terrace wall *ACZ* towards East and the walls *AEA* and *ADY* described above. To the North, the room measured only 0.80 m, in the northern part, 1, 80 m. The length of the room is 7.50 m. The back wall (= the terrace wall) is probably Archaic of the 6th century BC and is built into a natural depression in the bedrock (for description see above Chapter B.1) (for a reconstruction suggestion of the space see below Fig. 69). The room is not excavated to the North, so the extent of the room is not known.

Room V is a small, rectangular room measuring 3.4 × 2.3 metres or around 7.8 m^2. The wall/foundation is described above. Of the wall *to* the West, only one course is preserved, placed directly on bedrock, 30-40 cm above average floor level/bedrock in room V. The foundation is constructed by rather large, well-cut blocks measuring 30 to 50 cm in length and max. 30 cm in height. In addition, smaller, natural stones are used for fill. The wall is up to 50 cm wide. The fragmentary wall continues in the substantial stone wall *ADB*, the eastern limit of the narrow ring street around the Acropolis and the terrace wall which makes up the western limit of the narrow street.

At the western end of the wall *ATF* against the back wall, a rather substantial pillar consisting of three courses of sandstone slabs/ashlars probably makes up the one side of a doorway. The remaining construction of the wall *ATF* is much lighter with one course of natural slabs placed more or less in two parallel rows. The construction of the wall was described as "wattle and daub". Of the wall several pieces of wattles plastered with clay and mud were preserved. The wall facing room V was likewise covered with plaster.

Zone VI is the zone outside of room V on the eastside, limited by the prolongated wall, *AEK* and the eastern most corner of *ATF*. Large pieces of tile were found in the area and there seems no doubt that a shed roof covered the recess which was around 1.5 metres deep and thus deeper than the niche in front of room II.

(**Zone VII** is the ring street outside the terrace wall. See above p 88).

Room VIII is an almost totally square construction measuring 4.5 × 4.5 m or around 20.25 m^2. Of the back wall *ADB* (the stone wall against the ring street), a rather substantial part was preserved where the cross wall *ATD* joins *ADB*. More than ten courses are preserved to the height of around 1.75 m. Width between 0.50 and 0.60 m. The foundation of the wall consists of a line of large square/rectangular stone blocks, approximately 0.25 m high and resting on the bedrock. A line of flat slabs were placed on top of the foundation and on top of these, three courses of rather large, rectangular blocks were placed in an almost isodomic order. A further line of flat slabs separated this wall from the upper part of the preserved wall, consisting of five courses of rectangular blocks of smaller dimensions than the lower courses, but likewise laid out in horizontal bands. The foundation *ATD* joins *ADB* in a right angle. A maximum of 6 courses are preserved to a maximum height of 0.69 m, the width is around 0.40 m. It is constructed by rectangular medium sized stone blocks of H between 10 and 15 cm. The top of the foundation is flat and level consisting of two parallel lines of stones (Fig. 58). On top of the level surface a layer of broken tiles formed the bed for a mud brick construction. The foundation rests on bedrock. A 1,40 m wide section of larger stone blocks are placed on a soil packing approximately in the middle of the wall. This section seems to be a later filling of an originally broad doorway between room VIII and room X.

A large, flat stone plate, *ATY*, 0.70 × 0.80 m was situated in the SW corner of the room. In the northern part of the room, just 25 cm. from the wall *ATF*, a square stone construction *ATE* measuring approximately 0.90 × 1.00 m, was located (Figs. 58-60). The construction, which might be interpreted as an altar, is 0.62 m high and consists of rectangular, regular stones of various size. It rests on bedrock.

West of *ATE*, 23 flat stone slabs (*ATV*) cover an area of approximately 1.20 × 1.50 m and rest directly on bedrock. The construction might be a part of a larger pavement around the altar.

From the SW corner of *ATE* to the "door opening" in wall *ATD*, a groove was cut in the bedrock, 0.40 m broad and approximately 11.5 to 12.0 cm deep. The groove is probably connected with the groove/drain *ATM* running parallel and close to *ATD* in room X. A blocked door was found in wall *ATD* where the drain passes the wall.

ATC is a rather light stone construction which separates room VIII from the street. It consists of one row of medium sized stones resting on the bedrock. In a few instances smaller stones were situated on top of the basic row of stones. Like *ATF* in room V, pieces of wattle and daub were found in the surrounding area of *ATC* and it is likely, that the wall was a light construction. An almost square hole was cut into the bedrock along wall *ADB*.

Zone IX is the zone outside rooms VIII and X. In front of room X, a huge amount of tiles – of which one was totally preserved – was found, indicating the existence of a shed roof.

Room X measures 4.8 × 2.7 m or approximately 13.0 m^2. The foundation *ATH* (Fig. 61-62) is a rather low and less substantiated construction than *ATD*. It is built up to a maximum of 5 courses of irregular stones, it measures max. 0.41 m in height and rests on bedrock. The surface is level and broader than *ATD*, 0.50 m. Like *ATD* it must have been the foundation for a mudbrick wall. Towards the street the room is bordered by the construction *ATB* which consists of rather large square stone blocks, one is 0.40 × 0.22 m. The wall is preserved to a maximum height of 0.61 m in 3-4 courses resting on bedrock. Just outside the wall in AREA IX, a large square stone block was placed under the huge layer of tiles. In the northern end, the channels ATM drains out to the street.

The drain *ATM* is cut in the bedrock. Six terracotta slabs form the floor of the drain, while stones provide the southern wall. The drain was blocked by stones (when it went out of use). It was probably connected with the groove *ATX in room VIII.* Five holes were cut in the bedrock.

Room XI is a narrow room measuring 4.8 × 2.2 m or around 10.6 m^2. The back wall *ADB* is constructed as it is in room VIII with large rectangular blocks as foundation. In room XI this line is slightly protruding. On top of the base, more than ten courses of well-cut stone blocks, placed in an almost isodomic order were preserved, the wall measures up to approximately 2.5 m (Fig. 62).

The wall *AFO* is a substantial stone construction with nine courses preserved where the wall joins *ADB*. Two of the courses, however, consist of flat slabs. Towards the back wall *ADB*, the wall is preserved up to a height of 1.4 m. Towards the street, less of the wall is preserved. The width is 0.40 m and the stone wall rests on bedrock. *ATJ* is a circular structure in the corner between *AFO* and *ADB* – probably a silo for grain storage. The upper and lower part of a millstone was found on the floor in room XI (see Chapter E). No traces of separation between room XI and the street were found and we suggest that the front was open to the street.

Room XIV is a narrow storeroom for Laconian tiles connected with the somewhat broader, 2.3 metres wide

Room XV. The back wall *ADB/ACX* consists of 7-8 courses of stone slabs of very different size constructed in a more or less pseudo-isodomic order. The Southern end of the room is un-excavated.

RECONSTRUCTING THE ROOMS

As shown in the previous chapter the walls were built either entirely of stones or, as is the case of some of the inner constructions of mudbrick on stone foundations. In a few instances it seems possible, that wattle and daub were used in lighter constructions where walls had only one row of stones at the base. We have shown that the entire back wall (*AEA/ ADY/ADB/* ACX) of the rooms, was a stone wall, approximately 30 metres long, changing somewhat in construction technique (probably indicating different phases of construction). The same was probably the case, i.e. they were entirely stone built, with the end walls *ADO* and AFO and perhaps the cross-wall *AEK* and the wall *ADV* between rooms XIV and XV. Wattle and daub could have been used for walls *ATF* and *ATC*.

Doorways and passage ways

These are indicated on Fig. 44. As the wall constructions towards the street are less well preserved than the walls higher up the slope there are some uncertainties as to the placement of the openings in the walls. The courtyard (room I) might have had an opening of approximately 0.80 m onto the street. The wall was probably a very light and low construction. A doorway probably led from the street into room II, 0.80 m wide and the same for room V. Between room V and room VIII there was probably a passage close to the back wall *ADB* and a passage must have existed between room VIII and the street. Room X probably had only one entrance into room XI which could have had an open front onto the street. Finally the tiny room XIV had one passage opening onto the court AREA XIII and towards room XV – in both cases indicated by thresholds. A broad doorway led from room XV to the street. No fragments of the doors themselves were preserved.

Organization of the buildings

In AREA III we should thus reconstruct the general picture as follows: The fortification wall defines the border of the habitation around the Acropolis. A narrow street 1.0 to 1.4 m wide runs between the fortification wall and the back wall of the workshops. The houses are attached to the back wall on the east side and the shed roofs run from the back wall to the street. The iron nails found in the rooms are not abundant and were probably in use in wooden sub-constructions. The tiles lay on the wooden substructures: rafters, tie beams etc. – the pan tiles were placed on the rafters without nails and the slope was probably around 12 degrees.[99] There are traces which show that this general scheme was used for the habitation on a large area of the terrace on the northeast side of the Acropolis, and to the northwest probably at least until AREA I.

Behind the courtyard, room I and room II, a natural depression demanded another solution. The difference between the two walls *AEA* and *ADY* is of significance. The first is built of large square or rectangular blocks almost like the fortification wall and measures 0.50 m in width, while ADY is only 0.40 m wide and constructed with smaller stones placed in a more random manner, similar to the back wall further south. We consider the wide wall *AEA* was created to support an upper floor – and it might be older than *ADY*. In AREA IV the zone behind *AEA* was filled up with fragmentary tiles supposed to derive from a fallen roof. Fewer tiles were found behind room II indicating that the area was not roofed.

The above observations are shown on Fig. 66, a reconstructed section through the courtyard AREA I and the zone behind *AEA* to the terrace wall. We suggest that a wooden "bridge" had been constructed in order to allow the use of the ring street above the depression. The "bridge" was placed at a level of around 23 m.a.s. or slightly lower than the altitude of the ring street to the south, and the space below was around 1.5 m high. The water channel or drain *ADM* is evidence that water was coming from AREA IV, under the "bridge" into the drain. It probably came into AREA IV from the Acropolis, but the section

99 See *Kalydon* 2011, 583.

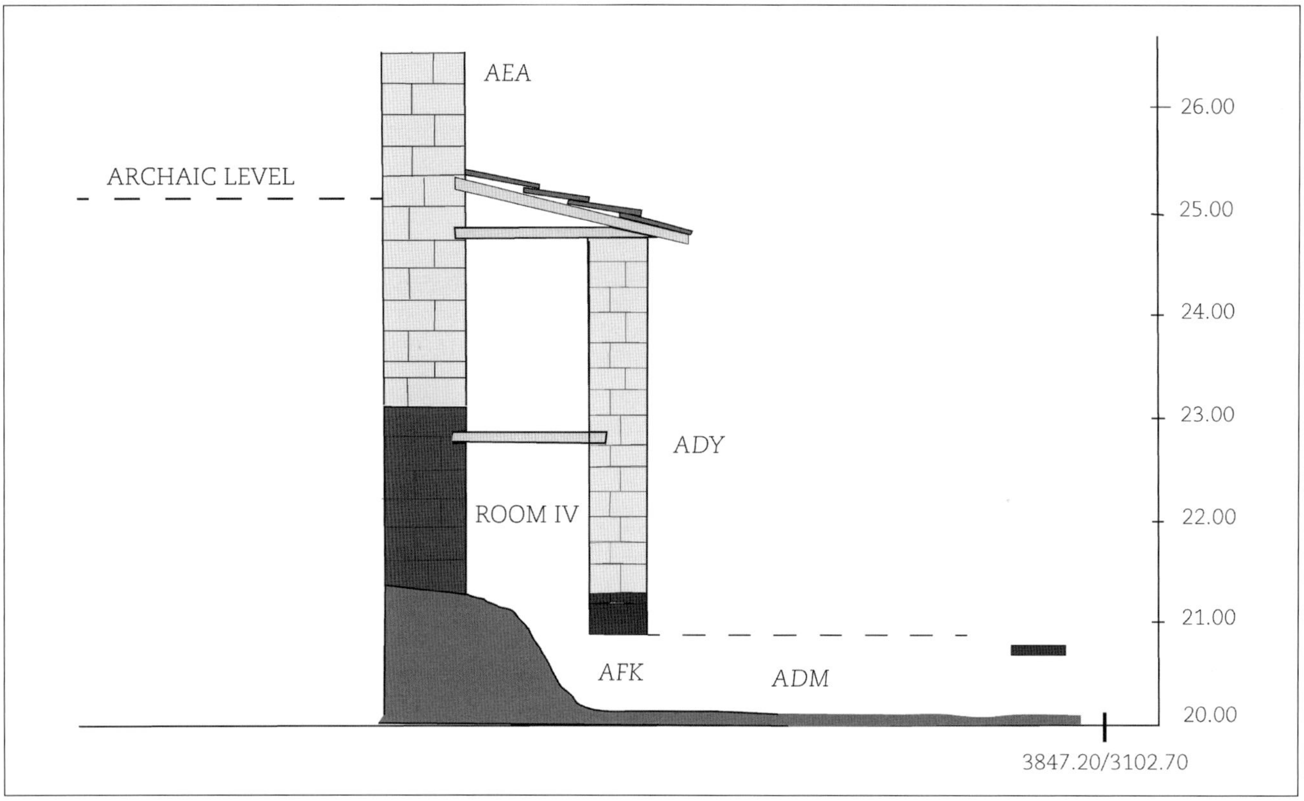

Fig. 66 *A reconstructed section through the courtyard room I and the zone behind the wall AEA. We suggest that a wooden "bridge" was constructed in order to facilitate the use of the ring street above the depression. Preserved wall structures are shown in black, reconstructions in grey.*

between the Acropolis and AREA IV to the North was unfortunately not excavated. As there is no natural spring on the sand stone mound of Aghia Triada we suggest that the water accumulated from rain fall especially during the winter season (the annual rain fall today in the Aitolian coastland is 750 mm or more than double the annual rain fall in Attica). If the water was collected in a cistern behind the rooms it could be used for longer periods of the winter. The upper, narrow passage was covered by a roof of Laconian pan tiles (as for the reconstruction of the fortification wall see below).

The two metre broad East-West trial trench, Tx1 was dug in the southern part of the Acropolis from the trench S9 to the Byzantine wall (Fig. 3). The trench is shown also on Fig. 43 where it is combined with the buildings in AREA III. The northern trench wall in Tx1 follows the east-west line 3830N which also crosses the southeastern corner of room X, and the wall *ATH* into room XI. On Fig. 67, the last approximately 3 metres of the section 3830N is depicted just before the trench was cut by the Byzantine fortification wall. The section goes down to almost 2 metres near the wall and four strata were recorded. The stratigraphy is approximately the same as in trench F15 on the northern end of the Acropolis. As for section 2990E in trench 15, the lower strata contain Archaic material as the most recent – in addition to a good quantity of Prehistoric material (Fig. 27). Fig. 68 shows a statistical representation of the sherds from trench Tx1. In the upper layer 1, there are almost the same number of Byzantine sherds as Archaic; Classical/Hellenistic are less represented. In stratum 2 the situation changes radically, the Classical/Hellenistic is well represented, there is less Archaic and no Byzantine. In the last two strata only Archaic was found (and less Prehistoric than in F15). The general picture is nearly the same as in F15 with a strong dominance of Archaic material,

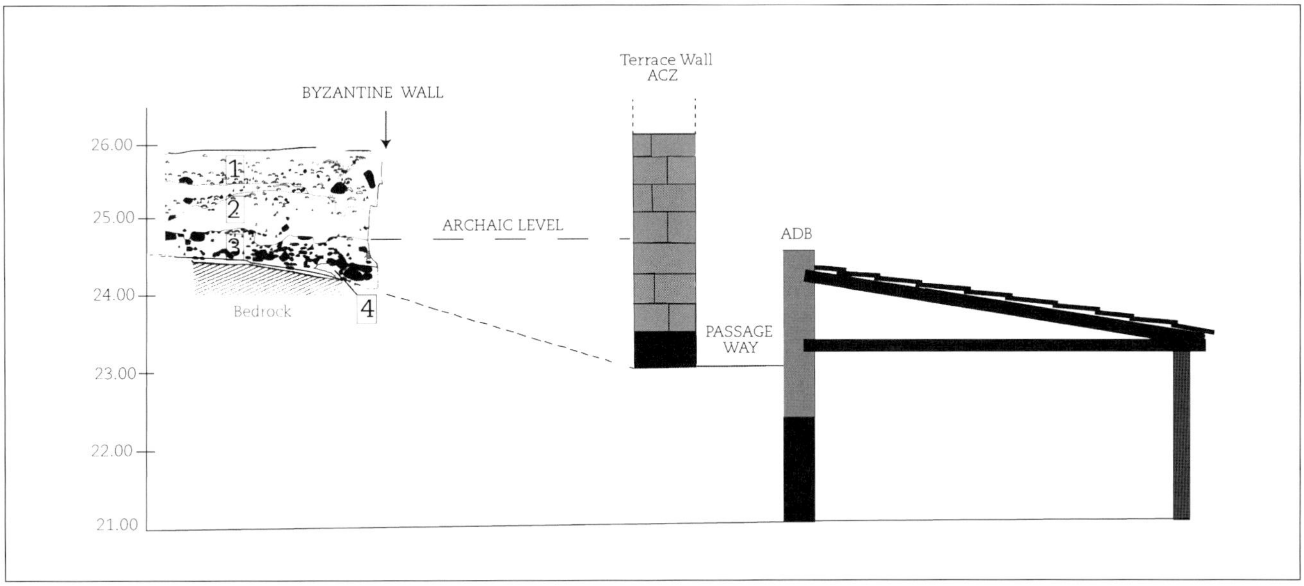

Fig. 67 *A reconstructed section following gridline 3830N. It runs along the north side of trench Tx1 and continues across the south-eastern corner of room X and wall ATH into room XI. The drawing shows c. 3 m of the section Tx1N to the west of the Byzantine fortification wall, where the section goes down almost 2 m next to the wall and four strata were registered. The late Classical/Hellenistic buildings are shown to the right with preserved structures in black and reconstructions in grey. Scale approximately 1:100.*

with Byzantine almost only in the upper stratum. It is, however, important that Classical/Hellenistic is found everywhere, if not abundantly. The building on the right side of Fig. 67 is a reconstruction of an "ideal" type house.

The upper level of stratum 3 is just below 25 m.a.s. – in F15 the same level was 27.38 m.a.s. reflecting that the bedrock in the northern part of the Acropolis is found at a considerable higher level that to the South. The conclusion is, that the fortification wall existed when the Archaic fill layer was deposited, and that the wall is thus older than the youngest Archaic sherds i.e. late 6th century BC. On Fig. 67 we have reconstructed the top of the wall to be approximately 1.4 m higher than the Archaic level. This is of course estimation and might reflect the situation of the wall at a later time – if, however, the wall functioned as fortification wall from the beginning, it is possible that it was already provided with a considerable parapet in late Archaic times. While only small sections of the Archaic wall is preserved, we believe the main part of the preserved wall and wall extensions were built in the first half of the 4th century BC when the defense system was fortified with the construction of the large walls in the Northeast corner of the mound. On the reconstruction Fig. 69 the wall is shown with merlons, as was usual in the early Late Classical period, even though we have no direct evidences for the existence of merlons (for a discussion of the fortification walls at Pangali see Chapter D).

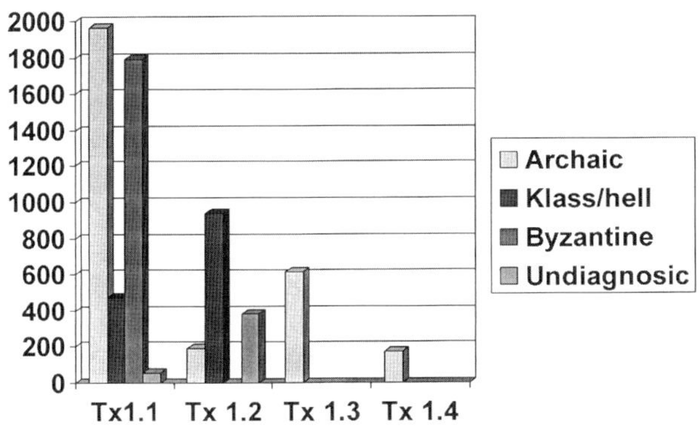

Fig. 68 *Statistical representation of sherd material from trench Tx1.*

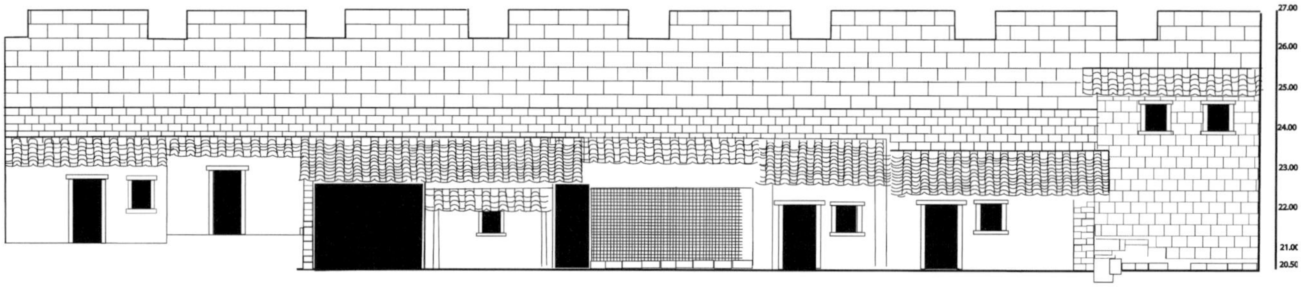

Fig. 69 *Schematic reconstruction of the workshops in AREA III as they could have looked in the Late Classical period and later. We suppose that the Archaic fortification/terrace wall was reinforced during the first half of the 4th century when the limestone walls in the North West corner was constructed. The wall, with the character of a fortification wall with a genuine parapet (here reconstructed to be around two meter above the level behind the wall (around 25 m.a.s.).*

On the elevation Fig. 69 we have tried to reconstruct the workshops and storerooms in AREA III according to the information and deliberations and conclusions above. The reconstruction reflects the area on the eastern terrace in the late 4th and 3rd century BC – but could partly reflect the situation in the Archaic and early Classical times – the buildings are "glued" to the wall limiting the passage way below the fortification (made somewhat higher than in Fig. 67).

C.3 Catalogue of selected roof-tiles from AREA III

Søren Dietz

Catalogue

1. Laconian tile (Figs. 70a-b)
Bag no. 1294/T6NA/ADZ-79/29.06.98
Biscuit: Light reddish brown (5YR 6/4). Coarse tempered with many white grits (less than 7 mm), grey grits and smaller black grits. *Surface*: Reddish yellow (5YR 7/6) smoothed (no colour). *Description*: Very curved, large Laconian tile. On the broad end there is a groove (2. 28 cm) on the convex side.

L: 103.50 cm. W (narrow end): 41.80 cm. W (broad end) (reconstructed – calculated): 50 cm. Th (in the middle): 2.45 cm. Th (at narrow end): 2.32 cm. Th (at broad end): 2.77 cm.

2. End piece of Laconian tile (Figs. 70a-b).
Bag no. 1314/T6NA/ADZ-86/29.06.98.
Biscuit: Light red (2.5YR 6/6). Medium coarse to coarse tempered with some voids, white stone inclusions (lime) (less than 10 mm) and a few black stone inclusions. *Surface*: Light red (10YR 7/6) with red (10R 5/6) paint on concave side and traces of the same paint on the convex side. *Description*: Flat, curved Laconian tile. Flat groove on the concave side: 2 cm broad.

L (preserved): 44.00 cm. W (end): 48.00 cm. W (in the broken end): 45.50 cm.

3. End fragment of Laconian tile (Figs. 70a-b).
Bag no. 7072/T6NA/ADZ/...-0052/...
Biscuit: Light red (2.5YR 7/6), medium tempered with brown/grey stones grits. *Surface*: Reddish yellow (5YR 7/8) surface with faint traces of dark red (2.5YR 4/6) paint on concave side. *Description*: Slightly curved Laconian tile.

L (preserved): 58.50 cm. W (end): 41.50 cm. W (at break): 46.50 cm. Th (middle): 2.19 cm. Th (end): 2.67 cm. Th (broken end): 2.34 cm.

Comments: On Laconian tiles the grooves, if found, are on the broad end.

4. End fragment of Laconian tile (Fig. 70a-b).
Bag no. 3071/T6NA/ADZ/....
Biscuit: Reddish yellow (5YR 7/6). Medium to coarse tempered fabric. White and black stone inclusions (less than 15.6 mm). *Surface:* Reddish yellow (5YR 7/6) perhaps covered with a thin white lime cover. *Description*: Slightly curved Laconian tile – no traces of groove.

L: (preserved max.): 64.50 cm. W (at preserved end): 47.50 cm. W (at broken end): 45.50 cm. Th (broken end): 2.00 cm. Th (at end): 2.60 cm.

5. End fragment of Laconian tile (Fig. 71a-b).
ADZ
Biscuit: Reddish yellow (5YR 7/6) medium tempered fabric. *Surface*: As fabric, soft surface (no traces of paint). *Description*: Curved, Laconian tile with curved groove (app. 1.2 cm broad) at the preserved end.

L (preserved max.): 66.60 cm. W (at preserved end): 49.50 cm. W (broken end – reconstructed): 43.50 cm. Th (preserved end): 3.44 cm. Th (mid): 1.39 cm.

6. End fragment of Laconian tile (Fig. 71a-b).
ADZ
Biscuit: Reddish yellow (5YR 7/6) medium tempered fabric, white and brown inclusions (less than 2.4 mm). *Surface*: *idem*. Red colour on concave side (2.5YR 5/6) (no traces of colour on convex side). *Description*: Curved Laconian tile with shallow groove (5.3 mm) – in the preserved end.

L (max.)(preserved): 54.00 cm. W (preserved end): 49.00 cm. W (broken end): 46.00 cm. Th (preserved end): 2.78 cm. Th (broken end): 1.55 cm.

7. End fragment of Laconian tile (Fig. 71a-b).
Bag no. 1083/T6NA7/ADZ/25.07.97.
Biscuit: Reddish yellow (7.5YR 7/6) medium tempered

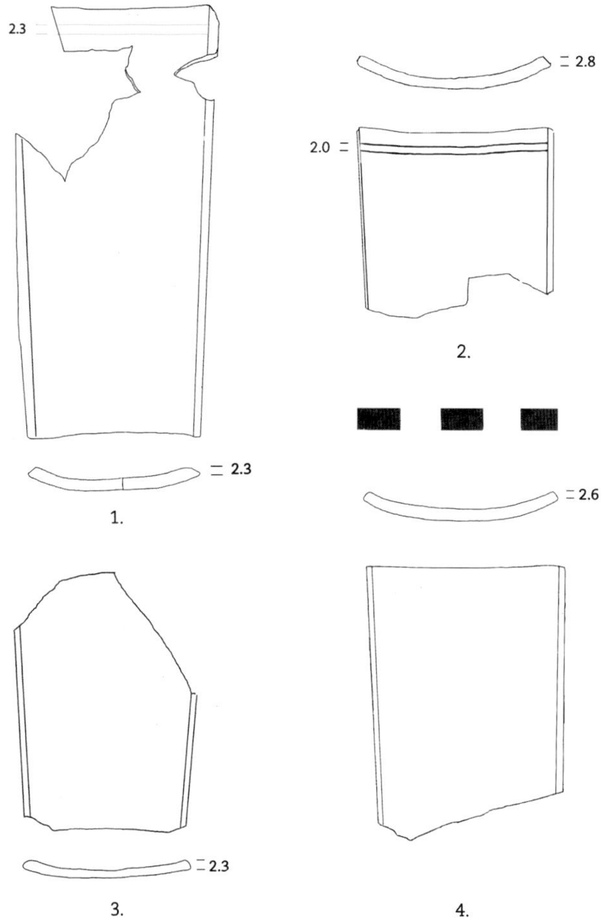

Fig. 70a *Selected Laconian pan tiles (catalogue nos. 1-4) from the workshops in AREA III. Drawing.*

Fig. 70b *Selected Laconian pan tiles (catalogue nos. 1-4) from the workshops in AREA III. Photos.*

fabric with black and a few white stone inclusions. *Surface*: *idem*. Traces of black paint on concave side. *Description*: Small curved Laconian tile. A thin groove along the preserved edge.

L (preserved): 39.50 cm. W (at preserved edge): 38.50 cm. W (at broken edge – reconstructed): 42 cm. Th (preserved edge): 2.32 cm. Th (middle): 1.90 cm.

8. End fragment of Laconian tile (Fig. 71a-b).
Bag no.: 1294
Biscuit: Reddish yellow (7.5YR 7/6) medium tempered with red and white stone inclusions. Surface: *idem* (no traces of paint). *Description*: Curved Laconian tile. No groove.

L: 60.00 cm. W (fragm. end – reconstructed): 45 cm. Th (preserved end): 2.36 cm. Th (middle): 1.99 cm.

Comments:

The catalogued tiles are mainly from the tile concentration *ADZ* in the southern end of AREA III. The concentration ATX in room XIV is supposed to be a tile storeroom. Only one of the tiles (catalogue no. 1) is preserved in its entire length, which was slightly more than 1 meter. The width in the broad (fragmented) end could be calculated as c. 50 cm while the narrow end measures slightly less than 42 cm. All catalogued tiles narrow from one end to the other, but it seems that the angle of taper differs; some tiles taper more

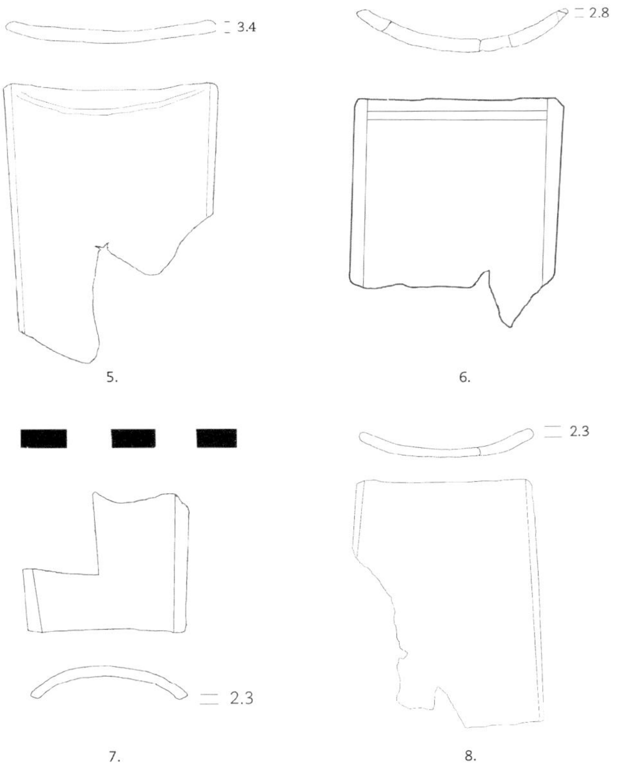

Fig. 71a *Selected Laconian pan tiles (catalogue nos. 5-8) from the workshops in AREA III. Drawing.*

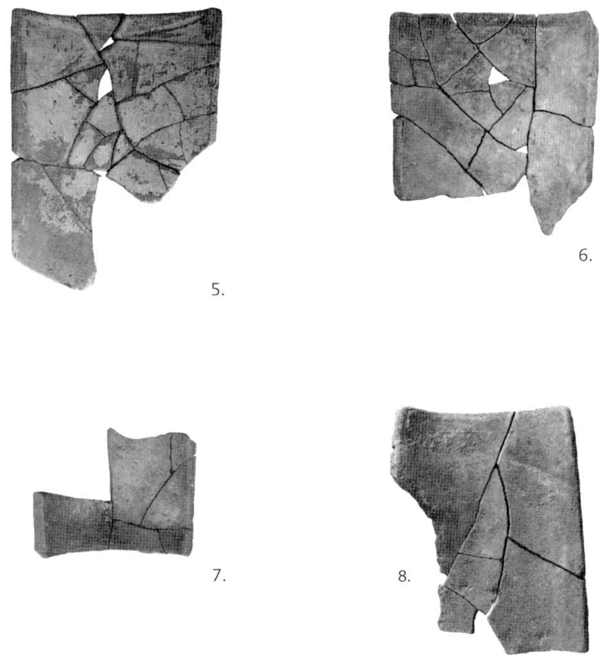

Fig. 71b *Selected Laconian pan tiles (catalogue nos. 5-8) from the workshops in AREA III. Photos.*

sharply than others. The widths of the (known) end vary, for the broad ends between 47.5 and 50 – and for the narrow ends between 38.5 and 41.8 cm. The broad ends are always thicker than the narrow ends and 2-5 cm broad grooves are usually found on the concave side on the broad end. The tiles are always curved, but the curve was more or less pronounced.

The tiles from AREA III were different in size, thickness and curving, indicating that several different moulds were used to produce them. At this time the tile production in the coastland was not standardized and no producers stamps were found as was the case in the peristyle building in Kalydon – some hundred years younger. As no cover-tiles were found, we presume that the tiles were placed alternately with the convex side and the concave side upwards with the black or red paint on the tiles creating a colourful impression of the roof.

C.4 The pottery in AREA III

Elizabeth Bollen

CLASSIFICATION OF POTTERY

Fabric

Given that there has been little to no evidence of installations or implements from local ceramic manufacture, beyond three kiln wedges (nos. 147, 148 and 189), the identification and discussion of a local fabric is based primarily on the frequency of certain fabric qualities across the assemblage. Fabric with comparable qualities in the different wares (fine, plain, cooking pot and coarse) helps support an identification of local production. Of course, given the geographical position of the settlement of Chalkis, and its likely economic reliance on the passing trade, a high number of imports can be expected and are, indeed, identified within the contexts on Agia Triada. With some of these 'imports' there would appear to be an established or regular trade, given that the same fabric type appears more than once, while others represent more sporadic or even eratic trade patterns. Others compare closely to material found at other sites in the area and suggest regional trade. No chemical analysis has been carried out on the material, so all observations are reliant on hand lens examination.[100]

The local ware is characterised first by its granular break, even in the fine ware the break is never more than 'fairly fine' and is, occasionally, hackly. The local production of fine wares does not achieve the smooth, clean profile of some productions and the category of vessel is defined more by function than fabric. The ware is commonly soft and has a rather powdery surface. This characteristic has contributed to the worn appearance of many of the local fragments and diminished the quality of the fragments. It also makes it a messy job to examine the pottery! Some examples have been produced with well-levigated clay and contain few inclusions, but voids often prevent a compact surface. Inclusions can be rare to common in the fine wares. White is the most common inclusion colour, grey, red and brown are also recorded. These inclusions are frequently angular/spherical but vary to sub-rounded and can be platy or tabular (often the fine size of the particles has prevented certain shape identification). There are some local fragments that carry light refracting particles. The colour of the fabric is a light-reddish pink, though the Munsell readings fluctuate somewhat due to the apparent irregularity of the firing process. There are also some fine ware examples that are a bright orange-pink or orange, similar to the fabric of the local cooking wares.

The plain ware fabric compares closely to that of the fine ware, though it is more often hard fired. The break is granular. Commonly the inclusions are few, around 3 %, and are most often white and angular/spherical, though grey and brown are also noted. These inclusions tend to be fine to small, though on no. 98 the size of the inclusions ranges to very large. There are occasional light-refracting particles in the local plain ware.

The typical cooking ware fabric at Chalkis is granular to hackly, with frequent white, brown and/or grey inclusions. The colour is a bright orange (5YR 5/6) or has a paler hue (5YR 4/4). Given the regularity of its appearance, this ware is likely to be produced near, if not at, the site. Other fragments add variety to the fabric types (as seen in the catalogue) indicating some importing of cooking pots to the site.

There are some 'imported' fabrics that would appear to be produced in the region of Aitolia and so are worth mentioning here. No. 291 does not differ much from the local fabric. It is thought to be regional due to the presence of a vessel from the same ware identified at Nafpaktos. It shares the granular fabric with some

100 Description of the fabric follows standards set out by Sanders, 1999, 477-480.

white inclusions, some mica and a Munsell reading of 5YR 6/6.[101]

FINE WARE

For the local ceramics at Chalkis, the term fine ware is comparative and does not necessarily indicate particularly fine clay or manufacture. Rather it is a term that is used to group vessels of a particular purpose or function, namely glazed table wares. Cups, plates, bowls, pouring vessels, toiletry vessels and miscellaneous vessels will be described.

The fine wares from the eight rooms on the eastern side of the mound of Agia Triada, ancient Chalkis, are produced in the Archaic, Classical and Hellenistic periods. The Archaic material is largely subsidiary and located in identifiable fills or post-use deposits, though in VIII the quantity and quality of the Archaic material indicates Archaic activity in the area.[102]

The Classical material is found throughout the houses, never in a particular concentration but rather distributed through the predominantly Hellenistic deposits. The Classical skyphos is common. Both Attic and Corinthian versions are found, the former identified by the torus foot, is more common. There is also one skyphos preserving the characteristic olive branches of an Attic owl skyphos, no. 288. The other red-figure fragments total only three and none are well preserved, nos. 106, 117 and 201. Classical kantharoi remain rare. Other Classical fine ware shapes include the Classical plate and the echinus, though the latter is more common in its Hellenistic form. The column krater, no. 200, is of this period.

Hellenistic fine wares date to the 3rd century and are all wheelmade products, the mouldmade vessels, popular throughout the Mediterranean in the late 3rd and 2nd century, have not been found at Chalkis. Hellenistic kantharoi are found, the one-piece kantharos being the more common on site, as it is in the rest of Aitolia and Central Greece. The pouring vessels are varied and infrequent and the occasional lekane rim provides the only possible krater-like wine-serving vessel. The plates are varied in their form, but are dominated by the plate with sharp inturned rim and the plate with rilled rim. Bowls are similarly varied, the echinus bowl (some now with quite straight walls) including the large version with grooved outer wall, and the bowl with folded rim are common in the deposits. Toiletry vessels are not numerous, but the major classes of Hellenistic toiletry vessels are identified, including the reversible lid, the pyxis, the unguentarium, the guttus and lekythos.

CUPS

Classical Kantharos or Cup Kantharos

The Classical kantharos, typically black glazed, is a familiar drinking cup of the Classical period. It has a high-stemmed foot, convex lower body with distinct junction to concave upper body and strap handles (the cup kantharos supporting, instead, high-swung handles).[103] The lower body can be ribbed and the interior floor is occasionally stamped. The shape continues to be produced in the first half of the 3rd century, as part of the black glaze assemblage, or adorned with West Slope garlands on the upper wall. In Athens a transition is noted in the first half of the 3rd century as the Classical kantharos is replaced by the sturdier Hellenistic versions.[104] In Aitolia, however, the Classical kantharos is never common, the locals preferring the skyphos in the 4th century and then the one-piece kantharos in the 3rd.[105]

The Classical and cup kantharos is an uncommon find in the rooms. Those that do appear are fragmentary. Still they can be compared to more complete versions and, in themselves, represent a range of date and type of kantharos present. The kantharos no. 301, from fill, issues from a vessel dating to the 4th century. The lower body is preserved and it carries incised regular teardrops that imitate the moulded ribbing found on some Attic kantharoi. The protruding node, if rightly

101 Nos. 217, 231, 291, 272. The stand no. 47, the reversible lid no. 83 share some of these characteristics, they have a paler colouring than the rest of the group though are quite similar to each other.

102 See S. Houby-Nielsen, report on T30 in *Chalkis Aitolias II.*

103 Rotroff 1997, p. 80-88; Sparkes and Talcott 1970, p. 117-124

104 Rotroff 1997, graphs 3 and 4.

105 *Kalydon* 2011.

identified as a handle, is circular in section, appropriate for the high-swung handle of a cup kantharos. The characteristics of fabric and glaze allow this piece to be made in the local region. With no. 209 we move into the Hellenistic period indicated both by the limited remains of West Slope decoration on the upper wall, and by the red-brown glaze. The glaze and fabric stand out from the majority of wares from the site, and the piece is identified as an import. No. 258 is a fragmentary example of novelty handle rests (this particular type called Herakles knot or double handle) that can be used to adorn the kantharos both in the Classical and early Hellenistic period.[106]

Classical Skyphos

The skyphos is common in all deposits of the rooms. The typical skyphos from Chalkis has the torus foot popular in Attic manufacture, differing from the ring or turned foot of the Corinthian version (or kotylai as the latter are also known).[107] The examples would seem to belong to the 4th century (and perhaps the 5th). In the 3rd century the one-piece kantharos appears to replace the Classical skyphos in the local assemblage.

No. 167 has a splaying foot that compares to some Corinthian versions and also carries a band of red paint above the black-brown glazed foot.[108] No. 154 carries a band of pale brown slip above its small foot and bands on the underside of the floor. The foot profile and the decoration owe something to Corinth, though the ring foot projects slightly indicative of the Attic torus. Nos. 154 and 167 both sport bands of glaze on the foot and floor. Nos. 1 and 314 carry a small but projecting foot profile that is further developed from that of no. 154. Nos.1 and 314 are too worn to allow certainty in the manner of their glazing on and under the foot. The base diameter of this first group of skyphoi falls within the range 4.4-6.6 cm.

The rest of the skyphoi bases have the broad torus foot of the Attic type. The selected examples, indeed, are mostly Attic imports. No. 274 is quite worn but retains the reserved area above the foot and is probably the earliest of this group. Nos. 41, 86 and 144 are all of Attic fabric and represent imports to the area. No. 41 is the largest of the group. These each have a torus foot with a glazed outer and inner face but a reserved resting surface. No. 86, a later version, has abandoned the torus foot profile and instead has a ring foot with a rather flat resting surface. The outer face of base no. 86 has a concave-convex profile. The skyphoi discussed in this paragraph are decidedly larger than those presented above, and have a base diameter range of 8.2-12 cm. These compare to 5th century versions published from the Agora.[109] Although the walls of the Chalkis examples are never preserved to a great height, none of these examples indicate the slight, or pronounced, concavity of the 4th century type A Attic cups, suggesting a 5th century date for most.[110]

The majority of rim fragments identified in the deposits are thin walled and have incurved to straight rims, classing them as the 5th century cups. Nos.70 and 84 display the range of features found. No. 70 preserves a rim with strong incurve and a bulbous body, while on no. 84 the curve of wall and rim is less pronounced. They both preserve the stem of a horizontal handle with circular cross section, that sits just below the handle. This contrasts to no. 199, a 4th century skyphos with flaring lip and a solid horizontal handle.[111]

No. 288 is the only skyphos to carry decoration.It is a rare example of red-figure from the site. No. 288 is an owl skyphos of Attic manufacture. It has a simple and in-turned rim with a rather thick wall, and unlike the other skyphos forms presented above, has a vertical strap handle. The decoration preserved consists of two olive leaves with a forked branch set between. This group of skyphoi date to the 5th century, with most

106 Chalkis: Eiring 2004, no. 36, pl. 150, fig. 74; Athens: Sparkes and Talcott 1970, nos. 715-718; Rotroff 1997, 94-100; On Hellenistic kantharoi: Rachi: Anderson-Stojanovic 1997, p. 15, pl. 5, no. IP 688; Corinth: Edwards 1975, nos. 380, 386-387, p. 74-76, pls. 15, 52, 82-3; nos. 451-57, pls. 15, 53.

107 Pemberton 1989, p. 25-28. Kotylai are a Corinthian form, distinguished from the skyphoi by their lighter foot. Skyphoi are an Attic form. Many of those at Chalkis are of composite forms, and thus it is deemed best to present the two simultaneously under the more common name.

108 Pemberton 1989, no. 395, p. 27, fig. 6, late 4th century.

109 Rotroff 1997, no. 342, fig. 4.

110 Compare with fourth century examples: Sparkes and Talcott 1970, nos. 349 and 352, fig. 4

111 This example compares with Rotroff 1997, no. 152.

produced in the middle years, though continuing to the last years, of that century.[112]

Cup Skyphos

The cup skyphos is by no means a common shape at Chalkis and does not appear as part of the local manufacturing assemblage, i.e. the examples are imported, no. 275 is certainly Attic. The two catalogued cup skyphoi share a concave lip and convex body and belong to the light-walled version of the shape, which, in Athens, is dated from the third quarter of the 5th century to the second quarter of the 4th.[113] On the smaller no. 275 the junction of lip and body is quite smooth, while on no. 109 the lip is set off from the body at a sharp angle. The handle stem preserved on no. 275 sits below the junction of rim and body, while that of no. 109 sits directly on the junction, which differentiates it from Attic examples. Both handle stems indicate that the handles were canted. The black slip covers the interior and exterior wall of both vessels with no variation to emphasize shape. There are no full profiles or identified lower body fragments to enable a complete understanding of this vessel form.

One-handler

Given the fragmentary nature of the material, determining whether a cup had two rather than one handle is difficult, so in some cases the identification, should be understood as tentative. A complete example of the one-handler was found in Grave 3.[114]

The most complete example of a one-handler from the rooms is no. 22 from a pit in Room I. It has a narrow ring foot, a smooth wall incurved to a simple lip and a horizontal strap handle that approaches a triangular form. The handle suggests a 4th century date, following Attic shape development.[115] A more extreme triangular and rising handle is found on no. 211 from Room X. The stems preserved on no. 142 allow a rising handle to be reconstructed. No. 142, found in VII, is a rather shallow bowl with a simple disc foot. While there is a possibility that this bowl had a second handle, the smooth curve of the wall is characteristic of the one-handler group.

Nos. 22 and 211 both carry black glaze, the former worn and mottled to grey, while no. 142 is coated in a thin brown slip.

Bolsal

In the lower levels of room XI a cup with a broad floor, rising vertical wall and horizontal handles was uncovered, no. 265. The shape of the body is characteristic of the bolsal.

The bolsal is produced from the late 5th century and through the fourth in Athens but does not continue in the 3rd century in that city.[116] This is not the case in Central Greece where examples of the bolsal with West Slope decoration demonstrate its continued production in the 3rd century.[117] No. 265 is a sturdy shape with a dull brown paint that preserves an occasional metallic sheen, making it a likely member of the Hellenistic assemblage.

No. 125 is a shallow cup with a rising horizontal handle. The handle stem is quite straight indicating a closer relationship with the bolsal rather than the one-handler for this fragment. It has a finer wall than no. 265 and a curved and shallow body. It shares this shallow and curved body with late 5th century Attic bolsals.[118]

112 Moore 1997, p. 64; nos. 1313-1322, pls. 122-123. For analysis of South Italian and Attic productions of vessels decorated with owls see Schaeunberg 1988.

113 Sparkes and Talcott 1970, p. 111; the same rim appears on the stemless cup "Class of Agora P 10359" which dates to 500-470 (Sparkes and Talcott 1970, nos. 454 and 456, p. 99, fig. 5) and the "large stemless cups with inset lip" which date 475-375 (Sparkes and Talcott 1970, nos. 494, 495, p. 101-102, fig. 5).

114 Eiring 2004, p. 114-117, figs. 32, 33. From the region: Thurreion: Zafeiropoulou 1979, pl. 366 e.f.; *Kalydon* (with out-turned rim) Papapostolou 1977, pl. 365 2nd row, 1st on left.

115 Rotroff 1997, p. 126.

116 Sparkes and Talcott 1970, p. 107.

117 Akraifias: Andreiomenou, A.K. 1994, pl. 94b; Demetrias: Furtwängler 1990, pl. 51-52, pl. 16a and 17d; Kabirion: Heimberg 1982, nos. 217-221, 226, 233, 234, p. 133-4, pls. 12, 50.3; Medeon: Bruneau 1976, no. 41.4, p. 38, figs. 35-36; no. 59B.2, pl. 46, figs 60-61; no. 60.4, p. 48, figs 68.69; no. 75.6, p. 62, figs, 109-110 (see figs. 157-163 for further examples of the form); no. 129B.2, pl. 72, figs 143-4; p. 83, fig. 156.

118 Sparkes and Talcott 1970, nos. 534, 538, fig. 6.

Hellenistic Kantharos, one piece

The one-piece kantharos is the most common Hellenistic kantharos type on the site, as it is in the rest of the region.[119] The cup has a wall that curves smoothly and somewhat tautly from foot to simple, inturned rim. There is a strong connection between the production of this shape and mid-4th century skyphoi, demonstrated at Corinth.[120] At Chalkis the one piece kantharos does replace the skyphos to become the common 3rd century drinking cup. The maximum diameter sits below mid-height and is not a pronounced feature of the shape. On no. 2 the maximum diameter is more pronounced than usual, allowing some comparison with the baggy kantharos of Attic manufacture. The wall can be articulated by light grooves, a feature that is particularly associated with those carrying West Slope decoration. One example from Chalkis, no. 210, carries horizontal ribbing on the lower wall. The vertical strap handles attach immediately below the rim and on the wall just above the maximum diameter. They can be unadorned strap handles (no. 43) or carry spurs (nos. 2, 210, 285 and 290) which tend to lie along the top of and follow the curve of the handle rather than projecting beyond or above the handle as they do in other productions. No. 39 has a higher ring foot and a slight stem, the two marked off from each other by a shallow groove. No. 210 preserves a moulded foot and narrow stem while no. 184 has a ring foot that kicks out to produce a more delicate profile. The majority of the kantharoi have a narrow and low ring foot with a very simple profile that along with the lower exterior wall, is often unglazed.

Many of the examples have similar form, fabric and slip qualities to suggest that they issue from the same production region, namely Western Greece (nos. 2, 42, 43, 44, 95, 192, 210, 247, 289 and 315). Also in this group are two fragments that carry incised garlands of West Slope ware, nos. 87 and 248. The other West Slope fragments, nos. 249 and 285, have glaze and fabric that stands out from the general assemblage and represent imports. Although red-glazed, the fabric of no. 289 is comparable to the local wares and the form and manner of the grooves is not unlike that of no. 315.

When comparing the local kantharoi to those four found in the Hellenistic burials on the other side of the hill, one is not immediately struck by similarities. All but the earliest of the grave kantharoi, which are dated through the 3rd century, have moulded feet while only one of our kantharoi does. The slight distinction between upper and lower wall of no. 43 is similar to grave kantharos no. 3, an emulation of the grave kantharos no. 2, which follows the Cyma kantharos wall articulation whilst maintaining the inturned rim.[121] The stylistic development suggested by the examples in the grave can not be easily implemented as a guide for the material from the rooms. The kantharoi from the rooms include the foot fragment no. 95, the lower wall is broad and the foot glazed, suggesting that it is the earliest version of the shape (date: 300-275). No. 42 is the broadest bodied cup with a low maximum diameter (date: 280 BC). Nos. 44, 210 and 247 have tauter bodies and therefore may date slightly later, given the tendency for attenuation in ceramic production (date: 250). If subtle influence from the Cyma kantharos can be argued for the one-piece kantharos, then the foot of no. 210 would fit with later 3rd century Corinthian products (250-225 BC).[122]

No. 235 stands out from the group and its identification as a one-piece kantharos is not certain. It does, however, have the slightly incurved rim characteristic of the shape. Two grooves define a decorative zone, the lower level of which is above the lower handle attachment. An incised line (not indicated on the drawing) could be the beginning of a West Slope garland. The handle itself is preserved, it has a spur that follows the line of the handle, the outer face of the handle carries two deep grooves. The glaze is a brownish red.

119 Chalkis: Eiring 2004, p. 100-105, fig. 11; *Kalydon*: Papapostolou 1977, pl. 365, 3rd row on right; Nafpaktos: Alexopoulou 1999, pl. 77d right. Further away, Medeon: Bruneau 1976, p. 38, no. 41.5, figs. 38, 39.

120 Edwards 1975, p. 75. The lack of the shape at Olynthos has been used to suggest that they developed toward the end of the fourth century, but the Hellenistic kantharos was never common in Northern Greece and so the lack of it at Olynthos is not definitive.

121 Eiring 2004, p. 100-105, fig. 11

122 Edwards 1975, no. 453, pl. 15.

Hellenistic Kantharos, straight walled

The straight-walled kantharos develops from the Kabeiric cup, a late 5th century Boeotian form.[123] This transition occurs in the Attic pottery industry and this is the first of the Hellenistic kantharoi forms in that production.[124] The Hellenistic version has a broad and low ring foot, a convex wall, often with grooves defining upper and lower zones and strap handles. Produced primarily in Boeotia and Athens, the straight walled kantharos is not a common form in the west.[125]

In T6NA/4d, in AREA XIII, three fragments of the lower wall of a cup, no. 267, prove the presence of the straight walled kantharos form on the site. From the same deposit the upper wall and handle fragment, perhaps of the same vessel, is also preserved, no. 268. The cup has a broad lower wall that has a sharp junction with a vertical upper wall. The junction is marked with a groove. The upper wall fragment preserves a rim to which the wall is slightly inclined but not curved. The handle is a simple strap. The fabric and glaze do not rule out the possibility that the shape is produced in the region, though the singularity of it is notable. A small pale body fragment, no. 88, preserves a small section of profile concurrent with this form. It carries incised scrolling ivy stems.

Two handle fragments, both of Attic fabric, attest to further examples of this form. No. 259 preserves a small section of rim and vertical upper wall and a handle with a very flat upper face that ends in a neat, pinched spur. Unlike the spur handles described above, this is not formed by an additional slab of clay laid on top of the handle proper, but rather the handle and spur are seamless. An ivy leaf handle attachment, no. 264, is of Attic fabric and would attach to the handle of either a straight walled or an angular kantharos.

Hellenistic Kantharos, angular

The angular kantharos developed from the straight walled version in the early 3rd century and continues in production until the last quarter of the 3rd century.[126] The angular kantharos has also been termed the articulated kantharos and the two terms can be used to identify two different versions of this form. The angular kantharos, as found in Athens, has a rounded lower body, while the articulated kantharos, as produced in Corinth, has a more conical lower wall.[127]

The angular kantharos is rare at Chalkis and here represented by one imported fragment of the concave upper body. No. 266 carries two grooves on the upper section of the fragment and one on the lower section. Between the grooves is a painted spearhead necklace. Though the decoration is fugitive, painted dots cling to the second upper incised band and pendants below. A second dot drips from the lower pendant. Despite our ignorance of the lower wall of this shape, the high concavity of the fragment suggests it follows the Attic form.

BOWLS

Conical bowl

The conical bowl is known from the second quarter of the 3rd century, but more common and more widely produced in the second half of that century.[128] The examples from Chalkis are of varied origin and indicate the trading position of the city on the Corinthian Gulf. Three out of the five inventoried examples carry distinct West Slope decoration and the other

123 For the development of the shape and progression of decoration see: Heimberg 1982, pp. 27-28; Braun & Haevernick 1981, pp. 1-74, pls. 1-18, 20-24; Wolters & Bruns 1940, pp. 95-128, pls. 17-19, 26, 44-59; for a discussion of the relationship to Attic production see: Rotroff 1997, pp. 97-98.

124 Rotroff 1997, p. 97-99;

125 Athens: Rotroff 1997, nos. 170-184, p. 97-100, figs. 13-14, pls. 16-17; Thompson 1934, B37, p. 342, fig. 22; Schöne 1991, p. 380, fig. 15; Knigge & Kovacsovics 1981, pl. 387, fig. 3, right; *Kerameikos XIV*, no. 122.6, p. 119, fig. 78.3; Townsend 1995, no. 219, p. 197, pl. 50; Braun 1970, nos. 9, 79, 80, 81, 101, 102, 114, pl. 79.2; Vierneisel 1964, col. 456, fig. 50 in col. 460. Boeotia: Heimberg 1982, no. 132, p. 131, pl. 8; no. 133, p. 131, pl. 8; no. 134, p. 131, pl. 8; Bruneau 1976, no. 219.2, p. 72, figs. 150, 151. Attic imports Rhodes: Patsiada 1989, p. 166-167; Kaninia 1998, p. 118-119, pl. 28b left; Aigina: *Walter, Felten & Smetana-Scherrer 1982*, no. 475, p. 69, pl. 37; no. 501, p. 71, pl. 39.

126 Rotroff 1997, p. 100-103, see footnote 81 for list of other examples of this shape. Edwards 1975, nos. 458-514, p. 83-86, pls. 16, 53.

127 For the distribution of this and other Hellenistic kantharoi see Bollen 2011.

128 For further discussion of this shape and decoration see, Bollen 2002, p. 95-108.

two show traces of fugitive paint, but the patterns are indiscernible.

No. 291 from Room XIV is the best preserved example and the one that is at least distance from its location of manufacture. This bowl finds a close parallel with an example from Nafpaktos.[129] It is of lower quality than the other fragments with a rather thick wall, dull glaze and thickly incised West Slope decoration. The bowl has a simple upright lip and smoothly curving shallow wall. Grooves on the interior wall divide the vessel into zones, but there are no corresponding grooves on the exterior.

Nos. 89 and 193 are both rim fragments. No. 89 has a sharp rim that runs smoothly into the straight wall, the transition marked artificially by a scraped groove. Two glazed grooves on the exterior similarly create a transition between upper and lower wall. No. 193 has a rounded lip and a wall that carries more of a curve than no. 89. A groove sits immediately below the rim on the interior and is followed by a second groove approximately one centimetre below. The zone between these grooves is likely to have held painted decoration. The fragment suggests a shallower form than no. 89.

No. 204 found in room X is from the same vessel as a fragment from room V, both are catalogued together. Although non-joining they are clearly from the same vessel. Both carry incised and painted wheat (or corn) ears on the mid-wall of the conical bowl. Grooves are used to define the zone both above and below the decoration. This decorative scheme is never common but is known on other conical bowls found in Athens, Corinth (and Rachi), Epiros and in Italy.[130] The Chalkis example bears closest resemblance to those from Corinth. The presence of the motif at Chalkis allows a line to be drawn from Corinth to Italy, via the Corinthian Gulf (and Epiros), along which this unusual motif traveled.

129 Alexopoulou 1999, p. 244, pl. 77a, right.

130 Athens: Metzger 1973, no. 83, p. 59, pl. 11; Attic import: Morel 1990, p. 22, pl. 1c; Corinth: Edwards 1975, no. 534, p. 92, pl. 55; Corinth Museum C-34-2498; Rachi: Anderson-Stojanović 2000, p. 383, pl. 204b; Anderson-Stojanović 1996, no. 21, p. 74, fig. 9; Kassope: Gravani 1986, p. 126, fig. 130.8 (left); Italy: Green 1979, p. 86, figs. 11, 12.

Hemispherical bowl

This shape is never common in Chalkis, and along with the absence of mouldmade (or Megarian) bowls, it points to the demise of the site in the late 3rd or early 2nd century. The one example no. 164 represents an early version of the shape, carrying as it does painted West Slope decoration on lustrous glaze. The rim is moulded and flares out slightly creating a concave-convex wall profile, a profile that troubles classification of this fragment to one of the canonical bowl types. Painted decoration is preserved in shadow on the exterior wall, consisting of a spearhead necklace and a bead and reel motif. Through comparison of the rim profile of the Chalkis piece, it would seem that this hemispherical bowl has more in common with late 4th early 3rd century bolster cups and cup with mould-made feet,[131] than with the late 3rd century mouldmade imitations.[132]

131 Cup with mouldmade feet: Aegina: *Walter, Felten & Smetana-Scherrer 1982,* no. 472, p. 69, pl. 36; no. 523, p. 72, pl. 40; no. 546, p. 74, pl. 41; Athens: Rotroff 1997, nos. 311-317, p. 275, fig. 20, ill. 1, pl. 32; no. 1659, p. 409, fig. 99, pl. 132; no. 1672, p. 411, fig. 100, pl. 133; Thompson & Scranton, p. 359, fig. 60a; Vogeikoff 1993, p. 44, A132-133, p. 79, B45; Eretria: Schmid 2000, no. 8, p. 364, pl. 181; Reber 1998, no. 252, p. 190, fig. 233; no. 461, p. 197, fig. 248; Metzger 1984, no. 31, p. 214; Thebes: Heimberg 1982, no. 171, p. 132, pl. 9; Medeon: Bruneau 1976, no. 42.3, p. 40, figs. 44, 45; Demetrias: Milojčić & Theocharis 1976, no. 136, p. 123, pls. 43.1; XIX.4; Mesopotamos: Ergon 1965, p. 55-56, fig. 60-61; Thessaloniki: Drougou 1991, nos. 5, 7, 8, p. 77-78, fig. 2a, c, d; Potidaea: Sismanides, K. 1990, p. 237, pl. 99b; Derveni: Themelis P.G. & I.P. Touratsoglou 1997, C3e, p. 96, pl. 107; Rachi: Anderson-Stojanovic 1993, nos. 89-90, p. 290, fig. 15, pl. 64; no. 116, p. 293, pl. 66; nos. 124-126, p. 294, pls. 66-67; Anderson-Stojanović 2000, p. 383, pl. 203e, g, h; Sparta: Karapanagiotou 2000, p. 137, pl. 59c,vii; Crete: Eiring 2001, p. 122, fig. 5e, pl. 1h,j; Watzinger 1901, no. 20, p. 75; Bolster cup: Samos: Isler & Kalpaxis 1978, no. 296, p. 118, fig. 9; Ephesos: Mitsopoulos-Leon 1991, B41-B51, p. 47, pl. 33-35; Gassner 1997, nos. 167, 168, 172, p. 63, pls. 10, 11; Athens: Rotroff 1997, no. 164-167, p. 259, fig. 13, pl. 15; no. 1365, p. 376, fig. 84, pl. 104; Schöne-Denkinger 1994, p. 36, pl. 11bi – bvi.

132 Corinth: Edwards 1975, nos. 527-529, p. 90, pl. 54; Isar Marvinci: Sokolovska 1986, p. 160, pls. 22.5, 9; 23.4, 5; 63.9; *Odigos tis Ekthesis Thessaloniki 1986*, p. 102.

PLATES

Classical Plate

Examples of Classical plates appear throughout the deposits under study, though they are not common. A small selection has been made for presentation that incorporates some interesting fragments whilst representing the typical forms. No. 287 from wall *ADF* gives a good indication of a typical Classical plate form. It appears to be of Attic production.[133] It has a broad ring foot with a curved outer profile. The floor is thick and fairly flat. Light glazed grooves run on the interior floor set just inside the foot diameter. The wall maintains the gradient of the floor, suggesting a broad and flat plate. On the underside of this piece an incised zigzag line forms part of a letter, perhaps a potter's mark, or a mark of ownership. The rim fragment of no. 3 preserves the upper zone of this plate type with thickened rim and a groove on the inner face. It corresponds to Athenian examples dated to the second half and last quarter of the 4th century.[134]

No. 91 comes from a similarly broad-floored plate, though of thinner wall than no. 287. No. 91 is a body fragment that is largely of interest given the band of rouletting that is preserved on the upper face of the wall. Rouletting is also preserved on no. 104. More elaborate decoration is found on no. 90, a plate that carries a series of glazed concentric circles set around the centre of the floor, encircled by linked arcs that are placed on the floor above the moulded, though only partially preserved, foot.

Plate, offset rim

The plate with offset rim is both imported and produced locally. There is some variation in the precision of the form, but all examples have a rim that is offset from the body of the plate by a groove and/or a ridge. The rim has a convex upper face so that it lifts up above the level of the wall of the plate before curving over and down. A ridge and/or a groove mark the other zone of the upper face of the rim. This plate is found in Athens, though here the rim regularly has a concave profile, something not found in Chalkis.[135] Rather our examples find closer correlation with those from Corinth with whom they share the concave upper profile.[136] The Chalkis examples do, though, have a wall that slopes gently from the rim, unlike the Corinthian examples. None of the fragments from Chalkis preserve the form beyond the mid-wall. For this reason the characteristics of the whole shape cannot be discussed.[137]

No. 110 is an imported version of the plate with lustrous black glaze on all preserved surfaces. It is thin walled. The rim is strongly concave with a ridge that divides it from the wall and a groove on the outer, overhanging edge. Also imported is no. 183. In this case the rim is less convex and the outer rim is horizontal rather than overhung. A ridge divides the rim from the wall and a second groove marks the outer rim. Between these two ridges lies an ivy wreath executed in neat West Slope technique with incised intersecting tendrils and painted heart-shaped leaves (now fugitive).

133 For comparable examples from the Agora see, Sparkes and Talcott 1970, nos. 1057-1060, fig. 10; and for Hellenistic versions, Rotroff 1997, fig. 46.

134 Sparkes and Talcott 1970, nos. 1058, 1059 and 1060, fig. 10.

135 Athens: Rotroff 1997, nos. 830-831, p. 326, fig. 56, pls. 69-70; Charitonides 1981, p. 173, pl. 41f1.

136 Edwards 1975, nos. 127-130, p. 39-40, pls. 4, 45; Pemberton 1989, no. 177, p. 104, pl. 19; no. 472, p. 164, pl. 48; Unpublished: C-38-717; C-39-390; C-63-86.

137 For further examples of this shape see: Aegina: *Walter, Felten & Smetana-Scherrer 1982*, no. 549, p. 74, pl. 41; no. 568, p. 75, pl. 43; Demetrias: Milojčić & Theocharis 1976, no. 50, p. 99, pls. 35.3; XVIII.5; Rachi: Anderson-Stojanović 1996, no. 50, p. 86, pl. 30; Anderson-Stojanović 2000, p. 384, pl. 204 e, f; Anderson-Stojanovic 1997, p. 16, pl. 8b; Perachora: Dunbabin 1962, nos. 3915-3917, p. 365, pl. 151; Eretria: S. Schmid 2000, no. 5, p. 364, pl. 181; Ducrey, Metzger & Reber 1993, no. 58, p. 109, fig. 156; no. 59, p. 110, fig. 157; Metzger 1969, nos. 9-11, 14, p. 57, pls. 16, 36, 37; nos. 44-46, p. 60, pls. 16, 40, a.b; no. 64, p. 61, pls. 16, 40 a, b; Reber 1998, no. 192, p. 189; no. 258, p. 191; no. 462, p. 197, fig. 247; Metzger 1984, nos. 2-4, p. 212, fig. 4; Themelis 1982, pp. 78-102, p. 99, pl. 84b; id., 1978, p. 77, pl. 39ci; Kabirion: Heimberg 1982, nos. 328-338, p. 137, pl. 15; Ithaca: Benton 1938, nos. 18-20, p. 33, fig. 17, pl. 15; Lissos: Eggebeht, Prendi, Korkuti, Ceka & Kohl *et. al.* 1988, no. 186, p. 307 (Alexandropoulou 2002), Ep 6, p. 209, pl. 6); Pella: Ancient Macedonia 1988, no. 287, p. 327; Aigeira: Mitsopoulos-Leon 1971-72, no. 17, p. 19, fig. 16:21; Ephesos: Mitsopoulos-Leon 1991, B96-B97, p. 50, pl. 46.

The local examples are larger and have thicker walls than the delicate imports. No. 316 is offset from the wall only by a ridge on the interior, the wall on the exterior runs smoothly to the rim. This rim form allows an alternative name, "Plate with flaring rim", to be applied. No. 316 carries a groove on the outer upper rim which corresponds to the imported examples with its strongly convex upper face and shiny black glaze. It shares with the other local examples the squared face of the outer rim face. Nos. 136 and 283 have worn glaze and are thick walled. They carry grooves on either side of the convex rim. The wall of no. 136 drops well below the level of the rim on the interior profile, and so is offset, a transition not reflected in the smooth outer wall.

There are two related plate rims preserved at Chalkis. No. 4 is a fine walled plate with groove on the outer, upper face and a very slight convexity. No. 159 has a convex upper face and a groove before the rim but, as would appear to be the case for no. 4, the wall runs smoothly into the rim.

Plate, grooved rim

The plate with grooved rim is a common serving vessel of Chalkis Aitolias. They compare to a plate with the moniker "rilled rim plate" in the Athenian Agora publications. In Athens, the shape is small and poorly made and predominantly found amongst the remains of sacrificial pyres, though a few do issue from domestic contexts.[138] Those of similar rim form manufactured at other sites tend to be larger, deeper and glazed.[139] It is worth noting that at Chalkis the grooved rim plate is one of the few examples of Hellenistic shapes found (and found repeatedly) amongst the largely Archaic ritual deposits of room VIII, highlighting a potential ritual link with the Attic versions.

The examples from Chalkis undergo a development of form. The earliest examples have a solid and upright rim that is offset from the wall on the exterior with a groove, no. 165, or a broad concave moulding, no. 111. Both early rims are decorated with two narrow grooves and the preserved surfaces are coated in glaze. On no. 165 the glaze between the two grooves is a reddish-brown, contrasting nicely to the black of the rest of the vessel. A date in the 4th century sits comfortably with these plates.

Later, the grooved rim becomes broader and projects beyond the wall of the plate. This develops from no. 317 that shares the strong curve of the interior wall of the earlier plates (as no. 111) and carries a groove to mark the exterior rim to wall profile (as on no. 165). No. 149 is a thick walled shape with a broad rim that carries the groove to mark the exterior wall junction. The interior junction to the wall is more angular than the concave section of the Classical version. A drilled and glazed hole pierces the wall right at its junction with the rim. An 'X' is incised on the exterior wall of this plate.

On no. 168, the rim now appears quite separate from the wall as though attached to it, rather than potted with it. The rim is thin in height, though the width is substantially greater. It has a pointed outer profile while the inner junction of the rim and wall has lost the concavity that characterized the earlier versions. The rim is still offset from the upper wall by a groove but the groove has risen to sit directly below the broad rim and is, therefore, virtually invisible. The broad upper face still carries two grooves. This profile is repeated by no. 45, though here glaze is used effectively to produce an appealing plate. The majority of the plate is glazed red, while brown glaze lies in the rim grooves and on the inner rim and upper wall. This contrast of colour highlights the form of the plate.

The last in the series, no. 169, has lost much of the original form. Here the thin rim projects well beyond the wall of the plate. There is no junction marked between the wall and rim either on the exterior or interior. The interior wall curves smoothly; a deep, bowl shape can be reconstructed.

No. 165 is an Attic import. The potter of no. 111 has taken some care to emulate the quality of Attic manufacture. No. 149 has similar fabric to no. 111, though here the form differs more markedly from the Attic type. No. 169 is likely to be of local production. No. 45 has similar fabric and glaze to the conical bowl no. 291 so is produced nearby. This may also be the case for nos. 168 and 317.

138 Rotroff 1997, p. 151

139 Rotroff 1997, p. 151, note 26.

A related plate, no. 276, is a cross between the Classical plate with rolled rim (see above) and the plate with grooved rim. The rim is set upright, following the curvature of the wall and only articulated by light grooves. A single groove is placed on the upper face of the rim. It dates to the 4th century. The fabric is similar to that of nos. 168 and 317.

Plate, fish plate

For a shape that begins as a black glaze shape around 400 BC and continues well into the Hellenistic period, it is remarkable that there is only one example of the fish plate identified from the rooms on the south east of Agia Triada.[140] No. 231 preserves the characteristic depression at the centre of the fish plate, thought to have drained the juices and dressings of fish and other foods into the centre of the plate, a feature to collect the liquid and to allow measured consumption. The lower wall rises above the depression to create a shallow, but broad saucer, a feature of the Hellenistic version of the plate. The profile is similar to one from nearby Kalydon.[141] The fabric of no. 231 suggests that the piece is imported, possibly from a nearby production in Western Greece.

Plate, rolled rim

The plate with rolled rim is a shallow plate that is the common dining vessel in the Chalkis deposits. The plate has a simple ring foot, and a shallow wall that is unarticulated. The rim is folded sharply at the top of the wall, a very different curve to that of the echinus bowl described above.[142] The rim diameter varies between 11 and 18 cm., most diameters sit within the range of 14.5-16.5 cm. The bowls that preserve the whole profile nos. 269 and 46 both share a height of 3.8 cm.[143]

No. 155 preserves a possible Classical or early Hellenistic forerunner to the shape with thick wall and rim rolled to an incurved point, a likely import. On the majority of examples the walls are thin and the curve is tight so that a thin groove sits between inner wall and rim. This groove would catch liquid if the vessel tipped to the side. This suggests that the consumption of food from the plate was carried out not through tipping and pouring but rather by using fingers or utensils. The plates are typically dip-glazed leaving the lower exterior wall and foot clay-ground. The glaze is invariably mottled and brown.

No. 23, an imported version, shows slightly more elaboration of form with a neater rim that is more clearly defined from the upper wall by light grooves on the interior and exterior.

BOWLS[144]

Echinus bowl

The echinus bowl is produced in the 4th century and continues into the third and is a common shape throughout the Greco-Roman world.[145] Rim fragments of bowls with inturned rim are collected here under the name of echinus bowl. The typical characteristics of this bowl include a simple ring foot and a wall that curves smoothly before reaching the maximum diameter just prior to the incurved rim. The Classical version with shallow form and decorated floor is not identified in the rooms complex at Chalkis, though an example, that compared to the long-lived Campanian version of the shape, was located in Grave 3.[146] On the first group of the bowls from Chalkis, the

140 For the development of the shape in Attica see Sparkes and Talcott 1970, 147-148 and Rotroff 1997, 146-149. Note, however, S. Rotroff, Rotroff 1997, p. 146, notes the difference of the profiles of these vessels in other regions and provides a list of references for comparison in footnote 13.

141 Dyggve, Poulsen & Rhomaios 1934, no. 16, p. 419, fig. 144.

142 Rotroff 1997, nos. 631-700, figs. 46-50, p. 142-145. The Attic Plate with rolled rim, however, develops to a form that corresponds with the Chalkis examples, only in the second century BC (see figs. 48-50). The Chalkis examples, however, must date earlier, see C1 General Stratigraphy. This form is also reported in Italy, it corresponds to Morel 1981, no. 2233a.1.

143 The forms are closely comparable to a *Kalydon* example, Dyggve, Poulsen & Rhomaios 1934, no. 13, fig. 144.

144 There is considerable variation in the serving vessels of the Hellenistic period site to site and region to region, making parallels difficult to unearth. When the parallels are found, their relevance is not always apparent.

145 Rotroff 1997, p. 161-164; see note 53 for further references to the shape.

146 The shallow version of this shape, although found in Grave 3, Eiring 2004, no. 10, is not identified amongst the rooms.

rim to wall junction is smooth and the bowl is deep. The second two groups date into the 3rd century: a deep bowl with a squared rim,[147] and a large bowl with a groove on the outer rim.[148]

The standard echinus bowl at Chalkis has a rim diameter range of 9.4-14 cm.[149] No. 126 has lustrous glaze and fabric suggest Attic production. The bowl is shallow and the wall thick, the Classical version of the shape. The local versions of the bowl are produced in the Hellenistic period and show a deep and broad bowl, no. 320. An example that shares this profile, no. 319, is made of a pale fabric that is clearly imported, allowing for an external source for this version of the shape.

No. 322 has a smaller diameter than the others. At 7 cm. this vessel belongs to the 'saltcellar' group.[150] The vessel has a very narrow foot and strongly incurved rim. It preserves a brown glaze on all surfaces.

No. 5 is much larger than the other examples with a diameter of 19.5 cm. It is coated in a good quality slip. On the exterior of the curving wall and outer rim are a series of light beveled facets, rather than the smooth curve found on no. 320 and the other examples mentioned above. This slight decoration on the exterior rim of larger bowls is a step toward the "large bowl with groove on exterior rim" variation of the shape.

The large echinus bowl with groove on exterior rim is common in the Chalkis deposits. These bowls have a diameter range of 17-34 cm. They are broad bodied, with smooth curving walls. Again the maximum diameter occurs just before the incurved rim. Grooves mark the position of the widest diameter, highlighting the division between rim and wall. On some (early?) examples this groove occurs on the smooth curve of the wall changing little of the profile of the canonical form (nos. 194, 260 and 277). On nos. 31, 38 and 304 the rim is thickened slightly above the groove. This helps to emphasize the incurve of the rim, which in profile is no longer so pronounced. No. 304 is a roughly made piece. The walls have an uneven surface and there is also attached extraneous patches of clay. On no. 156, the groove, combined with the thinning of the rim, creates a much more angular or sharp profile, a pleasing but different effect. The bowl no. 270 has a very tightly curved rim and the groove is moved from the maximum diameter to the upper face of the rim.

A variation of the echinus bowl with square rim develops in the 3rd century and its presence is apparent at Chalkis. This bowl, which probably dates to the second half of the 3rd century, shares the diameter range of the canonical echinus bowl (9.2-14 cm). Much of the shape is the same, with the simple ring foot and smooth curving wall. No. 212 still maintains a high maximum diameter, but the wall above this achieves a more vertical effect, particularly enhanced by the squared rim. This squared rim is also found on no. 150, a vessel that shares the slip characteristic of no. 212. On no. 150 the maximum diameter is positioned lower down the wall producing a deep bowl with a fairly upright rim. The upper body curves in slightly, but this is masked by the squared rim. Nos. 6 and 170 are rim fragments of the same version. No. 116 is a simple and somewhat rough, related version of this form. The link of this variation with the echinus bowl is strengthened by no. 157 a salt-cellar version of the shape with rim diameter of 5.8 cm., a disc foot, and walls that curve in slightly before a square rim.

Bowl, folded rim

The bowl with folded rim has a deep body that turns smoothly to a high maximum diameter before curv-

147 This shape conforms to that of Drougou &Touratsoglou 1991, p. 17, 22, fig. II, bowl A1; they place the introduction of the shape at the end of the third century. The appearance of this version at Chalkis argues for an introduction for this shape in Aitolia by the last quarter of the third century. Other comparisons include: Veroia: Drougou & Touratsoglou 1980, p. 129-131, fig. 21; Thessaloniki: Adam Veleni, Georgaki and Zografou 2004, pl. 61c; Panticapeum: Tolstikov & Zhuravlev 2004, pl. 93:20; Zaytsev 2004, p. 754, pl. 349.10.

148 Rotroff 1997, nos. 1034-1036, p. 164. The Athenian Agora examples are dated to the first quarter of the 2nd century. The Chalkis examples must date before this, given the evidence of abandonment of the site around the end of the third century see chapter C1 General Stratigraphy. Few parallels have been found for this shape, unusual, considering the frequency it appears at Chalkis.

149 Note the smaller versions of this shape from Grave 3, Eiring 2004, nos. 11, 12.

150 Rotroff 1997, p. 167.

ing to the rim. This is similar to the Hellenistic echinus bowls from the site. However, rather than having an incurved rim with simple lip, these bowls have a folded rim, that is beveled on the upper face and projects slightly beyond the exterior wall. The extremity of this projection varies with no. 261 being the most pronounced. These bowls are large with a range of rim diameters from 17-31 cm. There are no examples preserving the full profile from Chalkis so the discussion of the form is limited.[151]

Bowl, moulded rim

Nos. 92 and 113 both have upright upper walls with squared rims and two grooves on the exterior wall below the rim: a bowl with moulded rim.[152] No. 92 is a bigger and thicker walled version than the more delicate no. 113.

Bowl, projecting rim

Nos. 93 and 114 both carry lustrous glaze on their curving, shallow bodies. No. 93 ends with a narrow, beveled rim which projects slightly beyond the exterior wall, the junction to which is marked by grooves. No. 114 has, in contrast, a broad rim that continues to rise above the level of the wall. These two imported plates are made of a very similar fabric.

Saucer

No. 303 is a well-preserved, shallow bowl with a rim diameter of 11.2 cm. It has an open and flat body that sits on a simple ring foot. The upper wall rises from these and joins, without articulation, a squared lip. No. 271 preserves the rim and wall of a larger but comparable plate: the rim diameter is 29 cm. The junction of wall and floor is marked with a slight ridge. As the rim maintains the shallow curvature of the body, a saucer, rather than a plate or bowl form, results.

Bowl, outturned rim

The bowl with outturned rim is not common at Chalkis, as it is at other Hellenistic sites and both the fragments discussed below deviate from the standard version of that shape, as characterized by publications of Athenian examples.[153]

No. 115 has an outturned rim and slightly concave upper wall characteristic of the Attic form. The lower wall of this fragment, however, is not set at an angle from the upper wall, but rather the small section that is preserved has a convex bowl-like outer profile.[154]

Another fragment with an outturned rim, no. 32, carries incised and painted West Slope decoration. The rim has a rounded surface and projects beyond the wall. While the wall carries the horizontal convexity of a bowl, the vertical rise of the wall is quite straight. The rim diameter of 20 cm. indicates a broad form. The fabric indicates the piece is imported.

Base of bowl/plate

The bases of plates and bowls are found throughout the deposits and while clues to their original form are harder to discern than for the rim fragments, the vessels are nonetheless informative. The ring feet assembled represent a small selection of those preserved. Both nos. 306 and 213 have broad floors and rising walls of a Hellenistic plate. Both have simple, un-profiled ring feet.The more finely worked foot of no. 195 along with its darker glaze and thicker wall, places it earlier than the other examples. It has a drilled hole in the centre of the floor suggesting the re-use of this bowl/plate in the Hellenistic period.

151 Parallels include: Lemnos: Poggesi, Savona, Monaco & Monaco 1997, pl. 85 3.4; Asia Minor: Künzl 2004, pl. 339 S1-S6 (though these bowls carry mouldmade decoration)

152 The profile of the rim finds comparison with some Attic situla, such as Rotroff 1997 nos. 570-574, p. 134-135, fig. 40; a closer parallel issues from Panticapeum: Tolstikov & Zhuravlev 2004, pl. 93.21.

153 Sparkes and Talcott 1970, p. 128; Rotroff 1997, p. 156-160.

154 When comparing to the examples from the Athenian Agora the black and semi-glazed versions provide the best comparisons, particularly Rotroff 1997, nos. 948 and 959, fig. 61. It also finds some comparison to a piece from Kerkintida, Vdovichenko 2004, pl. 359.

LARGE BOWLS AND KRATERS

Krater, classical

There are two Classical kraters. One fragment is from a column krater, the other two fragments from the same bell krater. As on other sites, the Hellenistic assemblage at Chalkis does not include many kraters.[155]

The column krater was produced from the late 7th century and is a recipient first of black figure and then of red figured decoration in Attic production.[156] The context in which the Chalkis column krater, no. 200, is found sits above the tile smash of the rooms, and so is likely to have been originally located on the upper area of the Acropolis and displaced during the phases of collapse in the area. For that reason the krater cannot be said to be associated with the use phases of the rooms under study. No. 200 has a broad and horizontal rim that carries a dark brown to black slip which also coats the upper, interior wall. The upper wall has a concave outer profile that joins the convex and horizontal shoulder. The shoulder curves into a spherical bodied bowl. Two vertical handles sit between rim and shoulder, of the characteristic column form that gives the shape its name. The upper wall, shoulder and handles are unglazed apart from a dripping mark on one of the handles. The body of the vessels retains bands of a thin brown slip.The interior body shows no signs of glaze.

The rim of the bell krater no. 106 is preserved. The development of the bell krater coincides with the development of red figure.[157] It continues to be produced in the 4th century where it can be decorated or simply glazed.[158] On the interior of no. 106 the wall runs smoothly to the upper face of the rim, which it meets at an angular junction. The rim is rounded on its upper and outer face. It is divided from the exterior wall by a deep groove. Below this groove the very edge of a rough subsidiary pattern is preserved. A second fragment, no. 117, carries the same motif.[159]

Lekane

Glazed basins are not frequent in the assemblage at Chalkis, but they are present and perhaps provide a substitute for the krater, though the function of the lekane is not limited to the service of wine.[160] These large bowls, which also appear in plain wares, have wide disc feet supporting broad bodies and tall walls and are topped by projecting rims.

No. 96 is thin-walled. The outer profile of the outer wall is concave. The rim projects but is narrow and flat and set at a sharp angle from the interior wall. The upper face of the rim is marked with a broad groove at its outer limit.

POURING/SERVING VESSELS

Jug

Fine ware pouring vessels are neither common nor standardized shapes at Chalkis. Each example represents a new type.

No. 143 is a jug with a broad shoulder, a cylindrical neck, a flaring rim beveled to the interior and a strap handle attaching somewhat roughly to the rim. The handle rises above the level of the rim before curving to the outer shoulder. The glaze is uneven around the handle but is more uniform on other fragments of the jug. A pitcher is an apt name to describe this rather hearty-looking vessel.

Two other jugs share features with non-fine ware vessels. No. 138 has a broad-bodied form. The wall is constricted at a short neck before flaring to a rounded rim. The profile compares to the cooking ware chytra (see below p 128). The strap handle and projecting rim of no. 24, indicates a sturdy vessel that may be reconstructed with a short neck and ovoid body. It compares

155 Rotroff & Oakley 1992; Rotroff 1996; Edwards 1975, p. 45.

156 Moore 1997, p. 21.

157 Moore 1997, p. 31.

158 Sparkes and Talcott 1970, p. 55, note 12. McPhee 1997, pp. 99-145.

159 Comparisons of the shape and motif: Moore 1997, nos. 175-178 and 180-182, p. 161-162, pls. 26-27. These date the fragments to the first half of the fifth century 480-450. See p 133 for further discussion of the motif.

160 Rotroff 1997, nos. 1090-1105, p. 167-168, figs. 66-68 (here called Deep bowl, projecting rim); This shape is found in coarsewares (Edwards 1975, no. 616, pl. 21), plain wares and cooking wares (at Chalkis see p 125; Sparkes and Talcott 1970, nos. 1739-1843, p. 211-216, fig. 15). This same form is used as the decorated krater in Asia Minor, see, for example: Schäfer 1968, D33-D51, pls. 13-14; Z83, Z84, p. 154, fig. 18; Behr 1988, 155-159; Rotroff 2002, 97-115.

with the plain ware jar/stamnos (see below p 131). The function of no. 24 must overlap with its plain ware cousins.

In contrast to the other jugs, no. 292 is a small and delicate vessel, whose function is possibly more toiletry than drinking. The bulbous wall curves in to a brief concavity from which the simple rim flares.

Table amphora

The table amphora is a liquid serving or storage vessel. Like the transport counterpart, the table amphora has a cylindrical neck and broad body. The body of the amphora compares closely to the other liquid carrying vessels, as jugs, but the amphora can be distinguished from such pouring vessels by its projecting rim. The Hellenistic amphorae are commonly decorated on the neck and shoulder with West Slope ware, but no decoration, nor a substantial section of the decorative zones, is preserved on the Chalkis fragments.[161]

The examples identified here are all rim fragments. Nos. 7, 196 and 214 show cylindrical necks with flaring upper walls that flow, without articulation, into the rim. The rim is thickened and overhung and carries a moulded outer face. A small amount of glaze is preserved on no. 196. A groove sits under the rim of the heavily encrusted no. 7.

No. 185 is a finer-walled shape of higher quality glaze and fabric and precise potting. The vessel would contribute to a well-appointed table. It has a rim that projects horizontally, above a concave neck. The rim carries to light ridges on either edge of the upper face. These are now clay ground, perhaps due to wear rather than representing a subtle design.

161 In the Hellenistic period there are three types of decorated amphora: the Attic amphora, the Pergamene amphora (both discussed in Rotroff 2002, pp. 97-115; and the amphora produced in Epiros and Central Greece perhaps under Italian influence (discussed Alexandropoulou 2002), p. 149 ff; and Bollen 2011). The rim fragments from Chalkis are comparable to the Attic type amphora. Black glaze Hellenistic amphora are reported from Akraifias: Sabetai 2004, pl. 211c left; and Douroutis: Andreou 2004, pl. 280-281.

Dipper

From the channel in room I comes no. 33 a fragment that preserves the high loop handle, rim and upper wall of a dipper. It is a sturdy vessel. It has a worn and mottled red to brown slip. Although the dipper can be associated with wine consumption, used as a ladle to move liquid from one vessel to another, it could have a myriad of functions, including the movement of dried foods such as grains.

TOILETRY VESSELS

Reversible lid

The reversible lid is a vessel associated with female activities. It functioned as a lid for a jewellery box (the lekanis) or a palate for cosmetic application.[162] It was produced throughout mainland Greece and in Asia Minor, though variation in form can distinguish regional productions. The name of the shape derives from the two resting surfaces, which provide the reversible lid with a dual purpose. The vessel can function as a lid, when it stands on the rim, or as a bowl when it stands on the ring foot/knob. The shape has a Classical origin, yet it remains a favoured vessel type through the 3rd century when it is a common recipient of West Slope decoration.

This class of shape allows us to discuss one of the more extraordinary finds of the area, the near complete reversible lid no. 323. This lid was found in numerous fragments within room XV of trench T6NA. The scattered fragments around the door of the room suggest that it may have been a casualty of the packing and moving process of the inhabitants (or the result of a domestic feud!). It is of fine manufacture with well-executed West Slope decoration, both incised and painted. The shape could be labeled a lekanis lid rather than a reversible lid, given the stemmed and moulded knob. Such versions of reversible lid are found in other areas of Central Greece.[163] While the clay of no. 323 is

162 Rotroff 1997, p. 192.

163 Lamia: Baziotopoulou-Valavani, 1994, p. 53, pl. 24a; Demetrias: Papakonstantinou, M.-F. 1997, p. 52, pl. 36a, c; Phthiotic Thebes: Adrimi-Sismani 2000, p. 143, fig. 9. The form is also found in Campanian pottery: Morel 1981, nos. 4711a.1 and 4713a.1.

not greatly at variance with the local production the standard of production is so beyond the run-of-the-mill to prompt the need to look outside the town for its origin.

The rim of the lid no. 323 is slightly inclined to a diameter of 23 cm. The wall, set at an angle from the rim, begins with a groove above which is a concentric rectangles and checkerboard pattern. The lines of both motifs are incised and the alternate squares of the checkerboard are painted. A second groove provides an upper boarder to the decorative zone. The next zone carries further decoration, an egg and dart pattern with incised eggs filled with fugitive painted dots, and darts in the shape of tripartite leaves. The eggs are set below a groove and appear suspended from it. In this way they complement nicely the gradient of the wall. Four light, glazed grooves follow. The upper wall is undecorated until directly below the junction with the foot. Here another deep groove articulates the shape and suspended from this, dripping down the wall, a spearhead necklace with incised arcing chain and painted pendants. The stem of the knob is concave. The knob has a squared outer profile and a resting surface moulded by a deep groove on its upper face. Within the resting surface is a painted star flower, a design popular in such circular zones.

No. 324 is a small body fragment from a piece that bears some resemblance to no. 323, particularly in the glaze, the thin wall and the choice of motif, the egg and dart. The execution of said motif on no. 324 however, does not reach the standard of no. 323. West Slope decoration is found on no. 8, another body fragment, this time thick-walled. The motifs of this lid are incised lattice and stems for a scrolling ivy wreath, fugitive leaves can also be spotted by the astute. The groove holds a diameter of around 20 cm, which suggests the lid was of similar dimensions to no. 323 despite the solidity of its walls.

No. 81, the rim and wall of another reversible lid, has a slightly different profile to no. 323. It has a higher rim that is not inclined. The junction of the wall and rim are marked by two grooves. The wall of the rim is convex. It is a smaller shape with a diameter of only 12 cm. and this, rather than an alternate prototype, must account for its variation in form. It conforms to the regional production and has the familiar slightly coarse feel and glaze mottled brown to red on the exterior; the interior retains no glaze.

Pyxis

The pyxis is not common amongst the ceramics from Chalkis.[164] Two fragments nos. 9 and 166 provide examples. Both appear imported. No. 9 preserves the flanged rim and sections of wall above and below that are typical of the type B pyxis[165]. The type B pyxis is inherited from the Classical period, with some alteration (notably the loss of the moulded ovolo rim) and is the most common of the pyxis forms throughout mainland Greece.[166] No. 166 has a flanged rim, but the wall below is short and quickly terminates in a simple resting surface. The wall above the flange curves convexly, indicating a high dome. The glaze is lustrous and the potting refined with slight grooves defining the wall.

Lekanis

These broad and shallow bowls carry a flange on which would sit a lid, sometimes a decorated reversible lid as those described above.[167] These vessels are, like the pyxis, jewellery, cosmetics or keepsake boxes.

No. 145 preserves the inset rim and upper wall of a lekanis body. It retains no glaze. From examination of the cross-section of the break it would appear that the body curves smoothly to the flange but that the rim is carefully added and shaped to fit the incurving wall. The rim and flange produce a neat seat for a lid and no. 81, the reversible lid, fits snuggly, though the relationship between the two is more fortuitous than secure given the variation in their fabric. No more examples of this shape were noted in the examined contexts.

164 One complete example was found in Grave 3: Eiring 2004, no. 14, pp. 122-125.

165 Following the pyxis typology of Rotroff 1997.

166 For details of different groups of pyxides see: Kotitsa 1996. For a regional summary of mainland Greece see Bollen 2011.

167 For pairs of lidded lekanides from the region see: Kallipolis: Baziotopoulou-Valavani, 1994, p. 53, pl. 24a; Adrimi-Sismani 2000, p. 143, fig. 9; Papakonstantinou, M.-F. 1997, p. 52, pl. 36a, c.

OIL VESSELS

Guttus, Lekythos and Lagynos

There is an interesting variety in the few examples of perfumed oil containers from Chalkis. No. 215 preserves an almost full profile of a lekythos.[168] This jug has a broad bowl rim leading to a narrow neck, a short concave shoulder and a reasonably tall and narrow body with convex outer profile. The body has a low maximum diameter and thus has a slightly saggy appearance. The foot is a simple raised disc. The vessel is glazed on the interior and exterior with a dull black slip. Given that the glaze has reached the interior of this narrow necked vessel, it must have been dipped into the glaze, a common Hellenistic technique.

No. 151 is a small fragment. A flaring rim leads to a narrow cylindrical neck, a profile common for guttoi.[169] The wall fragment no. 153, which retains short incised stems of West Slope decoration, is a shoulder fragment from such a vessel.

No. 118 offers a different oil pouring vessel, this time with a broader neck for more liberal administration: a lagynos. The rim, neck and handle of this vessel are preserved. The rim flares out from the concave neck. A ridge, preserved on the very edge of the sherd, marks the junction with the shoulder. A double handle sits directly below the rim and is reconstructed to lift out to the height of the rim before dropping to the shoulder.

Unguentarium

No. 238 is a base of an unguentarium, the single identified fragment of the shape in the complex of rooms. This unguenatarium has a base that projects beyond the flaring and hollow stem.[170] Traces of black to brown glaze are preserved on and under the foot and on the lower wall.

168 The rim compares to Rotroff 1997, no. 11, fig. 69; Kotitsa 2004, pl. 63b left and pl. 66c. The body of the Chalkis example is much narrower and more angular, yet not elongated as the not too distant production of Elian Lekythoi, Kastler 2000, pp. 410-411.

169 For full profiles of this shape see Rotroff 1997, nos. 1140-1142, fig. 71.

170 The lower body compares to Camilli 1999, no. A24.1, p. 68, fig, 12 (dates to 300 B.C.); also p. 64, A 23.8, fig. 10 (no date given).

OTHER FINE WARE VESSELS

Lid

The lid, no. 272, does not belong to the reversible lid class. It is a conical lid with a narrow knob sitting at the apex. The knob is simple, though rises some distance above the wall of the lid. As it rises the knob increases in diameter making it sit firmly between a pinched grip (i.e. one can pinch it at its lower diameter and as the shape increases above the pressure point, the lid is held fast). The glaze is worn; that which is preserved is a brownish red.

Stand

This trumpet-like vessel, no. 47, was found along with a series of other well-preserved vessels in room II. It rests on a broad but somewhat irregular surface. The outer face of the foot is squared while the upper face is set off from the wall by a groove. The wall is concave, rising up into a hollow and increasingly narrow stem. Parallels for this shape suggest that it could have supported a lamp.[171] While lebes gamikoi and other larger vessels can also be supported by ceramic stands, no. 47 does not appear broad enough to provide a sturdy support for such a vessel. The glaze is very worn. Brown to grey glaze is preserved on the lower interior. Brown to grey glaze also coats the lower wall and rim but stops at an almost regular line approximately 2 cm. above the foot. On the upper exterior curvilinear lines of glaze are discernable allowing dark on light decoration, perhaps a ribbon, to be proposed, though dripping marks of glaze may also have produced these lines.[172]

171 Davidson 1942, fig. 1 shows terracotta lamp stands. The Corinthian stands are tall and narrow, similar to the Chalkis example. All have dip-glazing on the lower wall of the lamp stand. Broneer 1977, no. 137 (though this one is solid) with further parallels; Pemberton 1989, pl. 37, red figure lebes gamikos stands.

172 This apparent decoration was not clear enough to include it in the drawing of the piece.

PLAIN WARE

The plain wares from the Hellenistic rooms at Chalkis display a range of forms that have been gathered into the following categories for presentation: storage, serving and ritual. A typology of forms is not presented, but rather vessels of the same function are grouped together. The reason for this is simply that the plain ware vessels from Chalkis are quite varied and there are rarely multiple examples of any one type. Even for the transport amphorae, where a series of vessels are identified, the qualities and characteristics of these vessels are not uniform. Whilst a number of the deposits examined contain a lot of plain ware non-diagnostic fragments, particularly from amphorae, the diagnostics are not preserved or not to a state that can reveal much about the shape.[173] I have selected plain ware fragments that provide the greatest indication of the overall shape and give the range of forms and functions of vessels found on the site.

STORAGE

Transport Amphora

The transport amphora from Chalkis are varied both in form and in fabric, no doubt appropriate for a settlement set on the coast of the Corinthian Gulf, a major maritime trading route. A series of amphorae were found in Room XI, nos. 251, 252, 253, and 262. They, too, are of varied type, though their preservation suggests that they are contemporary and their context places them within the use phase of the room. A near-complete amphora was found within the tile smash in Room XV, no. 307.

The upper bodies of nos. 307 and 119 are similar in form, though the fabric of the latter is slightly darker. Both have a rolled rim and broad strap handle that is oval in section. The shoulder of no. 307 is broad and sloping. On both the arching strap handle is pressed just below the rolled rim, and on no. 307 the lower attachment is placed on the mid-shoulder. The toe of no. 307 provides a view to the whole profile – a piriform shape, though this has not, as yet, been reassembled. The toe is conical in form, running smoothly from the wall, and bulging at the tip. A similar toe, no. 34, has clay colouring that is associated with Corinth – a greenish exterior and a yellow core. Body fragments of this fabric were preserved, including one, no. 103, that had been reworked with a serrated edge. The small rim fragment no. 97 has a rolled rim and a pale buff fabric. The shape of these amphorae conforms with the Hellenistic Corinthian Type B amphora form, though the handles on the Chalkis examples, where preserved, do not rise above the rim.[174]

No. 262 also has a rolled rim, though here the fabric is quite distinctive with a brittle feel. It carries strong ribbing marks on the interior. The strap handle of no. 262 is narrower than nos. 307 and 119. No. 253 is the base of no. 262. The two share the same fabric and the same discoloration, probably caused by secondary burning. No. 253 is quite different than the other bases found on the site, being a broad toe with a slightly curved under-surface and walls that flare out to lead directly into the body.

The amphorae with mushroom rim comprise another group. No. 252 is well preserved. Here the rim is neatly folded to overhang slightly and to stand out from the wall. The strap handle is quite thick in section with a ridge on the interior that supports a strong handgrip. No. 98 displays less assured potting. The rim is turned to overhang, though adheres closely to the wall profile.[175] The handle stems show a rather thin strap, circular in section. The fabric with its white, red and brown inclusions allows one to suggest that this example is a local product. On no. 251 the taut rim is folded to a triangular section and projects out from the neck. It does not hold the 'overhang' of the two

173 Plain ware shapes are often sizeable vessels, a feature which can work against their preservation to a standard worthy of publication. Fine ware shapes tend to be smaller than plain ware shapes so that a fragment of a fine ware sherd preserves a higher percentage of the shape than does a similar-sized plain ware fragment, therefore fragments from smaller vessels often reveal more about the form of the vessel and are more often useful to the researcher.

174 For description of the Hellenistic version of the type B amphora, and its differentiation from the earlier forms, Koehler 1982, p. 286-287.

175 The profile compares to late 4th to 3rd century examples from the Athenian Agora, M. Lawall, *ΣΤ' ΕλλΚερ*, no. 30, p. 451-452, pl. 199.

described above.[176] The handle is a broad strap, oval in section. The shoulder curves smoothly from the cylindrical neck, the junction articulated by a groove. The very large and platy red sections in the clay make this ware quite distinctive. The folded rim of no. 239 introduces quite a different type of amphora. Here the rim is folded back along the wall profile for a distance of 5.7 cm. to the start of the handle. The handle stem is circular in section.

The amphora bases, in addition to those discussed above, are varied. No. 10 is a rough version of the piriform type. It lacks the broadening at the termination point of the Corinthian B group. Unlike the others, where the end of the toe is solid and provides a weight to the base of the vessel, no. 10 remains hollow, with the end of the toe being the same thickness as the rest of the lower wall. The fabric and the shape variations suggest that this example is locally produced.

Jar/Stamnos

Presented here are a group of vessels with broad body and narrow rim. The form is appropriate for the storage of goods, including grains. One can think of these vessels as small and portable versions of the pithos.

The three storage jars selected from the Chalkis material vary in their details but have the same general form. The rim stands up above a broad upper body. The body juts out, rather like a shoulder on an amphora, almost horizontal, yet declining. The rim stands above this wall, either rounded, like no. 327, squared, like no. 326, or projecting, like no. 279. The rim of no. 279 carries a series of narrow sharp grooves on the upper face. Below this the scar of a handle, circular in section, is visible. The other two are of much softer fabric and are undecorated, neither preserves evidence of a handle.

Lid

The two plain ware lids presented here are not similar in form. Both, however, would have functioned to stopper vessels, such as the storage jars described above.

No. 71 is a distinctive lid. It has a flat lower disc the outer zones of which provide a resting surface, the inner zones of which rise to a central point. The rim of the lid rises vertically above the body and has a ridge on the upper, outer face. The upper face of the lid is decorated with concentric ridges. In the centre of the upper face the wall thickens and a knob rises up. Unfortunately the knob itself is not preserved.

The second lid, no. 217, follows more the reversible lid prototype and when reversed appears as a simple bowl. It has a rounded rim, and a very shallow bowl body. The shallowness is increased by the wall, which thickens considerably as it reaches the ring foot/knob.

SERVING

Lekane

The lekane is a large bowl or basin that can be used both in the serving and the preparation of solid foods and of liquids, and no doubt could have come in handy for numerous other activities (consider the varied uses of a plastic basin or bucket). The fabric of the two catalogued lekanai suggests that they are products of two different external workshops.

No. 256 is of a pale fabric. The upper wall of the bowl is preserved. On the interior the wall runs smoothly from the concave body to the convex, flaring rim. On the exterior, a slight narrowing of the convex wall marks the transition of wall to rim. The rim is horizontal and thickened. It carries a groove on its upper and on its outer face.

No. 308 is a larger vessel with solid wall. The bowl is broad and runs to the flaring rim. The rim is thickened and has a squared outer face. A lug handle sits on the outer, upper wall.

Jug (plain ware)

Collected under this heading is a range of partially preserved profiles deemed appropriate for vessels of a pouring function. The fragmentary nature of these sizeable vessels makes certain identification problematic. For example the rim and vertical handle of a

176 Compares with, Lawall 2004, no. 20, p. 451-452, pl. 199; late 4th century.

hydria could be the rim and vertical handle of a jug. Furthermore, the base of a pouring or storage vessel is likely to be of much the same form.

The first jug fragment, no. 40, preserves a horizontal projecting rim, onto which the vertical strap handle attaches. The strap handle is broad but not overly thick. It falls from the height of the handle to join with the shoulder. One can reconstruct a cylindrical neck and sloping shoulder between the preserved rim and shoulder. This vessel is elegant, even in its fragmentary state.

Of very different appearance is no. 293. This jug has a broad ovoid shoulder that curves to an upright neck. The short neck leads to a rounded rim. At one break the rim appears to rise into attached clay, perhaps the start of a handle. The vessel is glazed, but the baggy shape decides against a fine ware classification.

No. 245 displays an ovoid body below a concave neck. A high loop handle links the rim (which is obscured by the handle attachment) and the body. The convex wall and concave neck meet at a sharp junction. Grooves on the handle make it tripartite in section. This juglet could have functioned both as a pouring and as a dipping vessel.[177]

On no. 48 the handle attaches below the flaring rim. The flaring rim brings to mind the fine ware amphora fragment, no. 185, with which it also shares a squared outer face. The placement of the strap handle, and its broad, oval form, is also appropriate for a table amphora. The thickness of the wall and the fabric itself are characteristic of plain ware.

The narrow neck and two strap handle stems of no. 49 suggest a narrow-necked flask, bottle or a small transport amphora. The rim is rolled, the diameter irregular, the neck narrow and cylindrical, and the handles oval in section.

No. 237 is a base fragment. The base has a broad floor and a broad but low and simple ring foot. The lower wall curves allowing a broad body and shoulder to be reconstructed above. The neck and handle fragments described in this section (except, one suspects no. 49) could have rested on such a base. The fragments no. 74 show a jug with low base (now very worn), above which the wall flares out to form a broad body. No. 325 has a simple disc base, with a diameter of 10 cm. (3 cm. less than no. 237). The wall is thin, appropriate for a smaller vessel.

No. 216, the only identified import amongst the jugs, has a narrower rim diameter and neck than the other jugs. The rim projects and is moulded on the outer face. Two handles rise from the neck, touching the handle as they rise up above its level.[178] At the height of the rim the handles are 2.35 cm. apart. One of the handles is preserved to a greater degree than the other. It rises just above the height of the handle. It curves over and down, inclined slightly toward the neck.

RITUAL

Thymiaterion

Thymiateria, incense burners, are used in ritual activities. No. 50 is a complete thymiaterion and the only identified example of the vessel from the rooms. It was found in room II and is associated with a series of other near complete vessels, including the stand, no. 47, and fine ware cups and lamps.

The thymiaterion has a bell-shaped lower stand with a flaring foot and a moulded band between foot and wall. The stand is hollow. Above the bell is a broad and solid flange that joins with an upright rim. This results in a shallow and elevated bowl on top of an elegant stand. The incense would sit within this bowl.[179]

The Chalkis thymiaterion is unglazed at first impression, but closer inspection reveals a thick layer of a white chalky substance preserved in one limited location (a little less than 1 cm. squared) under the flange. Such white paint is used on ceramic thymia-

177 Compare with: Edwards 1975, no. 273, pl. 10

178 For similar double handles see Edwards 1975, nos. 287-302, pl. 12.

179 A number of comparable thymiateria were found at the nearby site of *Kalydon*: *Kalydon 2011*, ch. 6.4. The flange and bowl of the Chalkis thymiaterion compares to the imported fragment found in the Athenian Agora: Rotroff 1997, no. 1567, fig. 95, 1st century context. The Attic thymiaterion, Rotroff 1997, no. 1442, also has a flange but the higher bowl and profiled stand differentiate it from no. **50** Radt 2000, fig. 1, shows another thymiaterion with similarities in the profile of the stand but the knob-like bowl of the Pergamene example, and furthermore its decoration, are quite different to the Chalkis example.

teria, to create the illusion of a marble vessel.[180] If this thymiaterion was coated in white then it probably originally held painted decoration.

COOKING POT WARE

The gritty fabric of cooking ware is common, if not plentiful, in the deposits under study. Bright orange fabric with frequent white, brown and grey inclusions, is typical of this ware. By far the most common shape is the lopas, a 'frying pan', with flanged rim, near-vertical upper wall, and shallow curved floor. Chytra, or 'stew pots', a deep and baggy-bodied form, are the other cooking pot that is common amongst the Chalkis Aitolias ceramics. Both these vessels have flanged rims that held lids, to assist in the cooking process. Some of these lids are preserved.

In addition to those vessels used on the fire, there are other pots that were made of the same fabric, though their function is possibly closer to that of plain ware. They are, however, classed here, and may be thought of as cooking vessels made 'not for use with heat".[181] Such vessels include jugs and jars, certainly vessels useful in the kitchen.

VESSELS USED ON THE FIRE

Lopas

The lopas is the most common cooking vessel in the Chalkis deposits. The examples are quite angular in form and have handles attached below the rim, attesting to their Hellenistic rather than Classical date.[182] They have a sharp flange separating wall from rim, and an angular junction between the upright upper wall and the very slightly curved lower wall. There are, however, no full profiles of the lopas at Chalkis. Many times it is only the rim and upper wall that is preserved. There are some fragments, though, where part of the lower wall and its junction with the upper wall can be seen.There are local and imported versions of the shape.[183]

The lopas varies in size, both in the height of the upper wall and in diameter. The majority fall in the range of 19-23 cm. (nos. 52, 128 and 187) in diameter, with three slightly larger measuring between 26-28 cm. and one very large example of 35 cm., no. 294. One is smaller at 17 cm. (no. 244), and a "single serve" pan, no. 218, has a diameter of only 13 cm.

When preserved there are a few different versions of the handle at Chalkis. The lopas handle is always circular in section and set flat against the wall and rim of the vessel. Most often at Chalkis, and on the sherds of local fabric, it is set in a curvilinear fashion (nos. 52 and 329). Other examples (all in imported fabric) include an angular, inverted V setting (found on no. 128) or a rectilinear handle with two sides rising perpendicular to the rim, squared by the third side which runs across the rim (found on no. 53).[184]

Apart from the type of handle, variation in form is minimal. The typical lopas of Chalkis is thin-walled. The rim, with rounded lip, stands above a flange. The flange varies slightly in its position (height on the wall), its angularity and the length of its projection. The lower wall meets the upper at an angular junction before curving to a shallow bowl. Variations include no. 294, which has a high rim, with a hint of concavity on the interior suggesting that it lies closer to the

180 White decoration: Romano 1994, no. 100, p. 95, pl. 30. Other thymiateria are decorated with mouldmade decoration, as those from Neapolis Scythian, Zaytsev 2004, pl. 356; while the profile of these has the basic form the Chalkis example with shallow bowl and high stem, the profile is made more elaborate by mouldings.

181 This category follows Edwards 1975, see p. 134.

182 The lopas documented for the Classical period has horizontal handles that stand above the rim of the lopas, such as Sparkes and Talcott 1970, fig. 18, nos. 1962, 1965, 1968 and 1970. These continue in the Hellenistic assemblage at Corinth: Edwards 1975, pl. 29. The transition to the attached handles is witnessed at both Athens and Racchi in the third century: Rotroff 2004, p. 459, pl. 207.1 and 207.2; Anderson-Stojanović. p. 624, the handle is set on the rim at the beginning of the third century but on the body by the end of the third century. Handleless lopades, which are not documented at Chalkis, appear in the mid-second century: Edwards 1975, p. 127-128, pl. 30; Rotroff 2004, p. 459, handless version dated 150.

183 Local: 28, 51, 52, 140, 146, 172, 173, 186, 218, 329. Imported: 53, 128, 187, 219, 244, 294, 309

184 Parallels for the curvilinear and V-shaped handles have not been found. The rectangular version compares to examples from Crete: Portale 2000, pl. 40a. 4.5; pl. 41c, pl. 42a; Hatzidakis 2000, pl. 76a.

Classical form than do others in the assemblage.[185] No. 294 is comparatively thick-walled. The grey ware vessel, no. 244, is thin-walled, sharp and shallower than is typical. The import no. 309 has a bevelled lip, which sets off the upper rim from the zone on which a lid would rest.

The fabric of no. 244 is similar to that of the spout, no. 76. The edge of the spout that would attach to a wall is well preserved but does not indicate its fusion with the shape (i.e. a hint of the wall to which it had attached) as one would expect of a pouring spout. There is a link between the spout, which is spool shaped in profile, and the lopas. At Corinth, Edwards has identified a non-functional spout on a lopas, suggesting that it could have held an inserted handle, perhaps wooden, effectively transforming the shape into a frypan.[186] Even without an inserted section of wood this spout could have made an effective handle. I do not think nos. 244 and 76 are from the same vessel, given the spout end is broader than the lopas wall, but they may issue from the same source.

Another addition to the lopas (or a handle variation for the frypan) is the loop handle found on no. 219.[187] This handle rises above the level of the rim and attaches just below. It would assist in lifting the vessel onto and off a hot surface, allowing ones hands to remain at a distance from the heat.

185 Concave lips, sometimes elaborate, are documented in the first half of the fourth century at Athens. In the late fourth century variation occurs in the rim zone and includes the concave Sparkes and Talcott 1970, no. 1968 and the angular, Sparkes and Talcott 1970, no. 1970. For Athens development compare Rotroff 2004 p. 459, pl. 207.a and 207.2. The Chalkis assemblage indicates that the angular version predominates in the third century.

186 Edwards 1975, no. 676, p. 125. Some Classical versions from the Athenian Agora have un-pierced spouts: Sparkes and Talcott 1970, no. 1968, p. 227; an imported example, no. 1969, p. 277 has a pierced spout.

187 This version is common in Laconia, see: Langridge-Noti 2002, nos. 13a, b, p. 65, fig. 21; Catling 1996, shape 47. The example from Chalkis shares the half-heart-shaped profile of the Laconian examples. Cypriot and Agora parallels listed by Langridge-Noti 2002 (as above) suggests 2nd century and Roman dates. Its discovery at Chalkis indicates a third century date for this shape in Aitolian production.

Chytra

Gathered under the term chytra are cooking ware vessels for which a deep ovoid body curving in to an upright or flaring rim can be reconstructed. This is a common form of cooking pot widely produced through the Classical and Hellenistic periods. Once again, given the fragmentary nature of the evidence, it is possible (indeed likely) that other related versions of cooking pots are represented amongst the fragments (including the stew pot, a chytra with vertical handles etc.). Some of the examples do not preserve burning marks that could allow those examples to have functioned as storage jars.[188] The range of fabrics is similar to that found with the lopas and includes what can be construed as local ware, alongside likely imports.[189]

There are different versions of the chytra represented amongst the finds. These two types, through comparison to other sites, indicate a development of the shape from the 4th to 3rd century. The distribution of the two forms at Chalkis, however, allows for concurrent use.

The first version, which compares to 4th century productions in other centres, has an ovoid body with a smooth curve to the constricted lower rim.[190] This rim has a strongly concave outer profile that flares away from the narrow neck to the lip. On no. 295 the lip is squared in section, which reinforces the impression of a projecting rim. The interior rim of no. 129 is set at two angles, with a distinct junction as the upper rim projects from the concave rim; this form must assist with supporting a lid. This angle can be extreme to produce a projecting rim above a low concave neck, as nos. 11, 27 and 330 (probably a 3rd century development).

No. 26 displays the characteristics of the second version. It has an upright rim that flares out slightly from the broad and ovoid body. The inner surface of

188 Nos. 11 and 152 do not have burning marks. However, 310, which is indisputably a chytra only has burning marks on one portion of the rim, providing support for the two unburnt fragments to remain in this class.

189 Local: 26, 27, 108, 129, 188, 281, 310, 330 and possibly, despite the slate grey colouring, 295; imports: 11 and 152.

190 Cf. Sparkes and Talcott 1970 nos. 1928, 1932, fig. 18; Monaco & Monaco 2000, p. 157, pl. 89.a.1; Eretria: S. Schmid 2000, no. 49, pl. 186.

the rim is slightly concave, a profile that would assist in the support of a lid.[191] The outer wall carries two light ridges just below the junction of rim and wall.[192] Related to this type is no. 188. It has the simple lip and upright rim, though it is a much shorter rim than no. 26 and it is not concave. No. 310 is of this type, with the short, vertical rim of no. 188, with no designated resting place for a lid. On no. 310 we see the body bulge out under the rim, and the short strap handle that loops from rim to outer shoulder. The handle sit close to the narrow neck, accommodating only one finger to loop through and pick up the vessel, therefore a second balancing handle on the other side can be reconstructed. The handle fragment no. 281 is of this type.

Nos. 108 and 152 lie somewhere between the two versions described above. They both have the tall rim with a rounded lip of version one, though the rim flares in a similar manner to the second version. The wall of no. 108 is preserved, though it does not join the rim. It has a concave upper section that runs to the ovoid lower wall and forms a distinct, if not sharp junction.[193]

STORAGE/POURING VESSELS

Storage vessel

No. 77 shares the upright rim and ovoid body of the chytra and it could be argued that it should be classed with them. However, its thick wall distinguishes it from that shape and cooking function. Rather this vessel would seem to lie closer in function to the plain ware jars and provide a storage bin for use in the kitchen. It is made of the local cooking ware fabric.

191 Cf. Edwards 1975, no. 651, pl. 27; Monaco & Monaco 2000, p. 157, pl. 89.a.3.

192 Similar ridges are reported on other comparable Hellenistic examples (in addition to those mentioned in previous footnote): Geraki: Langridge-Noti 2002, no. 11a; Athens: Rotroff 2004, pl. 206.1.

193 This profile is similar, though not quite as pronounced as an example from Beroia: Drougou & Touratsoglou 1980, Π 1379, see pages 120-122 for discussion of the local development of this shape at Beroia.

Jug

With a projecting rim with moulded outer surface, and the upper section of a cylindrical neck, no. 205 provides a different cooking ware vessel. Perhaps this vessel was not meant for use on the fire, though the inability to restore the lower body prevents certain identification of function. The inner rim is concave, and designed to hold a lid.

Lid

Both the lopas and the chytra, discussed above, are often designed to hold a lid. It is likely that lids were made to fit individual vessels. A number of cooking ware lids are found in the deposits at Chalkis, though they are not as frequent as the vessels with which they are paired. The lids can be made in the local fabric, or in fabric that appears to be imported.

The local fabric lids adhere to the same basic form with a broad and fairly flat wall rising slightly to a mushroom knob.[194] Nos. 35, 296 and 331 are examples of these. Often these simple discs are finished with a rounded lip, as seen on no. 75. No. 120 has a rounded ridge on the outer wall before curving to the rounded lip. The curve of the lower wall indicates the centre of the lid was elevated. No. 12 is slightly more elaborate with a vertical rim section with a deep moulding on the outer face. The wall rises up for a domed rather than disc lid. Similar lids are found in imported fabric including the very flat no. 311, which has a hollow knob with sharp profile, and the slightly domed no. 220, the knob of which has a central depression.[195]

In contrast to these is no. 297, a lid of cooking ware fabric that shares more in form with a fine ware reversible lid than the cooking lids described. It has a vertical rim, a smooth curving domed wall that reaches a height of 7.5 cm. before it breaks at the junction of the knob. The diameter at 28 cm. is too big for the majority of the lopades. There are some faint streaky brown curvilinear lines on the surface – possible slip or decoration? Is this, in fact a reversible

194 Compare with: Edwards 1975, nos. 694 and 695, pl. 31.

195 For knobs with central depression, see: Edwards 1975, nos. 696, 697, 698 and 699, pl. 31.

lid that is made in the 'wrong' ware? The quantity of micaceous particles in the fabric suggests that the piece is imported.

COARSE WARE

The coarse wares from Chalkis include pithos fragments and other vessels associated with food storage and preparation, such as the lid, the mortar, and the louterion. The latter can also have a ritual purpose. In addition to these there are some unusual vessels, likely to have been used for food preparation.

The majority of the coarse wares appear to be made out of the local fabric. They have a light reddish-pink fabric. They live up to the term "coarse" as the fabric contains very many inclusions. White, red, grey and sometimes brown inclusions, ranging from small to very large, were added to the clay to strengthen the walls of these vessels. The inclusions are hackly in the break and often on the surface. The surface tends to be powdery. On some examples the surface has been smoothed, perhaps with an added layer of finer clay. Decoration is preserved only on the louteria where painted, moulded or incised patterns are found. There are a few coarse ware pieces of imported fabrics, but most are locally made.

FOOD STORAGE

Pithos

Frequently pithoi fragments are found in the upper deposits of the site where they cannot be linked with any certainty either temporally or spatially. This is due largely to the size of pithoi fragments which keeps them kicking around on the surface. However, the collapsed roofs of the rooms at Chalkis have kept some pithoi within a secure deposit. It is these examples that have been selected for presentation. Pithoi represent a significant investment and are likely to be used for long years. The rim fragments of the pithoi from the rooms at Chalkis all have the solid projecting rim and convex interior wall that conforms to the neckless profile of Hellenistic pithoi.[196]

196 Cullen & Keller 1990; Boggess 1970, 73-78.

The examples from Chalkis vary slightly in their fabric. They all have a high quantity of inclusions, added to strengthen the large vessels. The qualities of the fabric are, however, recognizable from the other local wares. Nos. 54, 55 and 240 are of a fabric that compares to the local plain ware fabric, being a light reddish-pink with a powdery surface. The inclusions are hackly in the break, the surfaces of nos. 54 and 55 remain comparatively smooth. The inclusions of no. 312, also a light red fabric, protrude in a manner reminiscent of cooking ware. No. 56 also has characteristic in common with the local cooking ware, being orange in colour, and carrying the range of inclusions familiar from the fabrics of nos. 54 and 55.

The two base fragments, nos. 55 and 240 are disc feet. They share a diameter of 18 cm. No. 55 is moulded on the underside with a rounded resting surface and two moulded 'steps' leading to the raised centre. No. 240 has a simple disc base, though at the centre of the floor is a hole that appears to be part of the original design.

The rims all project beyond the upper wall. No. 54 is the largest of the rims with a diameter of 50 cm. It has a broad upper face, a squared outer face and a concave lower face that curves back to the wall.The inner face of the upper wall is slightly convex, the junction between the wall and rim is unmarked. The rim of no. 312 has a flat upper face, but not as broad as no. 54. The outer face is narrow and rounded, the underside (which would have been more visible than on the previous), is only very slightly concave. The cross section is triangular and the rim less heavy than no. 54. No. 56 is flatter in appearance than the others. It has a broad upper face, a squared outer face and a flat lower face that is inclined sharply and returns quickly to the wall. Although none of the rims are complete, the preservation percentage of the rim is similar in each to allow for their weights to be compared. The comparison reveals, better than the above descriptions, the dimensional differences of the above profiles: no. 54 which at 3395 grams is a much heftier vessel than nos. 312 and 56 at 1725 and 1315 grams respectively.

The body fragment no. 286 is the only example of a pithos with decoration. The fragment comes from the wall of a pithos. The wall is inclined and a relief band at the top of the fragment provides a definite junction between this and the next zone of the vessel, where the wall is reduced in thickness. Running just below the relief band are two grooves, 3 cm. below is another groove and 5 cm. below this are two grooves. Three bands, then, are preserved (one only partially) and these each hold an incised zigzag as decoration. Decorated pithoi are rare by the Hellenistic period and it would seem likely that this piece is residual.[197] Furthermore, the fabric of this fragment is a paler pink that compares more closely to fabrics from the site that date to the Archaic period than the other pithoi from AREA III.

Body fragments of the pithos, no. 257, were excavated from the lower levels of room XI. The combined weight of the fragments was 13.46 kg.

Lid

The lid no. 13 consists of a solid disc, the upper surface of which rises to a chipped mushroom knob, the wider upper diameter allowing for easy lifting. The fabric of this lid is heavy with added inclusions. It is the light reddish-pink of the pithoi and medium ware common on the site. The lid has a diameter of 17.6 cm. making it too small for a full-sized pithos. It is similar to those discussed as 'stamnos lids' from Corinth and like them lacks a certain partner vessel.[198]

The terracotta disc no. 58 may have functioned as a lid. The fabric shares the characteristics of the local coarse ware. There remains a possibility that this is part of an architectural, rather than ceramic, object.

FOOD PREPARATION

Deep spouted vessel

A large, local, vessel, no. 57, has a disc base, a thick wall that is convex and inclined creating a domed vessel. One wall opens to a spout, the outer zone of which is broken. A section of rim is preserved on the upper edge of this spout and suggests that the spout may have joined the, now missing, upper rim of this vessel. Two lug handles are preserved on either side of the vessel at ¼ and ¾ position on the wall with the spout located mid way between the two. The upper most wall preserved indicates that the break occurs where the wall changes direction and flares out, perhaps to the rim.

No. 57 was taken up during the removal of the tile smash in room II. It is an unusual vessel that prompts speculation of its use.[199] Although it is reminiscent of braziers it does not have a two-tiered form and furthermore there are no signs of burning. It is heavy, and though spouted it is difficult to consider pouring from this vessel. One could have used it effectively as a storage vessel, the wide spout providing an easy way of accessing the contents, but the position of the spout means that much of the vessel's storage potential is wasted. Furthermore, the vessel offers little protection and thus the preservation of contents was likely to be compromised. Perhaps a milk related production (yogurt or cheese manufacture), or some other similar process, may have utilized this vessel, where liquids (whey) had to be removed, via the spout, from solids which lay in the wide bottom of the vessel. The solids were then removed and stored in another vessel.

Dome

The reconstructed form of the two fragments of no. 36 remains uncertain. Certainly the thick wall of the coarse ware vessel rises in a dome. The lower section of the vessel is horizontal and perhaps worked to provide a base for the dome, though the dimensions and form of this base remain unclear.[200] The walls and the lower zone are uneven and this creates difficulties with

197 For a rare decorated pithos of Hellenistic date see: Boggess 1970, 73-78.

198 Edwards 1975 p. 105 ff; note the profiles do not compare closely.

199 Although not identical in shape there are some comparisons to be drawn between P 3310 from the Athenian Agora, Rotroff 2004, p. 458, pl. 204a. Both have broad bucket bodies and spouts, though the Chalkis example does not have the careful pouring spout of the Agora example but had, instead a narrower rim.

200 In its current form the outer edge of the dome 'base' is squared and so does not correspond at all with the circumference of the dome. It is likely that this represents a break and not the finished form, though given the coarse fabric and manufacture it is difficult to qualify this.

interpretation. The vessel form shows enough similarities with extant examples from other sites to suggest that it may have been used for food preparation, acting as a cover for food during the cooking stages, a kind of portable oven.[201] However, it is possible the ceramic object may have had an, as yet unidentified, industrial use.

Mortar

A mortar is identified in the fragment no. 14. This base has a diameter of 21 cm. The fabric does not hold the quantity of large inclusions that other coarse ware fragments have. The foot is broad and flat. The inner foot is only just set off from the floor of the basin.[202] The wall rises smoothly allowing a shallow, broad vessel to be reconstructed.

Louterion

Louteria are broad and shallow basins, characterized by their sizeable and often elaborately moulded rims. The basins sat on high stands, elevating the vessels. A louterion could function in a ritual context, holding sanctified water and/or providing for ritual bathing. It could also function within a household for bathing and for other water-related activities. Clay models show this vessel type to function without water instead providing a food preparation surface.[203]

The louteria from Chalkis can be divided into the two groups of ritual and household use. The ritual examples, nos. 82 and 83, are imported. They have a pale fabric, of a yellowish-pink (Munsel 'very pale brown) colour. The upper rim and inner surface of the bowl is smoothed with a fine clay that masks the coarse fabric. The rims have a broad upper surface that, on one edge, leads to the smooth, shallow curve of the bowl and, on the other, to a horizontal overhang that carries moulded bands. On no. 83 the moulding consists of a series of evenly spaced ridges with concave bands between. On the smaller no. 82, the moulding is more elaborate with two groups of three ridges and a broad band between. Red paint is preserved on the third ridge and between it and the second. These pieces fit with descriptions of the shape in 5th century Corinthian production and are likely to be imported from there.[204] Both of these two fragments are found in zone IV, between the Archaic/Classical terrace wall and the wall of the rooms, and it seems probable that both fragments are from vessels that were originally placed on the Acropolis and were used for ritual purposes.

The other louteria from the complex of rooms are of a more solid construction and lack the fine finish of nos. 82 and 83. Their fabric is similar to that of the pithoi described above, and it is thought to be local. No. 255 has a broad upper face, only the lower section is overhung, the upper zones are solid, making this a heavy vessel. The rim is decorated with two sets of ridges separated by a central recessed zone. On the lower edge of the outer rim are set a series of impressed dentils (short vertical line). This fragment is quite worn. No. 25 is better preserved. It too has a broad flat upper face. The wall of the basin meets this upper face at a sharp junction. The outer face is moulded and the lower half is overhung. Four ridges decorate the upper and mid-outer face with deep grooves between. On the lower edge the outer face carries an impressed garland of elongated leaves (olive or the like). No. 221 offers a variation on the form. Here the rim does not project but is thickened from the curve of the wall. The upper face is flat and the outer face is moulded, again with ridges and recessed zones. This outer face is inclined and runs into the outer wall. All these fragments come from deposits within the houses and under the tile smashes, allowing for a secular use.

201 Sparkes and Talcott 1970, nos. 2021 and 2022, fig. 19, though neither of these have the squared resting surface of the Chalkis example.

202 This foot type is seen Sparkes and Talcott 1970, no. 1898, fig. 16, though no. 14 has an outer profile more as no. 1907, fig. 16.

203 Sparkes and Talcott 1970, p. 218, note the terracotta figurines of bread-making occurring in such broad, shallow basins. The basin is elevated to waist level by the stand, providing a convenient bench.

204 Sparkes and Talcott 1970, nos. 1859-1861, p. 219-220, fig. 16. Dated 480-470, 430-415, late 4th century context.

MINIATURE VESSELS

The majority of the miniatures from the area come from the Archaic-rich deposits of room VIII and date to the Archaic period.[205]

No. 263 from room XI may be a miniature krater. It is coarsely made. It has a coarse base with a wall rising up above it to an irregular-shaped bowl. It feels moulded and certainly not wheel made. It is not properly fired. The fabric looks and feels like that of the figurines found in the area.

No. 59 is the only definite Hellenistic miniature from the complex of rooms.[206] The black glaze, the characteristic local Hellenistic fabric and the form support the date. It represents a bowl, with an incurving wall and a folded rim. Glaze covers the exterior and part of the interior wall.

DECORATED CERAMICS

Red figure

There are four pieces of red figure found within the rooms. All examples are imported.

Two appear to be from the same vessel. Nos. 106 and 117 are from a krater with rounded rim. They both preserve the same subsidiary motif, of short thick vertical lines alternating with thin vertical lines. A thick horizontal line provides a border for the motif, and, in both cases, a grooved articulation of the vessel follows. These pieces find comparison with examples from the Athenian Agora that date between 480-440 BC. Column kraters are the most common recipient in Athens of this so-called tongue pattern, but it is also recorded on a loutrophoros and a stamnos.[207]

Another red figure fragment, this time preserving a small section of the figure, is no. 201. It was found during the cleaning of wall *ADB* in room X. A hand can be identified and it appears to touch, but not grasp, a tubular object. Small sections of drapery are also identified.

The best-preserved piece of red figure is the owl skyphos, no. 288. The owl itself is not preserved, but one of the characteristic flanking olive branches is. These cups are produced in Athens from the second quarter of the 5th century to the end of the century.[208] Owl skyphoi were also produced in South Italy, but it is believed that the Chalkis example is Attic.[209]

WEST SLOPE WARE

The West Slope ware from Chalkis appears predominantly on drinking cups, though plates and toiletry vessels are also represented. Local and imported examples of this decorated fine ware group are found. The West Slope material from Chalkis belongs predominantly to the 3rd century. A few fragments may push back into the last decade of the 4th century, but there is nothing that, through comparison, dates beyond 200 BC.

There is one Classical kantharos, no. 209, that holds the edge of an incised stem. The glaze and the incision used to form the motif suggest that the piece belongs to the 3rd century.

The most popular drinking cup at Chalkis, the one piece kantharos, is also the most common recipient of West Slope decoration (nos. 42 (fugitive?), 87, 248, 235, 248, 249, 285, and 289). Painted, or painted-and-incised decoration decorates the upper wall. Often the decorative zone is defined by incised grooves, but on occasion, as on no. 87, the decoration is not presented in a frame. Incised ivy stems are preserved on no. 87. Slightly more elaborate are the elegant, elongated ivy stems of no. 249, with fugitive tripartite leaves set on their ends. More solid, tripartite leaves are preserved in shadow on no. 285. Here, rather than an incised stem, a painted undulating ribbon is partially preserved, curling between the leaves. No. 289 has a geometric bead and reel motif painted between grooves. Set below the rim and groove of no. 248 is an incised

205 The Archaic miniatures compare to Stillwell and Benson 1984, nos. 1769-1772, pl. 68.

206 For a collection of Hellenistic miniatures from Ambrakias, see, Andreou & Andreou 1997, pls. 149-156.

207 Moore 1997, loutrophoros, no. 78, p. 145-146, pl. 15; stamnos, no. 115, p. 150, pl. 19 (closest in painterly qualities to the Chalkis piece); column kraters, nos. 175-178 and 180-182, p. 161-162, pls. 26-27.

208 Moore 1997, nos. 1313-1322, p. 64, pls. 122-123; For closer study of the groups within these skyphoi see: Johnson 1955; Johnson 1953.

209 For an analysis of Attic and South Italian productions of vessels with owl motifs see Schauenberg 1988.

suspended line with a short tassel (or tie) set at its upper edge. This could be reconstructed as a spearhead necklace or similar pattern. A spearhead necklace is preserved on the angular kantharos fragment no. 266. Here the pendants appear suspended from the groove that marks the rim from the wall. No. 88, a straight walled katharos fragment, has incised ivy tendrils.

The conical bowl (nos. 193, 204 and 291) is produced in the first half of the 3rd century, but gains in popularity in the second half of the century. It often appears with West Slope decoration. Again incised grooves are used to define the shape. A combination of paint and incision is used on all examples. No. 291 is the most complete example of this shape. It carries rather broad incisions forming an elongated leaves motif on its rim, interrupted by a lattice wreath. Approaching the floor is a second zone of decoration, bordered by grooves, this time a wreath scrolling, intersecting stems and dot rosettes. No. 204 carries incised and painted wheat motif. This motif is less common than others on the site and can be linked to Corinthian production (see p. 113 conical bowl). The decoration on no. 193 is fugitive. The hemispherical bowl no. 164 holds a range of closely set but fugitive motifs. A spearhead necklace and elongated leaves are discernable.

Fine West Slope decoration is preserved on the plate with offset rim no. 183. Ridges define the decorative zone. Here the short scrolling and branching stems of an ivy wreath are incised through the glaze on the convex surface of the rim. Fugitive heart-shaped ivy leaves perch on the ends of tendrils. The unusual bowl/cup with out-turned rim, no. 32, is decorated with an ivy wreath with fine scrolling stems. The leaves are fugitive and now appear only as dots.

A guttus no. 153 holds a small, incised tendril, likely to be part of an ivy wreath.

The most impressive example of West Slope decoration at Chalkis decorates the reversible lid no. 323. This lid carries five different motifs on its wall and knob. Running around the outer circumference of the lid is the checkerboard, which is incised and painted, and alternates with incised concentric rectangles. Above this is an incised and painted egg and dart pattern, the darts painted tripartite leaves and the eggs formed by double incised lines with a central painted dot. Before the knob is a spearhead necklace with incised arcing chain and somewhat blobby pendants in yellow paint. On the lid a star flower motif is preserved. There are two other fragments of decorated reversible lids: no. 324 also carries an egg and dart, though here the darts are simple incised lines; and no. 8 preserves an outer band of lattice bordering a wreath with scrolling stems.

Of the fragments from unidentified shapes, no. 233 preserve the incised tendrils of an ivy garland. No. 202, however, adds another motif to the list, a scrolling wave pattern. The outline of the wave is incised.

The West Slope ware examples are predominantly imported to the site, and vary in their origin. The conical bowl, no. 204 is probably Corinthian. The other imports are of a mixed and uncertain origin. There are some local examples (nos. 42, 87, 153, 243 and 289), which allow ivy, bead and reel and the spearhead necklace to be counted as local motifs. The regional range is much greater, particularly boosted by the motifs on nos. 323 and 291. No. 324 is also counted amongst this regional group.

IMPRESSED DECORATION

Decoration that is impressed into the surface of the vessel is represented in both fine and coarse wares at Chalkis. The following focuses only on ceramics with decoration, for discussion of the stamps and incised decoration of loom weights see below.

Fine ware fragments with impressed decoration are not numerous in the houses at Chalkis. Common in the Classical period, the tradition of decorating black glaze vessel with stamps and other impressions, such as rouletting, falls out of common practice in the Hellenistic period. The examples found in the rooms at Chalkis are few in number and demonstrate the low number and limited variety of Classical material amongst the largely Hellenistic (and in Room VIII, Archaic) deposits excavated. Rouletting is preserved on no. 91, and the edge of a stamped palmette is visible. Rouletting, set between double incised lines, is preserved on the floor fragment of a thick walled plate, no. 104. The thin-walled plate fragment, no. 107, is decorated with a series of double lines that radiate using the centre of the plate as a (conceptual or actual?) mid-point. The plate no. 90 is more elaborate and preserves impressed arcs that surround the tondo, the arcs are open to the rim. Incised concentric circles at the centre provide further decoration. On the kantharos fragment no. 301, impressed decoration attempts to achieve the appearance of moulded ribbing.

The one piece kantharos, no. 210, carries horizontal ribbing on the outer lower wall. This would be achieved whilst the pot was still on the wheel: a hard, sharp object is held against the surface of the pot to create fine grooves. This technique would also have been used to produce the grooves on the upper body of kantharoi to define decorative zones, as well as the grooves on rims of plates and the like. On no. 210, though, the grooves are set close together to create a textured and subtle decoration.

The finest decoration on a coarse ware vessel is on the louterion rim no. 25, where, beneath the moulding typical of the shape, runs an impressed garland of elongated leaves (olive or myrtle). Another louterion fragment, no. 255, has vertical impressions that imitate architectural dentils. These are set below the horizontal moulding on the exterior face of the rim. The pithos fragment, no. 286, has a more freehand impressed decoration of at least three bands of incised zigzag below a thick, undecorated relief band.

GRAFFITI

Two plates carry graffiti. No. 287, a Classical plate, carries part of what may be restored as a 'Σ' under the foot. The rilled rim plate, no. 149 has an incised 'X' that is placed on the upper exterior wall, below the groove that marks the rim to wall junction and beside the drilled hole.

LAMPS

The lamps from the rooms at Chalkis are neither frequent nor well-preserved. The lamp fragments are found in rooms II, IV, V, X and XV.[210] They are of varied fabric. Some are locally made, their fabric corresponding to the local fine ware. Others are clearly imported. The lamps belong to the 4th and 3rd centuries.[211]

Classical lamps

The Classical lamps from the rooms fall into three groups. The first group consist of nos. 206 and 99, which are both from shallow-bodied lamps. Group 3, nos. 219 and 223, have deeper bodies and a more articulated form and provide a prototype for a number of the Hellenistic lamps (Group 4). No. 12, group 2, introduces a different form, with the broad body of the first group, but a depth common with the third group. The order groups 1-3 correspond to a likely chronology.

Only two of the lamps are potentially of the local production, nos. 99 and 223. They date to the 4th century. Others are imported from varied sources; no. 206 could be Corinthian.

Group 1

The imported no. 206 has a very shallow body and short nozzle. The unarticulated rim allows comparison with Isthmia no. 61, of type IVB, a long serving form that reaches into the 4th century BC.

Another Classical lamp comes from the lower levels of IV, no. 99. The nozzle and a section of the rim is preserved. The nozzle is broad and quite flat. It corresponds to *Isthmia* type V (*Agora* type 20), though appears to be of local production.

Group 2

The fragment no. 121 preserves the nozzle and a section of wall and rim. The nozzle is quite long. The flat upper face of the nozzle runs directly into the upper wall. The diameter of the body of this lamp is quite broad though shallow. It shares something of the form of *Isthmia* 83 (type V), though without the groove on the rim, like *Agora* IV 24A. A date in the second half of the 4th century is likely for this imported example.

210 One nozzle from the area outside room V is of uncertain type so is not discussed in detail. There are no lamp fragments found in rooms I, VIII and XI.

211 For dating the lamps, I have used Broneer 1977 in comparison with Howland 1958. To realign the dates to a more recent understanding of chronology I have used Rotroff 1997 pp. 493 ff.

Group 3

No. 222 provides the foot to rim profile of an imported lamp from room X. The foot is a raised disc and is set off from the wall by a deep groove. The wall is convex, with a fairly low maximum diameter. The rim and wall junction is marked by a light groove. The rim has a bevelled upper face, so that it appears to be hanging into the body of the lamp. Glaze (a mottled brownish black) coats all surfaces. The profile compares to type VI, *Isthmia*, no. 86 (*Agora* IV type 23 C).

The nozzle no. 223 from the same room is from a similar lamp. The nozzle increases in width at the wick hole, broadening from the narrow centre and equalled by the width of the nozzle at the wall. This example could be locally made.

HELLENISTIC LAMPS

The majority of the Hellenistic lamps are of the same type (group 4), but there is noticeable variation, and development within the group. These examples are found in rooms II, V and XV. They correspond to *Isthmia* type VII A and C, which date from the 4th to the 3rd century. In addition to this there is one Hellenistic lamp of a "lagynos type" profile,[212] no. 332 from Room XV, here Group 5.

Group 4

No. 334 is possibly the earliest of this group.[213] It retains some of the curvature of wall found in the Classical lamps of Group 3, though the maximum diameter has risen creating a squarer form. The rim is inset, defined from the incurving wall by a deep groove. An attached V-shaped handle is preserved on the upper wall. This example appears to be local.

No. 122 provides a squarer, yet comparable, profile.[214] This comparison of form, suggests no. 122 dates slightly later than no. 334. The horizontal rim is set inside the wall and the junction of the two is marked by a groove on the upper face of the rim.The wall is set at a right angle from the rim and has only a slight convexity. Again this lamp is of local fabric.

Another example of this form, though not from a secure context, is the imported no. 302. This lamp is fuller in profile. The rim is not inset, but is distinguished from the wall by a light groove. The maximum diameter is low, and the wall is inclined to the rim. The disc foot is solid with a convex inner profile.

No. 333 is a nozzle fragment that has the required height for such lamps. It is short and blunt with an angular lower profile and a flat upper face.

No. 60 is the latest of the type.[215] It was found within room II. The profile of the body is trapezoidal. The floor is a flat disc that is not differentiated from the lower wall. The wall is inclined. The horizontal rim is recessed so that the wall rises above to create a ridge. The nozzle is long and narrows as it approaches the wick hole. The fabric corresponds to the local wares.

Group 5

The upper wall and rim of no. 332 preserves another type of lamp. No. 332 shares both the form and the pale buff fabric of a group of lamps from Isthmia, identified as Corinthian.[216] The rim creates a narrow circular opening. Two light grooves distinguish the rim from the wall that curves smoothly out to a broad body. Most often these examples do not carry slip. On no. 332 there are remnants of a thin brown slip along with some white patches that may be incrustation or slip.[217]

LOOM WEIGHTS

Loom weights are a common find in the Hellenistic rooms of Chalkis. Those that are discussed here are from deposits that are associated with use phases, un-

212 Howland 1958, type 29 A and B. p. 94-97.

213 Broneer 1977, no. 109, type VIIa. Very similar but small fragment from *ADZ bag 926*.

214 Broneer 1977, p. 119, type VII C, 4th to 3rd century.

215 Compare with Broneer 1977, no. 125, Type VII C, 3rd century.

216 It compares with Broneer 1977, p. 214, type IXB 300-250 (*Agora* 28A and B, 300-190). This shape is found in the blister ware with dark grey and pink colouring, this is not one of those.

217 Howland 1958, p. 95, suggestion that type 28 A was made in the lagynos workshops.If the white matter on no. 332 is slip, one can draw a closer connection between the lamp type and the production of lagynoi.

less otherwise specified.[218] There are numerous examples from the fill of the strata above the destruction levels that will not concern us here. Given the difficulty dating loom weights, particularly without clear, local stratigraphic indicators, it remains possible that some of the loom weights presented here are earlier than the 4th and 3rd century. When viewing a compilation of the weights, four different sizes can be identified, small, medium, large and grand. Small loom weights weigh between 40-75 grams, medium weight between 75-130 grams, large between 130-230 grams and grand between 230-340 grams. These categories are defined by the weight of the complete examples.

There are three different categories of loom weight identified. Type 1 is the conical loom weight with circular base and walls that rises to a central point, often rounded. A single suspension hole is drilled toward the top of the loom weight. Type 2 is a pyramidal loom weight with a relatively square base and four faces of approximately equal width rising to a narrow rounded, or flat, top. A single suspension hole is drilled toward the top of the loom weight. Type 3 is also a pyramidal loom weight but has a rectangular base with two sides longer than the other two. This creates walls that are of unequal width, with two broad, and two narrow, that rise to a flat rectangular top. Two suspension holes are placed below the top of the weight. Type 2 is the most common, followed by type 1 and then by type 3.

There are thirteen example of type 1, the conical loom weight, though three of these do not preserve the full profile or weight.[219] Those that do, give a height range between 5.45 and 10.2 cm. Their weight ranges from 68 to 219 grams and so cover the small to large range. Some have a bevelled lower edge.[220] Most have a pointed top, but nos. 62 and 175 have a rounded top. All carry a single drilled hole. None are stamped. They appear in rooms I, II, V, VI, VIII, IX, X and XIII. They are always outnumbered by pyramidal loom weights, except when they appear in a deposit on their own (as in XIII (T27N/4d), VI (O27 zone II/3) and in the drain within room I (O26BD *ADM*)).

The most common loom weight at Chalkis is the type 2 pyramidal loom weight. There are 44 type 2 loom weights. Type 2 loom weights belong to small, medium, large and grand categories. The small examples are 5.5-7 cm. in height. There are fifteen examples of this type.[221] They appear in rooms I, III, IV, V, VIII, X, XIV. The examples have a tendency to have quite sharp edges, but no. 176 from Room VIII (T30D/7) has rounded edges. One carries stamps on all four walls, no. 182. No. 299 has a stamp on its top face. More frequent are incised marks: nos. 227 and 234 carry incised crosses; No. 100 has an incised border around one face. There are five loom weights of this type that are remarkably similar.[222] Three of them appear together in the same deposit in room XIV (T6NA/5e), the only loom weights in the deposit,[223]the others are in room V and room X. These five loom weights are from Hellenistic deposits.

Two small and unusual loom weights are from room VIII. No. 182 with stamps on all faces this comes from *ATX*, the drain in VIII that contains ceramics of the Archaic, and earlier, periods. Similarly the loom weight with rounded edge, no. 176, is from stratum 7 of this room, a deposit with predominantly Archaic ceramics.

There are twelve medium sized type 2 loom weights. They have a height range of 6.35-8.1 cm., which overlaps with the small examples. The weight of these examples ranges from 80 to 126 grams, though most fall between the 80-105 gram range. These loom weights vary in their form and their fabric. Four examples have softened corners and rounded tops.[224]Two loom weights have rather narrow bases with comparatively

218 Room I: O26BD/3, *AEV, ADM*; Room II: O26/3, O27/3, *AEP*; Zone III O27/3; Room IV: *ACZ-ADY/5*; Room V: O27/3; Zone VI: O27 zone II/3; *AGD*; Room VIII: T30/5, T30/7, *ATX*, T30/8; Zone IX: T31/4; Room X: T28/5, T28/6, *ATD*; Zone XII: T29/5; Room XI: *AFQ*; Zone XIII: T27N/4d, T6NA/5d; Room XIV: T27N/3, T6NA/5e.

219 Nos. 37, 61, 62, 123, 174, 175, 197, 224 and 225; fragmentary: nos. 139, 273 and 160. Although no. 197 displays a whole profile, it is too chipped for the weight to be included in the statistics.

220 Nos. 123, 174, 224 and 225.

221 Nos. 15, 78, 100, 130, 131, 132, 161, 176, 182, 226, 227, 234, 298, 299 and 300.

222 Unglazed: nos. 298 and 299. Glazed: nos. 132, 226 and 300.

223 Nos. 298, 299 and 300.

224 Nos. 16, 65, 73 and 207. The fragment no. 177 should also be classed in this group.

tall, though uneven walls, angular corners and a flattish top,[225] a fourth has a broader base but is otherwise comparable.[226] The remaining four are made of a fabric that is close to the local cooking pot ware.[227] They have square bases with defined but not sharp corners and horizontal but not flat tops. Two of this group were found together and carry the same stamp.[228] The medium sized loom weights are found in I, II (5 examples), IX, VIII (2 examples), X and XI (*AFQ*). Apart from the pair in bag 2192 (nos. 63 and 64), the comparable examples discussed in this paragraph are scattered through different contexts. Eight of the twelve medium loom weights have distinctive marks (stamps or incision) on their faces. Circular stamps: nos. 16 and 73; '+' incision: nos. 65, 66 and 246; 'Λ' incision: no. 177; flower stamp: nos. 63 and 64.

The large type 2 loom weights number twelve.[229] They range in height from 7.6-9 cm. and in weight from 144-209 grams. Six of the examples carry marks; only one has a stamp (no. 101), two have incised an incised 'A' on a face (nos 18 and 67), another a rough '+' (no. 29), two have drilled holes, one on the top (no. 178) and the other on the bottom (no. 17) of the weight. The majority have broad bases and soft corners, though no. 208 is more angular. The form of the top varies from broad and flat to an almost pointed face. No. 179 stands out from this group, it is more narrow and tall. The large type 2 loom weights are found in room I (3 examples), II, IV, VIII (4 examples) and X (3 examples).

The grand type 2 loom weights are a small group numbering only four, one of which is quite fragmentary.[230] They range in height from 8.35 to 11.2 cm. and in weight from 238-337 grams. They each come from a different AREA I, III, XII, XIV. The incomplete no. 79 has a circular stamp and a rough oval stamp is found on no. 30. A neat omega, placed at the height of the drilled hole on a non-drilled face, distinguishes no. 284.

There are seven type 3 loom weights.[231] Six of them are closely related, with a height range of 6.56-7.2 cm. and a weight ranging between 98-126 grams (this weight equates to the medium group). These examples have a rectangular base and top and angular junctions, only no. 134 shows softer angles between the faces. No. 141 represents a variation of the type. It is taller (9.35 cm.) and broader than the others with a weight of 247 grams. While the base is rectangular the top is curved. All have two drilled holes through the top, except for no. 282 which has no suspension holes. Three have distinctive markings: no. 20 carries a deep triangular impression; no. 21 carries a rosette stamp; and no. 282 is decorated with an oval stamp on one broad face and two impressions (that appear to be the result of an index finger and thumb pinching the clay) on the other broad face. These weights are found in I (3 examples), V (2 examples), VI and XIII.

Decoration

As has been noted, some of these loom weights carry identifying marks. There are seventeen impressed stamps preserved on thirteen loom weights. No. 20 has a deep triangular impression on the mid wall. On no. 79 and on one face of no. 30 a circular impression is left, on no. 16 three of these disc-impressions overlap. A more elaborate impression is found on all four faces of no. 182, where the disc is adorned with a central impressed dot. Nos. 30, 101 and 282, carry an oval impression. These, and no. 282 especially, may have carried more detailed decoration now worn away (no. 282 has a deep pinched impression on the other side). No. 73 has a deep ring impressed on one face, with the centre of the circle almost at the level of the weight face. More elaborate are the stamps on nos. 21, 63 and 64. These three stamps have a circular border with a many-petalled rosette set within. No. 299 has a series of impressed dots on its upper face that form a circle.

No. 284 preserves an omega stamp. This stamp is unusual as it is placed on the non-drilled face of the weight, and on the upper wall of the weight (a feature shared with both stamps on no. 30; all other stamps

225 Nos. 66 and 198.
226 No. 246.
227 Nos 63, 64, 190 and 191.
228 Nos. 63 and 64.
229 Nos. 17, 18, 29, 67, 101, 162, 163, 178, 179, 208, 228 and 229.
230 Nos. 30, 79, 241, 289.
231 Nos. 19, 20, 21, 133, 134, 141 and 282.

sit on the mid- to lower wall). When the weight was suspended the omega would be upside down. No. 241 has a stamp on the lower wall. It consists of two facing hooks that are conjoined. The hooks connect with the rather irregular, triangular border of the stamp. Nos. 17 and 178 have an impressed dot; no. 178 carries this on the top of the weight and no. 17 on the bottom.

Thirteen loom weights have marks on them that have been created by scraping the surface of the weight, i.e. incised decoration. Five of these are incised '+'s. On four examples the incision is placed on the lower wall of a drilled face.[232] On no. 246 and on no. 66 (its second incision) the '+' quarters the upper face of the weight. On no. 29 a rather irregular '+' is placed on the lower wall of one of the un-drilled faces. There are also examples of an incised 'A'. No. 67 carries an 'A' on its lower face, and a similar mark is partially preserved on the fragmentary no. 177. No. 18 is marked by a large 'A' that covers one un-drilled face. On one drilled face of no. 100, a thin line provides a border around the weight, set 0.3-0.5 cm from the edge of the face.

Use

The loom weights in rooms II, V, X and VIII are plentiful enough to discuss the combination of the loom weights found. However, each of these deposits has between six and twelve looms each, not, in themselves, enough for a full sized loom.[233]

It is noticeable when examining the weight of the examples in each of the rooms, regardless of category, that there is quite a balanced distribution. In room II, four medium loom weights are balanced by three large loom weights. In room VIII three small and three medium loom weights are set against six large. In room X there are four small and four large, joined by one medium.

In rooms II, VIII and X, the type 3 loom weight and the loom weight of grand weight is absent. Room V offers a different assemblage, where the type 3 loom weights are found and there is a low count of the larger loom weight groups. Here there are a total of six loom weights found. Two are of the type 3 form, one is conical and the three others are of type 2. The assemblage is still balanced with three small, two medium and one large. Room I has the type 2 and 3 loom weights but displays less balance in size, there is only one small, four medium and two large. A large and a grand example are found in the pit *AEP*.

OTHER WEAVING ITEMS

Spindle whorls

Two spindle whorls were found during the excavation of the rooms. One, no. 102, is from IV, the other, no. 180, from VIII. No. 102 is the larger of the two and weighs 47 grams. No. 180 weighs only 13 grams.

Spools

One spool is found, located in room X, along with nine loom weights. The spool, no. 230, stands at 3.75 cm in height.

FIGURINES

Figurines are rare within the Hellenistic rooms at Chalkis, though their presence on the site is attested in the Hellenistic grave GR3.[234] A series of drapery fragments that issue from the one figurine, were excavated within room XV, no. 313. The fragments are typical of 3rd century figurines. There is some white paint preserved on the fragments. In room V, a face of a figurine, quite worn, was discovered, no. 124. This female figure has her hair parted in the centre and wears a polos headdress. The face has been made in a mould, it is hollow, and the unworked side is rough. She dates to the 3rd century.[235] Two fragments of another figurine, were found in Room II, no. 68. One is of a small section of drapery, the other is very battered but maintains the form of a head and face.

232 Nos. 65, 66, 227 and 234.

233 Cahill 2002, p. 173; The finds from Olynthos suggest 20-40 loom weights were required per loom.

234 Eiring 2004.

235 Compare no. 124 with Davidson 1952, no. 260-261, 3rd century.

VARIOUS

Kiln objects

There are four roughly formed pieces of clay that could have functioned as kiln furniture, and thus provide some evidence (if out of context) for manufacture of ceramics or terracottas on site. They share irregular forms and often flattened faces set at angular junctions. No. 189 from room VIII has been placed over the 90 degree corner of a hard surface and pressed down while held between thumb, index and middle finger. No. 242 holds three finger impressions on an uneven faces, opposite two flat faces. Nos. 147 and 148 have also been pressed down over a corner. These last two come from a post-destruction level above room VIII.

Reworked sherds

Two reworked sherds have been identified, but they are quite different from one another. No. 135 displays the circular disc form, which is a common reshaped form. The other, no. 103, an amphora fragment of distinctive fabric, has been given a sharp, serrated edge.

UNIDENTIFIED

No. 69 at first glance could be mistaken for a type 2 (pyramidal) loom weight. On closer inspection, one notes that it lacks a drilled hole, and while this is also noted for the type 3 loom weight no. 282, no. 69 diverges further from the loom weight as the walls rise at uneven angles and the top is very narrow. The object has a more rectangular base than is typical of a type 2 loom weight and the two broad faces created by this are quite different in profile, one is flat and rises almost vertically, the other is slightly concave and is inclined to meet the other face at the pointed top. It appears that the object was designed to sit on its broad vertical (therefore horizontal) face and would act best as a wedge rather than a weight.

No. 181 is quite unusual, and its use, as yet, unidentified. Two faces are triangular in form, with smooth rounded edges, rather like a pyramidal loom weight. It is a flat strip of clay, however, with a slight bend as it lengthens (it looks somewhat like a long tongue). It shares the form of a stone axe head. This piece was found in room VIII.

CONCLUSION

The eight rooms and adjacent areas under examination in this report were constructed, or at least redeveloped, in the late 4th to early 3rd century BC. Pottery finds on the bedrock and at the base of the walls constructed in the area form the evidence for this proposal. The area had seen activity in other periods. Prehistoric, Archaic and Classical material is scattered throughout the Hellenistic deposits. Archaic and Classical material is found deposited above bedrock in rooms II and V, a possible redepositing of material to produce an even floor for the new rooms. More intensive Archaic occupation is reflected in room VIII, where largely undisturbed Archaic ceramics are preserved surrounding the platform *ATE*. This evidence points to an Archaic shrine that was left largely undisturbed, and possibly protected by wall and roof reconstruction, when the surrounding area was reoccupied in the late 4th century. The presence of occasional Hellenistic pottery and rather frequent Hellenistic coins (17 in total) suggests that 3rd century activity did occur beside, but did not disturb, the Archaic shrine.

The area was occupied until the end of the 3rd century. Clear tile layers document the collapse and destruction of the rooms. This destruction appears to have occurred at much the same time across the rooms and was concurrent with the abandonment of the site. Ceramic, lamp and coin finds can rarely be dated into the 2nd century and the abandonment of the town can be secured to the late 3rd century. What caused this abandonment is uncertain, though the political and economic reformation of the period, and the reconcentration of power, may have changed trading practices and affected the vitality of a small outpost.

The kiln objects found in zone XIII indicate that during the late 4th and 3rd centuries, pottery was produced at, or near, the settlement. This material follows the regional trends of Aitolia and broader Central Greece. Pottery is also imported to the site from a variety of productions, both those from the immediate region, and from further a field; products of Attic and Corinthian workshops are identified. The ceramics have been used to provide the chronology of the area, but they also reveal the use of the rooms and the activities of the people who inhabited them.

Religious activity in the area is not clearly reflected in the Hellenistic finds, though the position of the rooms beneath the Acropolis, the religious tradition of the area (i.e. Archaic shrine in VIII), and the mix of finds cannot rule this out completely. The thymiaterion in room II is the only certain ritual object from the area.

Food preparation and production occurred in the area. Cooking pot ware is found in quantity in rooms II, X, XIV and XV along with fire places. There is little cooking pot ware in I, apart from the material in pit *AEV*, another fire place. Little cooking pot ware is found in V and only a scatter is found across the Archaic deposits in VIII. Only worn cooking pot ware is recovered from XI. The broad spouted vessel in II along with a grindstone in XI, *ATL*, indicate some manufacturing of food occurred in the area. The less decorative louteria may also be food preparation vessels, these are found in rooms I, X and XI.

The storage of foodstuffs in the area is indicated by the pithoi. Fragments found in room II indicate two pithoi located within the room. Pithos fragments in XI and XV indicate storage in these areas. The pithos fragments in XII and the 6th century pithos fragment in room XIV may be residual. Room XIV appears to have been a store for materials used within room XV. A stack of tiles found within this room is of interest. Room XI contained a number of amphorae of different origins.

The concentration and preservation of dining wares is found in rooms II, V, X, XIV and XV (though fragmentary). Material for the preparation and consumption of food and drink is located within the same rooms. The fine wares are typical for the region and the period, with Hellenistic one piece kantharoi, echinus bowls and varied plates with shallow bowl bodies predominate. Room XV also held the impressive toiletry item, the reversible lid.

Rooms II, V and X are also the rooms that preserve lamp fragments. And loom weights were found in concentrated number in II, V, X and VIII.

CATALOGUE

Explanation of catalogue

Paradigma:
Cat no. Name of shape (Figure and Plate numbers in this volume)
Excavated Bag no.: Sherd/Object no. (e.g. 2248: 1)
Context (e.g. O26BD/3).
FABRIC: Description of clay following Sanders, G.D.R. 1999, "A Late Roman Bath at Corinth: Excavations in the Panayia Field, 199 -199 ", *Hesperia* 68, 477-478. Munsell colour. SURFACE: Description of glaze/coating/decoration. DESCRIPTION: Preservation. Appearance. Decoration.
Measurements
COMMENTS:
DATE:

ABBREVIATIONS:

FW = Fine ware
PW = Plain ware
CPW = Cooking pot ware
CW = Coarse ware

Room I

Stratum 3 was located underneath the rubble and was excavated to bedrock. Material in this layer is linked to the occupation of the houses, appearing, as it does, beneath the destruction deposits. The ceramic material consists of a large amount of medium ware, including a quantity of amphora fragments. The hollow toe fragment no. 10 of local manufacture is one of these amphora fragments. There was a low occurrence of cooking pot wares in the deposit.[236] The coarse ware vessels include no. 13, a lid, too small for a full-sized pithos, though presumably from a similar storage vessel, and the base of a mortar, no. 14. Notable is the absence of lamps and lamp fragments in this deposit.

The fine ware was numerous but the fragments generally small. Many of the fine wares are dining

236 Two fragments from the deposit are in the catalogue: Chytra **no. 11** and the lid **no. 12.**

vessels including plates, bowls, cups and one pouring vessel (nos. 1-7). In addition to the Corinthian-like skyphos these include two Classical versions of shapes common in the Hellenistic assemblage: the plate with rolled rim, no. 3, and the large echinus bowl, no. 5. Hellenistic shapes include no. 2, the one-piece kantharos with spur-handle, the deep and straight-walled bowl no. 6 (which represents a late 3rd century development of the echinus bowl), and the plate with offset rim no. 4. No. 7 is a rim fragment from a table amphora. Two toiletry vessels, a pyxis no. 9, and a fragment of a reversible lid with West Slope decoration, no. 10, broaden the assemblage. The fine wares suggest the use of room I spans the late 4th and 3rd century.

In addition to the ceramics, seven loom weights were found within stratum 3. They are all pyramidal. Three have rectangular bases and two drilled holes in the broad upper face (type 3), nos. 19-21. The rest have single drilled holes (type 2 – one small, one medium and two large), nos. 15-18. These four cluster within the room, set to either side of the break in wall *AFN*. Three carry stamps or other distinguishing marks: nos. 16, 20 and 21.

A dark deposit, called *AEV*, is located near wall *AEA* before the wall meets the baulk. It most likely represents a pit.[237] The vessels in this deposit are generally better preserved than those in stratum 3, and include some near-complete vessels. A marked increase in cooking ware fragments indicates the different make-up of *AEV* compared to stratum 3. One of these is no. 26, rim and body fragments from a Hellenistic chytra, no. 27, a chytra with a projecting rim, and the lopas no. 28. The deposit has a range of fine ware and plain ware sherds. The fine ware includes the one-handler no. 22, the jug no. 24 and the plate with rolled rim no. 23. There were also spur handle fragments. The louterion fragment with garland decoration, no. 25, was located within this darker deposit. There are two (type 2) pyramidal loom weights (nos. 29, 30), one large, one grand. No. 30 is decorated with a stamp. Again there are no lamps in this room.

The range of material within the channel *ADM* is very similar to that within the room itself. Again there is a quantity of medium ware, including the Corinthian Type B amphora toe no. 34. A lid, no. 35, is a rare example of cooking ware in the deposit. Two joining fragments of an unusual coarse ware vessel, no. 36, were excavated.[238] The object has a domed wall and a projecting section, perhaps a resting surface. This object has been interpreted as a cooking dome. It is possible, though, that in this context the objects actual function was to cover the drain alongside the tiles. Fine wares within the channel include an imported rim of a bowl with West Slope decoration no. 32, a red-glazed handle and wall of a dipper no. 33 and a large echinus bowl with a groove on the outer rim no. 31. A very similar bowl to no. 31 was found in association with one of the tiles (*AET*), no. 38 (again securing a 3rd century date for the deposit). A type 1 loom weight in *ADM*, no. 37, stands apart from those found in stratum 3, given that it is conical in form and may indicate earlier activity in the area. A deposit called *AEA*-1, with tiles and associated ceramics was interpreted as being displaced from *ADM*. A fine ware cup base and a plain ware jug are catalogued from this deposit (nos. 39 and 40). In *AFK*, the opening of *ADM* as it passes between *ADY* and *AEA*, non-diagnostic and plain ware fragments were found.

Discussion

The material found within the drain *ADM* is very similar to that found in the room, suggesting that despite the barrier, material did pass from the room and into the drain, and that I and IV were used simultaneously.

The ceramic finds within the room are not altogether well preserved, though the pit *AEV* produces some near-complete vessels. In comparison to the other rooms, a lack of cooking ware is noticeable accept in *AEV*. Fine wares and medium wares are numerous, but fragmentary, suggesting secondary dumping or random collection, rather than representing *in-situ*

237 In addition to the Classical/Hellenistic material inventoried there were a few Archaic sherds and two Prehistoric sherds (a rim and a base fragment both of different fabrics).

238 A similar fragment is found within stratum 3, now located in bag 1978.

destruction, which is recognisable in the neighbouring room II. Activities suggested by the ceramics are eating and drinking with limited preparation and storage of foods.

O26

O26BD/3

Pottery Bags: 1967, 1973, 1978, 1981, 1991, 2000, 2184, 2206, 2215, 2218, 2248, 2335

Pottery Statistics:

Total:	1333	%:	We: 9180
FW:	307	23	935
PW:	870	65	7120
CPW:	112	8.5	509
CW:	44	3.5	645

FW

1. Skyphos (Pl. 1).
Bag no. 2248: 1 O26BD/3.
FABRIC: Smooth, soft with no visible inclusions. Reddish yellow (5YR 6/6).
Base and lower wall fragment. SURFACE: Shiny black glaze on exterior, dull and mottled to brown on interior, thin remnants of slip on and under foot.
Base D: 4.4 cm; Pres. H: 2.2 cm.
COMMENTS: Local?
DATE: Classical.

2. Hellenistic kantharos, one piece (Pl. 1).
Bag no. 2335: 1 O26BD/3.
FABRIC: Granular, soft, with frequent fine, angular/platy white inclusions, rare small angular/spherical brown inclusions. Reddish yellow (5YR 7/6). SURFACE: Thin, worn, black to brown. DESCRIPTION: Rim, handle and wall. Spur handle.
Rim D: 10 cm; Pres. H: 5.8 cm.
COMMENTS: Local.
DATE: Hellenistic.

3. Classical Plate (Pl. 1).
Bag no. 2215: 1 O26BD/3.
FABRIC: Smooth, soft, with rare fine white inclusions, few voids. Pink (7.5YR 7/4).
SURFACE: Smooth and shiny black glaze mottled to brown, uneven thickness on interior, dripping marks on exterior. DESCRIPTION: Rim and upper wall fragment. Rolled rim.
Rim D: 17 cm; Pres. H: 2 cm.
COMMENTS: Local. Compare: Sparkes & Talcott, 1970, nos. 1058, 1059 and 1060, fig. 10.
DATE: Late Classical/Early Hellenistic, 350-300 BC.

4. Plate, offset rim (Pl. 1).
Bag no. 2218: 3 O26BD/3.
FABRIC: Fine, smooth, soft with no visible inclusions, few voids. Light reddish brown (5YR 6/4). SURFACE: Brown. DESCRIPTION: Rim fragment. Thin wall. Groove on upper outer rim.
Rim D: 20 cm; Pres. H: 0.9 cm.
COMMENTS: Local.
DATE: Hellenistic.

5. Echinus bowl (Pl. 5).
Bag no. 2218: 1 O26BD/3.
FABRIC: Smooth on some breaks, conchoidal on others, soft, rare fine white inclusions, few voids. Light brown to light red (7.5YR 6/4 and 2.5YR 6/6). SURFACE: Thick, black, lustrous interior, thinner and brown on exterior particularly on lower wall. DESCRIPTION: Large. Rim and upper wall (4 joining fragments). Bevelled on outer rim.
Rim D: 19.5 cm; Pres. H: 5.0 cm.
COMMENTS: Local.
DATE: Late Classical/Early Hellenistic.

6. Echinus bowl (Pl. 1).
Bag no. 2218: 2 O26BD/3.
FABRIC: Slightly granular, soft, with few fine white inclusions and voids. Light reddish brown (5YR 6/4). SURFACE: Thin, dull grey slip, fugitive on upper outer wall. DESCRIPTION: Rim and wall fragment. Deep bowl. Slightly projecting rim.
Rim D: 14 cm; Pres. H: 4.4 cm.
COMMENTS: Import.
DATE: Late 3rd century BC.

7. Table amphora (Pl. 1)
Bag no. 1973: 5 O26BD/3.
FABRIC: Granular, hard, with few fine angular/platy dark grey inclusions and rare small spherical white inclusions. Red (2.5YR 5/8).

DESCRIPTION: Rim to neck fragment. Moulded rim. Concave rim to neck profile. Rim moulded to a broader projection below. Ridge at junction between rim and neck.
Rim D: 14 cm; Pres. H: 28.0 cm.
COMMENTS: Local?

8. Reversible lid (Pl. 1).
Bag no. 2000: 1 O26BD/3.
FABRIC: Conchoidal, soft, with few fine grey inclusions and frequent voids. Pink (7.5YR 7/4). SURFACE: Thin brown slip. DESCRIPTION: Body fragment. West Slope decoration. Lattice on lower sherd, incised below a deep unglazed groove. Further up the wall ivy wreath with incised stems and fugitive heart-shaped leaves.
Pres. H: 1.7 cm
COMMENTS: Import.
DATE: Hellenistic.

9. Pyxis (not depicted).
Bag no. 2000: 2 O26BD/3.
FABRIC: Fine, smooth, soft with no visible inclusions. Reddish yellow (5YR 6/6). SURFACE: Shiny black to brown. DESCRIPTION: Rim and wall fragment from lid.
D of flange: 7.0 cm.
COMMENTS: Import.
DATE: Hellenistic.

PW
10. Transport Amphora (not depicted).
Bag no. 1991: 1 O26BD/3.
FABRIC: Granular, hard, common angular/spherical white, grey and brown inclusions, small and medium voids. Reddish yellow (5YR 6/6). DESCRIPTION: Toe fragment. Rounded lower, hollow toe. Wall rising direct from curve of toe, broadens quickly.
Pres. H: 9.3 cm.
COMMENTS: Local.

CPW
11. Chytra (Pl. 1).
Bag no. 1978: 1 O26BD/3.
FABRIC: Granular, hard, frequent fine and small white tabular-spherical/subrounded inclusions, few angular/tabular grey inclusions. Reddish brown to red (2.5YR 5/4-2.5YR 5/6), grey in core. DESCRIPTION: Rim and upper body fragment. Projecting rim, short concave neck, smooth transition to convex and broad upper body.
Rim D: 11.0 cm; Pres. H: 2.8 cm.
COMMENTS: Import. Other sherds in this bag from same vessel, 1978: 2 joins rim.

12. Lid (Pl. 1).
Bag no. 2206: 1 O26BD/3.
FABRIC: Granular, soft, with abundant small, angular/tabular white, brown and grey inclusions. Light brown (7.5YR 6/4) (unburnt) interior surface, dark grey (7.5YR 4/1) core. DESCRIPTION: Rim and wall. Rim has a moulded outer surface.
Rim D: 22.0 cm; Pres. H: 1.6 cm.
COMMENTS: Local, exterior shows signs of burning.
DATE: Hellenistic.

CW
13. Lid (Pl. 1).
Bag no. 2184 F98-1078 O26BD/3.
FABRIC: Hard, hackly, with abundant angular/tabular inclusions small to very large, grey-brown, grey, white, brown. Frequent small, large to very large voids, one very large void (1.5 cm.) with a white powdery inclusion partially preserved inside. Light reddish brown to reddish yellow (5YR 6/4-5YR 6/6). DESCRIPTION: Flat bottomed disc with slight rise to knob. Flat topped knob with concave profile. Chipped knob. Fresh break rim to body.
Rim D: 17.6 cm; Pres. H: 5.9 cm.
COMMENTS: Local.

14. Mortar (Pl. 1).
Bag no. 2218: 4 O26BD/3.
FABRIC: Smooth, hard, few medium angular/spherical, brown inclusions, frequent voids. Light reddish brown (5YR 6/4). Description: Base fragment. Broad, flat ring foot. Lower wall rising to broad bowl.
Base D: 21.0 cm; Pres. H: 2.5 cm.
COMMENTS: Local. Compare: Sparkes & Talcott, 1970, nos. 1898, 1907, fig. 16.

Loom weights

TYPE 2

15. Small pyramidal loom weight (not depicted).
Bag no. 2251; F98-1125
FABRIC: Smooth, soft with rare subrounded/spherical brown inclusions. Pink (5YR 7/4) (surface). DESCRIPTION: Complete. One drilled hole. Narrow top, slightly domed.
Pres. H: 6.65 cm; Base: 3.5 × 3.75 cm; top: 1.1 × 1.1 cm; We: 71 g.

16. Medium pyramidal loom weight (not depicted).
Bag no. 2254; F98-1128 O26BD/3.
FABRIC: Hackly, soft with small to medium subrounded/spherical grey, red and white inclusions. Light red (2.5YR 6/6). DESCRIPTION: One drilled hole. One corner and section above drill hole missing. Stamp on face not carrying drill hole, four overlapping impressions with a circular stamps (D: 1.4 cm).
Pres. H: 5.3 cm; Base: 4.6 × 4.15 cm; We: 84 g.

17. Large pyramidal loom weight (not depicted).
Bag no. 2255 F98-1129 O26BD/3.
FABRIC: Hackly, soft with subrounded/spherical large brown inclusions, abundant voids. Light brown (7.5YR 6/4).
DESCRIPTION: One drilled hole. Very chipped on two face and on top. Drilled hole on centre of base
Pres. H: 7.2 cm; Base: 4.75 × 4.3 cm; We: 129 g.

18. Large pyramidal loom weight (Fig. 83).
Bag no. 2259 F97-1132 O26BD/3.
FABRIC: Hackly, soft, common subrounded/spherical and some angular small to large red inclusions and small white inclusions. Reddish yellow (5YR 6/6). DESCRIPTION: Complete. One drilled hole. One undrilled face carries impressed line, forming an A.
Pres. H: 8.25 cm; Base: 5.65 × 5.3 cm; top: 2 × 1.85 cm; We: 209 g.
Type 3

19. Medium pyramidal loom weight (Fig. 83).
Bag no. 2252 F97-1126 O26BD/3.
FABRIC: Smooth, soft with few small to medium subrounded/spherical brown inclusions. Light red (2.5YR 7/6). DESCRIPTION: Two drilled holes. Chipped on one broad face.
Base: 5.2 × 3.7 cm; Top: 3.6 × 1.75 cm; We: 113 g.

20. Medium pyramidal loom weight (Fig. 83).
Bag no. 2253 F98-1127 O26BD/3.
FABRIC: Hackly, hard with frequent small and medium subrounded/spherical red, brown and grey inclusions. Reddish yellow (5YR 7/6). DESCRIPTION: Two drilled holes. Triangular impressed stamp on one broad face (each side of triangle measures 1 cm., impressed 0.5 cm. deep)
Pres. H: 6.66 cm; Base: 4.8 × 3.68 cm; We: 104 g.

21. Medium pyramidal loom weight (not depicted).
Bag no. 1979: 1 O26BD/3.
FABRIC: Hackly, soft, common small angular/spherical grey and red inclusions, very large subrounded/spherical green-brown inclusions. Reddish yellow (5YR 6/6). DESCRIPTION: Two drilled holes. Chipped on face. Worn stamp in circular frame (1.25 cm.) in centre of one drilled face, to the right and above is a second oval stamp (1 × 1.3 cm)
Pres. H: 6.56 cm; base: 2.9 × 4.8 cm; top: 3.65 × 2.05 cm; We: 98 g.

AEV

A dark deposit, likely to be a pit, located near wall *AEA* of room I. Associated with O26 BD/3, but distinguished through soil colour and an increase in cooking ware in the pit.

Pottery Bags: 2203, 2220, 2241, 2245
Pottery Statistics:

Total:	273	%:	We: 3145
FW:	59	21.5	280
PW:	107	39	940
CPW:	95	35	775
CW:	12	4.5	1150

FW

22. Cup, one-handler (Pl. 1 and Fig. 72).
Bag no. 2241: 1 *AEV*
FABRIC: Smooth, soft, with no visible inclusions but

Fig. 72 *Cup, one-handler. Catalogue no. 22.*

few voids. SURFACE: Thin worn black to grey on all surfaces. DESCRIPTION: Full profile and handle. Ring foot, inturned rim, handle is a softened triangle.
Rim D: 9.0 cm; Base D: 3.8 cm; Pres. H: 4.8 cm.
COMMENTS: Import? Compare: Rotroff 1997, p. 126
DATE: Classical, 4th century BC.

23. Plate, rolled rim. (Pl. 1).
Bag no. 2241: 3 *AEV*
FABRIC: Granular, hard with few fine subrounded/platy brown inclusions. Pinkish grey (7.5YR 6/2). SURFACE: Smooth black to brown glaze with some shine on interior and exterior. DESCRIPTION: Rim and upper wall.
Rim D: 15.0 cm; Pres. H: 1.7 cm.
COMMENTS: Import.
DATE: Hellenistic.

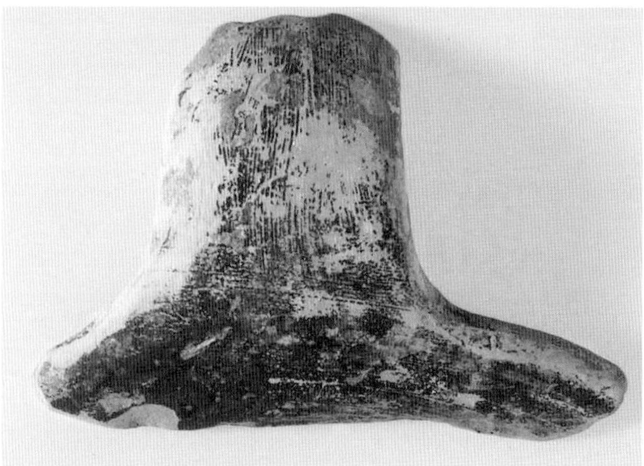

Fig. 73 *Jug. Catalogue no. 24.*

24. Jug (Fig. 73).
Bag no. 2241: 6 *AEV*
FABRIC: Smooth, soft, with no visible inclusions, few small voids. Pink (7.5YR 7/4). SURFACE: Thin brown. DESCRIPTION: Rim and handle fragment. Fine incised lines on top of rim.
Rim D: 19.0 cm; Pres. H: 9.6 cm.
COMMENTS: Local.

CW
25. Louterion (Pl. 2 and Fig. 74).
Bag no. 2245 *AEV*
FABRIC: Hackly, hard, with abundant small white and medium to very large grey and red angular/spherical inclusions. Light brown (7.5YR 6/4). DESCRIPTION: Rim fragment. Slightly overhanging rim with moulded outer face. Impressed elongated leaves motif on lower outer face of rim
Rim D: 56.0 cm; Pres. H: 6.3 cm.
COMMENTS: Local.

CPW
26. Chytra (Pl. 2 and Fig. 75).
Bag no. 2220 F98-1118 *AEV*
FABRIC: Laminar, hard, with frequent fine white inclusions and rare small spherical/angular brown inclusions. Red (2.5YR 5/8). DESCRIPTION: Rim and body. Simple lip, convex outer surface of rim, concave interior with a slight bulge at mid rim to hold lid. Sharp junction with ovoid body.
Rim D: 11.5 cm; Pres. H: 13.3 cm.

Fig. 74 *Louterion. Catalogue no. 25.*

Fig. 75 *Chytra. Catalogue no. 26.*

COMMENTS: Local. Compare: Edwards 1975, no. 651, pl. 27; Monaco & Monaco 2000, p. 157, pl. 89.a.3. (Grooves) Langridge-Noti 2002, no. 11a; Rotroff 2004, pl. 206.1.
DATE: Hellenistic.

27. Chytra (Pl. 2).
Bag no. 2241: 9 *AEV*
FABRIC: Granular, hard with common small sub-rounded/angular spherical white and grey inclusions. Dark grey (10YR 4/1). DESCRIPTION: Rim and upper body.
Rim D: 13.0 cm; Pres. H: 3.7 cm.
COMMENTS: Local.
DATE: Hellenistic.

28. Lopas (Pl. 2).
Bag no. 2241: 8 *AEV*
FABRIC: Hackly, soft with common small sub-rounded/tabular and spherical white, brown and grey inclusions. Yellowish red (5YR 5/6). DESCRIPTION: Rim, wall and lower wall. Burning on exterior rim and lower wall.
Rim D: 19.0 cm; Pres. H: 3.8 cm.
COMMENTS: Local.
DATE: Hellenistic.

Loom weight

Type 2
29. Large pyramidal loom weight. (not depicted).
Bag no. 2246; F97-1121 *AEV*
FABRIC: Hackly, hard with angular/spherical small, medium to very large brown and red inclusions and fine-small angular/tabular white inclusions. Red to light red (2.5YR 5/6-6/6). DESCRIPTION: One drilled hole, very off-centre. Slight chipping on base. Incised T (rope marks) on one undrilled face.
Pres. H: 7.6 cm; Base: 4.8 × 4.5 cm; top: 1.9 × 2.1 cm; We: 153 g.

30. Grand pyramidal loom weight (Fig. 83).
Bag no. 2243; F98-1120 *AEV*
FABRIC: Hackly, soft with small to very large sub-rounded/spherical red-brown and white inclusions, and angular tabular white/grey inclusions. Reddish yellow 5YR 6/6. DESCRIPTION: One drilled hole. Stamped. Base chipped. Oval stamps on each drilled face. One: 1.65 cm vertically and 0.9 cm horizontally and 0.4 cm deep. Other is 2.1 cm vertically (though tilted to left) and 1.55 cm horizontally, 0.2 cm. deep
Pres. H: 11.2 cm; max. pres. D: 5.7 × 5.4 cm; top: 1.65 × 1.45 cm; We: 337 g.

ADM
ADM is a channel dug into the bedrock. It runs beside the wall *ADO* and between the walls *AEA* and *ADY* and thus into AREA IV. The channel is lined with stone and covered with tiles.

Pottery Bags: 1981, 2134, 2296
Pottery Statisti

Total:	548	%	We: 7010
FW:	125	23	570
PW:	392	71.5	5220
CPW:	14	2.5	50
CW:	17	3	1170

FW
31. Echinus bowl, large with grooved wall (Pl. 2).
Bag no. 2134: 4 *ADM*
FABRIC: Granular, hard, with rare small grey and white inclusions, frequent voids. Red to light red

(2.5YR 5/6-2.5YR 6/6). SURFACE: Few remnants of a thin brown to red slip on exterior. DESCRIPTION: Rim and upper wall. Groove on exterior under rim.
Rim D: 24.0 cm; Pres. H: 7.0 cm.
COMMENTS: Local.
DATE: Hellenistic.

32. Bowl/cup, outturned rim (Pl. 2).
Bag no. 2134: 1 *ADM*
FABRIC: Smooth, soft with no visible inclusions. Pink (7.5YR 7/4). SURFACE: Smooth brown slip on all preserved surfaces. DESCRIPTION: Rim and upper wall. Slightly protruding rim and very straight upper wall. West Slope decoration. Ivy wreath with incised scrolling tendrils, one fugitive leaf and large dots preserved.
Rim D: 20.0 cm; Pres. H: 3.1 cm.
COMMENTS: Import.
DATE: Hellenistic.

33. Dipper (not depicted).
Bag no. 2134: 5 *ADM*
FABRIC: Granular, hard, with few small voids. Reddish yellow (5YR 6/6).
SURFACE: Thin brown to red-brown slip on handle and exterior wall. DESCRIPTION: Handle and upper wall. Loop handle, upper wall curves to a baggy body.
Pres. H: 6.5 cm.
COMMENTS: Local? Fabric compares to no. 7.

PW
34. Transport Amphora (Pl. 2).
Bag no. 2134: 3 *ADM*
FABRIC: Hard, smooth, with few fine grey and rare small rounded red inclusions, frequent platy voids. Pale yellow (2.5Y 8/4). DESCRIPTION: Toe. Conical, broadens slightly near termination.
Pres. H: 11.0 cm.
COMMENTS: Import. Corinthian Type B Amphora.

CPW
35. Lid (Pl. 2).
Bag no. 2134: 2 *ADM*
FABRIC: Hard, granular, with common fine platy white and small subrounded/spherical grey inclusions. Dark grey (2.5Y 4/1). DESCRIPTION: Knob and wall. Top of knob is rounded.
Pres. H: 2.1 cm.
COMMENTS: Local. Compare: Edwards 1975, nos. 694 and 695, pl. 31.
DATE: Hellenistic.

CW
36. Dome (Pl. 2).
Bag no. 2296: 1 *ADM*
FABRIC: Hackly, hard, abundant angular/spherical small white, large to very large red and grey inclusions, common voids. Red to light red (2.5YR 5/6-2.5YR 6/6). DESCRIPTION: Body fragment.
Pres. H: 14.8 cm; Th: 1.55 cm; W: 22.0 cm.
COMMENTS: Local. Bag 1978 has a related coarse ware fragment. Compare: Sparkes & Talcott, 1970, nos. 2021 and 2022, fig. 19

Loom weight
Type 1
37. Large conical loom weight (Fig. 83).
Bag no. 2298; F98-1137 *ADM*
FABRIC: Hackly, hard with angular/tabular-spherical grey, brown and white inclusions. Reddish yellow (5YR 6/6). DESCRIPTION: Chipped base. Top with rounded point. One drilled hole. Slightly convex walls.
Pres. H: 6.61 cm; Base: 5.4 cm; We: 142 g.

AET
COMMENTS: ceramics and tiles associated with *ADM*.

Pottery Bags: 2201, 2256, 2257
Pottery Statistics:

Total:	8	%:	We: 140[239]
FW:	4	50	70
PW:	-	-	-
CPW:	2	25	10
CW:	2	25	60

FW
38. Echinus bowl, large with grooved rim (not depicted).
Bag no. 2257 *AET*
FABRIC: Smooth, hard with frequent angular/tabular

239 No weight recorded for bag 2201 (pithos fragment).

white inclusions. Light red (2.5YR 6/6). SURFACE: Mottled brown to red, worn, dull on exterior, some fragments retain glaze on underside of lid. DESCRIPTION: Rim and wall. A deep glazed groove marks the junction of the wall and the rim. Fine glazed incisions decorate the wall.
Rim D: 34.0 cm; Pres. H: 3.5 cm.
COMMENTS: Found in association with tile: *AET*-2. Also fragments of this vessel from O26 *AET* 2256:1 And 1803: 2 O26/3 a bag associated with the area outside of Room II.
DATE: Hellenistic.

AEA-1
COMMENTS: ceramics and tiles displaced from *ADM*.

Pottery Bags: 1085
Pottery statistics:

Total:	3	%:We not available:
FW:	3	100

39. Hellenistic kantharos, one piece (Pl. 3).
Bag no. 1085: 2 *AEA-1*
FABRIC: Smooth, soft, with rare fine white and small grey inclusions. Pink (5YR 7/4-7.5YR 7/4). SURFACE: Dull greyish brown on interior and exterior, stops ca. 1.3 cm. from foot. DESCRIPTION: Ring foot, very slight stem between foot and lower wall.
Base D: 5.0 cm; Pres. H: 2.5 cm.
DATE: Hellenistic.

PW
40. Jug (Pl. 3).
Bag no. 1085: 1 *AEA-1*
FABRIC: Hackly, hard, with few fine and small angular/platy inclusions. Yellowish red (5YR 5/6). Rim and handle with shoulder attachment.
Rim D: 10.0 cm; Pres. H: 13.0 cm.
COMMENTS: Local.

AFK
COMMENTS: The opening of *ADM*, as it passes between *ADY* and *AEA*. Non diagnostics and plain ware fragments found.

Pottery Bags: 1801
Pottery Statistics:

Total:	26	%:	We: 560
FW:	–	–	–
PW:	24	92.5	480
CPW:	2	7.5	80
CW:	–	–	–

Room II
Room II crosses two trenches, O26 and O27. Large stones collapsed from the fortifications and buildings above, and a layer of Laconian tiles (excavated as deposit *ADG*) covered the trench, stratum 1 and 2 (the tile layer *ADG* lay between strata 2 and 3). The third stratum was a soft, yellowish soil and was excavated to bedrock.

Two coarse ware vessels protruded from the top of the occupation level, stratum 3. One, a Hellenistic pithos represented by a rim and a base fragment, very probably from the same pithos, nos. 54 and 55. The body fragments of the pithos were found within the tile deposit, *ADG*. Judging by the rim, this would seem to be the largest of the pithoi found within the rooms. The foot, which carries moulding on its underside, is distinctive. The second coarse ware vessel found in the deposit, no. 57, is a large domed vessel with a broad spout and two horizontal lug handles and may be associated with food production. The terracotta disc, no. 58, of uncertain use, was located within stratum 3. A second pithos rim fragment, no. 56, was found in stratum 3 of the baulk between O26 and O27.

A layer of well-preserved vessels and coins was discovered within the third stratum of the trench. A number of these were grouped in the northwest region of the room (the pithos and jar being the obvious exception, found south of the centre of the room).[240] It is possible that they represent material that was stored on a shelf or bench, and were displaced during the collapse of the room. Fine wares and cooking wares are well preserved within this level. They date to the 3rd century.

240 Pottery nos. 42, 43, 46, 47, 50, 51, 53 and the lamp no. 60 are located in the north west of the room, no. 45 is set to the south of this group along wall *ADY*. Nos. 51 and 54 (the jar and pithos) are set just south of the centre of the room. As for the coins see *SPR* and *TPR*.

Three one-piece kantharoi, nos. 42-44, produce a homogenous set of vessels, all of local manufacture. The walls are fine, and the overall effect pleasing, if simple with unarticulated ring feet and dip-glazed bodies. The plate with rolled rim, no. 46, provides a full-profile of a very popular shape in the local assemblage, and its appearance complements the cups. The plate with grooved rim, no. 45, is an attractive vessel that lifts the finds above the stock production. This is achieved largely by the effective glazing, which while dull in finish and not altogether evenly applied, contrasts brown slip on the borders of the rim with a bright red-brown on the rim's upper face and on the body. It is a striking piece.

In addition to these Hellenistic drinking and eating vessels are the three lopades nos. 51-53. The numerous fragments of no. 52 suggest a near complete form that, given the soft fabric of the local cooking pots, has proved difficult to reconstruct. All vessels show the marks of use on the fire.

The lamp, no. 60, has an inclined wall, of a type not infrequent amongst the deposits under study. This particular lamp displays the most developed of the local examples, with a flat disc floor, inclined walls, recessed rim and long nozzle. The burning on the nozzle indicates that it, too, was used. The lamp attests to a mid- to late 3rd century date. Other lamp fragments were found within the deposit.[241]

An element of ritual is found in the find level, represented most clearly by the incense vessel, or thymiaterion, no. 50. Also of a religious nature is the black glaze miniature of a bowl with folded rim, no. 59. The imported no. 47 is a 'special' vessel, if not a religious one; a stand for a lamp or other pot, elegantly elevating the vessel and allowing the form to be appreciated.

Hellenistic material continues to be found, though the skyphos base, no. 41, dates to the Classical period. The flask, no. 49, and the plain ware table amphora, no. 48, are vessels of more practicality. Fragments of a figurine are also identified.[242]

Loom weights are plentiful and are scattered in the northern half of the room.[243] There are seven examples. Five are pyramidal (type 2) and the remaining two are conical (type 1). Of the type 2 loom weights four are medium and one large. The weight of the two conical examples places them within the large category. In total there are four of medium weight and three of large weight.

The iron and charcoal rich deposit, *AEP*, is located within the third stratum of Room II. This location, coupled with cross-joins between the ceramics within *AEP* and the third stratum, link this deposit strongly with the occupation of the room.[244] *AEP* is located near the corner of walls *ADY* and *ADO*. The deposit covers an area of about 1.45 m NW-SE and 1.30 m NE-SW. The ceramics within the deposit includes the skyphos rim and handle, no. 70, and the miniature vessel of Corinthian fabric, no. 72, along with uncatalogued Hellenistic kantharoi. The best-preserved vessel in the deposit is the lid no. 71. It is of unusual form being a flat disc with a horizontal rim that project above the level of the body. This object shows some evidence of burning. One medium pyramidal loom weight, no. 73, was found within *AEP*. A nearby pit *AEQ* contained plain wares, no. 74, cooking pots, no. 75, and some small fragments of glazed wares.

An area close to wall *ADI* differed slightly from the rest of stratum 3, and it was excavated as stratum 3, fourth pass.[245] The material in this deposit correlated with that found beneath the clay packing *AED*.[246] In both deposits, Hellenistic ceramics are not easily identified, but rather Classical and Archaic material is plentiful.[247] The decline in the amount of cooking ware also distinguishes these deposits from those already discussed.

AEO a deeper deposit in the corner of O26 and the baulk with O27, a pit, contained nothing distinctly

241 In bag 2186. These are very fragmentary and not catalogued but are Hellenistic lamps that belong to Groups 4 and 5 (see Lamps).

242 No. 68 is a fragment of a figurine, probably the face of a female, but very battered, a fragment of drapery accompanies this piece.

243 Conical loom weight nos. 61and 62; Pyramidal loom weight: no. 63 (stamped), no. 64 **(stamped), nos. 65, 67 (stamped) and no. 66 (stamped).**

244 Cross-joins include those of fragments in bag 2002 joining with the kantharos no. 43.

245 This material is in bag 2213.

246 Bags 3385, 3390, 3388.

247 A plain ware base with broad squared foot in bag 3390 and lopas fragments in 3385 are Hellenistic.

Hellenistic, beyond the spout of the cooking vessel no. 76. The assemblage in the pit differs from the rest of the trench with little cooking ware beyond that catalogued. This pit appeared to extend under *ADY*. It contained some Hellenistic material but the ceramics were predominantly Classical and Archaic in date.

Discussion

Room II was a roofed space. The many Laconian tiles that were excavated above the find layer attest to this, as do the presence of lamps, needed to light an interior space. There is a high quantity of cooking ware within the room, and the charcoal-rich deposit of *AEP* provides a space on which these vessels were used.

The objects in the find layer were in such condition as to suggest that they were complete and *in-situ* when the room collapsed. A number of good quality ceramics were still within the house when the roof collapsed.

The lower level of the third strata excavated as pass four close to *ADI* contains an assemblage that is different from that found within the room proper. Given that pass four is at a lower level, the earlier date of the material is not surprising, though suggests that it represents a separate layer to stratum 3. The pit *AEO* also contains material that dates earlier than that in stratum 3. It supports the interpretation of pass 4 as a deposit associated with the construction of the room and contains predominantly Classical and Archaic material with nothing that is definitely of Hellenistic date, though the amount of pottery is not substantial.

O26/3; O27 baulk; O27/3 AREA II

COMMENTS: Bags 3385, 3390 and 3388: O26/3, pass 4, represents an earlier phase of activity in the area.

Pottery Bags: O26/3: 1080; 1081; 1907; 1909; 1910; 1912; 1915; 1923; 1926; 1928; 1934; 1935; 1936; 2014; 2186; 2193; 2213; 3385; 3388; 3390; O27 baulk: 2816; O27/3 AREA II: 2870

Pottery Statistics:

Total:	1831	%:	We: 11958[248]
FW:	570	31	1610
PW:	828	45	5660
CPW:	345	19	1562
CW:	88	5	3126

FW

41. Skyphos (Pl. 3).
Bag no. 2014: 1 O26/3.
FABRIC: Granular, soft with frequent fine white inclusions rare large white/grey angular/spherical inclusion. Red (2.5YR 6/6). SURFACE: Dark brown glaze, smooth and lustrous on exterior, worn on interior. DESCRIPTION: Base and lower wall. Broad projecting foot with flat upper and rounded outer face.
Base D: 12.0 cm; Pres. H: 3.3 cm.
COMMENTS: Import – Attic.
DATE: Classical, 5th century BC.

42. Hellenistic kantharos, one piece (Pl. 3 and Fig. 76).
Bag no. 1935; F98-1014 O26/3
FABRIC: Smooth, hard, with few fine subrounded/platy white inclusions. Light red (2.5YR 6/6). SURFACE: Black to brown glaze, now streaky in adherence, no glaze on exterior lower wall and foot. DESCRIPTION: Rim to foot (no handle) preserved. West Slope decoration? A fugitive dot rosette and a (suspended) elongated leaves motif on mid wall.
Rim D: 8.6 cm; Base D: 5.0 cm; Pres. H: 10.4 cm.
COMMENTS: Local.
DATE: Hellenistic.

43. Hellenistic kantharos, one piece (Pl. 3).
Bag no. 1910; F98-1036 O26/3
FABRIC: Fine, smooth, no visible inclusions. Light red (2.5YR 6/6). SURFACE: Black, smooth, slightly shiny. DESCRIPTION: Rim, upper wall and handle. Simple strap handle attaches on rim. Groove under rim. There is a distinct transition between upper and mid wall apparent on interior and exterior, the diameter of the mid wall is ca. 1 mm. less than that of the upper wall.
Rim D: 10.0 cm; Pres. H: 5.8 cm.

248 Weight not recorded for finds: 1080, 1081, 1907, 1909, 1910, 1912, 1915, 1926, 1928, 1934, 1935, 1936.

Fig. 76 *Hellenistic kantharos. Catalogue no. 42.*

COMMENTS: Local. Joins from bag 2002, O26 *AEP.*
DATE: Hellenistic.

44. Hellenistic kantharos, one piece (?) (Pl. 3).
Bag no. 1926; F98-1 O26/3
FABRIC: Conchoidal, hard, rare small angular/spherical white inclusions and voids. Light red (2.5YR 6/6). SURFACE: Thin worn brown slip on interior. No trace of slip on exterior lower walls or foot. DESCRIPTION: Base and lower wall. Simple ring foot, convex lower walls indicating a narrow and deep cup shape.
Base D: 4.0 cm; Pres. H: 3.0 cm.
COMMENTS: Local.
DATE: Hellenistic.

45. Plate, grooved rim (Pl. 3 and Fig. 77).
Bag no. 1909; F98-1028 O26/3
FABRIC: Hard, smooth, with very rare small subrounded/spherical inclusions. Pink (5YR 7/4), margins: Light reddish brown (2.5YR 7/4). SURFACE: Red on body, brown in grooves of rim and on rim to wall junction. DESCRIPTION: Rim and upper wall. The two toned glaze provides an effective decoration, highlighting the shape of the plate.
Rim D: 20.5 cm; Pres. H: 2.1 cm.

Fig. 77 *Plate with grooved rim. Catalogue no. 45.*

COMMENTS: Import – western Greece?
DATE: Hellenistic.

46. Plate, rolled rim (Pl. 3 and Fig. 78).
Bag no. 1936; F98-1015 O26/3
FABRIC: Laminar, hard, with few small subrounded/platy white inclusions and frequent irregular voids. Light reddish brown (5YR 6/4). SURFACE: Mottled black to brown on interior and over rim to mid wall, lower wall and foot unglazed. DESCRIPTION: Full profile. Simple, rough ring foot. Unarticulated walls rising from concave floor, inturned sharply at rim.
Rim D: 14.5 cm; Base D: 5.0 cm; Pres. H: 3.8 cm.
COMMENTS: Local. Compare: Dyggve, Poulsen & Rhomaios 1934, no. 13, fig. 144.
DATE: Hellenistic.

Fig. 78 *Plate, rolled rim. Catalogue no. 46.*

47. Stand (Pl. 3).
Bag no. 1928; F98-1009 O26/3
FABRIC: Smooth, soft, with rare fine subrounded/spherical grey and white inclusions. Pink (7.5YR 7/4 -7.5YR 8/4). SURFACE: Thin brown to dark brown slip preserved on lower exterior foot and on interior. DESCRIPTION: Hollow pedestalled foot. Narrow, cylindrical upper zone flaring to a broad foot. Groove defines the foot from the wall. Resting surface is flat, but slightly uneven and the clay is pushed over the inner wall to form a groove. Remnants of slip on the cylindrical wall suggest a garlanded decoration.
Base D: 10.0 cm; Pres. H: 17.7 cm.
COMMENTS: Import. In the preliminary report, *SPR* p. 246, it was suggested that this could be a loutrophoros rim and neck. There are no handle scars on this shape. The rim is not that of an oil pouring vessel, or of a pouring vessel of any kind given the deep groove between the inner wall and the 'rim'. Furthermore the rough finish of the 'rim' is more typical of a foot rather than a rim, particularly of a specialty vessel as a loutrophoros.
Compare: Lamp stand: Broneer 1977 137 (though this one is solid) with further parallels. Davidson 1942 fig. 1.
DATE: Hellenistic.

PW
48. Jug (Pl. 3).
Bag no. 2014: 3 O26/3
FABRIC: Granular, soft, with fine and small subrounded/spherical white inclusions. Pink (7.5YR 7/4). DESCRIPTION: Rim, upper neck, handle stem. Flaring rim.
Rim D: 16.0 cm; Pres. H: 4.7 cm.
COMMENTS: Local.

49. Jug (Pl. 3).
Bag no. 1923: 5 O26/3
FABRIC: Granular, soft, few small angular/spherical grey and white inclusions. Pink (7.5YR 7/4). DESCRIPTION: Flask. Rim, neck, handle stems. Rolled rim, cylindrical neck, thick vertical strap handles. Rough, uneven form.
Rim D: 4.75 cm; Pres. H: 6.3 cm.
COMMENTS: Local.

Fig. 79 *Thymiaterion. Catalogue no. 50.*

50. Thymiaterion (Pl. 3 and Fig. 79).
Bag no. 1934; F98-1013 O26/3
FABRIC: Hackly, hard, with frequent small to medium brown, grey and white angular/spherical inclusions. Margins: Reddish yellow (5YR 6/6); grey in core; Surface: Reddish yellow (5YR 7/6).
SURFACE: One small section of thick white slip, presumably had covered outer surface of vessel. DESCRIPTION: Full profile, chipping on receptacle and flange. Tall, hollow, pedestalled foot with moulding on and above foot. Broad projecting flange between foot and receptacle. Receptacle has an upright wall without moulding, concave on interior.
Rim D: 6.0 cm; Base: D: 9.0 cm; Pres. H: 10.4 cm.
COMMENTS: Import; Compare: *Kalydon* 2011, Ch. 6.4, nos. 16, 17, 26, 35, 36, 37, 38, 39, 40, 41, 42, 43, 44 and 3.4; Rotroff 1997, no. 1567, fig. 95.
DATE: Hellenistic.

CPW
51. Lopas (Pl. 4).
Bag no. 1907; F98-1026 O26/3
FABRIC: Hackly, hard with common angular/spherical fine to medium white, brown and grey inclusions

rare light refracting particles. Red (10R 5/8). DESCRIPTION: Rim, upper wall and floor. Sharp flange.
Rim D: 23.0 cm; Pres. H: 5.5 cm.
COMMENTS: Local – though fabric is more brittle and keeps a sharper shape than is typical for the finds from the site.
DATE: Hellenistic.

52. Lopas (Pl. 4).
Bag no. 1912; F98-1031 O26/3
FABRIC: Granular, soft, with common fine and small brown and white inclusions, and light refracting particles. Red (2.5YR 5/8). DESCRIPTION: Sherd 1: Rim, upper wall and handle. Attached curving ribbon handle.
Rim D: 26.0 cm; Pres. H: 4.4 cm.
COMMENTS: Local. Numerous other rim and wall fragments from same vessel preserved in bag.
DATE: Hellenistic.

53. Lopas (Pl. 4).
Bag no. 1915; F98-1032b O26/3
FABRIC: Granular, soft, with fine white inclusions and light refracting particles. Brown (7.5YR 5/3). DESCRIPTION: Rim, upper wall and handle. Attached squared ribbon handle.
Rim D: 21.6 cm; Pres. H: 3.4 cm.
COMMENTS: Import. Other fragments of same vessel found in the deposit including 1914 (F98-1032a) and 1923. Handle is not of a typical shape but rather squared; fabric also unusual. Compare: (Handle) E.-C. Portale 2000, pl. 40a. 4.5; pl. 41c, pl. 42a; Hatzidakis 2000, pl. 76a.

CW
54. Pithos (Pl. 4).
Bag no. 1081: 1; F97-3050 O26/3
FABRIC: Granular, hard with frequent small to very large subrounded/spherical red inclusions, small subrounded/spherical brown inclusions and very large subrounded/tabular white inclusions. Light red (2.5YR 7/6). DESCRIPTION: Rim and upper wall fragment. Broad flat upper surface, squared outer surface, concave profile to upper wall.
Rim D: 50.0 cm; Pres. H: 9.8 cm; We: 3395 g.
COMMENTS: Local.

55. Pithos (Pl. 4).
Bag no. 1081: 2; F97-3050 O26/3
FABRIC: Hackly, hard with abundant inclusions: fine to small white subrounded/spherical, medium angular/tabular red and brown inclusions, large to very large angular/tabular grey inclusions. Pink (7.5YR 7/4) outer margin, light red (2.5YR 6/6) inner margin. DESCRIPTION: Base fragment. Rounded resting surface, three-stepped underfloor surface. Interior unfinished surface.
Base D: 18.0 cm; Pres. H: 4.1 cm.
COMMENTS: Local.

56. Pithos (Pl. 4).
Bag no. 2816: 1 O26/3
FABRIC: Hackly, soft, abundant medium to very large subrounded/spherical red, white and grey inclusions. Light red (2.5YR 6/8). DESCRIPTION: Rim fragment. Projecting rim, flat upper surface, flat outer surface before incline to wall.
Rim D: 42.0 cm; Pres. H: 6.5 cm; We: 1315 g.
COMMENTS: Local.

57. Deep Spouted Vessel (Pl. 4).
Bag no. 1080; F97-304 O26/38
FABRIC: Hard, hackly, common very large red, medium brown and small white subrounded/spherical inclusions. Reddish brown (2.5YR 5/4). DESCRIPTION: Base, handle, spout wall. Broad flat base, convex lower wall swells out before inclining inwards. At break there is some indication that the wall curves out perhaps to rim. Horizontal strap handle preserved on mid wall at same level as spout. Scar for second horizontal handle opposite preserved example. Part of rim of spout preserved as it attaches to wall.
Base D: 30.6 cm; Pres. H: 31.0 cm; Spout is 14 cm across and begins 14 cm. from base.
COMMENTS: Local. General features shared with Rotroff, *ΣΤ' ΕλλΚερ*, p. 458, pl. 204a.

58. Lid (Pl. 5).
Bag no. 2186: 1 O26/3
FABRIC: Hackly, hard, with abundant large to very large angular/spherical grey and brown inclusions and few small to large subrounded spherical white inclusions. Light red (2.5YR 6/8). DESCRIPTION:

Terracotta disc. Rim and body ca. 1/8 preserved.
Rim D: 33.0 cm; Pres. H: 3.0 cm.
COMMENTS: Local.

Miniatures

59. Miniature vessel, bowl (Pl. 5).
Bag no. 2193: 1 O26/3
FABRIC: Granular, hard with few small subrounded/spherical grey/white inclusions. Light brown (7.5YR 6/4). SURFACE: Black glaze on exterior wall, rim and half of preserved interior wall. DESCRIPTION: Rim and upper wall fragment. Rolled and slightly projecting rim. Convex wall.
Rim D: 4.0 cm; Pres. H: 2.0 cm.
DATE: Hellenistic.

Lamps

60. Lamp (Fig. 80 and Pl. 5).
Bag no. 1924; F98-1010 O26/3
FABRIC: Laminar, soft, rare small white and grey angular/spherical inclusions, frequent voids. Reddish yellow (5YR 7/6). SURFACE: some red slip preserved on base and on wall. DESCRIPTION: Base to rim and section of nozzle, fragment with nozzle rim none joining. Flat base with slight rise to inclined wall, inset rim, long nozzle. Burning on nozzle.
Rim D: 2.35 cm; Base: D: 4.3 cm; Pres. H: 2.65 cm.
COMMENTS: Local. Compare: Broneer 1977, no. 125, Type VII C, 3rd century.
Date: Hellenistic.

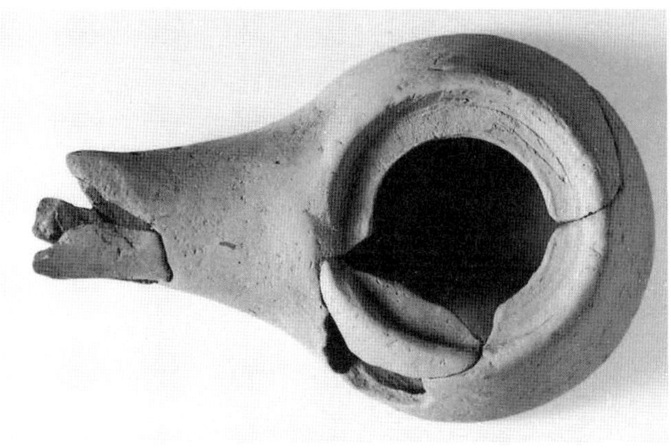

Fig. 80 *Lamp. Catalogue no. 60.*

Loom weights

Type 1
61. Large conical loom We (Fig. 83).
Bag no. 1902; F98-1027 O26/3
FABRIC: (surface) smooth, hard, with frequent small to medium brown and rare medium white subrounded/spherical inclusions. Pink (7.5YR 7/4). DESCRIPTION: One drilled hole. Concave base. Pointed top. Complete.
Base D: 5.3; Pres. H: 7.8; Weight: 140

62. Large conical loom weight (not depicted).
Bag no. 2190; F98-1079 O26/3
FABRIC: Hackly, soft, abundant small to very large angular/tabular grey and subrounded/spherical white and red inclusions. Light red (2.5YR 6/6). DESCRIPTION: One drilled hole. Rough based, chipped. Rounded top.
Pres. H: 8.3 cm; pres D: 5-5.45 cm; We: 177 g.

Type 2
63. Medium pyramidal loom weight (Fig. 83).
Bag no. 2192: 2; F98-1081 O26/3
FABRIC: (surface) Granular, soft, common subrounded/spherical white, grey, brown, red-brown inclusions. Light red (2.5YR 6/8). DESCRIPTION: One drilled hole. Complete. Stamp 9-petalled flower (or star) with a depressed irregular (circular) zone, heavy incrustation.
H: 6.9 cm; Base: 4.1 × 3.9 cm, top: 1.4 × 1.55 cm; We: 98 g.

64. Medium pyramidal loom weight (Fig. 83).
Bag no. 2192: 1; F98-1081 O26/3
FABRIC: (surface) Granular, soft, common subrounded/spherical white, grey, brown, red-brown inclusions. Light red (2.5YR 6/8). DESCRIPTION: One drilled hole. Complete. Stamp. 9-petalled flower (or star) with a depressed irregular (circular) zone.
Pres. H: 6.35 cm; Base: 4 × 3.8 cm; We: 96 g.
COMMENTS: Found with second loom weight with same stamp, no. 68.

65. Medium pyramidal loom weight (Fig. 83).
Bag no. 2018; F98-1100 O26/3
FABRIC: Granular, soft, no visible inclusions. Pink

(5YR 7/4). DESCRIPTION: One drilled hole. Complete. On one drilled face '+' incised across face.
Pres. H: 7.45 cm; Base: 3.9 × 3.8 cm, top: ca. 1.5 × 1.5 cm; We: 96 g.

66. Medium pyramidal loom weight (not depicted).
Bag no. 2329; F98-1152 O27/3
FABRIC: Hackly, hard, small to medium angular/spherical brown and angular/platy white inclusions. Light reddish brown (5YR 6/4). DESCRIPTION: Single drilled hole, off centre. Chipped base. Incised '+' on one face (without drill hole) and on the flat upper face of the loom weight.
Pres. H: 8.1 cm; base: 3.5 × 3.6 cm; top: 1.75 × 1.85 cm; We: 81 g.

67. Large pyramidal loom weight (not depicted).
Bag no. 1903; F98-1022 O26/3
FABRIC: (surface) Smooth, soft, with rare small white angular/spherical inclusions. Reddish yellow (7.5YR 7/6). DESCRIPTION: One drilled hole. Stamp. Complete. An incised 'A' on lower wall of one face with drilled hole – Height of letter: 2.1; width 2.35.
Base D: 8.35 cm; Pres. H: 8.3 cm; Base: 4.7 × 4.45 cm, top: 1.75 × 1.45 cm; We: 144 g.

Figurine

68. Head, female and section of drapery. 2 fragments, badly preserved. (not depicted).
Bag no. 1923: 6 O26/3
FABRIC: Hackly, very soft with few small subrounded/spherical grey, white and brown inclusions and voids. Light reddish brown (5YR 6/4).
Pres. H: 2.7 cm; W: 1.95 cm.
DATE: Hellenistic.

Various

69. Unidentified (Pyramidal wedge) (Fig. 83).
Bag no. 2214; F98-1111 O26/3.
FABRIC: Hackly, soft, medium angular/tabular grey, brown and red inclusions. Pink (7.5YR 7/4). DESCRIPTION: Complete.
Pres. H: 6.45 cm; Base: 4.5 × 3 cm; We: 57 g.
COMMENTS: At first this looks like a narrow-sided pyramidal loom weight but the lack of a drilled hole suggests that it is a wedge. It sits easily on one of the broad faces.

AEP
COMMENTS: Iron and charcoal rich deposit in room II. Ceramic joins indicate its close relation with O26 stratum 3.

Pottery Bags: 2002, 2198
Pottery Statistics:

Total:	154	%:	We: 630[249]
FW:	46	30	100
PW:	39	25.5	210
CPW:	67	43.5	300
CW:	2	1	20

FW
70. Skyphos (Pl. 5).
Bag no. 2002: 2 AEP
FABRIC: Granular, soft, few fine white inclusions. Light red (2.5YR 6/6). SURFACE: Shiny black to brown on all surfaces. DESCRIPTION: Rim and handle fragment.
Pres. H: 3.0 cm.
COMMENTS: Local.
DATE: Classical, 5th century.

PW
71. Lid (Pl. 5 and Fig. 81).
Bag no. 2198; F98-1086; AEP-5
FABRIC: Granular, soft, with no visible inclusions but frequent voids. Light brown (7.5YR 6/4). DESCRIPTION: Rim to knob stem profile, 50 % preserved. Knob missing. Flat bottomed except for an impression under knob, raised upright rim with groove on outer and upper face, upper body of lid carries 4 concentric ridges between the rim and knob. Surface has grey mottling, probably discolouration caused by slight exposure to fire/smoke.
Rim D: 16.2 cm; Pres. H: 2.2 cm.

249 Weight of 2198 not included.

Fig. 81 *Lid. Catalogue no. 71.*

Miniature

72. Miniature cup (Pl. 5).
Bag no. 2002: 4 AEP
FABRIC: Granular, soft, no visible inclusions. Pale red (2.5Y7/2). DESCRIPTION: Base and lower wall.
Base D: 2.2 cm; Pres. H: 0.9 cm.

Loom weights

Type 2
73. Medium pyramidal loom weight (Fig. 83).
Bag no. 2001; F98-1089 AEP
FABRIC: (Surface) smooth, soft, few medium to large subrounded/spherical white and red inclusions. Reddish yellow (5YR 7/6). DESCRIPTION: Complete. One drilled hole. Stamped. Rounded top. Single stamp on one face with drilled hole. Stamp consists of an impressed circle outline, the centre of the circle is only slightly impressed – donut stamp.
Pres. H: 7.4 cm; Base: 3.3 × 3.65 cm; We: 82 g.

AEQ
COMMENTS: Pit within O26/3.
Pottery Bags: 2017; 2211
Pottery Statistics:

Total:	10	%.	We: 200
FW	4	40	10
PW	3	30	180
CPW	3	30	10
CW	–	–	–

PW
74. Jug/amphora (Pl. 5).
Bag no. 2017; F98-1099 AEQ
FABRIC: Granular, soft with few fine to medium, subrounded/spherical grey inclusions, frequent voids. Red (2.5YR 5/6). DESCRIPTION: Base and lower wall. Foot flares out from lower wall, rounded and worn resting surface, low floor.
Base D: 10.6; Pres. H: 9.7

CPW
75. Lid (Pl. 5).
Bag no. 2211: 1 AEQ
FABRIC: Hackly, hard with frequent fine and small angular/spherical white and brown inclusions. Brown (7.5YR 4/3), very dark grey to dark grey (7.5YR 3/1-4/1). DESCRIPTION: Rim and wall fragment
Rim D: 22 cm; Pres. H: 1.6 cm.
COMMENTS: Local.

AED
COMMENT: Clay packing in and below stratum 3. Material in /3, pass 4 excavated in association with this deposit is in bags 3385, 3390 and 3388. The pottery range includes some Hellenistic fragments mixed with Classical and Archaic material.

Pottery Bag: 3384
Pottery Statistics:

Total:	26	%:	We: 90
FW:	9	35	20
PW:	10	38	40
CPW:	7	27	30
CW:	–	–	–

AEO
COMMENTS: A pit in the corner of *ADY* O26/3.
Pottery Bags: 2187, 2005
Pottery Statistics:

Total:	86	%:	We: 520[250]
FW:	22	25.5	40
PW:	49	57	360
CPW:	8	9	80
CW:	7	8.5	40

250 Weight for 2005 not included.

CPW

76. Lopas? Spouted cooking pot (Pl. 5).
Bag no. 2005; F98-1092 *AEO*
FABRIC: Granular, hard, abundant small to large angular/spherical, white, grey and brown. Grey (10YR 5/1).
DESCRIPTION: Hourglass-shaped spout. Angle of attachment suggests that the spout was placed on the shoulder of an ovoid vessel.
Rim D: 2.9 cm; Pres. H: 3.5 cm.
COMMENTS: Compare: Edwards 1975, no. 676, p. 125; Sparkes & Talcott, 1970, no. 1969, p. 277.

Zone III

Zone III, outside of rooms I and II, contained layers of tiles, structure *AFC*. This tile layer lay close to wall *ADI* and is spillage from the destruction of room II.[251] The zone contained ceramics comparable with those from inside the rooms and within drain *ADM*.[252] This material included a mix of Prehistoric, Archaic, Classical and Hellenistic sherds. The western section of the zone had a deeper deposit of soil and in the lower level, 2nd pass, a quantity of Archaic material mixed with Classical, Hellenistic, no. 77, and the occasional Prehistoric sherd was excavated.[253] Two loom weights were found in III, nos. 78 and 79. They are both pyramidal (type 2), one is small the other grand. The material from outside the rooms is similar to that found within, though it is of less quality, both in its level of preservation and the security of its context.

O26/3a; O27/3
COMMENTS: Area outside rooms I and II. Mixed deposit.

Pottery Bags:
1803; 2139; 2260; 2302; 3375; 3367
Pottery Statistics:

Total:	707	%:	We: 6090
FW:	270	38	1155
PW:	310	44	3500
CPW:	113	16	555
CW:	14	2	880

CPW

77. Storage vessel (Pl. 5).
Bag no. 3375: 1 O27/3
FABRIC: Hackly, hard, common fine to small angular/platy white, large to very large angular/spherical red and grey inclusions. Red (2.5YR 5/8), outer margin dark grey (5YR 4/1). DESCRIPTION: Rim and body fragment.
Rim D: 26.0 cm; Pres. H: 6.6 cm.

Loom weights

Type 2

78. Small pyramidal loom weight (not depicted).
Bag no. 2875; F99-3075 O27/3
FABRIC: Surface: smooth, hard, common medium to large, angular/platy grey, few small to medium angular/spherical white inclusions. Reddish yellow (5YR 6/6). DESCRIPTION: Complete. One drilled hole. Flat top. Stamped?
Pres. H: 5.7 cm; Base: 3.2 × 3.3 cm; Top: 1.35 × 1.2 cm; We: 56 g.

79. Grand pyramidal loom weight (Pl. 79).
Bag no. 2874; F98-3071 O27/3
FABRIC: Surface: granular, very soft, with frequent small to medium angular/spherical red, grey and white inclusions. Reddish yellow (5YR 6/6). DESCRIPTION: One drilled hole. Stamped. Top missing, one face chipped. Circular stamp on one drilled face, D 1.5 cm.
Pres. H: 6.8 cm; Base: 5.9 × 5.15 cm; We: 196 g.

Room IV

The excavation of the zone behind *AEA* and *ADY* was combined and the zone called *ACZ-ADY*. The wall *AEA* and *ACZ* run into the northern baulk. This area is defined as Room IV.

251 While in O27 this area was excavated as a distinct zone, called AREA IV, this was not distinguished in the O26 excavations.

252 Fragments of the same vessel are found in 2257 (*AET*) and in 1803 (see no. 38).

253 The material from stratum 3, 2nd pass is in bag nos. 3375 and 3367. The Archaic material includes kotyle handles, some in Corinthian fabric, and Archaic pedestalled cup. A jar, no. 77, (the only catalogued sherd from the area), a lopas rim and a Hellenistic pyxis fragment are also within these bags.

The upper levels of *ACZ-ADY* contained a mix of rubble and tiles, including architrave and metope pieces that provide fragmentary evidence of the buildings once situated on the Acropolis. In stratum 3 a tile layer was excavated along with a mix of Archaic and Hellenistic pottery fragments, including the catalogued plate no. 80. Stratum 4, beneath the collapse of the tiles, contains the fine louterion fragments nos. 82 and 83. The quality of the pieces suggests their original function might have been as ritual objects on the Acropolis. Along with them are Hellenistic amphora and plain ware fragments, a lopas rim, a Hellenistic cup and the reversible lid, no. 81.[254] Archaic and Classical fragments are mixed with these Hellenistic vessels.

Stratum 5 sat on the bedrock and is associated with the cutting of the rock for the wall construction. This material has significance as it provides a chance to date the construction of rooms I and II. There is a significant amount of material in this stratum. Much of it consists of medium ware body fragments, including those from amphorae, such as nos. 97 and 98 and the reworked amphora sherd no. 103. Amongst the fine ware are some Archaic fragments and a number of Classical sherds.The Classical material includes the decorated plates nos. 90 and 91, the skyphos rim no. 84, skyphos base no. 85 and the bowls nos. 92 and 93. The skyphos base, no. 86, with its oddly squared foot suggests a late Classical date. The lamp no. 99 is a Classical form. The West Slope kantharos fragment with incised ivy wreaths, no. 87, secures the deposit to the 3rd century. The conical bowl rim, no. 89, with a shadow of painted West Slope decoration belongs to the 3rd century. The late Classical-Hellenistic span of the deposit is nicely displayed by the two base fragments no. 94 and no. 95, the latter following the Classical standards of a complete coating of glaze, the former showing the characteristic Hellenistic semi-glazing. A heavier concentration of Classical material is evident in the layer just above bedrock: though the lekane with grooved rim and thin glaze no. 96 appears Hellenistic and the skyphos foot mentioned above, no. 86, suggests a late Classical date.[255]

There are two loom weights in stratum 5, nos. 100 and 101. These are both type 2, pyramidal loom weights, one is small the other large and both carry distinctive marks. A spindle whorl, no. 102, also issues from this deposit.

Discussion

The evidence in this deposit, suggests that the walls were constructed in the late 4th/early 3rd century and that they were used during the middle years of the 3rd century. There is very little cooking ware when compared to the deposits within the rooms, particularly in room II.

O26 *ACZ-ADY*/3
COMMENT: Layer includes tiles and a mix of Archaic and Hellenistic pottery.

Pottery Bags 1194, 1229, 1779
Pottery Statistics:

Total:	146	%:	We: 1240[256]
FW:	72	49	300
PW:	55	38	740
CPW:	13	9	20
CW:	6	4	180

FW
80. Plate, rolled rim (Not depicted).
Bag no. 1194 O26 ACZ-ADY/3.
FABRIC: Granular, soft, with rare small subrounded/spherical brown inclusions. Pink to reddish yellow (5YR 7/6-5YR 7/4). SURFACE: Mottled black to dark red brown on interior and on exterior just over rim.
DESCRIPTION: Rim and upper wall.
Rim D: 18.0 cm; Pres. H: 4.5 cm.
COMMENTS: Local.
DATE: Hellenistic.

O26 *ACZ-ADY*/4
COMMENT: Mix of Archaic, Classical and Hellenistic fragments, some apparently dislodged from the Acropolis above.

254 Reversible lid, no. 81, is the only catalogued amongst this list, the others are in bag 1650.
255 The last bags of pottery collected from the stratum are 1811, 1804 and 1733.
256 Weight for 1194 not recorded.

Pottery Bags 1650, 1657
Pottery statistics:

Total:	275	%:	We: 4120
FW:	74	27	260
PW:	158	57.5	3050
CPW:	39	14	180
CW:	4	1.5	630

FW
81. Reversible lid (Pl. 5).
Bag no. 1650: 1 O26 ACZ-ADY/4.
FABRIC: Granular, soft and powdery, no visible inclusions. Reddish yellow (7.5YR 7/6). SURFACE: Mottled red to brown. DESCRIPTION: Rim and wall fragment. Vertical rim, two grooves on wall edge.
Rim D: 12.0 cm; Pres. H: 2.7 cm.
COMMENTS: Local?

CW
82. Louterion (Pl. 5).
Bag no. 1657: 1 O26 ACZ-ADY/4.
FABRIC: Hackly, hard with common medium to very large/angular spherical brown, grey inclusions, tabular voids. Very pale brown (10YR 8/3). SURFACE: Smooth yellowish surface. DESCRIPTION: Rim. Flat upper face, moulded outer face. Red paint in bands on moulded face of rim.
Rim D: 54.0 cm; Pres. H: 4.1 cm.
COMMENTS: Import. Compare: Sparkes & Talcott, 1970, nos. 1859-1861, p. 219-220, fig. 16.
DATE: Classical, 5th century.

83. Louterion (Not depicted).
Bag no. 1650: 6 O26 ACZ-ADY/4.
FABRIC: Hackly, hard with large and very large tabular/angular brown and grey inclusions. Very pale brown (10YR 7/4). SURFACE: Yellow-pink slip on upper rim and inner wall, smooth and powdery. DESCRIPTION: Rim and upper wall fragment. Overhanging rim with moulded outer face.
Rim D: 80.0 cm; Pres. H: 6.4 cm.
COMMENTS: Import -Corinth. Compare: Sparkes & Talcott, 1970, nos. 1859-1861, p. 219-220, fig. 16.
DATE: Classical, 5th century.

O26 and O27 *ACZ-ADY*/5

COMMENT: Material set on the cut bedrock behind walls *ADY* and *AEA*. Deposit linked to construction of the rooms.

Pottery Bags 1733, 1741, 1757, 1759, 1804, 1811
Pottery Statistics:

Total:	805	%:	We: 12100
FW:	197	24.5	720
PW:	483	60	9160
CPW:	37	4.5	250
CW:	88	11	1970

FW
84. Skyphos (Pl. 5).
Bag no. 1741: 1 O26 *ACZ-ADY*/5.
FABRIC: Fine, soft, no visible inclusions, few rounded platy voids. Light brown (7.5YR 6/4). SURFACE: Black, shiny. DESCRIPTION: Rim and handle
Rim D: 10.0 cm; Pres. H: 2.2 cm.
COMMENTS: Local.
DATE: Classical, 5th century.

85. Skyphos (Pl. 6).
Bag no. 1733: 2 O27 *ACZ-ADY*/5
FABRIC: Hackly, soft, no visible inclusions. Reddish yellow (5YR 6/6). SURFACE: Remnants of black slip on and under foot. DESCRIPTION: Base fragment. Projecting profile of ring foot.
Base D: 10.0 cm; Pres. H: 1.5 cm.
COMMENTS: Local?
DATE: Classical.

86. Skyphos (Pl. 6).
Bag no. 1804; F98-1005 O26 *ACZ-ADY*/5.
FABRIC: Smooth, hard with few fine white inclusions. Light red (2.5YR 7/6). SURFACE: Lustrous black glaze on inner and outer wall and inner foot. Reserved outer foot, red wash under floor. One patch of reddish-brown on inner wall. DESCRIPTION: Base and lower wall. Groove between lower wall and foot. Profile bulges before squared resting surface.
Base D: 9.0 cm; Pres. H: 3.6 cm.
COMMENTS: Import – Attic? Note the square profile of this foot, perhaps indicating late version of this Classical shape – the onset of the Hellenistic foot type.
DATE: Classical.

87. Hellenistic kantharos, one piece (Not depicted).
Bag no. 1759: 12 O26 *ACZ-ADY*/5
FABRIC: Smooth, soft, no visible inclusions. Reddish yellow (5YR 6/6). SURFACE: Black to brown. DESCRIPTION: Rim and upper wall. West Slope decoration – incised stems of ivy wreath.
Rim D: 7.0 cm; Pres. H: 2.5 cm.
COMMENTS: Local.
DATE: Hellenistic.

88. Hellenistic kantharos, straight walled (Not depicted).
Bag no. 1759: 14 O26 *ACZ-ADY*/5.
FABRIC: Smooth, soft with rare fine rounded/tabular red inclusions. Very pale brown (10YR 7/4). SURFACE: Brown to black, dull. DESCRIPTION: Body fragment. Decoration: West Slope decoration. Two incised tendrils.
Th: 0.2 cm; L: 1.3 cm; W: 2.1 cm.
COMMENTS: Import.
DATE: Hellenistic.

89. Conical bowl (Pl. 6).
Bag no. 1759: 10 O26 *ACZ-ADY*/5.
FABRIC: Smooth, hard, no visible inclusions. Yellowish red (5YR 5/6). DESCRIPTION: Rim and upper wall fragment. Groove on interior rim below rim. Two grooves on exterior 2.75 below rim. Shadow of West Slope wreath.
Rim D: 20.0 cm; Pres. H: 3.5 cm.
COMMENTS: Import.

90. Classical Plate (PL. 6).
Bag no. 1811: 8 O26 *ACZ-ADY*/5.
FABRIC: Smooth, hard, few fine white inclusions. Light reddish brown (5YR 6/4). SURFACE: Brown slip, worn, on all preserved surface. DESCRIPTION: Floor and part of moulded foot. Stamped decoration on upper floor. Decoration: Two grooves around centre of plate floor, then arcs set side by side with open face pointing out forming a circle that coincides with the foot of the plate.
Rim D: 3.1 cm; Pres. H: 1.3 cm.
COMMENTS: Classical.

91. Classical Plate (Not depicted).
Bag no. 1759: 13 O26 *ACZ-ADY*/5.
FABRIC: Conchoidal, soft, with fine white inclusions. Pink (5YR 7/3). SURFACE: Brown, smooth, shiny. DESCRIPTION: Body fragment, floor of plate. Rouletting band and upper leaves of a palmette stamp preserved. (The stamp does not have a distinct border).
Th: 0.65 cm; L: 5.15 cm; W: 2.8 cm.
COMMENTS: Import.
DATE: Classical-Hellenistic.

92. Bowl, moulded rim (Pl. 6).
Bag no. 1746: 4 O26 *ACZ-ADY*/5.
FABRIC: Granular, soft, no visible inclusions. Reddish yellow (7.5YR 7/6). SURFACE: Black, some shine, worn. DESCRIPTION: Rim and upper wall. Decoration: Two grooves on exterior below rim.
Rim D: 19.4 cm; Pres. H: 3.2 cm.
COMMENTS: Import?
DATE: Hellenistic.

93. Bowl, projecting rim (Pl. 6).
Bag no. 1746: 2 O26 *ACZ-ADY*/5.
FABRIC: Granular, soft with no visible inclusions. Light red (2.5YR 6/6). SURFACE: Black, thick and lustrous. DESCRIPTION: Rim and body fragment (only small section of rim preserved). Rim projects slightly beyond the wall with flat upper face, two grooves on outer wall mark the junction with the rim. Grooves on outer wall below rim, light grooves on outer wall and mid wall.
Rim D: 30.0 cm; Pres. H: 3.2 cm.
COMMENTS: Import (same fabric as 114).
DATE: Classical-Hellenistic.

94. Base of cup (Hellenistic kantharos, one piece) (Pl. 6).
Bag no. 1759: 1 O26 *ACZ-ADY*/5.
FABRIC: Granular, hard with few fine and small angular/spherical white and grey inclusions. Reddish yellow (5YR 7/6). SURFACE: Dull dark brown slip on interior and exterior wall. No slip on or under foot. DESCRIPTION: Simple, narrow, elevated ring foot. Lower wall rises smoothly from concave floor.
Rim D: 4.0 cm; Pres. H: 2.1 cm.
DATE: Hellenistic.

95. Base of cup (Hellenistic kantharos, one piece) (Pl. 6).
Bag no. 1741: 2 O26 *ACZ-ADY*/5.
FABRIC: Granular, soft, with no visible inclusions but few irregular voids. Reddish yellow (5YR 6/6). SURFACE: Black to brown, shiny, on all preserved surfaces. DESCRIPTION: Narrow, simple ring foot with concave outer profile and flat resting surface, walls rise quickly from concave floor.
Rim D: 3.9 cm; Pres. H: 2.0 cm.
COMMENTS: Local.
DATE: Classical-Hellenistic.

96. Lekane (Pl. 6).
Bag no. 1811: 4 O26 *ACZ-ADY*/5.
FABRIC: Granular, hard with common small to medium angular/spherical white and grey inclusions. Margin: Light reddish brown (5YR 6/3); Core: Reddish brown (2.5YR 5/4). SURFACE: Dull black glaze on rim, inner wall and under rim. DESCRIPTION: Broad projecting rim with groove on outer border and rounded outer profile. Outer wall: smooth transition from rim, concave profile.
Rim D: 30.0 cm; Pres. H: 3.9 cm.
COMMENTS: Local.
DATE: Hellenistic.

PW
97. Transport Amphora (Pl. 6).
Bag no. 1741: 3 O26 *ACZ-ADY*/5.
FABRIC: Granular, hard with rounded tabular brown inclusions, platy voids. Pink (7.5YR 7/4). DESCRIPTION: Rim and neck fragment. Rounded, rolled rim.
Rim D: 9.0 cm; Pres. H: 6.1 cm.
COMMENTS: Import? Classical-Hellenistic. Corinthian Type B Amphora.

98. Transport Amphora (Pl. 6).
Bag no. 1811: 5 O26 *ACZ-ADY*/5.
FABRIC: Granular, hard, with small to very large angular/spherical white and brown inclusions, rare light refracting particles. Reddish yellow (5YR 6/6). DESCRIPTION: Rim, neck and handle stem. The mushroom rim is triangular in section with a flat outer profile, cutting back in to wall. Handle circular in section.
Rim D: 10.0 cm; Pres. H: 6.8 cm.
COMMENTS: Local. Compare: Lawall 2004, no. 30, p. 451-452, pl. 199.

Lamp
99. Lamp (Not depicted).
FABRIC: Smooth, soft, no visible inclusions. Reddish yellow (5YR 6/6). SURFACE: Black glaze. DESCRIPTION: Nozzle and body. Broad and shallow nozzle.
Pres. H: 1.7 cm; L: 3.65 cm; W: 3.3 cm.
COMMENTS: Local. Compare: Broneer 1977 type V.
DATE: Classical.

Loom weights

Type 2
100. Small pyramidal loom weight (Not depicted).
Bag no. 1819; F98-1004 O26 *ACZ-ADY*/5.
FABRIC: Granular, hard with frequent small rounded/spherical brown-white inclusions (some hollow), medium to large angular/tabular frequent dark brown and grey and rare white inclusions. Pale red (10R 6/3). DESCRIPTION: One drilled hole, decorated. Slight chipping on top. The resting surface is not flat resulting in an asymmetrical loom weight. Near complete. Two incised grooves that run parallel to each edge of the weight on one face with drilled hole.
Pres. H: 6.0 cm; Base: 3.25 × 3.45 cm; top: 1.4 × 1.4 cm; We: 65 g.

101. Large pyramidal loom weight (Not depicted).
Bag no. 1753; F98-1002 O26 *ACZ-ADY*/5
FABRIC: (Surface) Smooth, soft with small to very large angular/spherical white, brown, red, grey inclusions. Light red to reddish yellow (2.5YR 6/6 – 5YR 6/6). DESCRIPTION: One drilled hole. Stamped. Top broken at drilled hole, chipped base. Oval stamp on one face with drilled hole: 1.5 cm long, 1 cm broad.
Pres. H: 6.5 cm; Base: 4.7 × 4.45 cm; We: 143 g.

Other weaving objects
102. Spindle whorl (Not depicted).
Bag no. 1758; F98-1001 O26 *ACZ-ADY*/5.
FABRIC: Light red (2.5YR 7/6). DESCRIPTION: Single hole drilled through centre. Chipping of wall, but full profile preserved in part.

Pres. H: 3.0 cm; Max D: 4.5 cm; D drilled hole: 0.65 cm; We: 47 g.

Various

103. Transport Amphora (Pl. 6).
Bag no. 1757: 2 O26 *ACZ-ADY*/5.
FABRIC: Granular, very hard, few small subrounded/tabular brown inclusions, few voids
Colour: Core: Very pale brown to pale yellow (10YR 8/4 -2.5Y 8/4); exterior surface: Pale yellow (5Y 7/3).
DESCRIPTION: Handle and body fragments. Reworked sherd. One of the body sherds has an unfinished edge that has been reworked into sharp scallops that are reminiscent of a serrated knife edge, quite crisp and sharp.
Length of serrated area: 3 cm; each serration 0.75 cm in length and 0.2 cm in depth.
COMMENTS: Import. Corinthian Type B Amphora.

Room V

The first and second strata excavated in this trench represented fill and collapse likely to have fallen down the slope onto the already destroyed houses. Stratum 3 is reached and continues to bedrock.

The tile layer *AEZ* covered much of the room.

With the removal of the tile layer, a high concentration of finds both pots and 'non-pots' were found in stratum 3, set immediately below the tile smash, corresponding to the similar layer in room II.[257] There is a high quantity of fine ware, including high-quality examples, but many of them are small fragments. Cups, plates, bowls and a lagynos are catalogued (nos. 109-118). From the limited selection of cooking pot ware found in the deposit is the lid no. 120. The plain ware fragments are represented in the catalogue by the amphora no. 119. A number of fragments in the deposit are Archaic and Classical and the Hellenistic material does not extend beyond the mid-3rd century.[258] This material includes the two lamps nos. 121 and 122.

Bedrock appeared in the west of the trench near *AEJ* soon after the removal of the tiles and then in the centre of the room on the first day of digging the second pass of stratum 3. After bedrock was revealed the ceramic fragments were small with a balance of fine ware, small medium ware fragments and rare cooking ware. Archaic and Classical fragments (Classical vessels include nos. 125 and 126) are common and the Hellenistic wares are rare. The third pass contains a great mix of material ranging in date from Prehistoric to Hellenistic. The excavator reports a concentration of sherds near wall *AFI* including the lekane/strainer no. 127. The range is similar to that of the second pass, but the appearance of the Hellenistic fragments is further reduced (lopas no. 128 and chytra no. 129). The lopas, no. 128, was found in the quarter of the trench approaching the corner of *AEK/AEZ* and *AEJ*. Both nos. 128 and 129 are unworn and would appear to have hardly been used before deposition. Their presence in this deposit, as the only late 4th to 3rd century fragments, is significant in interpreting the use and date of the room.

Loom weights are found throughout stratum 3, totalling one conical (type 1) no. 123, three pyramidal (type 2) nos. 130-132, two pyramidal (type 3) nos. 133 and 134. The pyramidal loom weights are from the lower levels. The three type 2 loom weights are small, while the type 3 weights are medium and the conical loom weight, the heaviest of its type, belongs to the large group. The majority of loom weights are collected in the northern section of the room, along wall *AEK*.

A female figurine face, no. 124, from a 3rd century terracotta figurine was located within the second pass of stratum 3.[259]

Discussion

The roof of the room collapsed after occupation in the 3rd century period. There are no ceramics underneath the tile smash *AEZ* that reach beyond the last quarter of the 3rd century. This date limit is supported by the collection of coins that were excavated within the third stratum of the deposit, particularly in the area under-

257 The finds level was excavated on the 13th, 14th and 15th of July 1999.

258 Archaic: 2826: 7, 2826: 1; Classical: A red figure fragment in the stratum (not well-preserved), no. 117, compares to one found above the tile layer, no. 106. Also from the upper level is the Classical/Hellenistic plate fragment no. 104.

259 Compare with Davidson 1952, no. 260-261, 3rd century

neath the tile smash, and contributing considerably to the identification of a 'finds layer'. The coins issue from a range of places. The majority of the coins were manufactured in the 4th and 3rd centuries and only one (no. 93) must date after the mid 3rd century.[260] Naturally coins can be in circulation some time before ending their days under a tile smash in a small settlement in Aitolia, however, combined with the ceramic evidence we can certainly propose a mid to late 3rd century collapse of the buildings.

The differentiation in the material in stratum 3 (the occupation and construction layer) allows the possible interpretation, that the Hellenistic layer of finds represents the last of a series of occupations in the rooms, and, that the uneven bedrock was levelled with a fill containing Classical, Archaic (and some geometric and Prehistoric sherds) and rare, unworn Hellenistic material (suggesting a late 4th – early 3rd century date) to provide a floor level to the room. It is significant that the loom weights belong to the lower levels, suggesting that they formed either part of the fill or represented earlier, that is non-Hellenistic, activities in the area.

The gap between walls *ATF* and the east-west stretch of *ATC* allow a direct route from room V to room VIII. The Archaic material is found in both rooms (see below), but the ceramics in V indicate more intensive Hellenistic use.

O27/3 Upper Level
COMMENT: Material excavated above tile layer *AEZ*.

Pottery Bags: Upper Level: 2088, 2097, 2224, 2229, 2235, 2233, 2240
Pottery Statistics:

Total:	367	%:	We: 5355
FW:	149	40.5	990
PW:	175	47.5	3420
CPW:	34	9.5	175
CW:	9	2.5	770

FW
104. Classical Plate (Not depicted).
Bag no. 2235: 1 O27/3.
FABRIC: Slightly granular, soft, rare small angular/spherical white inclusions. Light red (2.5YR 6/8). SURFACE: Brown on interior, red on exterior. DESCRIPTION: Body fragment, floor of plate. Decoration: Thick band of rouletting (3-4 rows) between double incised lines on either side.
T: 0.7 cm; L: 2.8 cm; W: 4.6 cm.
COMMENTS: Import. Upper zone of stratum 3.
DATE: Classical-Hellenistic.

105. Bowl, folded rim (Pl. 6).
Bag no. 2224: 1 O27/3.
FABRIC: Granular, soft, with rare small angular/spherical white inclusions. Reddish yellow (5YR 7/6). SURFACE: Black to brown, worn and dull. DESCRIPTION: Rim and upper wall. Upper wall curves in, lip folded over onto outer wall with a flattened upper face.
Rim D: 30.0 cm; Pres. H: 2.2 cm.
COMMENTS: Local. Other examples of this shape found in this context. Upper zone of stratum 3.

106. Krater, Classical
Bag no. 2088: 2 O27/3.
FABRIC: Granular, soft, no visible inclusions. Reddish yellow (5YR 6/8). SURFACE: Brown to black, lustrous. DESCRIPTION: Bell krater (?). Rim and upper wall. Decoration: Edge of a subsidiary red figure pattern, thick vertical lines alternate with thin vertical lines on reserved background.
D: Rim. 33.0 cm; Pres. H: 2.0 cm.
COMMENTS: Import – Attic. Compare: Moore 1997, nos. 175-178 and 180-182, p. 161-162, pls. 26-27. Same vessel as no. 117.
DATE: Classical, 480-450.

AEZ
COMMENTS: Tile layer in Room V

Pottery Bags: 2380; 2584; 2600; 2645; 2634; 2805
Pottery Statistics:

Total:	154	%:	We: 1390
FW:	48	31	150
PW:	60	39	480
CPW:	32	21	170
CW:	14	9	590

260 TPR and figures at back of this chapter.

FW
107. Classical Plate (Not depicted).
Bag no. 2805: 1 O27/3 associated with *AEZ*.
FABRIC: Slightly granular, soft, rare fine white inclusions. Reddish yellow (5YR 6/6). SURFACE: Black, worn. DESCRIPTION: Body fragment, floor of plate. Long impressed rays formed by double incised lines, radiating from centre of plate.
T: 0.35 cm; L: 2.5 cm; W: 2.1 cm.
COMMENTS: Import. Bag is excavated as O27/3, associated with *AEZ*, the tile spill, through review of diary combined with ceramic analysis.
DATE: Classical.

CPW
108. Chytra (Pl. 7).
Bag no. 2380; F99-3001 *AEZ*.
FABRIC: Hackly, hard, frequent angular/spherical small white and grey inclusions and few large white inclusions. Red (2.5YR 5/6). DESCRIPTION: Rim, upper wall, numerous body fragments.
Rim D: 13 cm; Pres. H: 3.2 cm.
COMMENTS: Local. Compare: Drougou & Touratsoglou 1980, Π 1379, p. 120-122.
DATE: Hellenistic.

O27/3 Middle
COMMENTS: Area excavated below the tile spill. Excavated between 12-15 July 1999. Occupation level.

Pottery Bags: 2817, 2884, 2882, 2826, 2892, 2889, 2891
Pottery Statistics:

Total:	970	%:	We: 4620[261]
FW:	481	49.5	1390
PW:	233	24	2330
CPW:	240	25	740
CW:	16	1.5	160

FW
109. Cup Skyphos (Pl. 7).
Bag no. 2817: 5 O27/3 Middle.
FABRIC: Smooth, hard, rare spherical voids, no visual inclusions. Light reddish brown (5YR 6/4). SURFACE: Brown, mottled, dull. DESCRIPTION: Rim, handle stem and wall.
Concave lip with sharp junction to concave wall. Handle sits on junction.
Rim D: 12.0 cm; Pres. H: 5.5 cm.
COMMENTS: Import.
DATE: Classical.

110. Plate, offset rim (Pl. 7).
Bag no. 2817: 9 O27/3 Middle.
FABRIC: Smooth, soft with few fine angular/platy white inclusions. Light yellowish brown (10YR 6/4). SURFACE: Black, fairly lustrous. DESCRIPTION: Rim set from wall by ridge. Upper face of rim convex to overhanging lip, groove on outer rim.
Rim D: 18.0 cm; Pres. H: 1.8 cm.
COMMENTS: Import.

111. Plate, grooved rim (Pl. 7).
Bag no. 2826: 4 O27/3 Middle.
FABRIC: Slightly granular, soft, frequent very fine white inclusions. Pink (7.5YR 7/4).
SURFACE: Brown, shiny. DESCRIPTION: Rim and upper wall. Thick wall. Rim offset from wall. Two grooves on upper rim.
Rim D: 22.0 cm; Pres. H: 1.7 cm.
COMMENTS: There is another fragment of the same shape in this same bag. It has a bigger rim with deep grooves on it.
DATE: Classical-Hellenistic.

112. Plate, Rolled rim (Pl. 7).
Bag no. 2817: 8 O27/3 Middle.
FABRIC: Laminar, very soft, no visible inclusions. Light red (2.5YR 6/6). SURFACE: Dark brown mottled to red brown. DESCRIPTION: Rim and upper wall.
Rim D: 11.0 cm; Pres. H: 2.4 cm.
COMMENTS: Local.
DATE: Hellenistic.

113. Bowl, moulded rim (Pl. 7)
Bag no. 2817: 4 O27/3 Middle.
FABRIC: Smooth, hard, rare fine white inclusions, few fine voids. Light reddish brown (5YR 6/4). SURFACE: Black to brown, shiny on interior, dull on exterior. DESCRIPTION: Rim and upper wall. One deep and

261 This does not include the weight of Amphora 2889.

two shallow grooves on exterior wall below rim.
Rim D: 12.0 cm; Pres. H: 2.5 cm.
COMMENTS: Import.
DATE: Hellenistic.

114. Bowl, projecting rim (Not depicted).
Bag no. 2826: 5 O27/3 Middle.
FABRIC: Granular, soft, few fine angular/spherical dark inclusions. Red (2.5YR 5/6). SURFACE: Smooth and shiny black glaze. DESCRIPTION: Rim and upper wall. Rim has a slightly concave upper face. The outer rim to wall junction marked with two grooves but otherwise quite smooth. Interior junction is angular as the inner wall drops to a concave body and thin wall. The rim does not project horizontally but rather rises up above the body whilst projecting slightly.
Rim D: 28 cm; H: 1.3 cm
COMMENTS: Import (same fabric as 93).
DATE: Classical.

115. Bowl, out turned rim (Pl. 7).
Bag no. 2817: 6 O27/3 Middle.
FABRIC: Smooth, hard, no visible inclusions. Light reddish brown (5YR 6/4). SURFACE: Metallic grey/brown slip. DESCRIPTION: Rim and upper wall. Outturned lip. Upper wall thicker than lower wall and the junction is marked due to this.
Rim D: 15.0 cm; Pres. H: 4.3 cm.
COMMENTS: Import (same fabric as 1746:2 and 2826:5). Piece from same vessel in bag 2284. Compare: Rotroff 1997, nos. 948 and 959, fig. 61; I. Vdovichenko 2004, pl. 359.
DATE: Notes: Hellenistic.

116. Bowl (Echinus bowl) (Pl. 7).
Bag no. 2817: 2 O27/3 Middle.
FABRIC: Granular, very soft, frequent small angular/spherical brown inclusions. Reddish yellow (5YR 7/6). SURFACE: Brown very mottled. DESCRIPTION: Rim and upper wall. Rather rough production.
Rim D: 9.0 cm; Pres. H: 3.7 cm.

117. Krater, Classical (Pl. 7).
2826: 3 O27/3 Middle.
FABRIC: Granular, soft, no visible inclusions. Reddish yellow (5YR 6/8). SURFACE: Brown to black, lustrous. DESCRIPTION: Body sherd. Subsidiary red figure pattern, thick vertical lines alternate with thin vertical lines on reserved back ground, with continuous thick vertical line as base.
COMMENTS: Import – Attic. From the same vessel as no. 106. Compare: Moore 1997, nos. 175-178 and 180-182, p. 161-162, pls. 26-27.
DATE: Classical, 480-450.

118. Lagynos (with strap handle) (Pl. 7).
Bag no. 2826: 2 O27/3 Middle.
FABRIC: Granular, soft, few fine dark, few small subrounded/spherical white inclusions. Pink (5YR 7/4 – 7.5YR 7/4). SURFACE: Black, metallic slip on all exterior surfaces and on interior rim and neck. DESCRIPTION: Rim and handle. Flaring rim, double handle attached directly below rim, carination with lower body marked with ridge. Slight ridges on interior rim.
Rim D: 6.0 cm; Pres. H: 3.9 cm.
COMMENTS: Import.
DATE: Hellenistic.

PW

119. Transport Amphora (Pl. 7).
Bag no. 2892: 1 O27/3 Middle.
FABRIC: Granular, hard, common subrounded/spherical-tabular small and fine white inclusions. Red (2.5YR 5/6). DESCRIPTION: Rim, neck and handle. Rim rolled and slightly projecting.
Rim D: 11.0 cm; Pres. H: 11.4 cm.
COMMENTS: Import. Corinthian Type B Amphora.

CPW

120. Lid (Not depicted).
Bag no. 2892: 4 O27/3 Middle.
FABRIC: Hackly, hard, frequent angular/spherical small white and grey inclusions. Red (2.5YR 5/6). DESCRIPTION: Rim and wall. Moulding on upper face of rim.
Rim D: 19.0 cm; Pres. H: 2.0 cm.
COMMENTS: Local.
DATE: Hellenistic.

Lamp

121. Lamp (Pl. 7).
Bag no. 2817: 3 O27/3 Middle.
FABRIC: Slightly granular, soft, no visible inclusions. Pink (5YR 7/4). SURFACE: Thin brown to red brown. DESCRIPTION: Nozzle, wall and rim. Broad lamp, narrow disc.
Pres. H: 2.6 cm; Interior D: 4.5 cm.
COMMENTS: Import. Compare: Broneer 1977, 83.
DATE: Hellenistic-Classical.

122. Lamp (Pl. 7).
Bag no. 2826: 11 O27/3 Middle.
FABRIC: Smooth, soft, few fine rounded/spherical voids. Light red (2.5YR 6/6). SURFACE: Black to grey and brown. DESCRIPTION: Rim and body fragment. Groove at junction of rim and wall.
Rim D: 3.0 cm; Pres. H: 2.3 cm; max. D: 5.0 cm.
COMMENTS: Local. Compare: Broneer 1977, 119, type VII C, 4th to 3rd century.
DATE: Hellenistic.

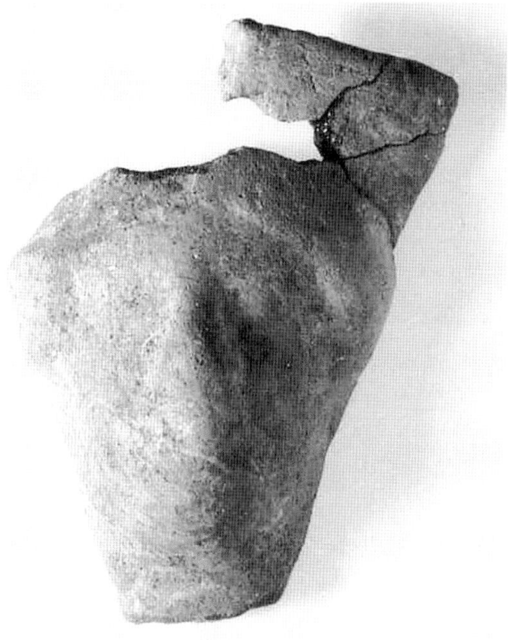

Fig. 82 *Face of female. Catalogue no. 124.*

Loom weight:

Type 1
123. Large conical loom weight (Fig. 83).
Bag no. 2819; F99-3010 O27/3 Middle.
FABRIC: Granular, hard, with common small rounded/spherical brown-white inclusions (some hollow, some platy), medium angular/spherical brown, white and grey inclusions. Light reddish brown to pink (5YR 6/3 – 5YR 7/3). DESCRIPTION: One drilled hole. Chipped base. Pointed top, bevelled to base.
Pres. H: 10.2 cm; max. pres. D: 6.0 cm; We: 219 g.

Figurine

124. Face of female, some neck and hair also preserved, hollow behind. (Pl. 7 and Fig. 82).
Bag no. 2945; F99-3042 O27/3 Middle
FABRIC: Hackly, hard, few small angular/spherical white, grey and brown inclusions. Red (2.5YR 5/6). DESCRIPTION: Worn, nose, chin and hairline still distinct but eyes, mouth etc are not.
Pres. H: 4.65 cm; W: 3.75 cm; We: 19.0 cm
COMMENTS: Compare: Davidson 1952, no. 260-261, 3rd century.
DATE: Hellenistic, 3rd century.

O27/3 Lower Layer
COMMENTS: Excavated 16-19th July, after the appearance of bedrock in the western area of the trench. Contains an increased amount of Archaic and Classical material along with rare Hellenistic sherds.

Pottery Bags: 2901, 2854, 2895, 2858, 2856, 2865, 2897
Pottery Statistics:[262]

Total:	449	%:	We: 2240
FW:	207	46	1030
PW:	147	33	830
CPW:	78	17	280
PW:	17	4	100

125. Bolsal (Pl. 8).
Bag no. 2858: 2 O27/3 Lower layer.
FABRIC: Granular, hard, few fine tabular/angular

262 These statistics do not include Bag 2865.

white and grey inclusions, few small and medium irregular voids. Light reddish brown (5YR 6/4). SURFACE: Black mottled to brown, some shine. DESCRIPTION: Rim, wall and handle. Thin walled, simple lip, handle attached to rim.
Rim D: 8.0 cm; Pres. H: 2.7 cm.
COMMENTS: Local. Compare: Sparkes & Talcott, 1970, nos. 534, 538, fig. 6.
DATE: Classical.

126. Echinus bowl (Pl. 8).
Bag no. 2858: 1 O27/3 Lower layer.
FABRIC: Smooth, soft, no visible inclusions. Light red (2.5YR 6/6). SURFACE: Black, lustrous. DESCRIPTION: Rim and upper wall. Thick walled, indication of transition to foot (suggests broad footed, shallow bowl).
Rim D: 9.4 cm; Pres. H: 2.2 cm.
COMMENTS: Import – Attic.
DATE: Classical.

127. Lekane/strainer (Pl. 8).
Bag no. 2897; F99-3055 O27/3 Lower layer
FABRIC: Slightly laminar, hard with few small angular/spherical brown inclusions and irregular voids, light refracting particles. Reddish yellow (5YR 7/6). SURFACE: Thin brown on interior, brown to red on exterior wall, reserved band above foot. Foot and under floor carry a smooth wash and three circles in brown paint mark the centre on the under floor. DESCRIPTION: Base, lower wall. 4 drilled holes in floor. Disc foot profiled to look like ring foot, slight elevation to floor on underside of foot. The drilled holes are placed in the floor more or less symmetrically where the floor measures 4.7 cm. in diameter.
Rim D: 12.8 cm; Pres. H: 8.9 cm.
COMMENTS: There is a rim fragment in the bag, but it is not from the same vessel, it belongs to another krater with a painted zigzag on the neck below the rim; it dates to the Geometric/Archaic period.
DATE: Classical.

CPW
128. Lopas (Not depicted).
Bag no. 2856: 1 O27/3 Lower layer
FABRIC: Granular, very hard, few small white angular/spherical inclusions. Dark reddish brown (2.5YR 2.5/3). DESCRIPTION: Rim, upper wall and handle. Attached handle secured below rim, rises up to height of rim, folded and angles sharply down (50 degree angle).
Rim D: ca. 26 cm; Pres. H: 2.5 cm.
COMMENTS: Import.
DATE: Hellenistic.

129. Chytra (Not depicted).
Bag no. 2865: 2 O27/3 Lower layer
FABRIC: Granular, soft with common small subrounded/spherical white and black inclusions. Red (2.5YR 5/8). DESCRIPTION: Rim and upper wall. Projecting rim, angular inner junction with smooth curving wall.
Rim D: 16.0 cm; Pres. H: 3.7 cm.
COMMENTS: Local.
DATE: Classical, 4th century.

Loom weight:

Type 2
130. Small pyramidal loom weight (Fig. 83).
Bag no. 2900; F99-3057 O27/3 Lower layer.
FABRIC: Surface: smooth. Pink (5YR 7/4). DESCRIPTION: One drilled hole. Flat top. Complete.
Pres. H: 5.55 cm; base: 3.45 × 3.3 cm, top: 1.15 × 1.2 cm; We: 57 g.

131. Small pyramidal loom weight (Fig. 83).
Bag no. 2863; F99-3064 O27/3 Lower layer.
FABRIC: Surface, smooth, common fine sub-rounded/spherical-platy white inclusions. Reddish yellow (7.5YR 7/6). DESCRIPTION: One drilled hole. Flat top. Complete.
Pres. H: 5.5 cm; Base: 3.9 × 3.8 cm; top: 1.3 × 1.15 cm; We: 68 g.

132. Small pyramidal loom weight (Fig. 83).
Bag no. 2862; F99-3062 O27/3 Lower layer.
FABRIC: Surface smooth, hard. Pink (5YR 7/4). SURFACE: Black to brown slip, thick in places. DESCRIPTION: One drilled hole. Flat top and base. Complete.
Pres. H: 6.5 cm; base: 3.5 × 3.45 cm; top: 1.55 × 1.3 cm; We: 65 g.

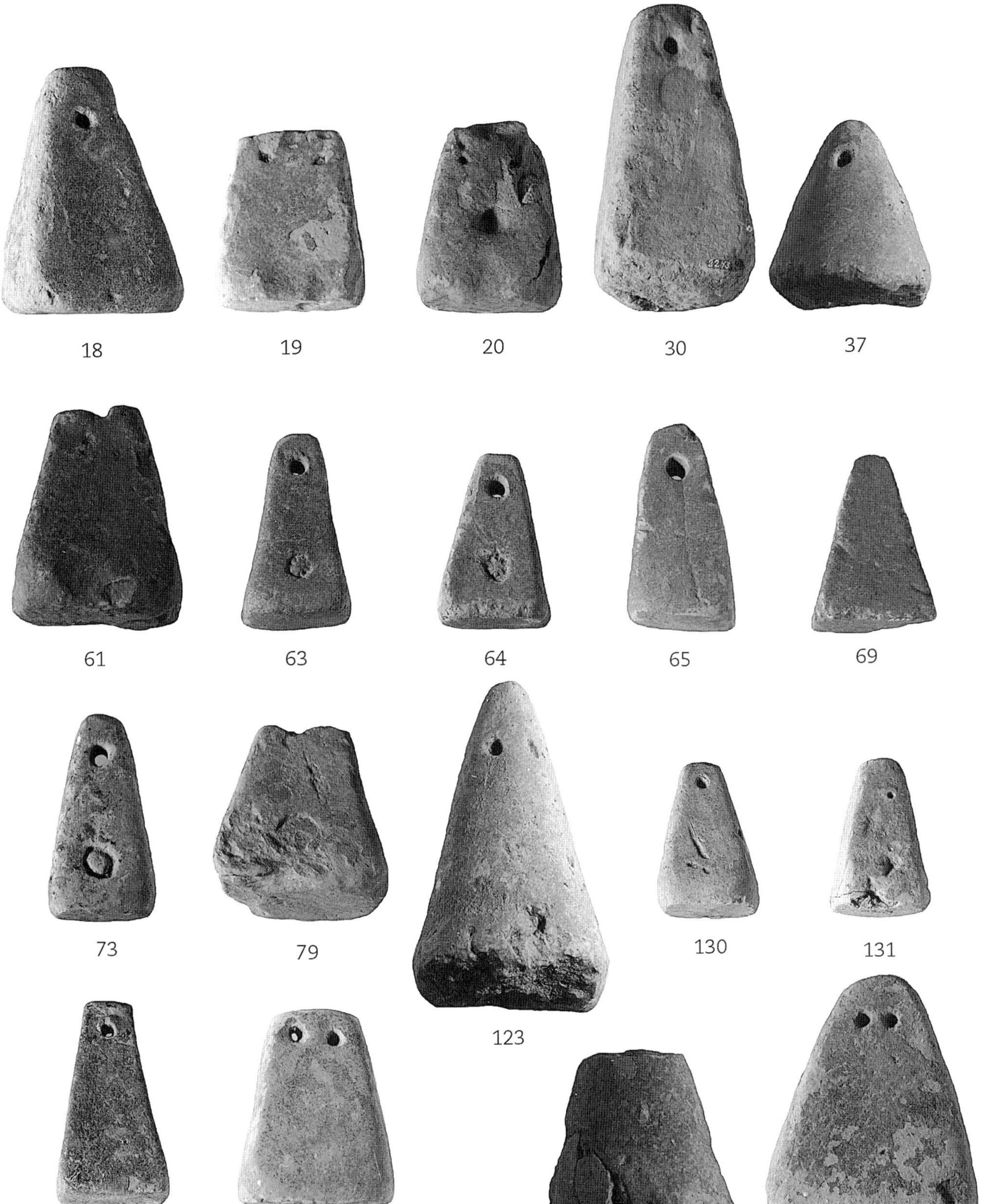

Fig. 83 *Loom weights from AREA III.*

Type 3
133. Medium pyramidal loom weight (Fig. 83).
Bag no. 2864; F99-3067 O27/3 Lower layer.
FABRIC: Smooth, soft, few small subrounded/spherical grey and brown inclusions. Pink (7.5YR 7/4). DESCRIPTION: Two drilled holes (these holes are placed at a fairly even level on one face, but come through very unevenly on the other). Chipped near top on one face.
Pres. H: 7.0 cm; Base: 5.3 × 3.4 cm; top: 3.1 × 1.5 cm; We: 111 g.

134. Medium pyramidal loom weight (Not depicted).
Bag no. 2857; F99-3060 O27/3 Lower layer.
FABRIC: Granular, hard, small to very large subrounded/spherical red, grey and white inclusions. Pink (5YR 7/4). DESCRIPTION: Two drilled holes. Rounded top. Complete.
Pres. H: 7.2 cm; Base: 4.4 × 2.9 cm; We: 105 g.

Various

135. Reworked sherd (Not depicted).
Bag no. 2858: 3 O27/3 Lower layer.
FABRIC: Granular, hard, with few small rounded/spherical grey inclusions. Pink (5YR 7/4). SURFACE: Thin brown on one surface. DESCRIPTION: Body fragment shaped into a rough circle
T: 1.65 cm; Max D: 6.3 cm.

Zone VI

Zone VI is the area in front of room V that is recessed from the front of the neighbouring rooms II and VIII. Therefore it is protected on its north by the end of wall *AEK* and on its south by the wall *ATC*. The majority of this zone is located in O27 (excavated in 1999 as zone II stratum 3), the southern zone is in T31 (excavated in 2000 asT31b stratum 4). The upper layers of fill are common across the zone but in the third stratum of VI the material offers little remarkable. A single coin, dated to the 4th century,[263] is found near *AFI* and a conical (type 1) loom weight, no. 139, is also from stratum 3. The ceramics are found in some quantity and like those on the other side of the wall include Hellenistic materials, nos. 136, 137, 138, along with earlier ware. Archaic material is plentiful in the area just to the north of *ATC*, reminiscent of what is found within room VI. This includes an Archaic cup and other fine body fragments along with an Archaic cooking pot fragment. Prehistoric fragments are also in evidence.[264]

Within the zone a cut into bedrock, *AGD*, is found in, or rather below, the third strat. The material within the cut consisted largely of cooking wares, including the lopas fragment no. 140. The uncommonly large type 3 loom weight no. 141 with two drilled holes was also found within this cut.

Discussion

The material in VI represents a similar date range as that in the room V. The lack of a distinct find layer to match that within the adjacent room V prompts an interpretation of this space not as a room, but as a sheltered but outdoor area. As with the strata in rooms V and VIII there is evidence of Archaic and Classical activity within the zone, but Hellenistic sherds appear on the bedrock, including the cooking wares in *AGD*.

O27 zone II /3
Pottery Bag: 2870
Pottery Statistics:

Total:	269	%:	We: 1430
FW:	159	59	530
PW:	52	19.5	620
CPW:	49	18	200
CW:	9	3.5	80

FW
136. Plate, offset rim (Not depicted).
Bag no. 2870: 4 O27 zone II /3.
FABRIC: Granular, hard, with few small white angular/tabular-spherical inclusions. Reddish yellow (5YR 6/6). SURFACE: Thin grey on interior. DESCRIPTION: Rim and body. Broad rim, overhanging, not offset from outer wall, but offset from inner wall by ridge and deep groove, second groove on outer upper face.
Rim D: 22.0 cm; Pres. H: 2.5 cm.

263 See *SPR* and *TPR*.

264 In bag 4797.

COMMENTS: Local.
DATE: Hellenistic.

137. Plate, rolled rim (Pl. 8).
Bag no. 2870: 3 O27 zone II /3.
FABRIC: Laminar, soft, few small white angular/spherical inclusions. Reddish yellow (5YR 6/6). SURFACE: Brown, mottled and thin. DESCRIPTION: Rim and upper wall
Rim D: 16.5 cm; Pres. H: 1.8 cm.
COMMENTS: Local.
DATE: Hellenistic.

138. Jug (Pl. 8).
Bag no. 2870: 2 O27 zone II /3.
FABRIC: Slightly hackly, hard, rare angular/tabular fine white and grey inclusions and frequent voids. Light reddish brown to pink (5YR 6/3 – 5YR 7/3). SURFACE: Brown, thin and dull. DESCRIPTION: Rim and upper wall. Flaring rim, small globular shape.
Rim D: 9.0 cm; Pres. H: 3.3 cm.
COMMENTS: Local.
DATE: Hellenistic.

LOOM WEIGHT:
Type 1
139. Conical loom weight (Fig. 83).
Bag no. 2869 O27 zone II /3.
FABRIC: Hackly, hard, common large and very large angular-subrounded/spherical red and brown inclusions. Red (2.5YR 5/6). DESCRIPTION: One drilled hole. Top missing from drilled hole. Base chipped. Poor preservation.
Pres. H: 6.65 cm; max. D base: 5.7 cm.

AGD
COMMENTS: a cut into bedrock within VI. Cooking wares.

Pottery Bags: 3379
Pottery Statistics:

Total:	65	%:	We: 150
FW:	35	54	80
PW:	12	18.5	30
CPW:	18	27.5	40
CW:	–	–	-

CPW
140. Lopas (Pl. 8).
Bag no. 3379: 3 AGD.
FABRIC: Granular, hard, frequent small white and brown angular/spherical inclusions. Reddish brown (5YR 4/4). DESCRIPTION: Rim, upper wall and carination to lower wall.
Rim D: 19 cm; Pres. H: 4.8 cm.
COMMENTS: Local.
DATE: Hellenistic.

Loom weight

Type 3
141. Grand pyramidal loom weight (Fig. 83).
Bag no. 3378; F99-3083 *AGD.*
FABRIC: Surface: smooth, soft, frequent small to large angular/spherical white, red and brown inclusions. Pink to reddish yellow (5YR 7/4 – 5YR 7/6). DESCRIPTION: Two drilled holes. Chipped bottom, rounded top. Faces holding drilled holes are much broader than the other faces – broad, flat loom weight.
Pres. H: 9.35 cm; base: 7.6 × 3.8 cm; We: 247 g.
COMMENTS: Unusual loom weight form

Zone VII

To the west of room V is a narrow zone between the back wall and the Archaic/Classical terrace wall, zone VII. Bedrock rises up in this area. The zone is excavated to stratum 2, where a 2a, 2b and 2c are excavated as distinct layers. In 2a, the one-handler no. 142 and the jug no. 143 were located. 2b refers to a hard-packed deposit and contained a quantity of ceramics. This material included Archaic and Classical/Hellenistic material; included in the catalogue are Classical fragments, the skyphos no. 144, the lekanis no. 145, and the lopas rim no. 146 and one base of a miniature vessel, uncatalogued and of uncertain date. No ceramic material was recovered in stratum 2c, which was located directly on the bedrock.

COMMENT: Area between the back wall of room V and the Classical wall.

ACZ-AEJ O27/2a

COMMENT: Zone is a fill and material is likely to be from the Acropolis above.

Pottery Bags: 1564, 1565, 1566

Pottery Statistics:

Total:	22	%:	We: 290[265]
FW:	5	23	10
PW:	17	77	280
CPW:			
CW:			

FW

142. One handler (Pl. 8).
Bag no. 1566; F98-4002 *ACZ-AEJ* O27/2a.
Rim to foot profile.
FABRIC: Granular, soft, small platy voids, no visible inclusions. Pink (7.5YR 7/4). SURFACE: Dull brown on interior, exterior dark brown and red. Worn. DESCRIPTION: Disc foot, horizontal handle stems indicate rising handle.
Rim D: 9.0 cm; Base D: 3.8 cm; Pres. H: 3.7 cm.
COMMENTS: Import.
DATE: Hellenistic.

143. Jug (Pl. 8).
Bag no. 1565; F99-4003 *ACZ-AEJ* O27/2a.
FABRIC: Granular, soft (powdery surface) few small angular/tabular-spherical white inclusions angular/spherical grey inclusions. Reddish yellow (5YR 7/6). SURFACE: Brown slip, mottled, on exterior wall, dripping marks around handle. Interior rim band of glaze mottled to red, some dripping marks on interior neck, but largely unglazed. DESCRIPTION: Rim, neck and handle. Rim flaring, simple lip. Short, broad cylindrical neck, concave profile, flares out to junction with rounded shoulder. Handle rises above rim, slightly moulded.
Rim D: 14.0 cm; Est. Rest. H: 9.6 cm.
COMMENTS: Local. F98-4004 in bag 1564 is the same vessel and the description here combines the two.
DATE: Classical-Hellenistic.

265 Weight not recorded for find bags 1565 and 1566, (nos. 142 and 143).

ACZ-AEJ *O27/2b*

COMMENT: Stratum 2b linked to the use phase of the rooms in front of VII.

Pottery Bags: 1589

Pottery Statistics:

Total:	477	%:	We: 4660
FW:	80	17	190
PW:	342	71.5	2920
CPW:	15	3	80
CW:	40	8.5	1470

FW

144. Skyphos (Pl. 8).
Bag no. 1589: 1 *ACZ-AEJ* O27/2b.
FABRIC: Fine, smooth with no visible inclusions. Light red (10R 6/6). SURFACE: Black, lustrous, reserved on resting surface, band of brown glaze on inner face of ring foot. Red wash under floor. DESCRIPTION: Base and lower wall. Foot with rounded and slightly protruding profile.
Base D: 12.0 cm; Pres. H: 3.6 cm.
COMMENTS: Import.
DATE: Classical, 5th century.

145. Lekanis (Pl. 8).
Bag no. 1589: 4 *ACZ-AEJ* O27/2b.
FABRIC: Smooth, soft, with rare fine white sounded/spherical inclusions and few voids. Light red (2.5YR 6/6). SURFACE: No slip preserved. DESCRIPTION: Rim and upper wall.
Rim D: 13.0 cm; Pres. H: 2.2 cm.
DATE: Classical.

CPW

146. Lopas (Not depicted).
Bag no. 1589: 8 *ACZ-AEJ* O27/2b.
FABRIC: Hard (but brittle), hackly, frequent small to large white and small grey angular/spherical inclusions. Red (2.5YR 4/8). DESCRIPTION: Rim. Tall rim with slightly concave profile rises above narrow flange. The flange has a convex lower face as it curves back to join the wall.
Rim D: 21.0 cm; Pres. H: 2.0 cm.
COMMENTS: Local.
DATE: Classical.

Room VIII

Room VIII sits between rooms V and X and has common walls with them both. A gap between the east-west section of the *ATC* wall and its continuation *ATF* provides a potential doorway between rooms VIII and V (see Fig. 43). Room VIII crosses trenches T28, T29, T30 and T31, excavated in 2000. With the removal of the tile layer ATG, which appeared below stratum 3,[266] the area was redefined so that room VIII was excavated as one unit called T30. A significant feature in the room is the dry stone platform, *ATE*.

ATI, the mudbrick deposit, was located to the north of platform *ATE* and across the east-west section of wall *ATC*. It can be reconstructed as the upper courses of wall *ATC*. Some ceramic material was taken up along with the mudbrick. The fine ware was preserved in larger fragments than in the other T30 deposits. There were a few Archaic fine ware sherds, though Hellenistic examples were the best preserved; these included a plate with rilled rim, no. 149, a Hellenistic echinus bowl, no. 150, and the rim of a guttus, no. 151. Cooking pots were also located within this deposit, represented in the catalogue by no. 152, a clean and remarkably fresh-looking chytra (or jar) fragment. These indicate 3rd century pre-destruction activity.

Stratum 4, below the tile layer *ATG*, is a thin layer with rather few finds. The pottery has a similar appearance to that in stratum 3, with worn medium ware non-diagnostics and a mix of Archaic, Classical and Hellenistic fine wares. These include a West Slope fragment from a guttus, no. 153.

Stratum 5 contains a variety of finds, including coins that date from the 4th and 3rd centuries, lead, bronze, loom weights and ceramics. Stratum 5 corresponds to the finds layers in the previous rooms and like them is considered pre-destruction. The objects are found in the east of the trench, along wall *ATC* and around platform *ATE* extending west to wall *ADB*. The five complete miniature kraters indicate a deposit of a distinct character and raise questions of cultic activity in the vicinity, particularly when combined with the platform *ATE*.[267] Three of the miniature kraters span the distance between the eastern corner of *ATE* and wall *ATD*, while the fourth lies to the southwest of the platform. Both fine and plain ware fragments tend to be worn and, apart from the miniatures and the salt cellar no. 157, their fragmentary preservation and lack of homogeneity does not present a clear use phase for the room. The material combines Prehistoric and Archaic, with Classical/Hellenistic material.[268]

Four loom weights are found within this deposit. No. 160 is conical (type 1) the others are type 2, one is small, no. 161, the other two examples are large, nos. 162 and 163.

Unlike the previous rooms where this same stratum situated below the tile layer was dug to bedrock, in room VIII additional strata (6, 7 and 8) are identified.[269] Stratum 6 is a small deposit. The finds remain as those in stratum 5 with a fair proportion of glazed wares of Classical and Hellenistic date (including the West Slope bowl no. 164, plate no. 165 and the pyxis no. 166) mixed with Archaic and Prehistoric fragments.

Stratum 7 is the second finds-rich deposit in Room VIII. It covers the whole trench and the finds are located in all areas of the room.

There is a heavy concentration of Archaic ceramics in stratum 7. Where Archaic material has been mentioned before it is in low numbers and appears residual, here the Archaic ceramics dominate. The ceramics are largely fine wares, particularly from Archaic drinking vessels (kotylai, cups and kantharoi), a number of which carry decorative painted bands. There are very few plain ware fragments and almost no cooking pots. The Archaic material is very fragmentary, but the fine walls and decorative glazes remain attractive. The Classical and Hellenistic material is scanty, and accounts for the only cooking pots found in the deposit.

The division of the room into the trench quadrants

266 This stratum 3 corresponds to stratum 2 in the other trenches. An 'additional' strata is amounted here as the first layer was removed as stratum 1 and not as "surface" as was the case in the other trenches. The stratum represents fill, but within this are two kiln wedges, nos. 147 and 148.

267 4585; 4586; 4590; 4596 and 4579: 1. Above Fig. 59.

268 The catalogued Classical and Hellenistic vessels are: nos. 154-159.

269 2796: 1; 4613: 4; 4618: 2; 4618: 5; 4624: 3; Miniature: 4612: 6. As for the Archaic material see Sanne Houby Nielsen in *Chalkis Aitolias II* (forthcoming).

allows for some pattern to be sort amongst the ceramic finds. There is very little Classical (a skyphos base, a handle and a rim fragment) and no definite Hellenistic ceramic fragments found in N (the quadrant around platform *ATE* and between walls *ADB* and *ATF*), given the amount of Archaic material from here (420 fine ware sherds in N alone), this absence is significant. In quadrant B the Hellenistic material is limited to a lopas rim along with two black glaze Classical/Hellenistic fragments. Quadrants D and A, both of which lie along the wall *ATD*, offer more Hellenistic material.

The Hellenistic shapes include cooking wares, as the lopas rims nos. 172 and 173. The fine wares include an early Classical skyphos base no. 167,[270] and Hellenistic bowl with folded rim, no. 171, echinus bowl, no. 170, and two plates with grooved rim, no. 168, and the distinctly Hellenistic no. 169. These catalogued pieces represent close to all the Classical or Hellenistic fragments in stratum 7, a paltry collection given the quantity of ceramics found.

There are six loom weights in stratum 7. There are two large conical (type 1) nos. 174 and 175, loom weights. The others are type 2 pyramidal loom weights: one small, no. 176, one medium, no. 177, and two large, nos. 178 and 179. These are joined by the spindle whorl, no. 180, and terracotta wedge, no. 181.

A channel *ATX* runs from *ATE* across the trench through quadrants N, D and A to wall *ATD*. It is dug into bedrock. The material within this channel predates our period of focus considerably. The latest dating sherds in this deposit are Archaic, and include a kantharos rim and a fragment from a conical oinochoe. There is also one small type two loom weight that carries stamps on all four faces, no. 182.

Stratum 8 is located only in quadrant D. The levels taken for stratum 8 place it at the same height as stratum 7 which continues to bedrock in the rest of the trench. As it is excavated through the quadrant it appears an artificial division. A considerable number of finds are located here including two coins,[271] and two medium, type 2 loom weights (nos. 190, 191) alongside the ceramics. The pottery bags hold lots of small Archaic fragments as in stratum 7, including a fine Archaic knob (2799), an Archaic kantharos fragment (2795: 2) and an Archaic cup (2795: 3). Proportionally there is more Hellenistic material in stratum 8. There are lopades, nos. 186 and 187, chytra no. 188, a high quality table amphora no. 185, the base of a cup with profiled foot suggesting an early Hellenistic date, no. 184, and, the sherd that is undeniably from the 3rd century (though again early), the West Slope plate fragment, no. 183. This plate is a fine example of West Slope ware. Its position, just above bedrock in a trench that has been dominated with Archaic material is somewhat puzzling! Certainly, I would suggest that the area within this room along wall *ATD* (so quadrants A and D), saw more Hellenistic activity than did the other quadrants of the room, perhaps associated with wall *ATD*, which joins the more distinctly Hellenistic space of room X (see below).

Discussion

Room VIII is a distinct space in this row of buildings.To begin with it is distinguished by the platform *ATE*. The miniatures found in stratum 5 supported an interpretation of *ATE* as a dedicatory space and room VIII as having a ritual function. The large quantity of Archaic material which includes the miniatures,[272] is largely uncontaminated in the areas around *ATE*, with only an occasional, intrusive Classical fragment. The channel *ATX*, which is cut into the bedrock and lies underneath these deposits, and the flooring *ATV*, allows an early Archaic date for initial activity.

However, the entire room is not uniform in its apparent use, with the quadrants (D and A) along the wall *ATD*, providing more examples of Hellenistic and Classical material mixed with the numerous Archaic fine wares. This continues to bedrock, with examples in the stratum 8 dug in quadrant D. There is no evidence in the ceramics vessels of the Hellenistic period in this room that they represent continued use of a ritual space.

There are twelve loom weights found in the use phases of this trench (strata five to eight, not counting the one from *ATX*). At some time in its history the

270 There are two other scrappy skyphos bases not catalogued.

271 Coins date before 251 and 371-357. See *SPR* and *TPR*.

272 The miniatures compare to Stillwell & Benson 1984, nos. 1769-1772, pl. 68.

space may have been used for weaving or the loom weights could form part of the dedications in the area. Three are conical, the rest are of type 2. In total, there are three small, three medium and six large. No form of decorative details are found on these loom weights which distinguishes them from the loom weights in other rooms (this could reflect a difference in date).

The coins in the room include 4th and 3rd century examples. There is a higher ratio of 4th century dates amongst these, but there are at least three coins that date from the 3rd to 2nd century. The coins unlike the ceramics provide comparable types and a similar date range with those found in the other rooms.

T30/3
Comment: This strata is post-destruction fill that corresponds to the level of stratum 2 in other trenches. It lies above tile layer *ATG* and mud brick deposit *ATI*.

Pottery Bags: 4471, 4459, 4336, 4289
Pottery Statistics:

Total	570	%	We: 10665g
FW:	177	31	955
PW:	354	62	5020
CPW:	8	1.5	50
CW:	32	5.5	4640

Various
147. Kiln wedge/waster (Not depicted).
Bag no. 4289: 1 T30/3.
FABRIC: Reddish yellow (5YR 7/6) but more pale. DESCRIPTION: Rough T-shaped
Pres. H: 3.0 cm; L. 5.4 cm; W: 2.65 cm.

148. Kiln wedge/waster (Not depicted).
Bag no. 4289: 2 T30/3.
DESCRIPTION: Partially preserved. Two preserved flat faces at 90 degree angle to each other.

ATI
COMMENT: Mud brick deposit and related finds within room VIII.

Pottery Bags: 4525, 4583
Pottery Statistics:

Total:	61	%:	We: 490
FW:	31	51	160
PW:	16	26	280
CPW:	14	23	50
CW:	-	-	-

FW
149. Plate, grooved rim (Pl. 8).
Bag no. 4525: 4 ATI.
FABRIC: Slightly granular, hard, no visible inclusions. Light reddish brown (5YR 6/4). SURFACE: Dark brown, mottled. DESCRIPTION: Rim and upper wall. Graffiti on exterior wall. Two grooves on upper face of rim. Groove on exterior at rim to wall junction. Rim set above wall on interior. Drilled hole preserved on wall just below rim. Drilled hole is glazed, therefore not a repair hole. X incised on exterior beside drilled hole.
Rim D: 20.0 cm; Pres. H: 2.2 cm.
COMMENTS: Import.
DATE: Classical-Hellenistic.

150. Echinus bowl (Not depicted).
Bag no. 4583: 1; F00-1037 *A.I.*
FABRIC: Granular, hard, few small white angular/spherical white inclusions. Light red (2.5YR 6/6). SURFACE: Red to brown, mottled on interior and exterior, including foot, dark brown on upper face of rim, grey under foot. DESCRIPTION: Full profile. Rounded rim projects very slightly on exterior. Foot has flat resting surface. Convex outer profile.
Rim D: 9.2 cm; Base D: 4.35 cm; Pres. H: 5.6 cm.
COMMENTS: Local.
DATE: Hellenistic.

151. Guttus (Pl. 9).
Bag no. 4525: 6 *ATI.*
FABRIC: Slightly granular, hard, few voids, no visible inclusions. Reddish yellow (5YR 6/6). SURFACE: Black, lustrous. DESCRIPTION: Rim. Flaring rim with rounded upper and outer face. Ridge on exterior at junction with cylindrical neck.
Rim D: 3.4 cm; Pres. H: 0.85 cm.
COMMENTS: Compare: Rotroff 1997, nos. 1140-1142, fig. 71.
DATE: Classical-Hellenistic.

CPW
152. Chytra (Jar) (Not depicted).
Bag no. 4525: 5 *ATI.*
FABRIC: Granular, common small white and grey angular/spherical inclusions. Red (2.5YR 4/6). DESCRIPTION: Rim and upper wall. Flaring rim.
Rim D: 10.0 cm; Pres. H: 2.7 cm.
COMMENTS: Import.

T30/4
COMMENTS: Thin layer below tile deposit *ATG.* Worn pottery Archaic, Classical and Hellenistic.

Pottery Bags: 4523, 4591
Pottery Statistics:

Total:	98	%:	We: 925
FW:	47	48	330
PW:	39	40	510
CPW:	7	7	25
CW:	5	5	60

153. Guttus (Pl. 9).
Body fragment. Convex wall profile.
Bag no. 4591: 1 T30/4
FABRIC: Granular, very soft, few small rounded spherical voids. Reddish yellow (5YR 6/6). SURFACE: Mottled brown to black, some shine. DESCRIPTION: West Slope decoration of incised tendrils.
Pres. H: 3.0 cm.
COMMENTS: Local.
DATE: Hellenistic.

T30/5
COMMENT: Variety of finds including miniature vessels. Fragmentary plain and fine wares. Prehistoric, Archaic, Classical, Hellenistic. For Archaic material in this and following deposits see report by S. Houby-Nielsen in Chalkis Aitolias II (forthcoming).

Pottery Bags: 4579, 4585, 4586, 4588, 4593, 4590, 4596, 4598
Pottery Statistics:

Total:	601	%:	We:3750[273]
FW:	228	38	880
PW:	232	38.5	1950
CPW:	125	21	550
CW:	16	2.5	370

FW
154. Skyphos (Pl. 9).
Bag no. 4593: 1 T30/5.
FABRIC: Smooth, soft, no visible inclusions. Reddish yellow (5YR 6/6). SURFACE: Lustrous black glaze on exterior to reserved band above foot, brown on interior, black on ring foot, bands of glaze painted on under floor. DESCRIPTION: Base, lower wall and floor. Blob of clay in centre of upper floor.
Base D: 4.5 cm; Pres. H: 2.1 cm.
COMMENTS: Import.
DATE: Classical.

155. Plate, rolled rim (Pl. 9).
Bag no. 4593: 3 T30/5.
FABRIC: Granular, hard, small angular/spherical white inclusions and voids. Reddish yellow (5YR 6/6). SURFACE: Black to brown on all preserved surfaces. DESCRIPTION: Thick walled. Drilled hole in wall of plate.
Rim D: 16.0 cm; Pres. H: 1.9 cm.
COMMENTS: Import.
DATE: Classical-Hellenistic.

156. Echinus bowl, large with grooved wall (Pl. 9).
Bag no. 4579: 3 T30/5.
FABRIC: Laminar, very hard, with few white rounded/tabular inclusions. Light red (2.5YR 6/6). SURFACE: Black to brown, smooth, uneven dipping line on exterior wall, sections of wall unglazed. DESCRIPTION: Rim and wall.
Rim D: 24.0 cm; Pres. H: 4.8 cm.
COMMENTS: Import.
DATE: Hellenistic.

157. Echinus bowl (Pl. 9).
Bag no. 4598; F00-1057 T30/5.
FABRIC: Granular, soft, no visible inclusions. Light red (2.5YR 6/6). SURFACE: Grey, metallic interior, exterior mottled grey-brown. DESCRIPTION: Full profile. Small, salt cellar variation. Rim only slightly

273 Weight not included for miniature vessels 4585, 4586, 4590, 4596, and bowl 4598.

incurved.
Rim D: 5.8 cm; Base D: 3.6 cm; Pres. H: 3.1 cm.
COMMENTS: Import.
DATE: Classical.

158. Bowl, folded rim (Pl. 9).
Bag no. 4593: 2 T30/5.
FABRIC: Smooth, hard, no visible inclusions. Reddish yellow (5YR 7/6). SURFACE: Interior and over rim thick blackish-brown glaze slight shine, below rim thin wash of grey, lower wall unglazed. DESCRIPTION: Rim and wall.
Rim D: 17.0 cm; Pres. H: 4.4 cm.
COMMENTS: Import.
DATE: Hellenistic.

159. Plate, offset rim (Pl. 9).
Bag no. 4588: 1 T30/5.
FABRIC: Smooth, very hard, few small rounded/platy white and hollow grey inclusions. Red (10R 5/6). SURFACE: Thin brown on interior, rim and upper exterior wall, lower exterior wall unglazed. DESCRIPTION: Rim and upper wall. Wall flares smoothly to projecting rim, groove sits on upper face of rim. Fine walled.
Rim D: 17.6 cm; Base D: 1.0 cm; Pres. H: 1.6 cm.
COMMENTS: Import. This shape lacks the strongly convex upper rim surface and distinct upper to lower wall carinated junction that characterises the other examples of this plate form.

Loom Weight

TYPE 1
160. Conical loom weight (Not depicted).
Bag no. 4592 T30/5.
FABRIC: Hackly, hard, common large angular/spherical red, white and brown inclusions and voids. Red (2.5YR 4/6). DESCRIPTION: Top and upper wall. One drilled hole. Poor preservation.
Pres. H: 4.55 cm; max pres D: 3.2 cm; We: 35 g.

TYPE 2
161. Small pyramidal loom weight (Not depicted).
Bag no. 4582 T30/5.
FABRIC: Surface: smooth, soft, common small angular/spherical grey inclusions and few angular/platy red inclusions. Reddish yellow (7.5YR 7/6). DESCRIPTION: One drilled hole. Chipping around base.
Pres. H: 6.2 cm; Max W: 3.7 × 3.2 cm; We: 68 g.

162. Large pyramidal loom weight (Fig. 84).
Bag no. 4601 T30/5.
FABRIC: Hackly, hard, few large angular/spherical white and red inclusions, frequent very large grey angular/platy inclusions (laminar construction) and voids. Reddish brown (2.5YR 4/3). DESCRIPTION: One drilled hole. Very chipped, broken at drilled hole, half of base and two lower faces missing.
Pres. H: 5.95 cm; We: 116 g.

163. Large pyramidal loom weight (Not depicted).
Bag no. 4597; F00-1053 T30/5
FABRIC: Hackly, soft, common large angular/spherical red, white and brown inclusions and voids. Reddish yellow (5YR 6/6). DESCRIPTION: One drilled hole. Half of base and two lower faces missing.
Pres. H: 8.65 cm; We: 168 g.

T30/6
COMMENT: Small deposit in Room VIII, closely related to stratum 5.

Pottery Bags: 4600
Pottery Statistics:

Total:	240	%:	We: 1490
FW:	88	36.5	300
PW:	111	46.5	950
CPW:	25	10.5	160
CW:	16	6.5	80

164. Hemispherical bowl (Pl. 9).
Bag no. 4600: 8 T30/6.
FABRIC: Granular, hard, few fine white angular/tabular inclusions. Light reddish brown (2.5YR 6/4). SURFACE: Black, shiny slightly metallic sheen. DESCRIPTION: Rim and upper wall. Spherical body, rim flares out, moulding on outer face. West Slope decoration: shadow of a spearhead pendant, suspended dot necklace and elongated leaves.
Rim D: 9.0 cm; Pres. H: 2.9 cm.
COMMENTS: Import.
DATE: Hellenistic.

Fig. 84 *Loom weights from AREA III.*

165. Plate, grooved rim (Pl. 9).
Bag no. 4600: 2 T30/6.
FABRIC: Smooth, hard, no visible inclusions. Pink (5YR 7/4). SURFACE: Black, shiny with some mottling to reddish brown on rim. DESCRIPTION: Rim and small section of upper wall. Two grooves on upper face of rim. Deep groove on exterior at junction of wall and rim.
Rim D: 19.0 cm; Pres. H: 1.1 cm.
COMMENTS: Import-Attic.
DATE: Classical.

166. Pyxis (Pl. 9).
Bag no. 4600: 1 T30/6.
FABRIC: Smooth, hard, frequent small rounded/spherical voids. Light brown (7.5YR 6/4). SURFACE: Lustrous black. DESCRIPTION: Rim sits directly below flange, wall rises up with concave profile.
Rim D: 8.9 cm; Pres. H: 3.25 cm; max. D: 10.5 cm.
COMMENTS: Import.
DATE: Classical.

T30/7
COMMENT: Concentration of Archaic ceramics.

Pottery Bags: 2796, 4612, 4613, 4618, 4619, 4623, 4624, 4790, 4791
Pottery Statistics:

Total:	1805	%:	We: 9985
FW:	776	43	2450
PW:	648	36	5260
CPW:	278	15.5	1115
CW:	103	5.5	1160

FW
167. Skyphos (Pl. 9).
Bag no. 4612: 1 T30/7.
FABRIC: Smooth, soft, no visible inclusions. Pink (5YR 7/4). SURFACE: Black on interior and outer face of foot, wall just above foot carries red wash, also on underside of foot, resting surface reserved, inner floor the glaze is mottled to brown. DESCRIPTION: Base and lower wall. Foot has rounded lower surface, kicks out to somewhat sharp outer face.
Base D: 6.6 cm; Pres. H: 1.2 cm.
COMMENTS: Import. Compare: Pemberton 1989, no. 395
DATE: Classical.

168. Plate, grooved rim (Pl. 9).
Bag no. 4612: 4 T30/7
FABRIC: Smooth, hard, rare fine rounded/spherical grey inclusions. Pinkish grey (5YR 6/2). SURFACE: Thin brown. DESCRIPTION: Rim and upper wall. Light glazed grooves on upper face of rim, deep groove at rim and exterior wall junction.
Rim D: 21.0 cm; Pres. H: 1.0 cm.
COMMENTS: Import – Western Greece.
DATE: Hellenistic.

169. Plate, grooved rim (Pl. 9).
Bag no. 4623: 3 T30/7.
FABRIC: Granular, very soft, no visible inclusions. Light red (2.5YR 6/6). SURFACE: Black to brown preserved on interior wall and in first groove, brown wash/shadow of glaze on rest of rim and on exterior. DESCRIPTION: Rim and upper wall. Groove at junction of rim and interior wall and two further grooves on upper face of rim.

Rim D: 20.0 cm; Pres. H: 1.5 cm.
COMMENTS: Local.
DATE: Hellenistic.

170. Echinus bowl (Pl. 9).
Bag no. 4623: 4 T30/7.
FABRIC: Smooth, hard, few small angular/spherical white inclusions, frequent spherical and tabular voids. Red (10R 5/6). SURFACE: Thin grey on interior, brown on exterior rim and upper wall only. DESCRIPTION: Rather upright inturned rim.
Rim D: 12.0 cm; Pres. H: 4.5 cm.
COMMENTS: Local.
DATE: Hellenistic.

171. Bowl, folded rim (Not depicted).
Bag no. 4612: 8 T30/7
FABRIC: Granular, soft, with frequent fine and small angular/spherical white inclusions. Light red (2.5YR 6/6). SURFACE: Brown to grey, worn. DESCRIPTION: Rim and upper wall.
Rim D: 25.0 cm; Pres. H: 2.2 cm.
COMMENTS: Import.
DATE: Hellenistic.

CPW
172. Lopas (Not depicted).
Bag no. 4623: 6 T30/7.
FABRIC: Hackly, soft, common small angular/spherical white and grey inclusions. Red (2.5YR 5/6-5/8). DESCRIPTION: Rim and upper wall. Small fragment.
Rim D: 21.0 cm; Pres. H: 2.3 cm.
COMMENTS: Local.
DATE: Hellenistic.

173. Lopas
Bag no. 4623: 5 T30/7
FABRIC: Granular, soft, common small angular/spherical white and grey inclusions. Brown (7.5YR 5/3). DESCRIPTION: Rim and upper wall. Flange worn.
Rim D: 20.0 cm; Pres. H: 3.0 cm.
COMMENTS: Local.
DATE: Hellenistic.

Loom weight

Type 1
174. Large conical loom weight (Not depicted).
Bag no. 4780; F00-1116 T30/7.
FABRIC: Surface: smooth, soft, frequent small angular/spherical grey and white inclusions. Reddish yellow (5YR 6/6). DESCRIPTION: Wall bevelled to base. Narrow, flattened top (perhaps with impression). Chipped base.
Base D: 5.0 cm; Pres. H: 8.2 cm; max. D: 5.35 cm; We: 143 g.

175. Large conical loom weight (Not depicted).
Bag no. 4626; F00-1112 T30/7.
FABRIC: Granular, hard, frequent medium angular/spherical grey, white and red inclusions. Pink (5YR 7/4). DESCRIPTION: One drilled hole. Flat resting surface, broad top. Slight chipping on wall.
Base D: 5.0 cm; Pres. H: 7.1 cm; We: 144 g.

Type 2
176. Small pyramidal loom weight (Not depicted).
Bag no. 4620; F00-1105 T30/7.
FABRIC: Surface: smooth, hard, abundant small subrounded spherical red inclusions. Pink (5YR 7/4). One drilled hole. Rounded edges to flat base, rounded top. Complete.
Pres. H: 7.0 cm; Base: 2.8 × 2.8 cm; We: 53 g.

177. Medium pyramidal loom weight (Not depicted).
Bag no. 4618: 4 T30/7.
FABRIC: Granular, very soft, small to medium angular/spherical white, brown and grey inclusions. DESCRIPTION: Fragment of face. Incised impression/stamp. Two incised lines form the peak of a triangle or Λ.
Pres. H: 2.2 cm; W: 3.9 cm.

178. Large pyramidal loom weight (Not depicted).
Bag no. 4614; F00-1094 T30/7.
FABRIC: Surface: smooth, soft, few medium angular/spherical white inclusions. Light red (2.5YR 6/8). DESCRIPTION: One drilled hole. Flat base pointed top. Stamped circular impression on top of loom weight, 0.5 cm. in diameter. Chipped base, chipped face.
Pres. H: 8.85 cm; Base 5.15 cm; We: 162 g.

179. Large pyramidal loom weight (Not depicted).
Bag no. 4617; F00-1097 T30/7.
FABRIC: Surface: smooth, hard, abundant small subrounded spherical red inclusions. Light red (2.5YR 7/6). DESCRIPTION: One drilled hole. Flat base and top. Complete.
Pres. H: 9.0 cm; Base: 3.8 × 3.95 cm; Top: 1.95 × 1.8 cm; We: 132 g.

Other weaving objects
180. Spindle whorl (Not depicted).
Bag no. 4615; F00-1095 T30/7.
FABRIC: Surface: granular, hard, frequent small to medium angular/spherical white and grey inclusions. Reddish brown (2.5YR 5/4). DESCRIPTION: Spherical bead with broad drilled hole.
Pres. H: 2.0 cm; D: of body 2.6 cm; D: of drilled hole: 0.65 cm; We: 13 g.

Various
181. Unidentified object (Not depicted).
Bag no. 4782; F00-1117 T30/7.
FABRIC: Granular, soft, frequent subangular/spherical white and brown inclusions. Red (2.5YR 5/8). DESCRIPTION: Triangular shaped face (as pyramidal loom weight but almost two dimensional), rounded surfaces. One side is slightly concave, the other convex.
L: 1.25 cm; Max. W: 5.3 cm; T: 1.35-1.5 cm; We: 79 g.

ATX
COMMENT: Channel runs through Room VIII from platform *ATE* to wall *ATD*.

Pottery Bags: 4788
Pottery Statistics:

Total:	41	%:	We: 320
FW:	20	49	160
PW:	13	32	80
CPW:	3	7	20
CW:	5	12	60

Loom weight

Type 2
182. Small pyramidal loom weight (Not depicted).
Bag no. 4789; F00-1130 *ATX*.
FABRIC: Surface: Smooth, soft, abundant small to large angular/spherical and platy grey inclusions, few large angular/spherical white inclusions. Pink (7.5YR 8/3). DESCRIPTION: Single drilled hole. Stamped on all four faces. Flat base and top. Complete. Each face carries a circular stamped impression (D: 1.4-1.6 cm), in centre of circle is a small circular indent (0.25 cm. diam).
Pres. H: 4.9 cm; Base: 2.75-3 × 3.1 cm; top: 1.55 × 1.55 cm; We: 42 g.

T30/8
COMMENT: Excavated in one quarter of Room VIII. Occasional Hellenistic fragments mixed with Archaic ceramics.

Pottery Bags: 2795, 2797, 2799, 4781
Pottery Statistics:

Total:	380	%:	We: 2020[274]
FW:	140	37	540
PW:	159	42	1220
CPW:	68	18	170
CW:	13	3	90

FW
183. Plate, offset rim (Pl. 9).
Bag no. 2795: 1 T30/8.
FABRIC: Granular, very hard, no visible inclusions. Red (2.5YR 5/6). SURFACE: Black, thick, shiny. DESCRIPTION: Rim and upper wall. Ridge on upper face before lip and at rim to wall junction. West Slope decoration: incised scrolling and intersecting tendrils, fugitive painted ivy leaves.
Rim D: 22.0 cm; Pres. H: 1.5 cm.
COMMENTS: Import.
DATE: Hellenistic.

184. Base of cup (Hellenistic kantharos, one piece) (Pl. 9).
Bag no. 2795: 5 T30/8.
FABRIC: Granular, hard, rare angular/spherical small white and grey inclusions, frequent voids. Light red

274 This weight does not include the fine ware finds 2797 and 2799.

(2.5YR 6/6). SURFACE: Mottled brown to red glaze. DESCRIPTION: Base and lower wall. Profile of base flares out, creating impression of short stem.
Base D: 4.2 cm; Pres. H: 3.5 cm.
DATE: Hellenistic.

185. Table amphora (Pl. 9).
Bag no. 2797; F00-1126 T30/8.
FABRIC: Smooth, hard, rare small or medium angular/spherical white inclusions, few voids. Red to yellowish red (2.5YR 5/6 – 5YR 5/6). SURFACE: Black with some mottling to black and brown, slight metallic sheen. DESCRIPTION: Rim and neck. Projecting rim, concave, cylindrical neck. Projecting rim, slight groove on outer, squared face, second slight groove on upper face of rim. Neck has concave exterior profile.
Rim D: 8.6 cm; Pres. H: 2.9 cm.
COMMENTS: Local.
DATE: Hellenistic.

CPW
186. Lopas (Not depicted).
Bag no. 4781: 5 T30/8.
FABRIC: Hackly, hard, common small white angular/spherical inclusions. Red (2.5YR 4/6) burnt to reddish brown (2.5YR 5/3). DESCRIPTION: Rim and upper wall, small fragment. Smooth concave rim to flange junction.
Pres. H: 2.8 cm.
COMMENTS: Local.
DATE: Classical-Hellenistic.

187. Lopas (Not depicted).
Bag no. 4781: 4 T30/8.
FABRIC: Hackly, hard, common small white and grey angular/spherical inclusions. Dark reddish brown (2.5YR 3/4). DESCRIPTION: Rim and upper wall. Chipped outer wall.
Est. Rim D: 28.0 cm; Pres. H: 2.8 cm.
COMMENTS: Import.
DATE: Hellenistic.

188. Chytra (Not depicted).
Bag no. 2795: 7 T30/8.
FABRIC: Granular, hard, small angular/spherical white and grey inclusions. Reddish brown (2.5YR 5/4). DESCRIPTION: Rim and wall.
Rim D: 10.0 cm; Pres. H: 2.8 cm.
COMMENTS: Local.
DATE: Hellenistic.

Various

189. Kiln waster/wedge (Not depicted).
Bag no. 2795: 8 T30/8.
FABRIC: Surface: smooth, soft, few medium subrounded/tabular red and small to large angular white-grey inclusions. Pink (7.5YR 7/4). SURFACE: Very small remnant of red slip. DESCRIPTION: A sub-spherical piece of clay pushed against a 90 degree corner with thumb and two fingers.
Pres. H: 2.8 cm; L: 4.1 cm; W: 3.65 cm.

Loom weight

Type 2
190. Medium pyramidal loom weight (Not depicted).
Bag no. 4783; F00-1121 T30/8.
FABRIC: Surface: smooth, soft, few small angular/spherical white inclusions. Light red (2.5YR 6/8). DESCRIPTION: One drilled hole. Slight chipping on base. Flat top and base.
Pres. H: 6.25 cm; Base: 3.6 × 3.65 cm; Top: 2.9 × 2.95 cm; We: 84 g.

191. Medium pyramidal loom weight (Not depicted).
Bag no. 4787; F00-1129 T30/8.
FABRIC: Hackly, soft, few medium angular/spherical white and grey inclusions. Red (2.5YR 5/8). DESCRIPTION: One drilled hole. Chipped base and face.
Pres. H: 7.3 cm; Top: ca. 1.65 × 1.65 cm; max pres W: 4.4 cm; We: 103 g.

Zone IX

Zone IX sits outside of room VIII. Excavated in trench T31, it is defined as a distinct zone at stratum 4. The strata that are excavated above this (1-3) are associated with the destruction of the buildings in the zone (particularly VIII) and the subsequent fill. The tile layer that characterises the destruction deposit within the room VIII does not exist outside the room. While there are tiles found in stratum 2 and 3 they do not form a concentrated deposit in IX. Stratum 4 is excavated to bedrock. Stratum 4 represents a use context rather than a fill and is level with stratum 7 within the room VIII.

Within this stratum are a range of finds, including a coin, nail, bronze fragments, two knuckle bones and two loom weights: nos. 197 and 198. The ceramics date to the Classical and Hellenistic period, nos. 192-196, so quite different from the Archaic deposits within room VIII.

Discussion

The material outside the house does not correspond to the same use phase as the majority of that within the room VIII. It does, though, show continued use of the zone in the Hellenistic period, further indicating that the room VIII remains somewhat of an anomaly within the complex. This zone that runs outside the rooms would have served as a path between the rooms.

T31/4
Pottery Bags: 4793, 4795
Pottery Statistics:

Total:	641	%:	We: 6510
FW:	158	24.5	530
PW:	430	67	5780
CPW:	51	8	150
CW:	2	0.5	50

FW
192. Hellenistic kantharos, one piece (Not depicted).
Bag no. 4795: 4 T31/4.
FABRIC: Granular, soft, few fine angular/spherical grey inclusions. Pink (5YR 7/4). SURFACE: Worn black glaze. DESCRIPTION: Rim and upper wall.
Rim D: 9.0 cm; Pres. 2.3 cm.
COMMENTS: Local.
DATE: Hellenistic.

193. Conical bowl (Pl. 9).
Bag no. 4795: 5 T31/4.
FABRIC: Granular, soft no inclusions but few small voids. Light red (2.5YR 7/6). SURFACE: Black to brown, slight shine. DESCRIPTION: Rim and upper wall. Interior wall carries groove below rim. West Slope decoration: Elongated leaves set on either side of interior groove below rim.
Rim D: 11.0 cm; Pres. 1.8 cm.
COMMENTS: Import.
DATE: Hellenistic.

194. Echinus bowl, large with grooved wall (Not depicted).
Bag no. 4795: 3 T31/4.
FABRIC: Conchoidal, soft, no visible inclusions. Light red (2.5YR 6/6). SURFACE: Brown to black on all preserved surfaces. DESCRIPTION: Rim and upper wall.
Rim D: 20.0 cm; Pres. H: 2.7 cm.
COMMENTS: Local.
DATE: Hellenistic.

195. Base of bowl/plate (Pl. 9).
Bag no. 4795: 6 T31/4.
FABRIC: Granular, very soft, few fine angular/spherical grey inclusions. Reddish yellow (5YR 6/6). SURFACE: Brown, mottled, dull, interior only. DESCRIPTION: Base and lower wall. Ring foot with concave-convex profile – the appearance of a short stem. Drilled hole in base of plate.
Base D: 4.6 cm; Pres. H: 1.6 cm.
COMMENTS: Local.
DATE: Classical-Hellenistic.

196. Table amphora (Not depicted).
Bag no. 4795: 2 T31/4.
FABRIC: Granular, soft, fine angular/spherical white and red inclusions. Red (2.5YR 5/6). SURFACE: Remnants of black glaze on interior rim. DESCRIPTION: Rim and neck. Flaring rim with moulded overhang.
Rim D: 9.0 cm; Pres. H: 3.5 cm.
COMMENTS: Local.
DATE: Hellenistic.

Loom weight

Type 1
197. Large conical loom weight (Not depicted).
Bag no. 4799; F00-1138 T31/4.
FABRIC: Granular, very soft, few angular/platy brown inclusions. Surface carries frequent light refracting

particles. Light brown (7.5YR 6/4). DESCRIPTION: One drilled hole. Chipped wall and base, but full profile preserved.
Base D: 7.0 cm; Pres. H: 9.3 cm; We: 173 g.

Type 2
198. Medium pyramidal loom weight (Not depicted).
Bag no. 4798 T31/4.
FABRIC: Granular, hard, few small angular/spherical white inclusions, few voids. Margin reddish yellow (5YR 6/6) to light red (2.5YR 6/6) with burnt core. DESCRIPTION: One drilled hole. Slight chipping on base, full profile preserved. Concave impression on mid wall of face as though squeezed between thumb and forefinger.
Pres. H: 7.35 cm; Base: 3.5 × 3.6 cm; We: 81 g.

Room X

The tile layer *AGC* and the stone packing *AFQ* are common to rooms X and XI. In room X the tile layer lies underneath the third stratum excavated. Thus strata 1-3 are post-destruction deposits and their finds consist of a mix of material, including the column krater no. 200, the skyphos no. 199, a red-figure fragment no. 201 and the West Slope fragment no. 202, along with pithoi, amphorae and other fine ware fragments of Archaic, Classical and Hellenistic date. Stratum 4, excavated in conjunction with the removal of the tiles and containing an amount of tile and charcoal, belongs to the destruction phase of the building. The pottery is worn and consists of medium ware with some black glaze fragments. One fragment of West Slope ware, no. 204, provides a mid- to late 3rd century *terminus post quem* for the destruction of the room.

Stratum 5 moves us into the use phase of the building, lying as it does, beneath the destruction deposits described above. The pottery is quite scrappy with medium, fine and cooking ware fragments (the latter represented by no. 205). The lamp no. 206, which belongs to the Classical type of lamps from the site, is from stratum 5. Two type 2 loom weights, nos. 207 and 208, one medium, one large, are found in this deposit.

The majority of ceramics in stratum 6 are fine or medium ware, mainly non-diagnostics and some cooking pots. The one-handler, no. 211, has a triangular handle of late 4th century production and extends the range of the deposit. The two lamps are also of the late 4th century, nos. 222 and 223. The majority of the material is of 3rd century date. No. 210 is a Hellenistic one-piece kantharos. It is more elaborate than the typical examples of this shape from the site with a profiled and stemmed foot and horizontal ribbing on the lower wall.[275] The glazing on the lower body is somewhat patchy. The attenuation of the shape would see it placed in the mid 3rd century. An imported Classical kantharos, no. 209, with West Slope decoration is of a mid-3rd century date. The Hellenistic echinus bowl, no. 212, a deep vessel with thickened rim, is dip glazed and carries distinct and roughly decorative stacking marks on the interior. The base fragment, no. 213, is from a broader bowl or plate but is of comparable manufacture. The rim of a table amphora, no. 214, completes the table wares of room X. In addition to the Hellenistic drinking and dining vessels in this deposit is a vessel for pouring oil, the lekythos, no. 215. The date and preservation of these vessels compares to the third stratum of Room II, indicating a similar date of destruction for the two rooms.

Plain wares include amphora fragments (though fragmentary and infrequent when compared to the amphora-rich deposits in room XI). There is a double-handled pitcher no. 216 and a reversible lid no. 217. A small lopas, no. 218, a frypan, no. 219, and a lid, no. 220 are the catalogued representatives of the mix of cooking pot wares found within the deposit. A coarse ware louterion rim, no. 221, with moulded but not elaborate rim, adds to the domestic cooking/food preparation activities that may have occurred in this room.

Six loom weights are found in the sixth stratum in room X (in addition to the two found in stratum 5). Four are pyramidal type 2 loom weights (two small:

275 Comparable but uncatalogued fragments within the same deposit include: a profiled foot in bag 4571, and a rim, wall to handle fragment in 4561. Horizontal ribbing is common on bowls with conical profile (see below), but is less common on kantharoi, where vertical ribbing is the norm. Horizontal ribbing is occasionally used on Calyx cups: Vickers, Impey & Allan 1986, pl. 19, above.

nos. 226 and 227; two large: nos. 228 and 229) and two type 1 conical (one small: no. 224; one large: no. 225), none are decorated. There is also a terracotta spool found in the room, no. 230.

The pit *ATK* identified in stratum 6, contained quite a lot of potsherds of 4th and 3rd century date, including the fishplate, no. 231.[276]

Only one bag of ceramics was excavated as part of structure *ATD*, bag 4931, and it contains only five fragments in total (fine, cooking and coarse wares) along with a small, type 2, pyramidal loom weight, no. 234.

Discussion

The use of room X is closely comparable to that of room II, both in the date range of objects and the objects themselves; both contain well-preserved cups and bowls accompanied by cooking and plain wares, that date from the late 4th but predominantly in the 3rd century. The scattering of loom weights is also common.

In room X there are 9 loom weights in total. Seven loom weights are of type 2, the two others are conical. Of these, four are small, one is medium, and four are large. There is also a terracotta spool located alongside these loom weights.

T28/3
Pottery Bags: 4343, 4455, 4510, 4334, 4473
Pottery Statistics:

Total:	562	%:	We: 7765[277]
FW:	173	31	870
PW:	337	60	5360
CPW:	21	3.5	175
CW:	31	5.5	1360

FW
199. Classical Skyphos (Pl. 10).
Bag no. 4334: 3 T28/3.
FABRIC: Smooth, soft, no visible inclusions. Pink (7.5YR 8/4). SURFACE: Black to brown, mottled, smooth. DESCRIPTION: Rim, upper wall, handle. Rim flares out to rounded lip. Horizontal handle.
Est. Rim D: 10; Pres. H: 4.5 cm.
COMMENTS: Compare: Rotroff 1997, no. 152
DATE: Classical-Hellenistic.

200. Krater, Classical (Not depicted).
Bag no. 4343; F00-1023 T28/3.
FABRIC: Granular, soft, rare small rounded-angular/spherical white and brown inclusions. Reddish yellow (5YR 6/6). SURFACE: Brown, thin on rim and upper half of interior neck. Dripping on upper handles. Bands of thin brown slip on upper wall. DESCRIPTION: Column krater. Rim, handle, upper wall and shoulder. Flat broad rim, constricted straight neck, convex shoulder swelling to the bowl of the body. Column handle linking rim to shoulder.
Rim D: 54.0 cm; Pres. H: 11.9 cm.
COMMENTS: Import. Given the deposit in which this is found, it is associated with material on the Acropolis, rather than within the area of the houses.
DATE: Classical.

201. Fragment: Body sherd (Not depicted).
Bag no. 4473: 1 T28/3.
FABRIC: Granular, soft, no visible inclusions. Reddish yellow (5YR 6/8). SURFACE: Brown to black, lustrous. DESCRIPTION: Large vessel. Red figure decoration: hand, tubular object, drapery?
T: 0.6 cm; L: 4.1 cm; W: 4.8 cm.
COMMENTS: Import – Attic.
DATE: Classical.

202. Fragment (Pl. 10).
Bag no. 4334: 2 T28/3.
FABRIC: Granular, soft, no visible inclusions. Light red (2.5YR 6/6). SURFACE: Black, some shine on interior and exterior. DESCRIPTION: Body fragments. Light glazed grooves provide decorative zone. West Slope decoration: incised scrolling wave pattern on exterior.
Pres. H: 2.6 cm; W. 2.5 cm.
COMMENTS: Import.
DATE: Hellenistic.

276 The two other catalogued fragments are the Classical bowl with horizontal handle, no. 232, and the West Slope fragment no. 233.

277 Weight does not include find 4343 (no. 200).

Loom weight

Type 1

203. Medium conical loom weight (Not depicted).
Bag no. 4347 T28/3.
FABRIC: Granular, hard, frequent voids. Light red (2.5YR 6/6). DESCRIPTION: One drilled hole. Almost half of base and lower wall missing.
Base D: 6.0 cm; Pres. H: 5.45 cm; W: 99 g.

T28/4

COMMENT: Ceramic material from the destruction layer of the room, mixed with tile.

Pottery Bags: 4578, 4594

Pottery Statistics:

Total:	80	%:	We: 2560
FW:	18	22.5	90
PW:	54	67.5	4430
CPW:	8	10	40
CW:	–	–	–

FW

204. Conical bowl (Pl. 10).
Bag no. 4578: 1 T28/4 and 2235:4 O27/3.
FABRIC: Smooth, hard, no visible inclusions, no voids. Reddish yellow (5YR 6/6). SURFACE: Brown, smooth. DESCRIPTION: Body fragment. Grooves on interior wall marking zones (wall to rim?). West Slope decoration: wheat motif, incised hairs, paint of head of wheat is fugitive but dots for the seeds have left a shadow. Incision above groove in next zone edge of concentric rectangles on 2235:4 and below wheat for tondo zone on 4578:1.
Pres. H (2235:4): 2.2 cm; Pres. H: 2.3 cm; D: Groove (2235:4): 12 cm.
COMMENTS: Import – Corinth? Compare: Athens: Metzger 1973, no. 83, p. 59, pl. 11; Attic import: Morel 1990, p. 22, pl. 1c; Corinth: Edwards 1975, no. 534, p. 92, pl. 55; Corinth Museum C-34-2498; Rachi: Anderson-Stojanović 2000, p. 383, pl. 204b; Anderson-Stojanović 1996, no. 21, p. 74, fig. 9; Kassope: Gravani 1986, p. 126, fig. 130.8 (left); Italy: Green 1979, p. 86, figs. 11, 12.
DATE: Hellenistic, mid to late 3rd century.

T28/5

COMMENT: Below the tile smash. Worn material.

Pottery Bags: 4371, 4372, 4373, 4501

Pottery Statistics:

Total:	97	%:	We: 510
FW:	30	32	80
PW:	45	46.5	340
CPW:	19	19.5	80
CW:	2	2	10

CPW

205. Storage vessel (Pl. 10).
Bag no. 4372: 1 T28/5.
FABRIC: Granular, hard, frequent fine angular/spherical white-grey inclusions. Dark grey (10YR 4/1). DESCRIPTION: Slightly flanged flaring rim with square outer face that carries grooves.
Rim D: 8.0 cm; Pres. H: 3.1 cm.

Lamps

206. Lamp (Pl. 10).
Bag no. 4371: 1 T28/5.
FABRIC: Granular, very soft with rare small angular/spherical brown inclusions. Very pale brown (10YR 8/2). SURFACE: Black to brown. DESCRIPTION: Nozzle on wall of body. Low body.
Pres. H: 1.4 cm.
COMMENTS: Import-Corinth? *Isthmia* no. 61, of type IVB.
DATE: Classical.

Loom weight

Type 2

207. Medium pyramidal loom weight (Not depicted).
Bag no. 4374; F00-1069 T28/5.
FABRIC: Granular, hard, frequent small to medium angular/spherical red and white inclusions. Pink (7.5YR 7/4). DESCRIPTION: One drilled hole. Flat base, rounded top. Slight chipping on face.
Pres. H: 7.65 cm; Base: 4.6 × 4.2 cm; We: 126 g.

208. Large pyramidal loom weight (Not depicted).
Bag no. 4375; F00-1070 T28/5.

FABRIC: Granular, hard, few angular/spherical small to medium brown and white inclusions. Yellowish red (5YR 5/6). DESCRIPTION: One drilled hole. Flat top. Chipped base.
Pres. H: 7.15 cm; Top: 6.6 × 2.5 cm; We: 145 g.

T28/6
COMMENT: Occupation layer of room X. Rich in finds.

Pottery Bags: 4571, 4574, 4605, 4563, 4561, 4562
Pottery Statistics:

Total:	907	%:	We: 7100
FW:	273	30	1090
PW:	456	50	4300
CPW:	168	19	670
CW:	10	1	1040

FW
209. Classical kantharos (Pl. 10).
Bag no. 4562: 1 T28/6.
FABRIC: Smooth, hard, with few fine angular/spherical white inclusions. Light red (2.5YR 6/6). SURFACE: Brown, lustrous. DESCRIPTION: Upper wall fragment. Edge of West Slope decoration, incised tendril.
Pres. H: 3.7 cm.
COMMENTS: Import.
DATE: Hellenistic, mid 3rd century.

210. Hellenistic kantharos, one piece (Pl. 10).
Bag no. 4574: 4; F00-1085 T28/6.
FABRIC: Granular, hard, few small angular/spherical white inclusions. Light red (2.5YR 6/6). SURFACE: Black to brown, mottled particularly on lower body where the clay is visible through a thin wash. DESCRIPTION: Full profile. Spur handle, simple lip and smooth convex body, slightly stemmed foot with moulded outer profile flaring to flat resting surface. Horizontal ribbing on lower wall, to maximum diameter.
Rim D: 11.0 cm (irregular); Base D: 5.3 cm; Pres. H: 12.1 cm.
COMMENTS: Local.Compare: Edwards 1975, no. 453, pl. 15
DATE: Hellenistic, mid-late 3rd cent.

211. One handler (Not depicted).
Bag no. 4571: 3 T28/6.
FABRIC: Granular, soft with no visible inclusions. Reddish yellow (5YR 7/8). SURFACE: Black to brown, shiny. DESCRIPTION: Rim, upper wall, handle. Simple rounded lip, slightly incurved. Horizontal strap handle rises above level of rim.
Rim D: 12.0 cm; Pres. H: 2.5 cm.
COMMENTS: Import?
DATE: Classical-Hellenistic.

212. Echinus bowl (Pl. 10).
Bag no. 4575: 1 T28/6.
FABRIC: Granular, hard, with frequent small white angular/spherical inclusions. Light red to reddish yellow (2.5YR 6/6 – 5YR 6/6). SURFACE: Black on rim and inner upper wall with some mottling to red, distinct transition to red on mid wall to floor on interior. Exterior, black on rim mottled to red below, mid wall to foot unglazed. DESCRIPTION: Full profile. Rim squared upper profile with grooves on exterior. Ring foot flares out, flat resting surface. Deep bowl with depressed floor, nipple on underside of floor.
Rim D: 14.0 cm; Base D: 5.7 cm; Pres. H: 7.3 cm.
COMMENTS: Local. Fragments from other bags in the deposit including 4571, 4563, 4561.
DATE: Hellenistic.

213. Base of bowl/plate (Not depicted).
Bag no. 4571: 6a T28/6.
FABRIC: Granular, soft with rare small angular/tabular white inclusions. Light red (2.5YR 6/6). SURFACE: Red in centre of floor, red-brown on mid wall, some dark brown preserved, fairly distinct stacking mark on interior. Exterior red-brown glaze to resting surface. DESCRIPTION: Base and wall. Unprofiled ring foot with flat resting surface, wall rising into broad, shallow face.
Base D: 6.7 cm; Pres. H: 2.8 cm.
COMMENTS: Local.

214. Table Amphora (Pl. 10).
Bag no. 4574: 2; F00-1085 T28/6.
FABRIC: Granular, soft with few fine white inclusions. Light red (2.5YR 6/8). DESCRIPTION: Rim to upper neck. Outer rim moulded.

Rim D: 16.0 cm; Pres. H: 3.0 cm.
COMMENTS: Local.
DATE: Classical-Hellenistic.

215. Lekythos (Pl. 10).
Bag no. 4563: 1; 4605: 1 T28/6.
FABRIC: Granular, soft, with few fine angular/tabular white inclusions. Reddish yellow (5YR 6/6). SURFACE: Black, worn. DESCRIPTION: Base to shoulder, rim to neck. Flat base, narrow body with convex profile, slightly inset junction with shoulder. Incurved lip and bowl like rim, at break the rim drops into a narrow cylindrical neck.
Rim D: 4.8 cm; Base D: 5.0 cm; Pres. H: 8.4 cm; Pres. H: body 8.4 cm; Pres. H: rim 2.6 cm.
COMMENTS: Local. Compare: rim Rotroff 1997, no. 11, fig. 69; Kotitsa 2004, pl. 63b left and pl. 66c
DATE: Hellenistic.

PW
216. Jug, two handled (Pl. 10).
Bag no. 4575: 3 T28/6.
FABRIC: Granular, soft with few angular/spherical small white and brown inclusions. Pink (7.5YR 7/3 – 7.5YR 8/3). SURFACE: Thin reddish brown slip. DESCRIPTION: Rim, neck, two handles. Protruding rim above constricted cylindrical neck, strap handles attach to neck and rim, looping out at the level of the rim. At the rim the handles are set only 2.3 cm. apart.
Rim D: 8.0 cm; Pres. H: 3.9 cm; Pres. H (with handle): 5.4 cm.
COMMENTS: Import. Compare: (handles) Edwards 1975, nos. 287-302, pl. 12
DATE: Hellenistic.

217. Reversible lid (or shallow bowl) (Pl. 10).
Bag no. 4575: 2 T28/6.
FABRIC: Surface: smooth and powdery, soft, with few small to medium and rare very large angular/spherical white inclusions. Reddish yellow (5YR 6/6). SURFACE: Red slip, little preserved on outer rim and inner wall. DESCRIPTION: Full profile. Rim rolled in slightly, thick walled, ring foot with rounded resting surface.
Rim D: 14.0 cm; Base D: 5.8 cm; Pres. H: 4.2 cm; Height ranges 3.5-4.2 cm.
COMMENTS: Import. Fits perfectly the flanged rim of no. 218.

CPW
218. Lopas (Pl. 10).
Bag no. 4574: 1; F00-1085 T28/6.
FABRIC: Granular, soft, frequent angular/spherical small to large white inclusions, few angular/spherical medium grey inclusions. Light red (2.5YR 6/6 – 2.5YR 6/8). DESCRIPTION: Rim and upper wall. Rim flares out. Flange on inner rim indicates the vessel was lidded (lid no. 271 fits). Rim to upper wall concave profile, wall turns convex indicating bulbous shape.
Rim D: 13.0 cm; Pres. H: 3.1 cm.

219. Lopas, variation (Pl. 10).
Bag no. 4571: 7 T28/6.
FABRIC: Granular, soft, frequent small to medium angular/spherical white and rare brown-grey inclusions. Red (2.5YR 5/6). DESCRIPTION: Frypan, loop handle. Rim, upper wall and handle. Flanged rim above slightly concave wall, break at junction with lower wall which angles in and down. Handle attaches to and below rim and rises above rim.
Rim D: 20.0 cm; Pres. H: 3.2 cm; Height with handle 5.5 cm.
COMMENTS: Import. Compare: Langridge-Noti 2002, nos. 13a, b, p. 65, fig. 21; Catling 1996, shape 47.

220. Lid (Pl. 10).
Bag no. 4575: 4 T28/6.
FABRIC: Granular, hard, common small angular/spherical white and grey inclusions. Red (2.5YR 5/6). DESCRIPTION: Knob and wall. Mushroom shaped knob with depression in upper face.
Pres. H: 2.5 cm; W: 6.1 cm.
COMMENTS: Import. Compare (Knob) Edwards 1975, nos. 696, 697, 698 and 699, pl. 31

CW
221. Louterion (Pl. 10).
Bag no. 4562: 3 T28/6.
FABRIC: Hackly, hard, abundant medium to very large angular/tabular red, frequent medium grey and small white angular/spherical inclusions. Reddish yellow (5YR 7/6). DESCRIPTION: Rim fragment.

Convex-concave-convex moulding on outer face, each convex section carries groove, upper foot has smooth convex outer profile. Inner face smooth arc from broad, flat rim.
Base D: 59.6 cm; Pres. H: 8.5 cm.
COMMENTS: Local.

Lamps

222. Lamp. Base to rim (Pl. 11).
Bag no. 4571: 7 T28/6.
FABRIC: Granular, soft with rare fine angular/tabular white inclusions. Pink (5YR 7/4); Core: Grey (5YR 5/1). SURFACE: Brown to grey.
Base D: 3.2 cm; Pres. H: 2.8 cm.
COMMENTS: Import. Compare: Broneer 1977, type VI, no. 86.
DATE: Classical.

223. Lamp (Not depicted).
Bag no. 4571: 6b T28/6.
FABRIC: Granular, soft with rare fine angular/tabular white inclusions. Reddish yellow (5YR 7/6). SURFACE: Black to brown. DESCRIPTION: Nozzle.
COMMENTS: Local?
DATE: Classical.

Loom weight

Type 1
224. Small conical loom weight (Not depicted).
Bag no. 4565; F00-1075 T28/6.
FABRIC: Granular, soft, frequent rounded/spherical medium red, brown and white inclusions. Light red (2.5YR 6/6). DESCRIPTION: One drilled hole. Wall bevelled to base, top pointed. Complete.
Base D: 3.2 cm; Pres. H: 5.6 cm; Max. D: 4.0 cm; We: 68 g.

225. Large conical loom weight (Pl. 11).
Bag no. 4566; F00-1076 T28/6.
FABRIC: Hackly, hard, common small to medium angular/platy-spherical red and brown with few white inclusions. Reddish yellow (5YR 7/6). DESCRIPTION: One drilled hole. Wall bevelled to base, base concave face, top pointed. Chipping on base.
Base D: 5.8 cm; Pres. H: 7.4 cm; Max. D: 6.3 cm; We: 189 g.

Type 2
226. Small pyramidal loom weight (Not depicted).
Bag no. 4573; F00-1084 T28/6.
FABRIC: Surface: smooth, soft, few small to medium angular/spherical red and brown inclusions. Pink (7.5YR 7/4 – 7.5YR 8/4). DESCRIPTION: One drilled hole. Flat base, pointed top.
Pres. H: 7.0 cm; Base: 3 × 3.2 cm; We: 48 g.

227. Small pyramidal loom weight (Not depicted).
Bag no. 4568; F00-1080 T28/6.
FABRIC: Surface: smooth, hard, few small and occasional very large angular/spherical white chalky inclusions. Reddish yellow (7.5YR 7/6). DESCRIPTION: One drilled hole. Flat base and top. Incised '+' on one face with drilled hole. Complete.
Pres. H: 6.55 cm; Max. Dim. 3.6 × 3.3-3.5 cm; We: 73 g.

228. Large pyramidal loom weight (Not depicted).
Bag no. 4564; F00-1071 T28/6.
FABRIC: Surface: smooth, soft, small to medium angular/spherical abundant red and brown few white and rare blue-grey inclusions. Light red (2.5YR 6/6). DESCRIPTION: One drilled hole. Slight chipping on base. Flat base, rounded top.
Pres. H: 8.25 cm; Base: 5.35 × 4.9 cm; We: 178 g.

229. Large pyramidal loom weight (Not depicted).
Bag no. 4567; F00-1077 T28/6.
FABRIC: Surface: Hackly, hard, common small to large angular/spherical white, brown and red inclusions, rare examples of very, very large white. Light red (2.5YR 6/8). DESCRIPTION: One drilled hole. Flat base, rounded top\Slight chipping on base.
Pres. H: 8.15 cm; Base: 5.2 × 5.1 cm; W: 177 g.

Other weaving objects

230. Spool (Not depicted).
Bag no. 4572; F00-1083 T28/6.
FABRIC: Hackly, soft, common medium angular/spherical red, white and grey inclusions. Light red (2.5YR 6/6). DESCRIPTION: Two disc ends, walls

run smoothly with concave profile to produce stem. Some chipping on discs.
Pres. H: 3.75 cm; Disc D: 2.3 cm; We: 33 g.

ATK
COMMENT: Pit in the southwest corner of room X. Identified during the excavation of stratum 6.

Pottery Bags: 4560
Pottery Statistics:

Total:	97	%:	We: 700
FW:	38	39	320
PW:	28	29	280
CPW:	31	32	100
CW:	–	–	–

FW
231. Fish plate (Pl. 11).
Bag no. 4560: 3 ATK.
FABRIC: Granular, soft, no visible inclusions, mica on surface. Reddish yellow (5YR 6/6). SURFACE: Matt red on interior and on upper and mid wall, some dripping marks on exterior to foot. DESCRIPTION: Foot, floor and lower wall. Low ring foot with narrow cross section, flat resting surface, interior floor depressed, ringed with ridge and groove. Lower wall rises slowly to produce shallow bowl.
Base D: 8.0 cm; Pres. H: 3.1 cm.
COMMENTS: Import – Western Greece? Compare: Dyggve, Poulsen and Rhomaios 1934, no. 16, p. 419, fig. 144.
DATE: Hellenistic.

232. Bowl, folded rim (Pl. 11).
Bag no. 4560: 4 *ATK.*
FABRIC: Granular, soft, few fine angular platy white inclusions. Pink (5YR 7/4). SURFACE: Black, lustrous on body, worn on rim. DESCRIPTION: Rim, upper wall, handle, non-joining body fragments. Rim is bevelled, and thickened so it projects just beyond the inner and outer wall. Horizontal handle attaches below the rim but the height rises above the rim.
Rim D: 20.2 cm; Pres. H: 36.5 cm.
COMMENTS: Import.
DATE: Classical.

233. Fragment (Pl. 11).
Bag no. 4560: 1 *ATK.*
FABRIC: Slightly granular, soft, no visible inclusions. Outer margin: Pink (5YR 7/4); Inner margin: Grey (10YR 6/1). SURFACE: Black-brown smooth, metallic grey on interior. DESCRIPTION: Convex wall. Decoration: West Slope decoration, incised scrolling stems. Fugitive dot rosette and ivy leaf not shown on drawing.
Pres. H: 3.1 cm.
COMMENTS: Import.
DATE: Hellenistic.

ATD
COMMENT: Excavation of material associated with mud brick soil on and around wall *ATD.*

Pottery Bags: 4931
Pottery Statistics:

Total:	6	%:	We: 330
FW:	1	16.5	5
PW:	–	–	-
CPW:	1	16.5	5
CW:	4	67	320

Loom weight
Type 2
234. Small Loom weight, pyramidal (Not depicted).
Bag no. 4931:1 *ATD.*
FABRIC: Surface: smooth, hard, frequent small to medium subrounded-angular/spherical white and grey inclusions. Pink (5YR 7/4). DESCRIPTION: One drilled hole. Slight chipping on faces.
Pres. H: 5.75 cm; Base 3.3 × 3.3 cm; Top: 0.8 × 0.8 cm; We: 45 g.

Zone XII
Zone XII is located outside rooms X and XI.
The zone is not distinguished from room X in the excavation of the earlier layers, though in stratum 2 and 3 a tile deposit, *ATA*, is located to the east of *ATB.*[278] The collapse phase continues in stratum 4 with rocks fall-

278 The West Slope kantharos no. 235 and the lamp no. 236 are from these strata, accompanied by loom weights 3944, 4291 and 4329; these loom weights are not included in the catalogue.

en from *ATB* located through it. The scrappy ceramics are part of this collapse. Stratum 5 is the pre-destruction deposit of the zone. A range of finds are located in the dry and olive yellow soil, including coins, and loom weights. The ceramics are mixed and worn and in this are dissimilar to those found in the room: jug base no. 237; unguentarium: no. 238; amphora rim and handle: no. 239. An unusual pithos base, no. 240, has a hole in the centre of the floor which appears part of the original construction of the pot, no. 241, a grand, type 2, pyramidal loom weight with stamp and no. 242, a clay waster, are recorded from zone XII, stratum 5.

In the zone outside room XI,[279] the finds include tile fragments, a coin and some ceramics. Amongst the fragments of ceramics, that include Geometric, Archaic, Classical and Hellenistic sherds, both mixed and worn, is the bolsal no. 265.

Discussion

Zone XII displays a worn and scrappy accumulation of materials. Most objects are likely to be out of their use positions, representing rubbish rather than activity.

T29/2

Pottery Bags: 3947, 3942, 3955

Pottery Statistics:

Total:	283	%:	We: 3190
FW:	65	23	375
PW:	198	70	2225
CPW:	13	5	30
CW:	7	2	560

FW

235. Hellenistic kantharos, one piece (or straight walled) (Pl. 11).

Bag no. 3955: 1 T29/2.

FABRIC: Granular, hard with no visible inclusions, but small voids. Reddish yellow (5YR 7/6). SURFACE: Brown to black, smooth. DESCRIPTION: Rim, upper wall, handle. Simple rounded rim, groove divides upper and lower wall. Spur handle, outer handle carries two grooves down the centre. Possible West Slope decoration: An incised groove that runs on the upper wall from under the handle could be the edge of a wreath.

Rim D: 13.0 cm; Pres. H: 4.5 cm.

COMMENTS: Import.

DATE: Hellenistic.

T29/3

COMMENT: Excavation of the stratum crosses between zone XII and room X. Associated with tile deposit *ATA*. Mixed fill.

Pottery Bags: 4287

Pottery Statistics:

Total:	114	%:	We: 1500
FW:	53	46.5	360
PW:	61	53.5	1140
CPW:	–	–	–
CW:	–	–	–

Lamps

236. Lamp (Not depicted).

Bag no. 4287: 3 T29/3.

FABRIC: Granular, soft with few fine angular/spherical white inclusions. Light brown (7.5YR 6/3). SURFACE: Black-brown. DESCRIPTION: Lower nozzle. Nozzle end is flattened (squared).

L: 4.0 cm; W: 2.5 cm.

T29/5

COMMENT: Pre-destruction deposit of the outdoor zone XII. Mixed and worn ceramics.

Pottery bags: 4801, 4802

Pottery Statistics:

Total:	335	%:	We:
FW:	56	16.5	200
PW:	246	73.5	1110
CPW:	26	8	80
CW:	7	2	60

FW

237. Jug (Not depicted).

Bag no. 4802: 5 T29/5.

279 It is excavated as T27A and called stratum 7 to relate it to the stratum 7 found within room XI, though there is no strata 4, 5 or 6. It is the equivalent of stratum 5 in T29 (XII) and stratum 4 in T31 (IX).

FABRIC: Granular, hard, few small angular/spherical white inclusions. Outer margin: light red (2.5YR 6/8).; Core: grey (7.5YR 5/1). DESCRIPTION: Base and lower wall. Broad ring foot with rounded resting surface, convex lower walls.
Base D: 13.0 cm; Pres. H: 3.1 cm.
COMMENTS: Local.

238. Unguentarium (Pl. 11).
Bag no. 4802: 2 T29/5.
FABRIC: Granular, soft with few voids and no visible inclusions. Light reddish brown (5YR 6/4). SURFACE: Black to light brown on all exterior surfaces. DESCRIPTION: Base and lower wall. Disc base protrudes beyond narrow lower wall which rises with a slightly concave profile.
Base D: 1.75 cm; Pres. H: 2.25 cm.
COMMENTS: Import. Compare: Camilli 1999, no. A24.1, p. 68, fig, 12; p. 64, A 23.8, fig. 10.
DATE: Hellenistic, 300 BC.

PW
239. Transport Amphora (Not depicted).
Bag no. 4802: 3 T29/5.
FABRIC: Laminar, hard, few small angular/tabular white inclusions. Pink to reddish yellow (7.5YR 7/4 – 7.5YR 7/6). DESCRIPTION: Rim, neck, handle stem. Rim folded over and attached to upper neck to height of handle attachment, cylindrical neck.
Rim D: 13.0 cm; Pres. H: 10.5 cm.
COMMENTS: Import.

CW
240. Pithos base (Not depicted).
Bag no. 4802: 4 T29/5.
FABRIC: Hackly, hard, abundant angular/tabular large to very large red, small to medium white and grey inclusions. Core: weak red (10R 5/4); margin: yellowish red to reddish yellow (5YR 5/6 – 5YR 6/6). DESCRIPTION: Disc foot with solid outer face but no profiling. Interior surface uneven (flaked?). The interior of the floor of the disc foot is depressed. At the centre of the foot is a circular cut through the floor.
Base D: 18.0 cm; Pres. H: 5.2 cm.
COMMENT: Local.

Loom weight

Type 2
241. Grand pyramidal loom weight (Not depicted).
Bag no. 4805; F00-1144 T29/5.
FABRIC: Hackly, hard, frequent small angular/spherical white and rare very large angular/spherical red inclusions. Reddish yellow (5YR 6/6). DESCRIPTION: One drilled hole. Stamp. Flat bottom, rounded top, wall bevelled to base. Chipped base.
Pres. H: 8.35 cm; Base: 6.0 cm; We: 238 g.

Various

242. Clay waster (Not depicted).
Bag no. 4802: 1 T29/5.
FABRIC: Surface: granular, very soft, small to medium angular/tabular-spherical white inclusions. Light brown to reddish yellow (7.5YR 6/4 – 7.5YR 6/6). DESCRIPTION: Clay lump, with two flattened surfaces and third surface punctured by three finger impressions.
Pres. H: 3.35 cm; L: 3.8 cm; W: 4.0 cm; We: 32 g.

Room XI

The ceramics within the tile layer *AGC* are plain ware and fine ware fragments, largely non-diagnostics. There is, though, no. 247, a Hellenistic kantharos base that is reminiscent of the cups found below the destruction levels in rooms II and X.

The material from T27B/4 includes bigger stones, tiles and few ceramics finds, though amongst these are no. 254, rim to floor fragments of a lopas with a distinctive grey fabric. *AFQ* is a stone packing, that includes displaced stones from *ACZ* and from structures of the Acropolis.The ceramic assemblage has a considerable amount of medium ware, including fragments from amphorae, thick walled black glaze fragments, the jug, no. 245, and a medium, type 2 loom weight, no. 246.

T27B/5 is excavated across room XI. It lies underneath the tile layer *AGC* and is closely associated with the pre-destruction phase of the building. This is followed by stratum 6 and stratum 7, excavated to bedrock. The pit *ATS* which also reaches bedrock, is discovered at this level. Cross joins in the ceramics between strata 5, 6 and 7 indicate that they represent the same period of use.[280]

The strata contain many finds, including some near-complete vessels. This room is set apart from the others by the number of amphorae found. These include amphorae that preserve diagnostic elements, nos. 252, 252,253 and 262 though the concentration of sherds indicate a higher number of amphorae in the room. While there is some dispersal of the fragments, and amphorae do account for some of the cross-joins between the strata, there is enough concentration to allow the amphora to have broken where they were stored, and left where they broke. That is, it would appear that the vessels were broken when the tiled roof collapsed on top of them.[281]

In addition to the amphorae there are some fine ware and coarse ware diagnostics and some cooking wares. These are not preserved to the level of the amphorae, nor to the standards of those vessels of the same ware found in the neighbouring room X or in room II. Room XI ceramics include 3rd century material as the imported West Slope kantharos, no. 249, the large echinus with exterior groove, no. 260, and the Classical/Hellenistic black glaze bowls with folded rim (nos. 250 and 261, the former with handle), and the spur and Herakles knot handle fragments (nos. 258 and 259). There is the plain ware lekane, no. 256 and the heavy coarse ware rim, no. 255, from a louterion. No. 263 is a fragment that does not appear to have been made on the wheel, it is catalogued as a miniature vessel though the fabric is similar to figurine fabric. Large body fragments, no. 257, indicate a pithos was located in this room. There are no lamps and no loom weights below the destruction level of this room, but a grindstone, given the structure number *ATL*, is set along wall *AFO*.

Lying along wall *ATH* is a pit *ATS*, which measures 0.4 × 0.3 m in its upper dimensions and 0.22 m deep. It contained some scraps of pottery, including black glaze fine ware, plain ware, coarse ware and some cooking pots.

There was little found within the structure *ATJ* beyond some worn ceramic fragments, including an ivy leaf handle attachment, no. 264.

Discussion

Room XI is characterised by the amphorae that are found within the pre-destruction deposits. These appear to have been stored within the room. They are better preserved than the fine wares in the area, a reversal of the assemblage in rooms X and II.

T27B/3

Pottery Bags: 2314, 2512, 2514, 2516, 2517, 2518

Pottery Statistics:

Total:	541	%:	We: 1380[282]
FW:	125	23	660
PW:	329	61	7190
CPW:	82	15	360
CW:	5	1	170

243. Hellenistic kantharos, one piece (Pl.11).
Bag no. 2518 T27B/3.
FABRIC: Smooth, soft, rare small angular/spherical brown inclusions. Reddish yellow (5YR 6/6). SURFACE: Black, dull with some mottling to brown on exterior, brown on interior. DESCRIPTION: Rim and upper wall. Groove under rim. West Slope decoration: Incised suspended ribbon and tie, spearhead necklace? Rim D: 11.0 cm; Pres. H: 2.1 cm.
COMMENTS: Local.
DATE: Hellenistic.

T27B/4 and T26/3

Comments: T27B/4 and T26/3 associated with the tile and stone destruction deposits (*AFQ* and *AGC*) in the trench. It includes bigger stones and tiles, few ceramic finds.

Pottery Bags: 3022, 2522, 2523, 3084.

Pottery Statistics:

280 However, they may represent the two levels of finds reported in the lower zones of other trenches, when no stratum change is made (as in II and V).

281 No. 262 (includes fragments in bags 4524, 4370, 4609); uncatalogued body fragments 4364 (joining fragments in 4370); uncatalogued handle fragment 4604. No. 251 (fragments in 4570) and nos. 252, 253, 262 (has body fragments taken up in bag 4609; no. 253 may be the toe of this same amphora).

282 Weight does not include 2516 or 2517.

Total:	178	%:	We: 1820[283]
FW:	43	24	140
PW:	121	68	1600
CPW:	10	6	30
CW:	4	2	50

CPW

244. Lopas (Pl. 11).
Rim, wall and lower wall. 4 joining fragments
Bag no. 3022: 1 T27B/4.
FABRIC: Hackly, hard with common small angular/spherical white, grey and brown inclusions. Dark grey (2.5Y 4/1).
Rim D: 17.0 cm; Pres. H: 3.1 cm.
COMMENTS: Import. Fabric compares to no. 76.
DATE: Hellenistic.

AFQ

Comment: Stone packing. Destruction of Room XI; excavated in T27B/4 and T26/3.

Pottery Bags: 3075
Pottery Statistics:

Total:	175	%:	We: 6930
FW:	6	3.5	30
PW:	166	95	5480
CPW:	1	0.5	10
CW:	2	1	1410

PW

245. Jug (Pl. 11).
Bag no. 3075: 1 *AFQ*
FABRIC: Granular, hard, few fine angular/spherical white inclusions. Reddish yellow (5YR 6/6). DESCRIPTION: Handle and wall. Upper wall inset above handle attachment and the profile changes from convex to concave. The strap handle is high and raises well above the level of the rim.
Pres. H: 12.8 cm (height includes handle).
COMMENTS: Local. Compare: Edwards 1975, no. 273, pl. 10

283 Does not include weight of 3022 and 2522.

Loom weight

Type 2
246. Medium Loom weight, pyramidal (Not depicted).
Bag no. 3080 *AFQ*.
FABRIC: Granular, hard, with frequent medium angular/tabular grey and angular/spherical red inclusions. Very pale brown (10YR 8/3). DESCRIPTION: One drilled hole. Stamp on upper face. Slight chipping on walls but profile complete. Impressed cross on upper face, bars travelling from mid wall to mid wall so forming a +.
Pres. H: 6.65 cm; Base: 4.5 × 4.1 cm; Top: 1.95 × 1.85 cm; We: 86 g.

AGC

COMMENTS: Tile layer in rooms X and XI. Ceramics are associated with the destruction and fill in the area, including T26B/4 and T26/3 in room XI.

Pottery Bags: 4504, 4509, 3090, 3296, 3089
Pottery Statistics:

Total:	125	%:	We: 2390
FW:	35	28	380
PW:	68	54	1850
CPW:	21	17	150
CW:	1	1	10

FW

247. Hellenistic kantharos, one piece (Not depicted).
Bag no. 3090: 1 *AGC* cleaning.
FABRIC: Smooth, hard, with rare fine angular/spherical inclusions, few voids. Pink (5YR 7/4). SURFACE: Brown, streaky and dull on interior. Thin brown wash on exterior. DESCRIPTION: Base and lower wall. Narrow ring foot, curving, taut lower wall.
Base D: 4.2 cm; Pres. H: 4.4 cm.
COMMENTS: Local.
DATE: Hellenistic.

T27B/5

COMMENTS: Lies beneath *AGC*. Pre-destruction layer in Room XI. Cross-joins with strata 6 and 7.

Pottery Bags: 4517, 4518, 4519, 4521, 4522, 4524, 4570, 4581
Pottery Statistics:

Total:	326	%:	We: 10345[284]
FW:	37	11.5	160
PW:	225	69	8580
CPW:	51	15.5	180
CW:	13	4	1425

FW

248. Hellenistic kantharos, one piece (Not depicted).
Bag no. 2518: 1 T27B/5.
FABRIC: Smooth, soft, rare small angular/spherical brown inclusions. Reddish yellow (5YR 6/6). SURFACE: Black, dull with some mottling to brown on exterior, brown on interior. DESCRIPTION: Rim and upper wall. Groove under rim. West Slope decoration. Incised suspended ribbon and tie: spearhead necklace?
Rim D: 11.0 cm; Pres. H: 2.1 cm.
COMMENTS: Local.
DATE: Hellenistic.

249. Hellenistic kantharos, one piece (Pl. 11).
Bag no. 4524: 1 T27B/5.
FABRIC: Slightly granular, soft, with few very fine white inclusions. Light red (2.5YR 6/6). SURFACE: Brown. DESCRIPTION: Rim and upper wall. West Slope decoration. Between two incised lines lies an ivy wreath. Incised curling stems with painted leaves, now fugitive. Elegant long stems, large leaves. Very light glazed groove at junction of upper and lower body.
Rim D: 12.0 cm; Pres. H: 6.8 cm.
COMMENTS: Import.
DATE: Hellenistic.

250. Bowl, folded rim (Pl. 11).
Bag no. 4517: 1; F99-1029 T27B/5.
FABRIC: Granular, hard, rare angular fine spherical white and grey inclusions. Yellowish red (5YR 5/6). SURFACE: Black to brown, matt. DESCRIPTION: Rim, wall, handle. Inturned upper wall, rolled rim with flat upper surface. Broad horizontal handle stem sits below and onto rim indicating handle rises above rim.
Rim D: 20.0 cm; Pres. H: 3.3 cm.
COMMENTS: Local.
DATE: Classical-Hellenistic.

284 This weight does not include the material in bags 4517, 4519 and 4522.

PW

251. Transport Amphora (Pl. 12).
Bag no. 4521; F99-1031 T27B/5.
FABRIC: Laminar, soft, frequent medium rounded/spherical brown, very large rounded/spherical red, small angular/tabular white inclusions. Very pale brown (10YR 7/4 – 10YR 8/4), patches of clay are light red (2.5YR 6/6). DESCRIPTION: Rim, neck, shoulder, handle and body fragments. Mushroom rim, angular profile.
Rim D: 11.5-12 cm; Pres. H: 21.5 cm.
COMMENTS: Import. Compare: Lawall 2004, no. 20, p. 451-452, pl. 199.
DATE: Late 4th century.

252. Transport Amphora (Pl. 12).
Bag no. 4519; F00-1030 T27B/5.
FABRIC: Hackly, soft, few small to medium angular/spherical brown, grey and white inclusions few platy voids. Reddish yellow (5YR 6/6). DESCRIPTION: Rim, neck and handle. Mushroom rim, angular profile.
Rim D: 13.0 cm; Pres. H: 9.4 cm; Pres. H: with handle 11.8 cm.
COMMENTS: Import.

253. Transport Amphora (Pl. 12).
Bag no. 4581: 1 T27B/5.
FABRIC: Hackly, hard, frequent small to medium angular/platy-spherical brown, red, grey, white inclusions, light refracting particles and voids. Reddish yellow (5YR 6/6) and burnt to brown (7.5YR 5/3). DESCRIPTION: Toe (body fragments from amphora in same bag). Hollow, broad toe with rounded resting surface.
Base D: 4.7 cm; Pres. H: 3.3 cm.
COMMENTS: Import.

CPW

254. Lopas (Not depicted).
Bag no. 3022: 1 T27B/5.
FABRIC: Hackly, hard with common small angular/spherical white, grey and brown inclusions. Dark grey (2.5Y 4/1). DESCRIPTION: Rim, wall and lower wall. 4 joining fragments.
Rim D: 17.0 cm; Pres. H: 3.1 cm.

COMMENTS: Import.
DATE: Hellenistic.

CW
255. Louterion (Not depicted).
Bag no. 4522 T27B/5.
FABRIC: Hackly, hard, frequent small to medium angular/tabular-spherical white and grey inclusions. Light red: 2.5YR 6/8. DESCRIPTION: Rim and inner wall. Moulded outer rim face, broad flat upper face, interior concave wall (broad, shallow bowl), vertical dentils impressed on lower outer face. Some chipping.
Est. Rim D: 77.0 cm; Pres. H: 6.5 cm; We: 1510 g.
Notes: Local.

T27B/6
Comments: Pre-destruction deposit in Room XI. Cross-joins with strata 5 and 7.

Pottery Bags: 4364, 4370
Pottery Statistics:

Total:	102	%:	We: 1180
FW:	37	36	170
PW:	40	39	730
CPW:	24	24	270
CW:	1	1	10

PW
256. Lekane (Pl. 12).
Bag no. 4370: 1 T27B/6.
FABRIC: Granular, hard, with angular/spherical red-brown and grey inclusions and voids. Very pale brown (10YR 7/4 – 10YR 8/4). DESCRIPTION: Rim and upper wall. Flaring rim inset from wall on exterior. Upper face carries groove, outer face squared. Lower wall curves to bowl. Part of drilled mending hole preserved at break.
Est. Rim D: 36 cm; Pres. H: 7.0 cm.
COMMENTS: Import.
DATE: Hellenistic.

CW
257. Pithos (Not depicted).
Bag no. 4606; F00-1088 T27B/6
FABRIC: Hackly, hard, common large angular/tabular red, brown, white and grey inclusions. Reddish yellow (5YR 6/6). DESCRIPTION: Large body fragments.
We: 13460 g.

T27B/7
COMMENTS: Pre-destruction deposit in Room XI. Cross-joins with strata 5 and 6.

Pottery Bags: 4570, 4604, 4609
Pottery Statistics:

Total:	368	%:	We: 2515[285]
FW:	72	19.5	170
PW:	225	61	1780
CPW:	64	17.5	215
CW:	7	2	350

FW
258. Classical kantharos (Not depicted).
Bag no. 4604: 2 T27B/7.
FABRIC: Granular, soft with no visible inclusions. Pink (5YR 7/4). SURFACE: Black, worn. DESCRIPTION: Herakles knot handle attachment.
Pres. H: 2.3 cm; L. 2.8 cm; W: 2.8 cm.
COMMENTS: Import.
DATE: Classical-Hellenistic.

259. Hellenistic kantharos, straight walled (?) (Not depicted).
Bag no. 4604: 3 T27B/7.
FABRIC: Granular, soft, no visible inclusions. Light red (2.5YR 6/6). SURFACE: Black, shiny. DESCRIPTION: Spur handle and rim. Simple, upright rim, circular strap handle with flattened upper face and protruding ledge.
Rim D: 11.0 cm; Pres. H: 2.0 cm.
COMMENTS: Import – Attic. Note that this example of the spur handle does not have a double layer of clay on the handle, one for the handle and the other the spur, but rather the spur is shaped from the handle itself.
DATE: Hellenistic.

260. Echinus bowl, large with grooved wall (Pl. 12).
Bag no. 4604: 1 T27B/7.
FABRIC: Smooth, hard, with frequent fine angular/

285 This weight does not include 4608 (no. 262).

tabular white inclusions. Yellowish red (5YR 5/6). SURFACE: Thin grey slip, very worn on exterior. DESCRIPTION: 5 joining fragments, rim and upper wall.
Rim D: 17.0 cm; Pres. H: 3.5 cm.
COMMENTS: Local. There is another rim fragment of this shape in the same bag with a black and slightly shiny glaze.
DATE: Hellenistic.

261. Bowl, folded rim (Pl. 12).
Bag no. 4570: 1 T27B/7.
FABRIC: Granular, soft, with no visible inclusions but few tabular and spherical voids. Reddish yellow (5YR 6/6). SURFACE: Grey-brown on walls, brown on rim. DESCRIPTION: Rim and upper wall.
Rim D: 31.0 cm; Pres. H: 2.4 cm.
COMMENTS: Local.
DATE: Hellenistic.

PW
262. Transport Amphora (Pl. 12).
Bag no. 4608; F00-1089 T27B/7.
FABRIC: Granular, hard with few medium angular/spherical grey and white inclusions and large spherical red inclusions, rare light refracting particles. Red to light red (2.5YR 5/6 – 2.5YR 6/6). DESCRIPTION: Rim, neck, handle, numerous body fragments. Lead joins on rim. Folded rim. Heavily ridged interior wall. Burnt on lower exterior wall.
Rim D: 12.0 cm; H: neck to rim 15.5 cm.
COMMENTS: Import. Body fragments also in bag no. 4609 F00-1090 T27B/7.

Miniature

263. Miniature cup (Pl. 12).
Bag no. 4570: 2 T27B/7.
FABRIC: Hackly, very soft with few small grey angular/spherical inclusions and irregular voids. Pink (7.5YR 7/4 – 5YR 7/4). DESCRIPTION: Base and lower wall. Very rough manufacture and irregular form. Broad foot rather like a fusiform unguentarium flaring at base, hollow interior. Rising convex outer walls.
Base D: 2.6 cm; Pres. H: 2.4 cm.

ATJ
COMMENTS: Stone lined quarter circle in the corner of walls *ADB* and *AFO*.

Pottery Bags: 4607
Pottery Statistics:

Total:	14	%:	We: 25
FW:	5	36	10
PW:	7	50	10
CPW:	2	14	5
CW:			

FW
264. Hellenistic kantharos, handle attachment (Not depicted).
Bag no. 4607: 1 *ATJ*
FABRIC: Smooth, hard, no visible inclusions, rare voids. Reddish yellow (5YR 6/6). SURFACE: Black, shiny. DESCRIPTION: Hellenistic kantharos, straight walled. Ivy leaf.
L: 2.2 cm;W: 2.15 cm.
COMMENTS: Import – Attic.
DATE: Hellenistic.

T27A/7
Pottery Bags: 4803, 4806
Pottery Statistics:

Total:	99	%:	We: 440
FW:	30	30.5	120
PW:	51	51.5	250
CPW:	16	16	50
CW:	2	2	20

265. Bolsal (Pl. 12).
Bag no. 4806 T27A/7.
FABRIC: Granular, soft, few small angular/spherical white inclusions and rare grey inclusions. Light red (2.5YR 6/6). SURFACE: Black, dull, on all surfaces. DESCRIPTION: Foot to rim profile, handle stem. 50 % preserved. Disc foot, broad floor rising to vertical upper wall and rim.
Rim D: 9.2 cm; Base D: 4.3 cm; Pres. H: 4.2 cm.
COMMENTS: Local.
DATE: Hellenistic.

Zone XIII

There is a mix of Archaic, Classical and Hellenistic material in zone XIII which is located outside rooms XIV and XV, sheltered to the north by wall *AFD*. The ceramics include some good quality black glaze of Classical and Hellenistic date. Occasional examples maintain the kind of preservation common within the rooms, such as the plate with rolled rim no. 269. The remaining ceramics are more fragmentary and many are worn. The fine wares all share a dining function, the exception, perhaps, being the lid no. 272. Most are Hellenistic (nos. 267-272, nos. 276-278), though the skyphos, no. 274, and cup skyphos, no. 275, date to the 4th century.[286] A jug, no. 279, a jar/stamnos, no. 280, and a chytra, no. 281, represent the numerous worn plain ware and cooking pot fragments in the deposit. There is a loom weight from the deposit, no. 282, a type 3 of medium weight (this is joined by a very fragmentary conical loom weight from stratum 4, no. 273).

The loosely packed pit *AGH* is located in zone XIII. It was not fully excavated. It contained a plate with offset rim, a worn Hellenistic sherd, no. 283.

Discussion

The preservation of some vessels links the zone to the interior spaces, though on the whole the ceramics are worn and fragmentary.

Area includes excavated zones T6NA and T27N.

T6NA/2d
COMMENTS: Tile and stone fragments in this well-packed deposit identify it as a destruction fill.

Pottery Bags: 489, 558, 617, 874
Pottery Statistics:

Total:	195	%:	We:1175
FW:	62	32	110
PW:	98	50	600
CPW:	31	16	25
CW:	4	2	440

286 Nos. 267, 268, 270, 271, 272, 276, 277, 278; Classical: Nos. 274; 275 (the date range of the material found in strata 4 and 5 does not differ).

FW
266. Hellenistic kantharos, angular (Pl. 13).
Bag no. 874: 1 T6NA/2d.
FABRIC: Hard, fine, smooth, no visible inclusions. Reddish yellow (5YR 6/6). SURFACE: Thin smooth slip, brown on exterior, black on interior. DESCRIPTION: Upper wall. West Slope decoration, spearhead necklaces. Paint is fugitive but pattern preserved in glaze (much of surrounding glaze has worn away). Double incised line as the chain, holds clay-painted dots where the spearheads descend, single dot painted under spearhead.
Pres. H: 3.3 cm.
COMMENTS: Import.
DATE:Hellenistic.

T6NA/4d and T27N/4d
Pottery Bags: 1962. 1770, 3298, 3311, 3517, 3523
Pottery Statistics:

Total:	545	%:	We: 2435[287]
FW:	125	23	240
PW:	255	47	890
CPW:	142	26	1065
CW:	23	4	240

267. Hellenistic kantharos, straight walled (Pl. 13).
Bag no. 1770: 3 T6NA/4d.
FABRIC: Fine, soft, smooth, rare fine white and grey inclusions. Light reddish brown to reddish yellow (5YR 6/4-5YR 6/6). SURFACE: Brown, dull with some shiny patches, worn, uneven on lower wall. DESCRIPTION: Body fragments of the junction between upper and lower body (straight-walled kantharos). Glazed groove above junction of upper and lower body. Some irregular incised curvilinear lines on the lower body of one fragment, though glazed.
Max. Pres. D: 11.0 cm (junction of upper and lower body).
COMMENTS: Local.
DATE: Hellenistic.

268. Hellenistic kantharos, straight walled (Pl. 13).
Bag no. 1770: 4 T6NA/4d.
FABRIC: Fine, hard, smooth, no visible inclusions,

287 No weight recorded for bag 1770 or 3523.

few voids. Pink (5YR 7/4). SURFACE: Thin, dull dark brown, worn. DESCRIPTION: Rim, upper wall and handle fragment. Strap handle without thumb-rest. Simple lip. Straight wall angles out to a junction with lower wall.
Rim D: ca. 10.0 cm.
COMMENTS: Local.
DATE: Hellenistic.

269. Plate, rolled rim (Pl. 13).
Bag no. 3523; F99-1030 T27N/4d.
FABRIC: Granular, soft, rare medium angular/spherical white inclusions. Reddish yellow (5YR 7/6). SURFACE: Brown, mottled dull on interior and over rim, no glaze on wall and foot. DESCRIPTION: Full profile. Simple, unprofiled ring foot, simple lip rolled inwards.
Rim D: 12.0 cm; Base D: 4.3 cm; Pres. H: 3.8 cm.
COMMENTS: Local. Compare: Dyggve, Poulsen & Rhomaios 1934, no. 13, fig. 144.
DATE: Hellenistic.

270. Echinus bowl, large with grooved rim (Not depicted).
Bag no. 3517: 1 T27N/4d.
FABRIC: Hard, granular, with rare small angular/spherical white inclusions. Light brown (7.5YR 6/4). SURFACE: Black with brown tinge on interior and upper rim, outer and lower rim on exterior coated by a thin wash, stops before mid wall. DESCRIPTION: Rim and wall. Rim curves over quite sharply. Groove on exterior rim "upper face".
Rim D: 30.0 cm; Pres. H: 6.3 cm.
COMMENTS: Import.
DATE: Hellenistic.

271. Saucer (Pl. 13).
Bag no. 1770: 5 T6NA/4d.
FABRIC: Fine, hard, few fine, white inclusions and voids. Light reddish brown (5YR 6/4). SURFACE: Smooth brown slip, thicker on interior than exterior where it is streaky. DESCRIPTION: Broad rim. Simple rounded lip. Depressed junctions to lower wall. Possibly a painted band, now fugitive, on interior upper rim.
Rim D: 29.0 cm; Pres. H: 2.5 cm.
COMMENTS: Local.
DATE: Hellenistic.

272. Lid (Pl. 13).
Bag no. 1770: 1 T6NA/4d.
FABRIC: medium fine, soft, granular with few voids, no visible inclusions apart from rare white light refracting particles. Reddish yellow (5YR 6/6). SURFACE: Thin red-brown slip, very worn, exterior only. DESCRIPTION: Body to knob. Cylinder knob. Domed upper wall.
Pres. H: 3.2 cm; Knob D: 1.8 cm.
COMMENTS: Import.
DATE: Hellenistic.

Loom weight

Type 1
273. Loom weight, conical (Not depicted).
Bag no. 3299; F99-1016 T27N/4d.
FABRIC: Hackly, soft, with few large reddish angular/spherical and rare angular/platy white inclusions, common platy voids. Reddish brown to red (2.5YR 5/4 – 2.5YR 5/6). DESCRIPTION: Only base and part of lower wall preserved. Wall bevelled to base.
D: Base 4.5 cm; Pres. H: 5.1 cm; Max. D: ca. 5 cm; We: 99 cm.

T6NA/5d
COMMENT: Mixed and worn sherds in this outdoor area. Archaic, Classical, Hellenistic. Range compares to /4d material.

Pottery Bags: 2282, 2292, 2314, 3322
Pottery Statistics:

Total:	615	%:	We: 4115[288]
FW:	193	31	685
PW:	228	37	1820
CPW:	175	29	610
CW:	19	3	1000

FW
274. Skyphos (Not depicted).
Bag no. 2292: 6 T6NA/5d.
FABRIC: Fine, soft, smooth, few fine white inclusions and platy voids. Light reddish brown (2.5YR 6/4 – 5YR 6/4). SURFACE: Smooth dark brown to black

288 Does not include weight for 3322.

slip on interior and lower wall, unglazed band above foot, the foot itself retains glaze on the outer and inner surface, but neither the resting surface nor the underside of the floor retain glaze. DESCRIPTION: Base and lower wall. COMMENTS: Local. Indication of the mixed layer of this deposit, in contrast to the cleaner layers inside the room XIV and XV.
Base D: 8.2 cm; Pres. H: 3.2 cm.
DATE: Classical, 5th cent.

275. Cup Skyphos (Pl. 13).
Bag no. 2292: 3 T6NA/5d.
FABRIC: Hard, conchoidal, rare white inclusions, platy voids. Light red to red (2.5YR 6/6 – 10R 5/8). SURFACE: Worn black to brown slip, smooth and shiny. DESCRIPTION: Rim upper wall and handle preserved. Simple rounded lip. Wall concave immediately below rim then convex at the height of the handle. Handle stem, circular in section, lower handle indicates rising horizontal handle.
Rim D: 9.0 cm; Pres. H: 3.2 cm.
COMMENTS: Import-Attic. Indication of the mixed layer of this deposit, in contrast to the cleaner layers inside the room XIV and XV. Compare: Sparkes & Talcott, 1970, p. 111
DATE: Classical.

276. Plate, grooved rim. (Pl. 13).
Bag no. 2314: 7 T6NA/5d.
FABRIC: Fine, soft, granular, with frequent very fine white and grey inclusions and rare voids. Very pale brown (10YR 7/3). SURFACE: Mottled dark brown to light brown slip on all preserved surfaces. DESCRIPTION: Rim flattened from wall and carries grooves, but does not project. Groove on upper surface of rim.
Rim D: 17.0 cm; Pres. H: 1.5 cm.
DATE: Hellenistic.

277. Echinus bowl (Not depicted).
Bag no. 2314: 6 T6NA/5d.
FABRIC: Fine, hard, slightly granular, few fine white inclusions, rare small brown inclusions, voids. Light reddish brown (2.5YR 6/4). SURFACE: Dark brown to black with a very slight metallic shine on interior, mottled to light brown and red on exterior. DESCRIPTION: Rim and upper wall fragments. Two ridges are placed to mark the junction of the exterior rim and wall lower and coincide with the maximum diameter of the bowl.
Max. D: 11.0 cm
COMMENTS: Local.
DATE: Hellenistic.

278. Plate, rolled rim (Not depicted).
Bag no. 2314: 5 T6NA/5d.
FABRIC: Fine, soft, no visible inclusions. Pink (5YR 7/4). SURFACE: Brown slip on interior and over rim, no slip on outer wall. DESCRIPTION: Rim and upper wall
Rim D: 16.0 cm; Pres. H: 1.8 cm.
COMMENTS: Import.
DATE: Hellenistic.

PW
279. Jar/stamnos (Pl. 13).
Bag no. 2292: 1 T6NA/5d.
FABRIC: Hard, granular, small angular/tabular grey brown and white inclusions. Red (10R 5/6). SURFACE: Thin matt brown slip on all preserved surfaces. DESCRIPTION: Rim and upper wall. Flat upper surface of projecting rim carries a series of sharp concentric grooves. Ridges on upper rim.
Rim D: 17.0 cm; Pres. H: 2.8 cm; L: handle frag. 5.1 cm, W handle fragment: 2.3 cm.
COMMENTS: Import. Double handle in same fabric, non joining. Unusual shape and fabric: hard firing, crisp preservation.

280. Jug (Pl. 13).
Bag no. 2292: 2 T6NA/5d.
FABRIC: Soft, powdery surface, hackly in break, few to frequent small white inclusions. Yellowish red to reddish yellow (5YR 5/6 – 5YR 6/6). SURFACE: Red glaze, very worn preserved in part on rim and inner rim and on handle. DESCRIPTION: 4 non-joining fragments from same vessel. Rim, rim and handle stem, handle, base. Handle holds a central ridge.
Rim D: 7.0 cm; Base D: 10.2 cm; H of handle fragment: 5.0 cm.

CPW
281. Chytra (Not depicted).
Bag no. 2292: 5 T6NA/5d.
FABRIC: Hard, granular, frequent small subrounded white and grey inclusions. SURFACE: Red (2.5YR 5/8) and reddish brown (5YR 4/3) in core. DESCRIPTION: Handle and rim fragment.
Pres. H: 6.0 cm; W: 2.5 cm.
COMMENTS: Local.

Loom weight

Type 3
282. Pyramidal loom weight. (Fig. 84).
Bag no. 2291; F98-5004 T6NA/5d.
FABRIC: coarse, hackly with frequent large to small red spherical/subrounded inclusions, few medium to small subrounded/tabular grey inclusions, small subrounded white inclusions. Reddish yellow (5YR 6/8). DESCRIPTION: Stamped. No holes drilled. Base slightly convex. One broad face has oval stamp with raised central bar; the other broad face holds a pinched zone of clay with two deep finger impressions.
Pres. H: 6.8 cm; Base: 5.6 × 4 cm, Top: 3.1 × 1.8 cm; W: 126 g.

AGH
COMMENTS: Loosely packed pit in zone XIII. Contained few potsherds.

Pottery Bags: 3534
Pottery Statistics:

Total:	16	%:	We: 70
FW:	8	50	30
PW:	7	44	20
CPW:	–	–	–
CW:	1	6	20

FW
283. Plate, offset rim (Not depicted).
Bag no. 3534: 1 *AGH.*
FABRIC: Granular soft, no visible inclusions, few voids. Reddish yellow (5YR 6/6). SURFACE: Dark grey to brown, dull, worn. DESCRIPTION: Rim. Groove on upper face.
Rim D: 22.0 cm; Pres. H: 1.7 cm.
COMMENTS: Local.
DATE: Hellenistic.

Room XIV
A number of ceramics were gathered with the removal of the *ADZ* tile deposit in room XV and XIV and there are cross joins between the two (see below for those in room XV). There are fewer finds in this layer than in room XIV, but a 3rd century date is indicated by the West Slope kantharos no. 285. A pithos fragment with incised decoration, no. 286, was found amongst the tiles. Other material included Archaic to Hellenistic black glaze scraps, cooking pot fragments and amphora fragments.

The fine wares from stratum 5 include the best example of red-figure from the site, the partially preserved owl skyphos, no. 288. The spur handle of a one-piece kantharos, no. 290 belongs to the late 4th to 3rd century. Securing the deposit in the 3rd century are the two West Slope fragments: the kantharos no. 289 and the conical bowl no. 291; the latter is most likely from the 2nd half of the century. Other black glaze vessels, though not well-preserved, include echinus bowls, plates with offset rim. A variety of jugs and amphora are preserved, including no. 292 and no. 293. Cooking pots are also common in this deposit. Chytra (including no. 295), lopades (represented by no. 294), lids (such as no. 296) and jars are found. The amount of cooking pot in this deposit is considerable. A lid of cooking pot fabric, but resembling a reversible lid in form, is the best-preserved vessel from the room, no. 297.

There are three, small, type 2, loom weights from stratum 5, all of very similar size and fabric, nos. 298, 299, 300.[289] These are found in different areas of the room.

Discussion

Room XIV sits as an alcove to room XV. The smaller room XIV holds a range of material, including fine, plain and cooking ware ceramics, in a reasonable, though not complete, state of preservation. The material within the room is more homogenous than

289 Also no. 284 found in stratum 3.

that found in zone XIII (there are fewer Archaic and Classical sherds). In many ways, the material in this room, display the range of material one would expect to find in a domestic context, with cooking wares, numerous plain vessels (particularly jugs and amphora fragments) and fine ware cups. The destruction in this room dates much to the same time as those in the adjacent rooms, sometime in the late 3rd century.

T27N/3

COMMENTS: Stratum 3 lies on top of /4d and /5e. Stratum 3 partly lies on top of tile layer *ADZ*, found in T6NA, and thus is a post-destruction deposit.

Pottery Bags: 2601, 2606

Pottery Statistics:

Total:	94	%:	We: 1510
FW:	39	42	210
PW:	20	21	600
CPW:	30	32	430
CW:	5	5	270

Loom weight

Type 2

284. Grand loom weight, pyramidal (Fig. 84).

Bag no. 2603; F99-1008 T27N/3.

FABRIC: Granular, hard, common small to large angular/spherical white inclusions, rare medium or large angular/spherical brown inclusions, platy voids. SURFACE: Reddish yellow (5YR 6/6). DESCRIPTION: One drilled hole. Stamped. Chipping around base. Stamp of an Omega at height of drilled hole on face without drilled hole.

Pres. H: 8.65 cm; Base: 5.6 × 5.5 cm; Top: 2.45 × 2.45 cm; We: 243 g.

ADZ

COMMENTS: Tile deposit within the area, between strata 3 and 4. Deposit covers both room XIV (T27) and XV (T6NA) and spills into AREA XIII. Cross joins with stratum 5. All ceramics from this deposit in both rooms one and two included in the statistics. For finds located in room XV *ADZ*, see below.

Pottery Bags: 926, 1016, 1019, 1025, 1028, 1031, 1033, 1050, 1070, 1072, 1074, 1084, 2066, 2617, 2625

Pottery Statistics:[290]

Total:	518	%:	We: 3405[291]
FW:	145	28	315
PW:	129	25	2120
CPW:	243	47	970
CW:	1	–	–

FW

285. Hellenistic kantharos, one piece (Pl. 13).

Bag no. 2617: 1 *ADZ*.

FABRIC: Smooth, hard, no visible inclusions, few voids. Red (2.5YR 5/6). SURFACE: Grey-brown exterior, brown interior, metallic shine. DESCRIPTION: Rim, upper wall. Spur handle. West Slope decoration: Between two grooves on upper wall is a painted garland with solid tripartite leaves, possibly set on either side of an undulating ribbon, Fugitive.

Rim D: 10.6 cm; Pres. H: 5.2 cm.

COMMENTS: Import. Joining fragment 2625: 1, Compare: Rotroff 1997 no. 1034, ca. 200 (near the beginning of the 2nd century).

DATE: Hellenistic.

CW

286. Pithos (Pl. 13).

Bag no. 2617: 2 *ADZ*.

FABRIC: Hackly, hard, with small to medium frequent angular/spherical grey, red and white inclusions. Pink to reddish yellow (7.5YR 7/4 – 7.5YR 7/6). DESCRIPTION: Wall fragment with relief band and incised decoration. Note the thickness of the wall above this band is half of that below the band. Raised band (coil) with convex outer surface attached at the shoulder. Below the band are a series of grooves followed by three bands of incised zigzags divided from each other.

Pres. H: 13.0 cm; T: 2.15 cm; W: 22.0 cm; T above relief band: 1 cm

COMMENTS: Local.

290 No statistics are recorded for bag 926.

291 No weight recorded for 1084 or for the finds 1019, 1025, 1028, 1031, 1033, 1070, 1072, 1074, 1025, 1050.

ADF

COMMENTS: Material found on top of the wall *ADF* is closely associated with the material excavated as stratum 5e.

Pottery Bags: 601, 1073

Pottery Statistics:

Total:	6	%:	We: [292]
FW:	3	50	
PW:	3	50	
CPW:			
CW:			

FW

287. Classical plate (Pl. 14).

Bag no. 1073; F97-2088 *ADF.*

FABRIC: Hard, conchoidal, rare small rounded/tabular grey and subrounded/tabular white inclusions. Light reddish brown to pink (5YR 6/4 – 5YR 7/4). SURFACE: Thick black shiny glaze on all preserved surface, slight mottling to brown under foot. DESCRIPTION: Base and floor. Broad foot and floor. Solid walls and foot. Foot has a convex outer profile and flat resting surface (though chipped). Two bands of two glazed grooves on upper floor of plate. Incised graffiti under foot M or Σ.

Base D: 14.0 cm; Pres. H: 1.9 cm.

COMMENTS: Import – Attic. Compare: Sparkes & Talcott, 1970, nos. 1057-1060, fig. 10

DATE: Classical.

T6NA/5e

COMMENT: Below the tile spills, stratum 5e preserves the materials used within room XIV.

Pottery Bags: 1244, 1246, 1389, 3300, 3310, 3316, 3518, 3519, 3522, 3525, 3530

Pottery Statistics:

Total:	1147	%:	We: 4540[293]
FW:	449	39	1540
PW:	344	30	2040
CPW:	352	31	910
CW:	2	–	50

292 No weight recorded for bags 601 or 1073.

293 Does not include finds 3530, 3522, 3519, 3316.

FW

288. Skyphos Pl. 14).

Bag no. 3300: 1a T6NA/5e.

FABRIC: Slightly granular, soft, no visible inclusions. Reddish yellow (5YR 6/6). SURFACE: Black to brown, lustrous. DESCRIPTION: Rim, upper wall and handle. Red figure: Owl skyphos. Red figure, upright olive branch preserved, twig that forks in two and two leaves on either side. Part of the familiar Owl skyphos decorative arrangement.

Rim D: 10.5 cm; Pres. H: 3.7 cm.

COMMENTS: Import – Attic. Compare: Moore 1997, p. 64, nos. 1313-1322, pls. 122-123.

DATE: Classical, 5th century.

289. Hellenistic kantharos, one piece (Pl. 14).

Bag no. 1389: 1 T6NA/5e.

FABRIC: Hard, granular, with no visible inclusions but common voids. Bands of colour through sherd. 1 = red (2.5YR 5/6); 2 = reddish yellow (5YR 6/6). SURFACE: Reddish brown with some dark brown mottling on exterior. Interior upper zone is dark brown mottled to reddish-brown on lower wall. Rim and upper wall. West Slope decoration: bead and reel between two incised grooves below rim. Paint fugitive.

Rim D: 11.0 cm; Pres. H: 4.4 cm.

COMMENTS: Local.

DATE: Hellenistic.

290. Hellenistic kantharos, one piece (Not depicted).

Bag no. 1389: 4 T6NA/5e.

FABRIC: Fine, hard, granular, few fine white and rare small grey inclusions, frequent voids. Light reddish brown to pink (5YR 6/4 – 5YR 7/4). SURFACE: Worn brown-black glaze. DESCRIPTION: Rim and handle. Spur handle.

Rim D: 8.0 cm; Pres. H: 1.5 cm.

DATE: Hellenistic, late 4th-3 century.

291. Conical bowl (Pl. 14).

Bag no. 3519; F99-1024 T6NA/5e

FABRIC: Granular, soft, common small white angular/platy-spherical inclusions. Reddish yellow (5YR 6/6). SURFACE: Dark brown on upper wall, red on lower wall both interior and exterior. DESCRIPTION: Rim to floor. West Slope decoration: between grooves un-

Rim D: 7.0 cm; Base D: 2.7 cm; Pres. H: 3.3 cm.
COMMENTS: Local.
DATE: Classical-Hellenistic.

323. Reversible lid (Pl. 16).
Bag no. 679; F97-2019 T6NA/5b.
FABRIC: Fine, slightly soft, very slightly granular, powdery surface, frequent fine white and grey inclusions. Pink to reddish yellow (7.5YR 7/4 – 7.5YR 7/6). SURFACE: Dull to shiny mottled brown, worn in places. DESCRIPTION: Almost complete, full profile, reconstructed from numerous fragments. Knob stemmed and close to that of a lekanis lid. West Slope decoration on upper face. On upper side of knob a semi-preserved star flower in clay paint. Around knob, below a groove, a spearhead necklace, incised chain with clay painted dots. Three fine grooves and broad groove, egg, dart (tripartite leaves mostly fugitive, some in clay paint, dots in eggs are all fugitive. Deep groove to outer zone, concentric rectangles and checkerboard incised. Checkerboard painted – fugitive.
Rim D: 23.0 cm; Pres. H: 8.5-8.8 cm.
COMMENTS: Import. Central Greece. Compare: Baziotopoulou-Valavani 1994, p. 53, pl. 24a; Papakonstantinou 1997, p. 52, pl. 36a, c; Adrimi-Sismani, B., 2000, p. 143, fig. 9. Campanian pottery: Morel 1981, nos. 4711a.1 and 4713a.1. For decoration: Rotroff 1997, no. 1272. For further discussion of this lid see Bollen 2013.
DATE: Hellenistic.

324. Reversible lid (Pl. 16).
Bag no. 1406: 3 T6NA/5b.
FABRIC: Soft, fine, no visible inclusions, few small voids. Light brown (7.5YR 6/4). SURFACE: Shiny black to brown glaze on interior, pale and thin brown glaze on exterior (originally as interior indicated by patches of preservation). DESCRIPTION: Body fragment. West Slope decoration. Egg and dart pattern. Somewhat irregular incised eggs and darts, an overpainted dot in centre of egg, now fugitive but glaze beneath is preserved.
Pres. H: 1.4 cm; T: 0.3 cm; L: 3.65 cm; W: 1.9 cm.
COMMENTS: Import. Western Greece.
DATE: Hellenistic.

PW
325. Jug (Not depicted).
Bag no. 712: 2 T6NA/5b.
FABRIC: Medium, with few small white inclusions and voids, soft and powdery. Reddish yellow (5YR 6/6). DESCRIPTION: Base fragment. Flat disc base and foot, lower wall profile indicates a broad bodied vessel.
Base D: 10.0 cm; Pres. H: 2.0 cm.
COMMENTS: Local.

326. Jar/Stamnos (Pl. 16).
Bag no. 1396: 4 T6NA/5b.
FABRIC: Medium hard, hackly, with frequent medium white and grey inclusions (tabular and sub-rounded). Yellowish red (5YR 5/6). DESCRIPTION: Rim and upper body preserved. Upright rim with flat and slightly projecting upper surface. The inner surface of the rim cuts away smoothly to the inner wall. The wall projects out and down from the rim with a slight curve, indicating a broad bodied shape.
Rim D: 35.0 cm; Pres. H: 4.9 cm.
COMMENTS: Import.

327. Jar/Stamnos (Pl. 16).
Bag no. 1396: 5 T6NA/5b.
FABRIC: Medium hard, laminar, frequent tabular voids, rare grey and white inclusions, rare light refracting particles. Light red (2.5YR 6/8). DESCRIPTION: Rim and upper wall preserved. Upright rim with rounded profile. Wall projects out from rim with slight convexity, indicating a broad-bodied shape.
Rim D: 13.0 cm; Pres. H: 4.2 cm.
COMMENTS: Local.

328. Fragment – Stand? (Pl. 16)
Bag no. 1396: 6 T6NA/5b.
FABRIC: Hard in break but powdery on surface. Hackly with frequent, medium white and grey inclusions. Red (2.5YR 5/8).
Rim D: 33.0 cm; Pres. H: 4.0 cm.

CPW
329. Lopas (Pl. 16).
Bag no. 1401 T6NA/5b.
FABRIC: Soft, laminar with abundant small white

angular/spherical inclusions, medium subrounded/spherical grey and red-brown inclusions. Red (2.5YR 5/6). DESCRIPTION: Numerous fragments including rim and handle. Conserved rim to carination with lower body. Burning marks on outer rim and handle.
Rim D: 23.0 cm; Pres. H: 4.0 cm.
COMMENTS: Local.

330. Chytra (Pl. 17).
Bag no. 1396: 2 T6NA/5b.
FABRIC: Hard, hackly with frequent small to medium white, grey and brown inclusions. Frequent voids in break and on surface. Yellowish red (5YR 5/6). DESCRIPTION: Rim fragment. Projecting rim with flat upper surface. Exterior wall concave under rim and then flares out to body. Burning marks on inner and upper rim and on exterior wall.
Rim D: 9.0 cm; Pres. H: 1.5 cm.
DATE: Hellenistic.

331. Lid (Lopas) (Not depicted).
Bag no. 609; 97-2022 T6NA/5b.
FABRIC: Soft in break, hard on surface, granular with abundant inclusions: medium red, grey subrounded spherical and tabular; small to angular medium white. Light red to reddish yellow (2.5YR 6/8 – 5YR 6/8). DESCRIPTION: Knob and upper wall preserved.
Pres. H: 3; Diam of knob: 2.7
COMMENTS: Local. Compare: Edwards 1975, nos. 694 and 695, pl. 31.
DATE: Hellenistic.

Lamps

332. Lamp fragment (Pl. 17).
Bag no. 722; 02-2047 T6NA/5b.
FABRIC: Soft, smooth, very fine with no visible inclusions or voids. Pink (5YR 7/4). SURFACE: Remnants of white (though could be incrustation). DESCRIPTION: Rim and upper shoulder.
Rim D: 2.0 cm; Pres. H: 1.8 cm.
COMMENTS: Import-Corinth. Compare: Broneer 1977, 214, type IXB 300-250 (Agora 28A and B, 300-190).
DATE: Hellenistic.

333. Lamp (Pl. 17).
Bag no. 710: 1 T6NA/5b.
FABRIC: Fairly fine, hard, granular, with frequent small subrounded grey inclusions and voids. Pink (7.5YR 7/4). SURFACE: Thin greyish brown slip, partially preserved. DESCRIPTION: Nozzle fragment.
Max. H: 2.3 cm; W Nozzle: 2.0 cm.
COMMENTS: Compare: Broneer 1977, types VI – VII some similarities with Broneer 1977, nos. 87 and 109, 350-3rd century.
DATE: Hellenistic.

334. Lamp (Pl. 17).
Bag no. 1200: 1 T6NA/5b.
FABRIC: Soft, fine, slightly granular, few fine white inclusions. Margins: Light red (10R 6/6). Core Light reddish brown (2.5YR 6/4). SURFACE: Shiny dark brown exterior, mid brown on interior. DESCRIPTION: Rim, upper body and handle. Attached wishbone-shaped handle.
Pres. H: 2.5 cm; Max. D: 6.0 cm.
COMMENTS: Local. Very similar but small fragment from *ADZ* bag 926. Compare: Broneer 1977, no. 109, type VIIa, 4th- early 3rd century.
DATE: Classical-Hellenistic.

Figurine

335. Figurine fragment (Not depicted).
Bag no. 1233 T6NA/5b.
FABRIC: Soft, medium, common medium white inclusions, rare medium to large rounded brown inclusions. Pink to very pale brown (7.5YR 7/4 – 10YR 7/4). SURFACE: Traces of white paint. DESCRIPTION: Moulded fragment.
Width: 3.0 cm.
COMMENTS: Uncertain of the section of figurine represented by this fragment.
Similar to fragments of drapery found in *ADZ* F97-2085, F97-2082 and no. 335 (F97-2055).
DATE: Hellenistic.

Room/AREA	Trench and stratum	Date ranges of coins	Publication nos. G.Z. Alexopoulou
I	O26BD/3	369-313	*SPR* – 24
II	O26 AEP9	279-168	*SPR* – 19, 5, 13, 14
II	O26 AFC	279-168	*SPR* – 16
II	O26/3	4th cent, 387-374, 279-168, 230-168	*SPR* – 26, 25, 23, 22, 21, 20, 18, 17, 15, 12, 11, 10, 9, 8, 4, 3, 2
II	O27/3 AREA II	4th cent	*TPR* – 69
III	O27/3 AREA IV	330-200	*TPR* – 74
V	O27/3; O27/3 AREA I	4th-3rd, 279-168, 271-191, 241-146, 362-300, after 370, before 251, 330-200, 369-338, 369-313, 371-357, 338-300, 302-286, 3rd	*TPR* – 87, 83, 64, 27, 23, 10; 5, 7, 15, 17, 18, 19, 30, 31, 47, 48, 52, 53, 54, 57, 58, 59, 60, 62, 70, 71, 72, 73, 81, 84, 85, 86, 89, 90, 93
VIII	T30(/3) ATI	279-168	*TPR* – 13, 25, 28
VIII	T30/5	Before 344, after 362, before 251, 330, 371-357	*TPR* – 51, 76, 79, 91
VIII	T30N/5	300-196	*TPR* – 2
VIII	T30/6	279-168	*TPR* – 11
VIII	T30/7	279-168	*TPR* – 16
VIII	T30A/7	350, 371-357	*TPR* – 49, 77
VIII	T30N/7	4th-3rd cent, 279-168, 325	*TPR* – 1, 34, 63
VIII	T30D/8	Before 251, 371-357	*TPR* – 50, 80
IX	T31/2	279-168	*TPR* – 41
X	T28A/5	279-168	*TPR* – 26
X	T28A/6	350-322	*TPR* – 88
X	T28/4	357-346	*TPR* – 55
X	T29/5	279-168, before 344	*TPR* – 4, 20, 37
X/XII	T29/4	279-168	*TPR* – 45
XI	T27B/4	279-168	*TPR* – 38
XI	T27B/6	79-168	*TPR* – 14
XII	T27A/7	4th-3rd cent	*TPR* – 65
XIII	T27N/4d	279-168	*TPR* – 46
XIII	T6NA/5d	279-168	*TPR* – 24
XIV	T27N/5e	279-168	*TPR* – 21, 22
XIV	T6NA/5e	369-313, 279-168	*TPR* – 29, 35, 43*, 56
XV	T6NA/5b	279-168, 238-168	*TPR* – 8, 42, 44*

Table 1: *Coins. Compilation of excavation and chronological information*

Room/AREA	Number of coins
I	1
II	23
III	1
IV	-
V	35
VI	-
VII	-
VIII	17
IX	-
X	3 (+1?)
XI	2
XII	1
XIII	2
XIV	6
XV	3

Table 2: *Tally of coins from rooms and zones*

	I	II	III	IV	V	VI	VII	VIII	IX	X	X	XI	XII	XIII	XIV	XV
	O26BD	O26, O27 AREA II	O26, O27 AREA IV	O26 *ACZ-ADY*	O27, O27 AREA I	O27 AREA II, T31b	O27 ACZ-AEJ	T30 A,B,N, D	T31	T28 A, N, D	T29	T27 B	T26 **T27A**	T6NA, T27N	T6NA, T27N	T6NA
Post	/1	/1	/1	/1	/1	/1		/1	/1	/1	/1	/1	/1	/1	/1	/1
Post	/2	/2	/2	/2	/2	/2	/2a	/2	/2	/2	/2	/2	/2	/2d	/2	/2
Post								/3	/3	/3		/3			/3e	/3b
Post																/4b
Dest		AGD	AFC	/3	/3 AEZ, AER, AFU			ATG, ATI		AGC, AFQ	/3 ATA	/4 AFQ, AGC	/3	/3d, /3	ADZ, ADE	ADZ
Dest								/4		/4	/4			/4d	/4 ATX	
Occ	/3	/3 AEP, AEO, AED	/3	/4	/3 1st pass, 2nd pass	/3	/2b, /2c	/5	/4	/5	/5	/5, /6, /7, ATS, ATJ	/5 T27A/7	/5d, AGH	/5	/5b, ADZ-**
Occ								/6								
Con				/5 ADY-AEA	/3 3rd pass	/4		*/7 ATX, ATT, ATY, ATU*		/6 ATN, ATK, ATM						
Con								*/8*								

Table 3: *Stratigraphic alignment of trenches in AREA III*

Key:
Post – Post Destruction layer.
Dest – Destruction layer.
Occ – Occupation layer.
Con – Construction layer.
Italics – previous occupation layers (Archaic) mixed with Hellenistic material

PLATES 1-17

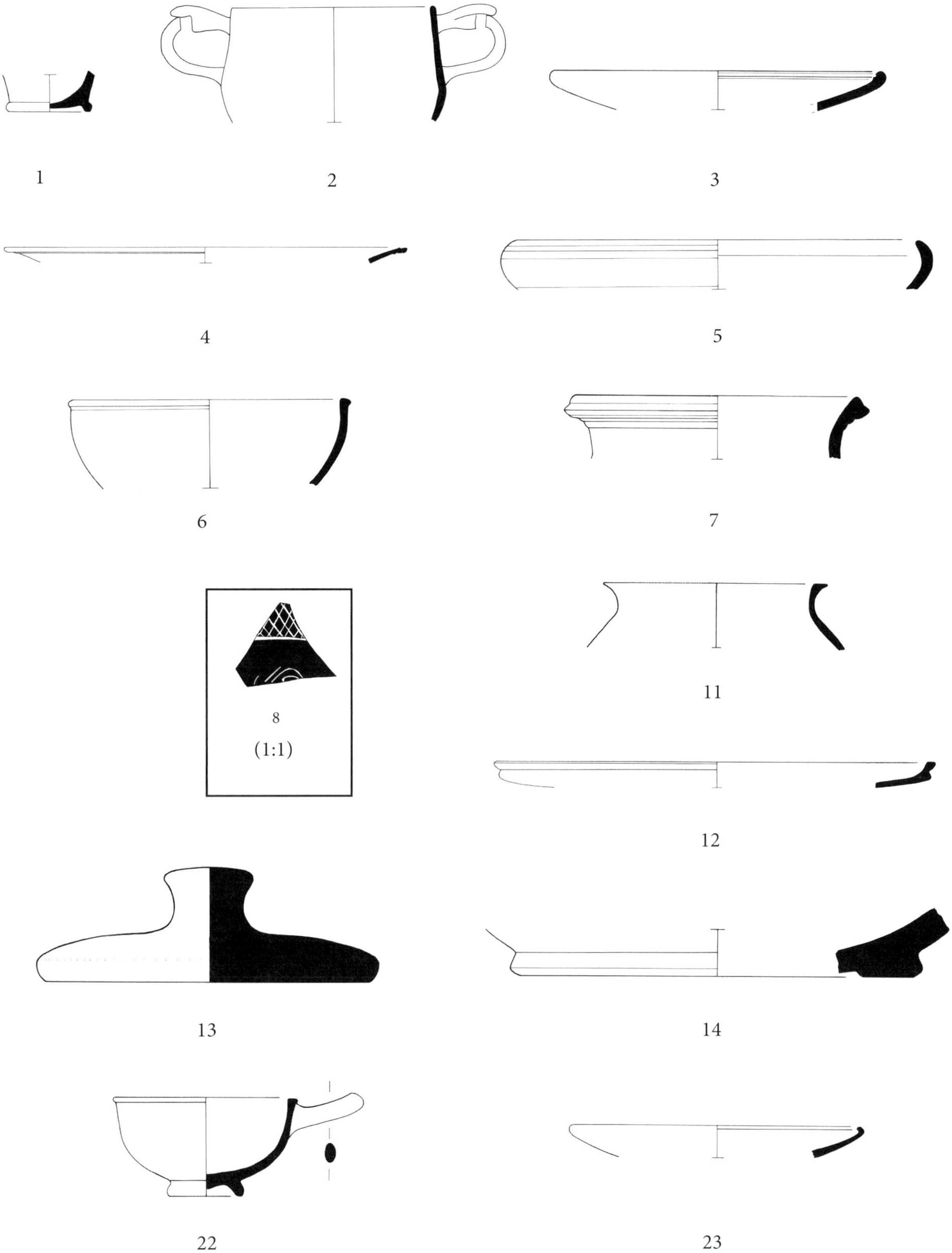

Plate 1 *Pottery from AREA III, room I. 1:3.*

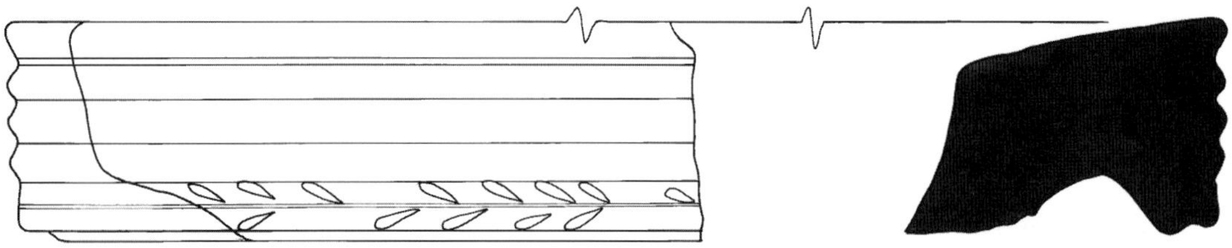

25 (1:4)

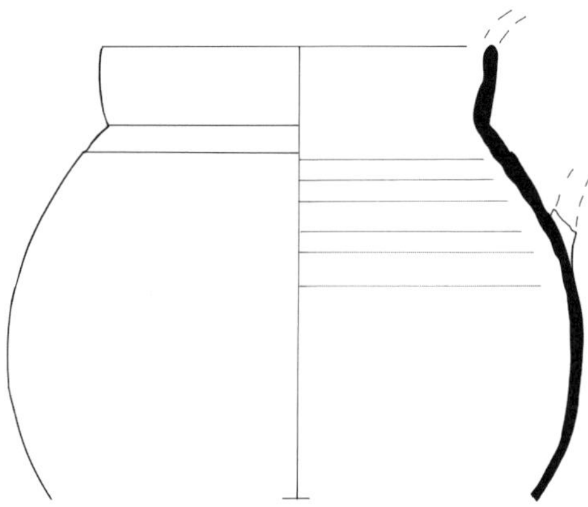

26

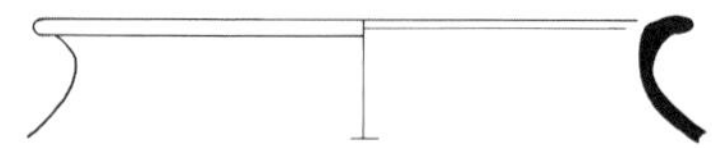

27

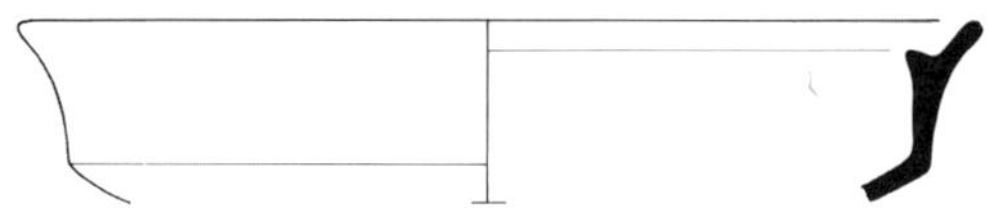

28

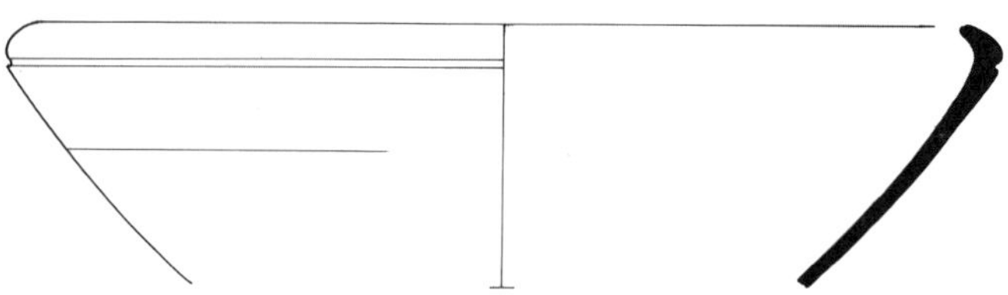

31

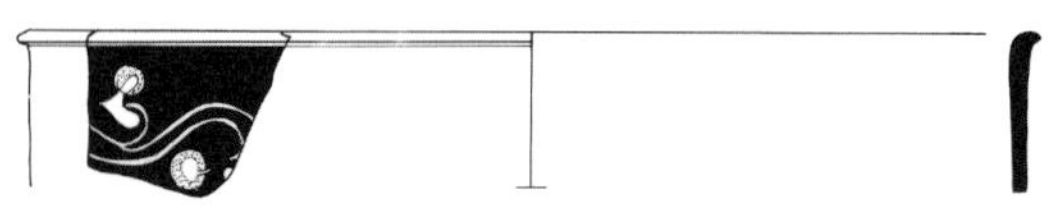

32

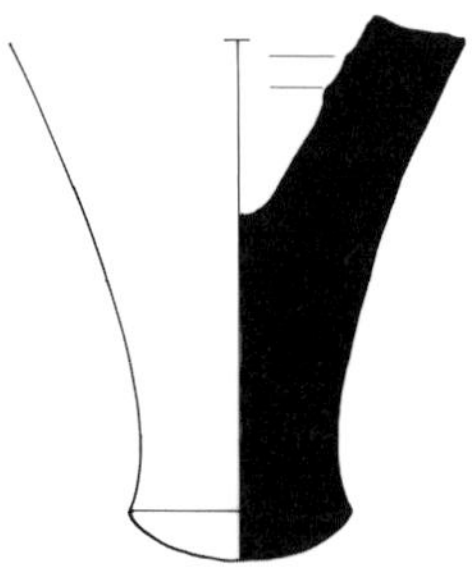

34

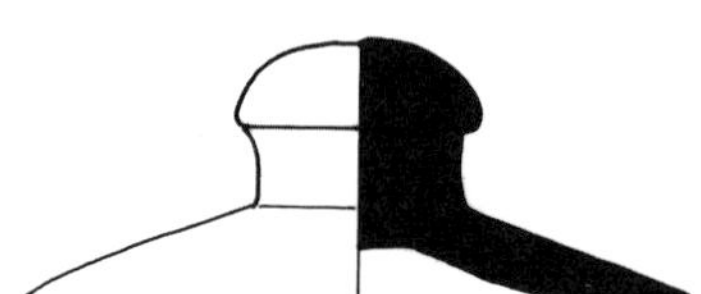

35 (1:1)

36

Plate 2 *Pottery from AREA III, room I (AEV and ADM). 1:3.*

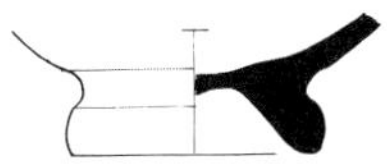

39

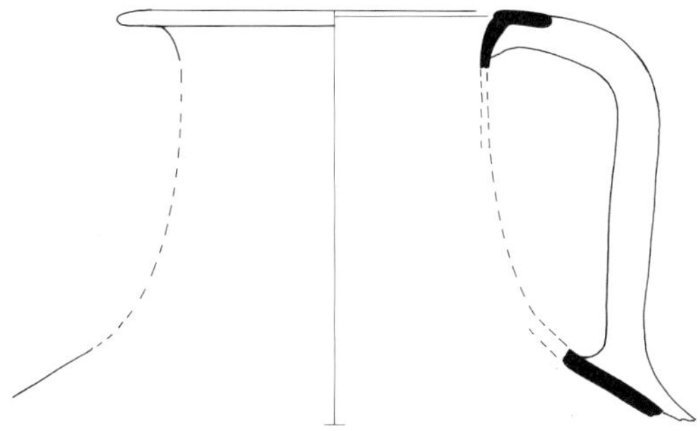

40

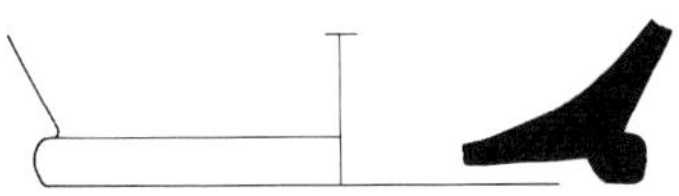

41

42

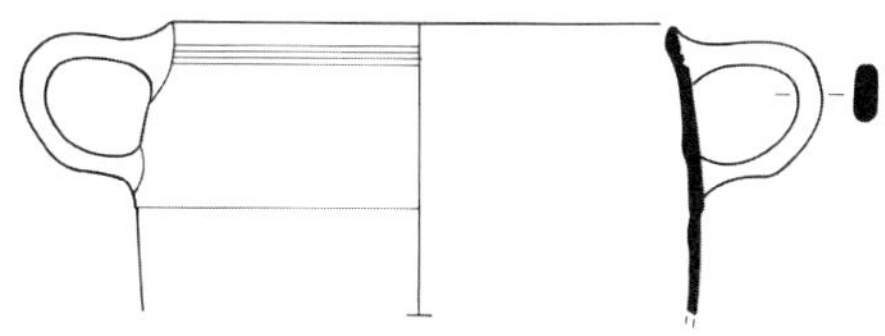

43

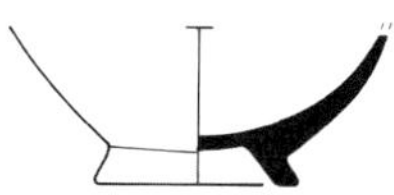

44

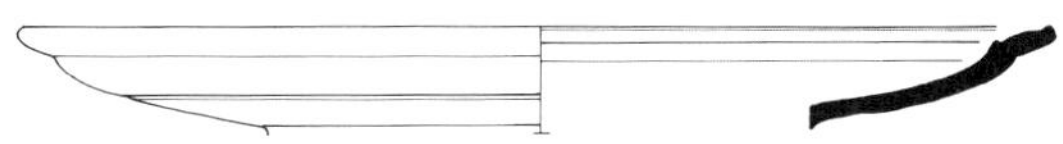

45

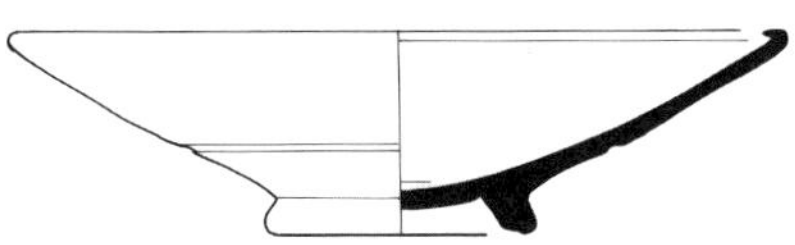

46

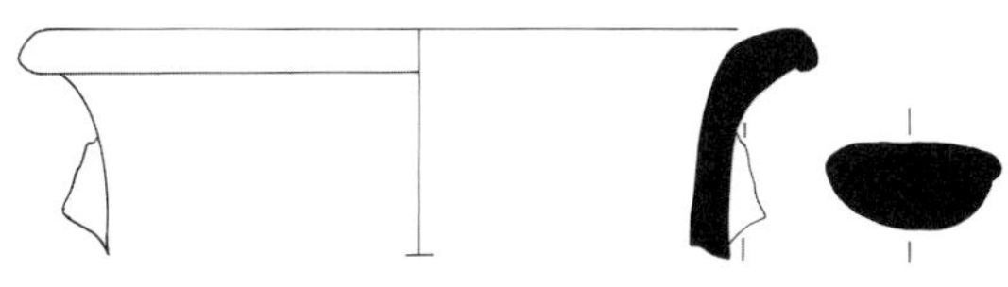

48

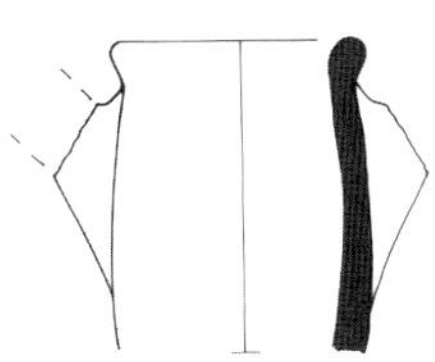

49

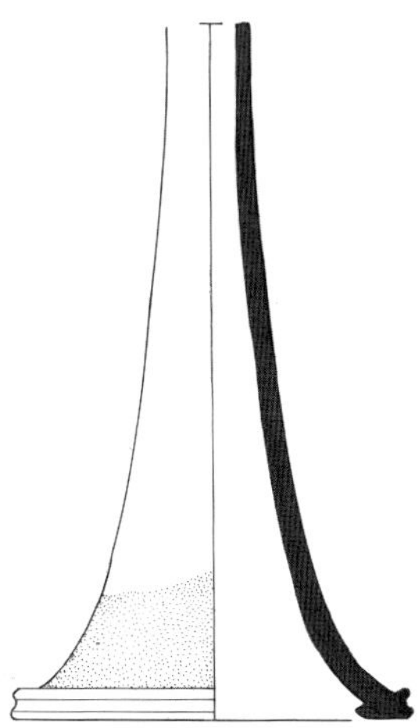

47

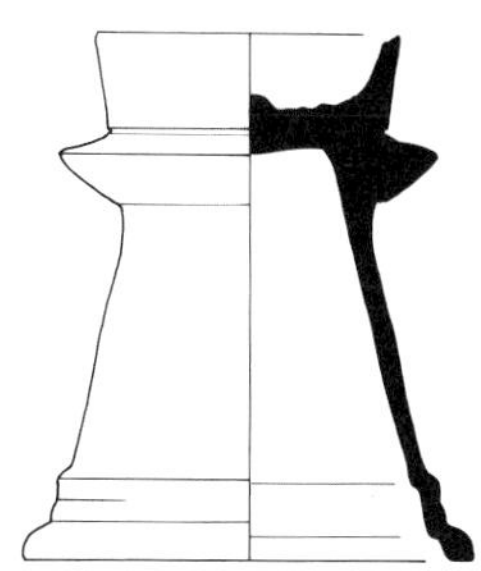

50

Plate 3 *Pottery from AREA III, room I (AEA) and room II. 1:3.*

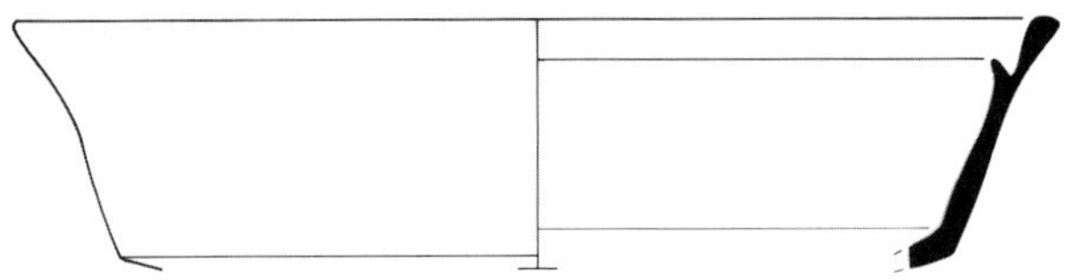

51

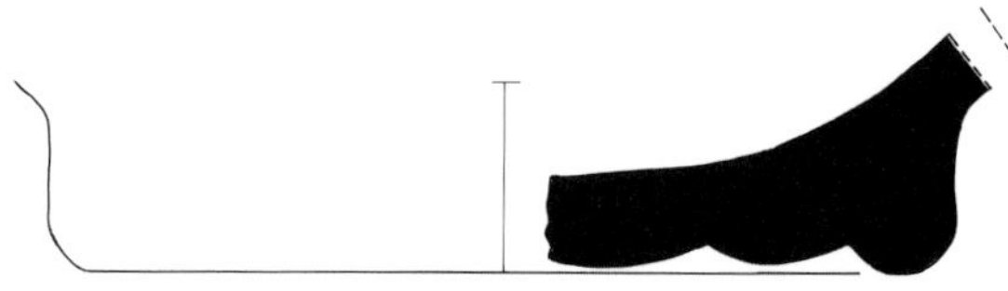

55

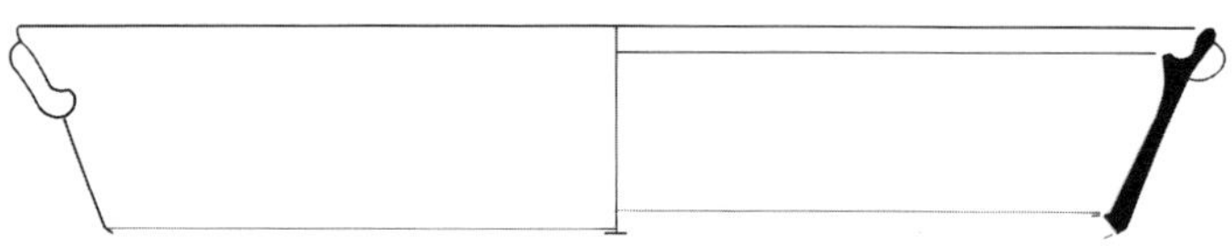

52

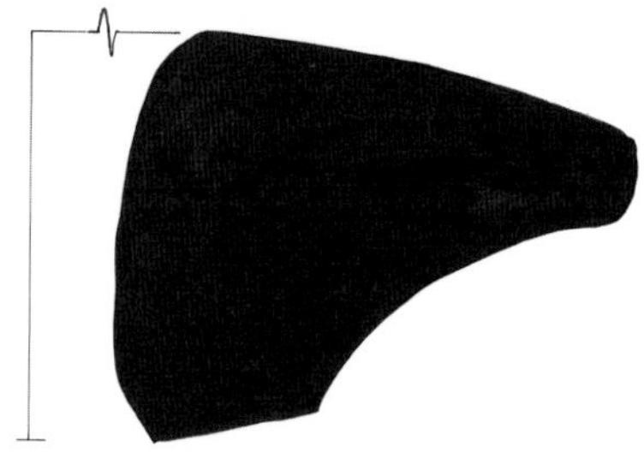

54

53

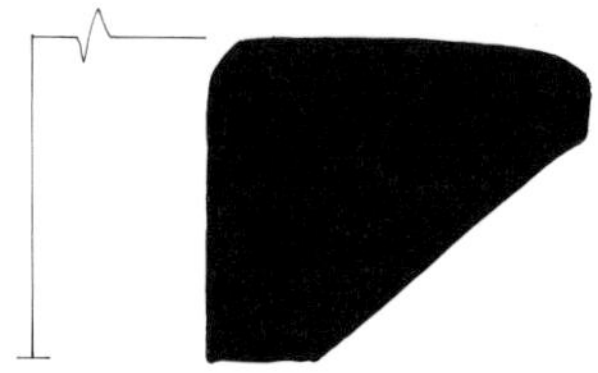

56

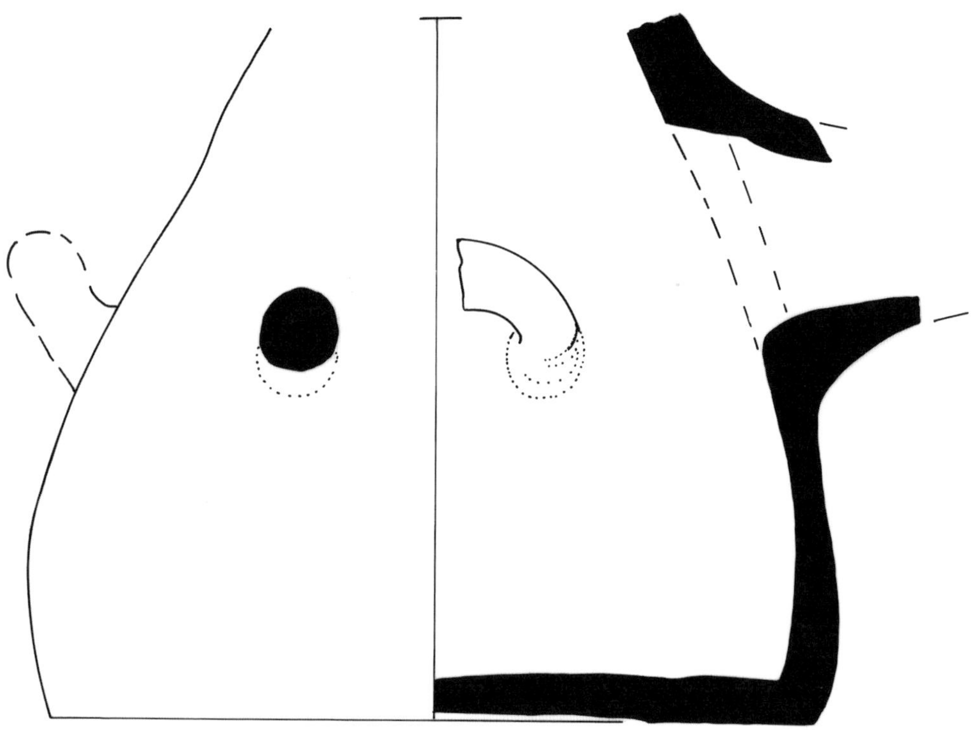

57

Plate 4 *Pottery from AREA III, room II. 1:3.*

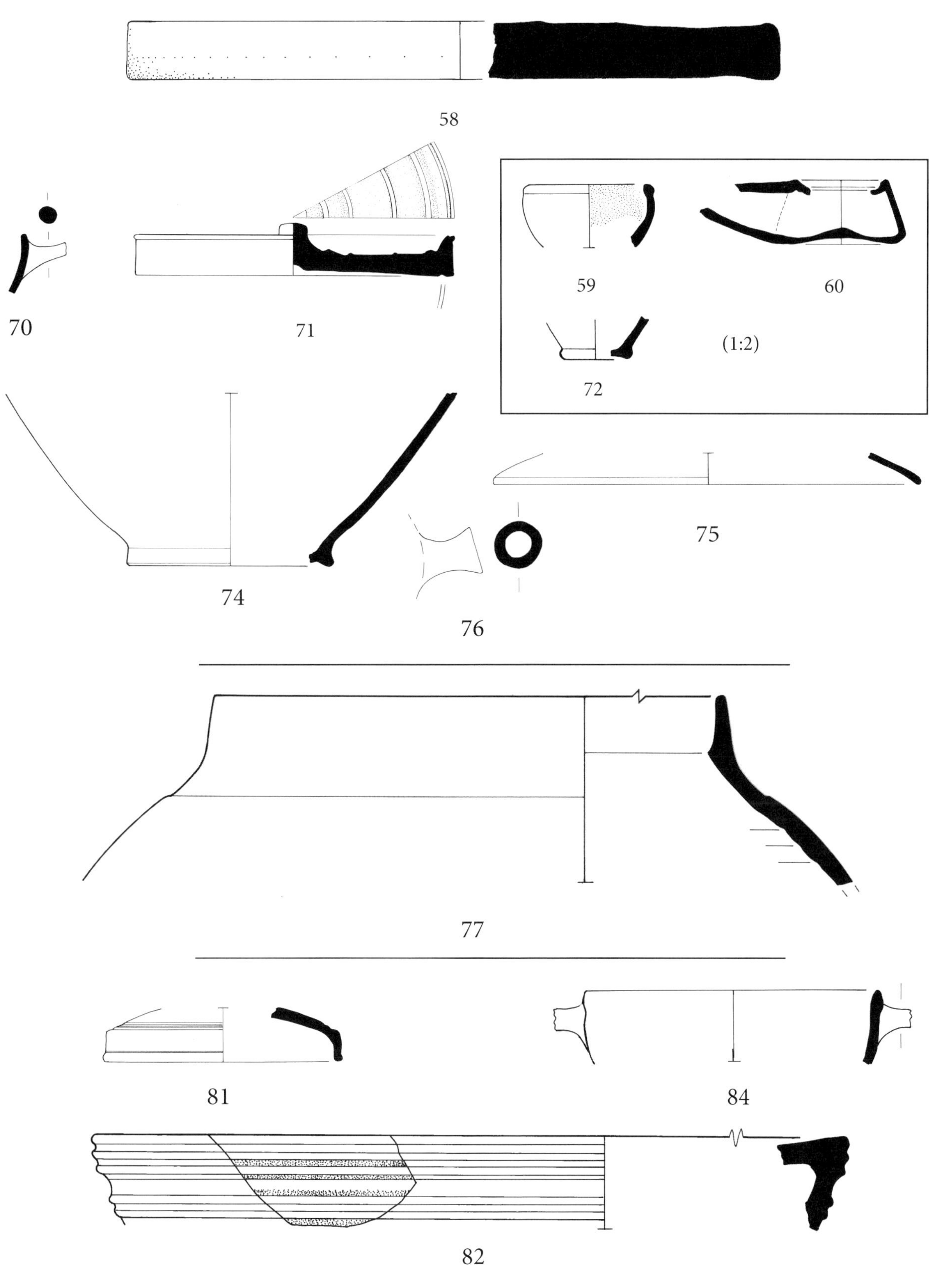

Plate 5 *Pottery from AREA III, room II and room IV. 1:3.*

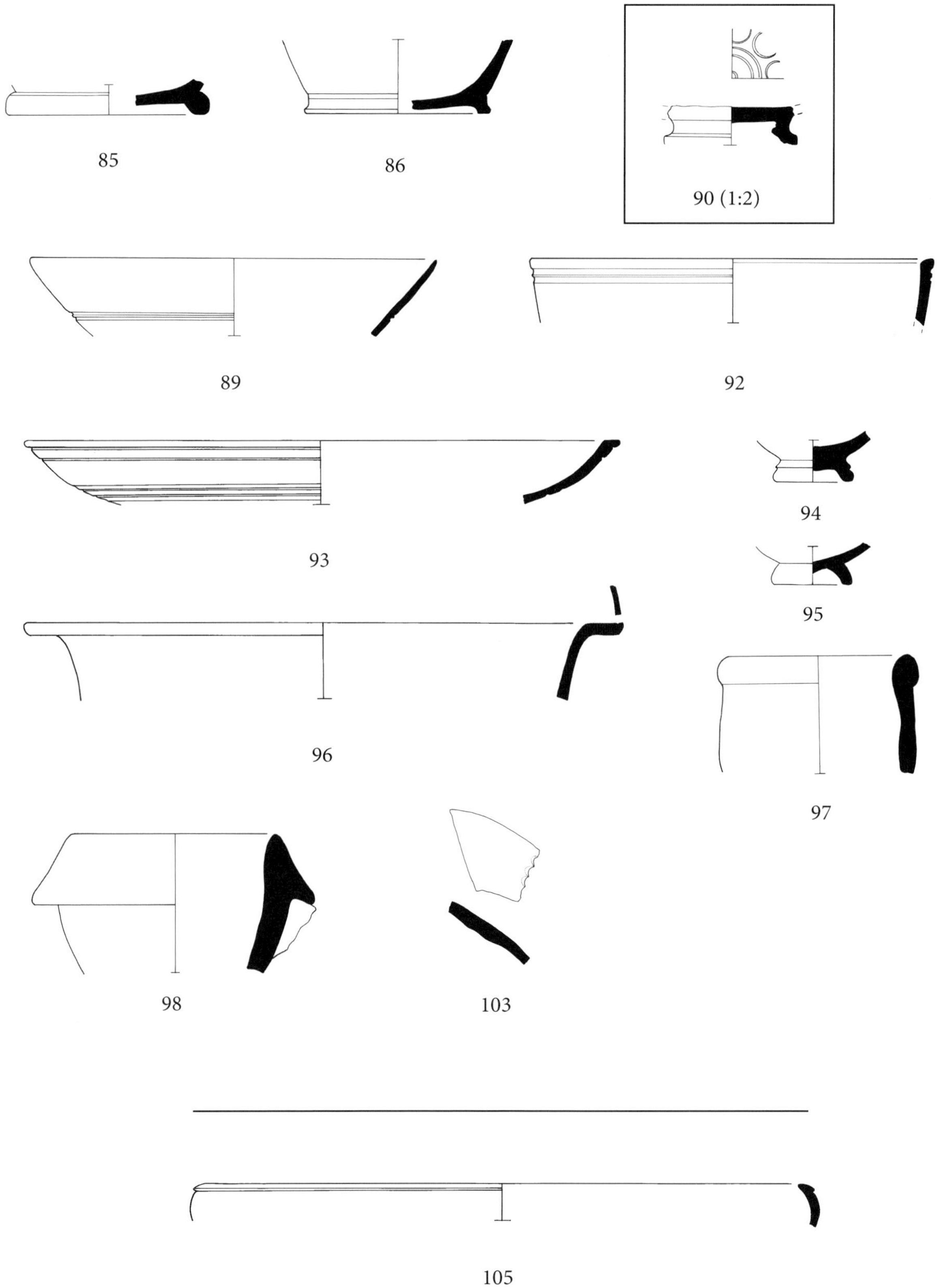

Plate 6 *Pottery from AREA III, room IV and room V. 1:3.*

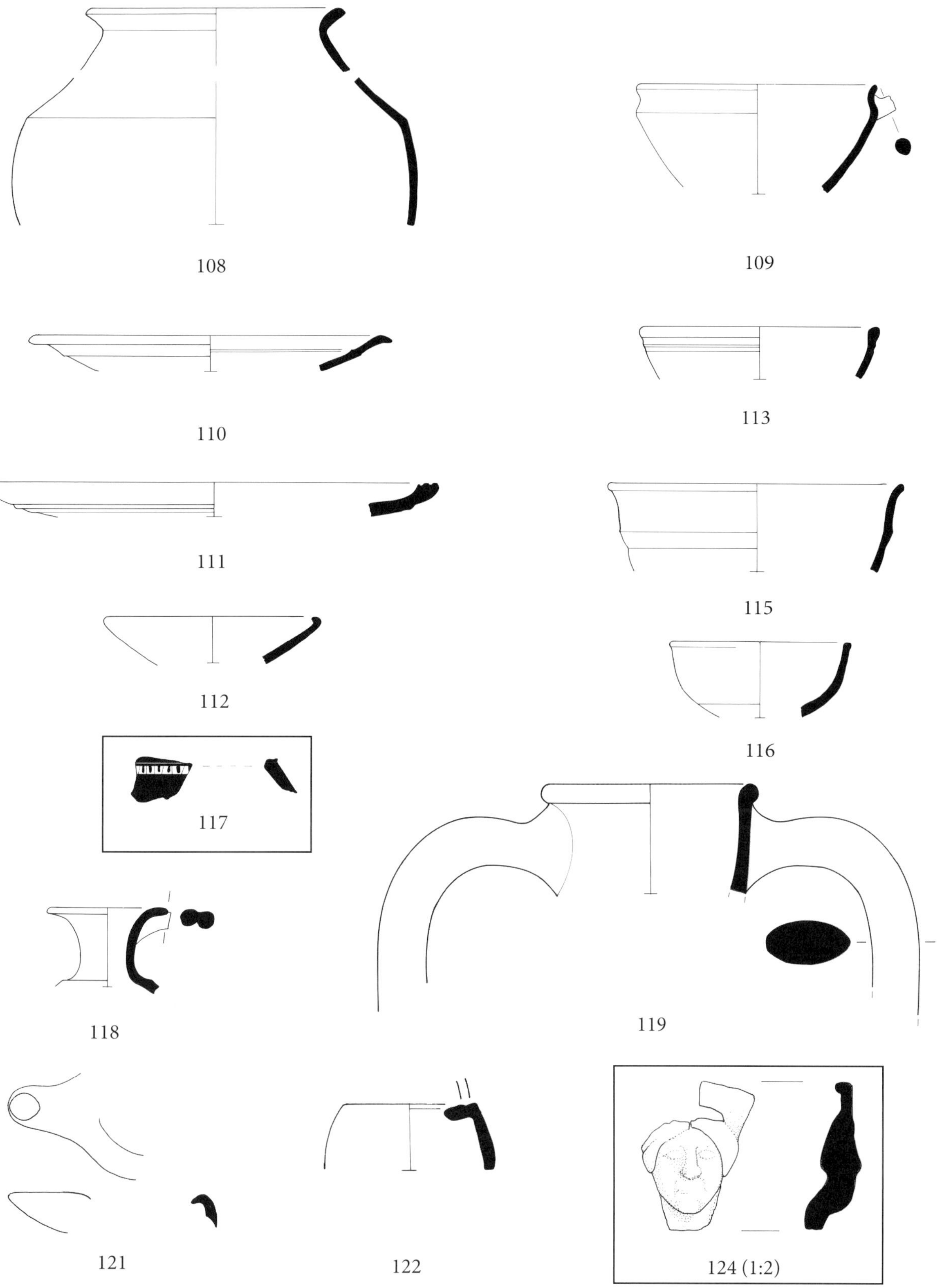

Plate 7 *Pottery from AREA III, room V. 1:3.*

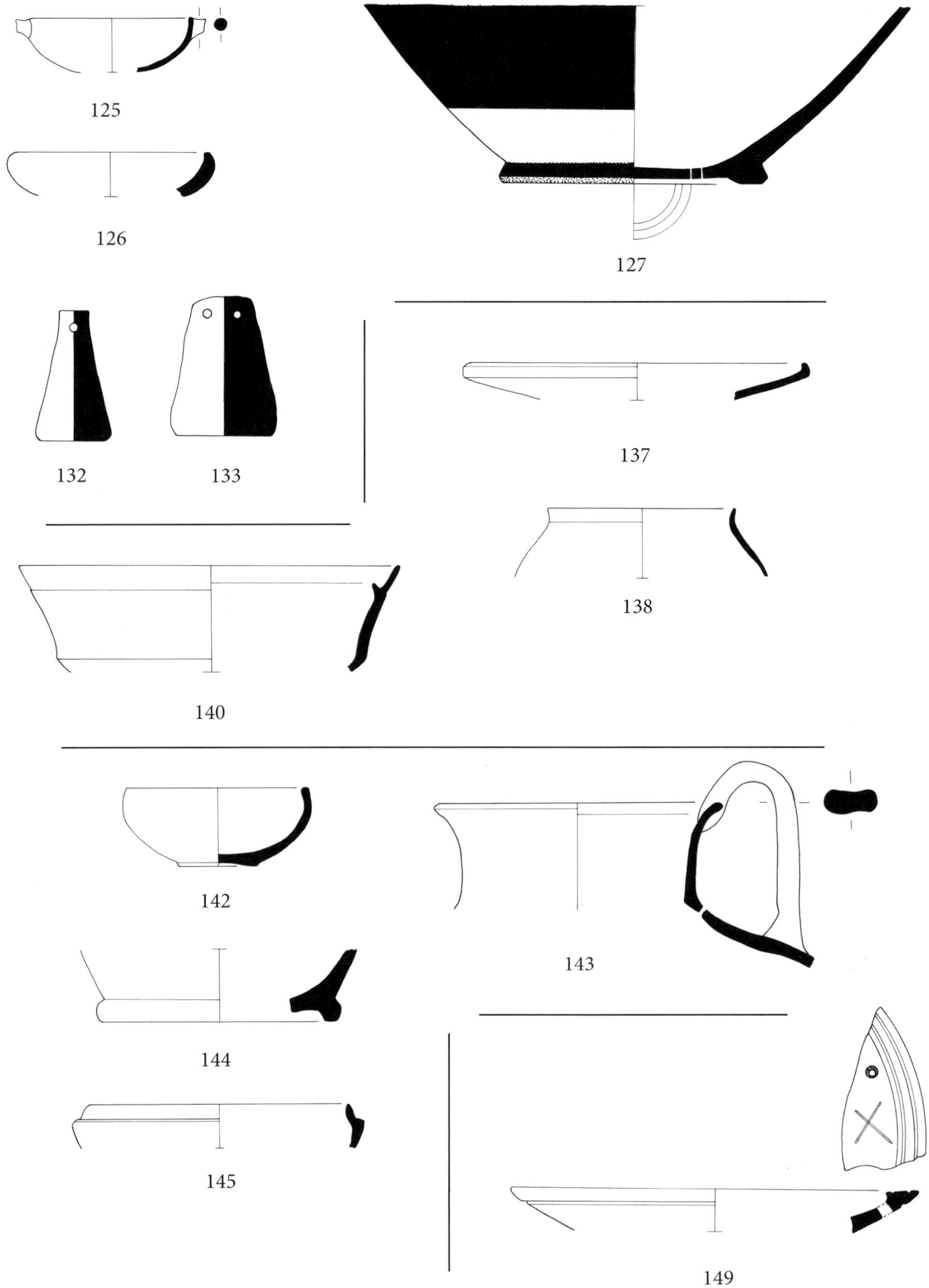

Plate 8 *Pottery from AREA III, room V, unit VI and room VIII. 1:3.*

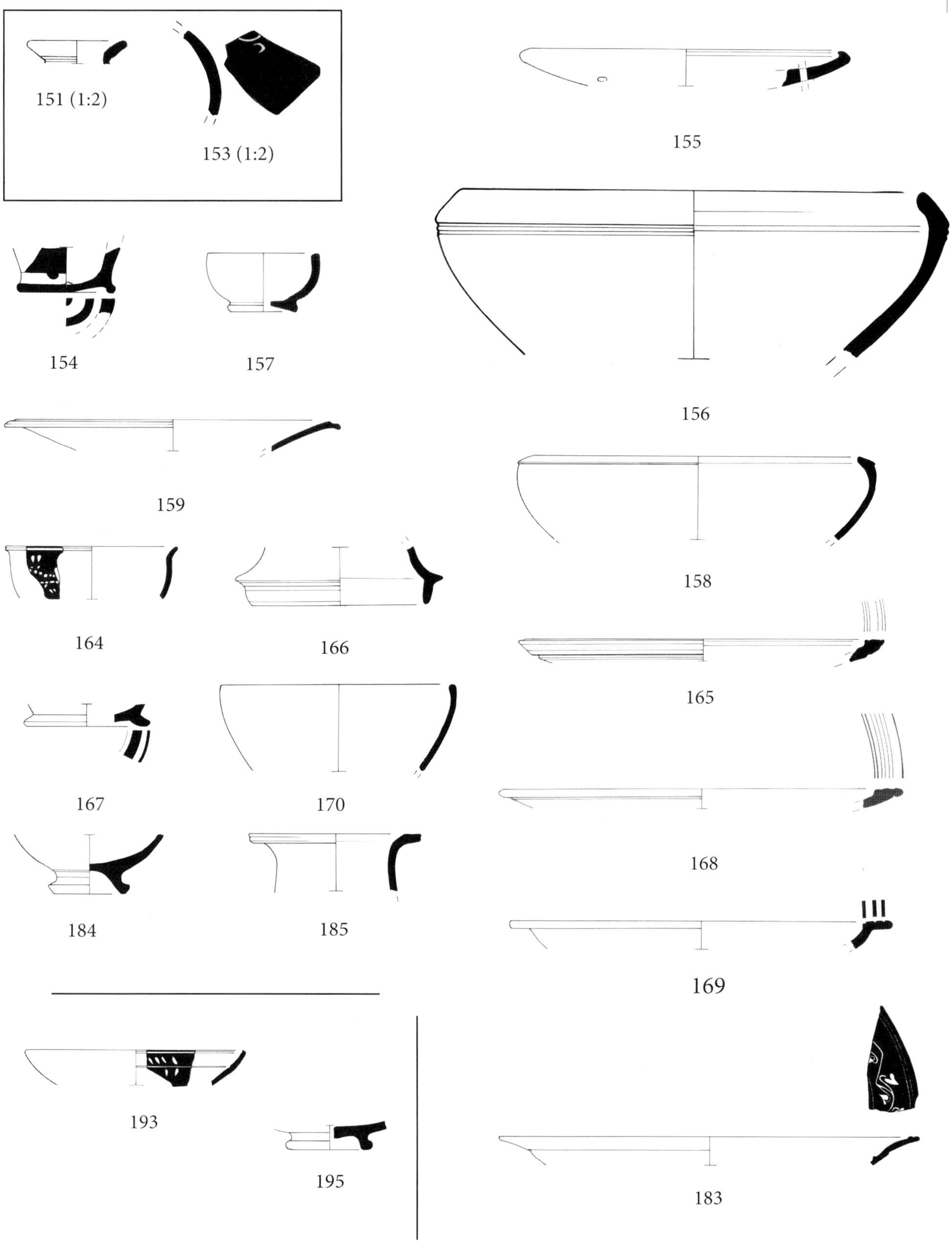

Plate 9 *Pottery from AREA III, room VIII and unit IC (?). 1:3.*

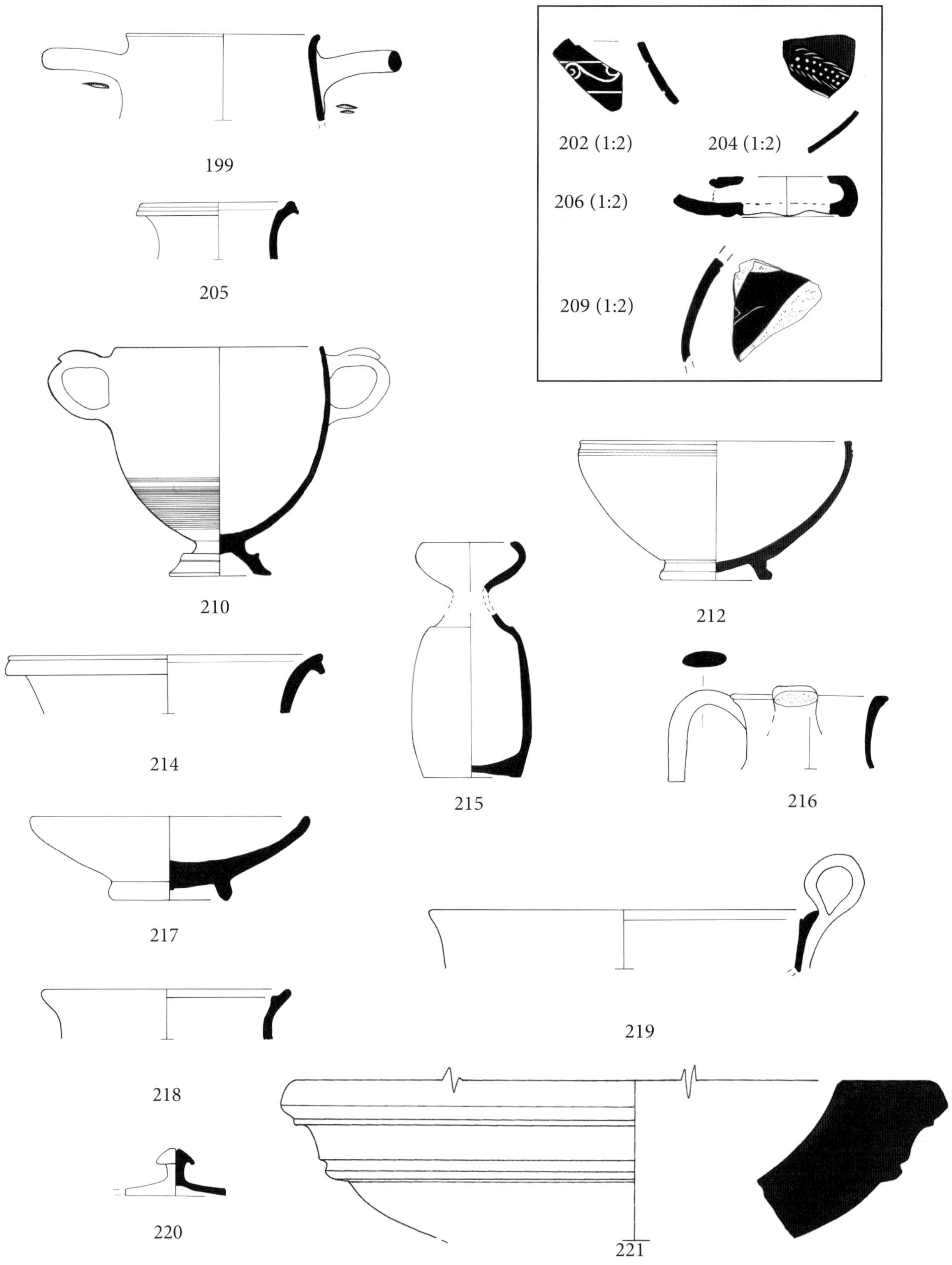

Plate 10 *Pottery from AREA III, room X. 1:3.*

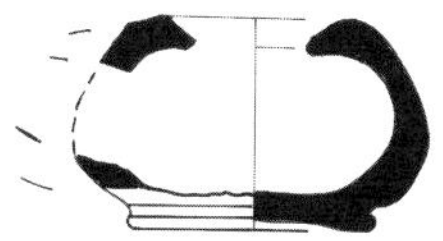

222 (1:2)

233 (1:2)

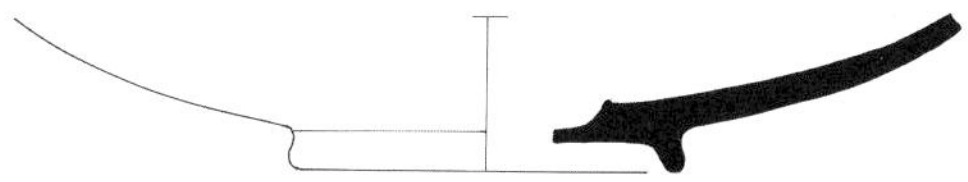

231

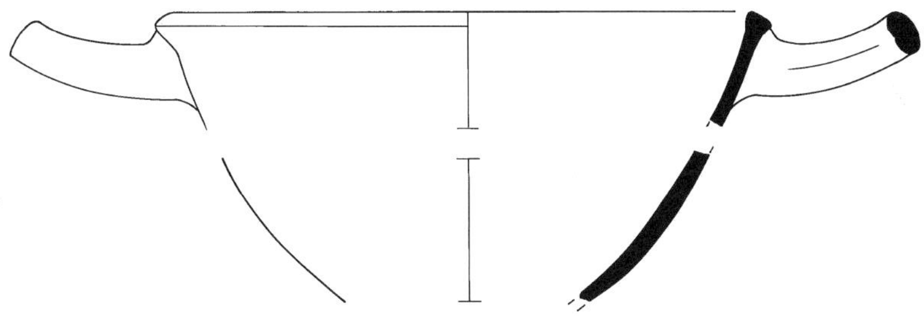

232

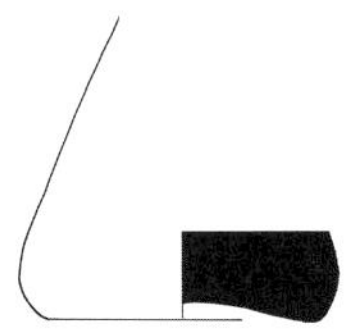

225

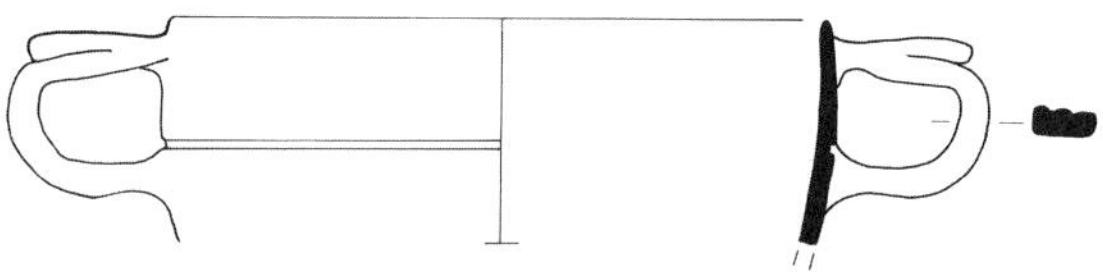

235

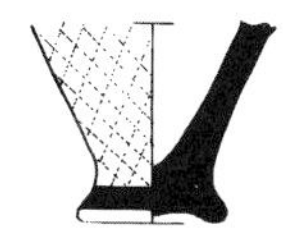

238 (1:2)

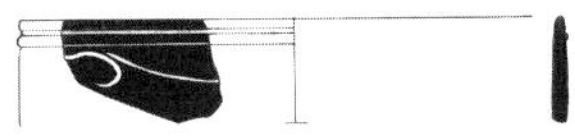

243

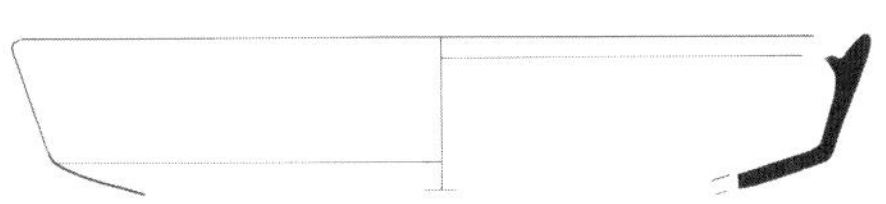

244

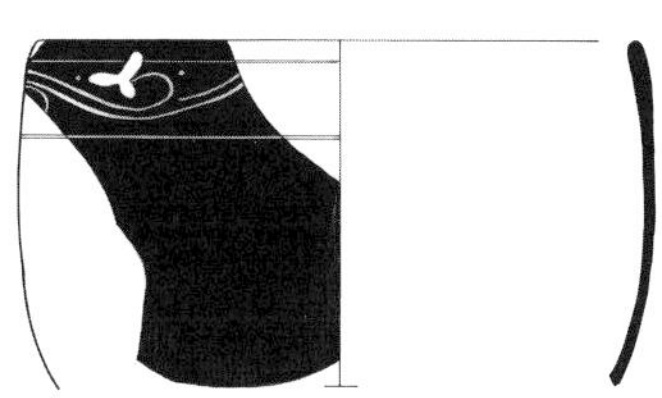

249

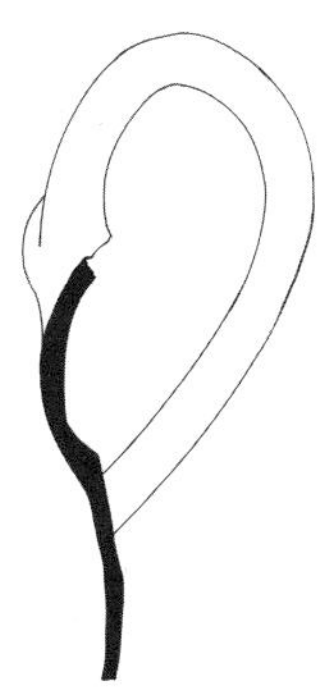

245

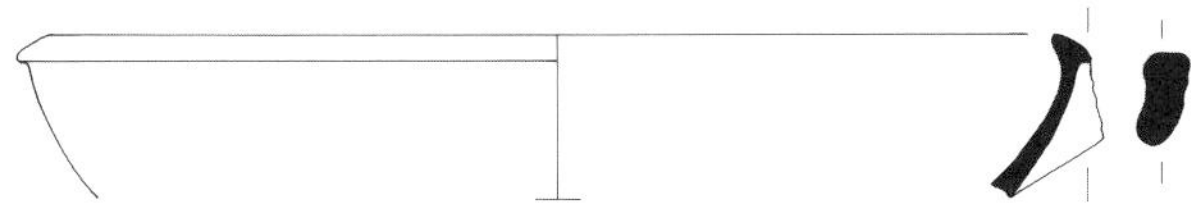

250

Plate 11 *Pottery from AREA III, room X and unit XII. 1:3*

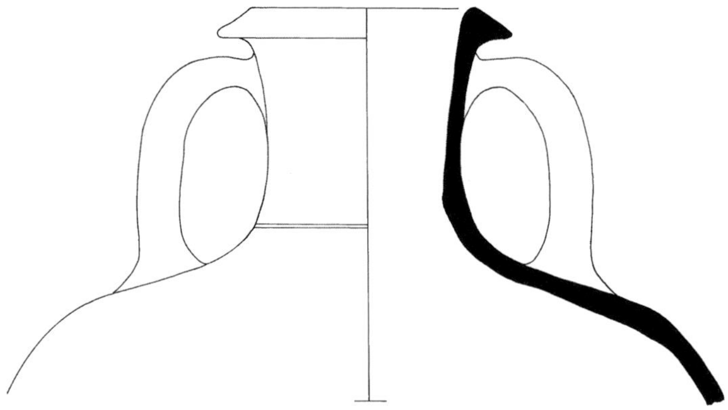

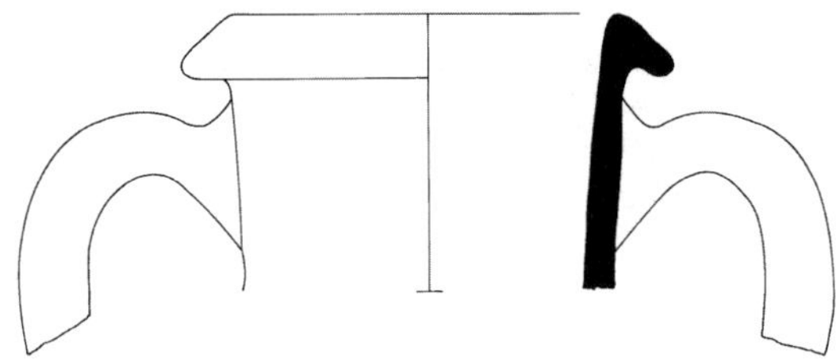

252

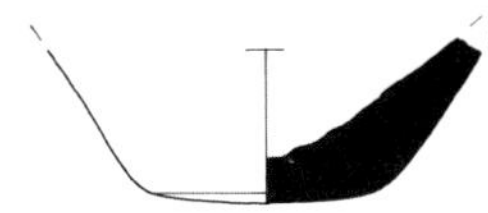

251

253

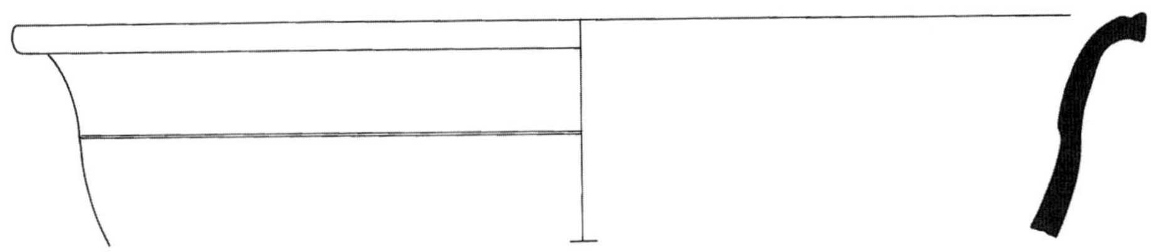

256

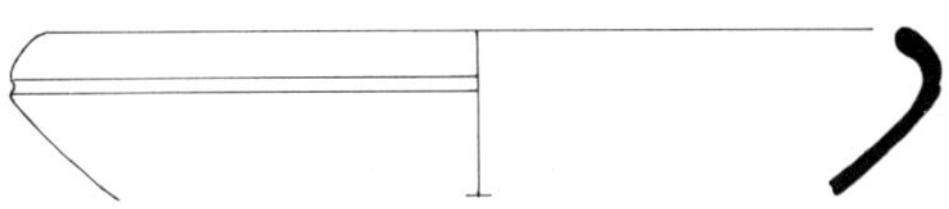

260

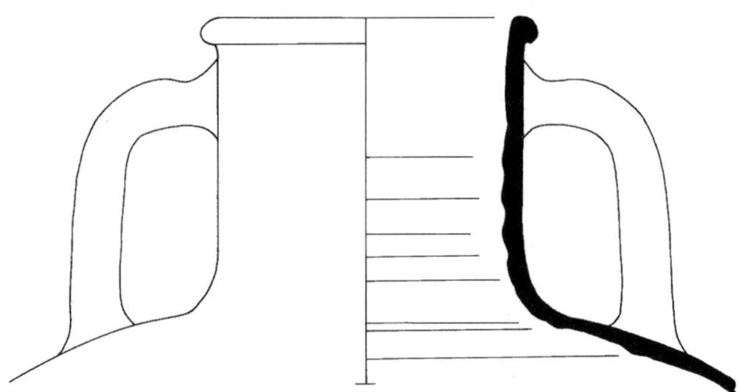

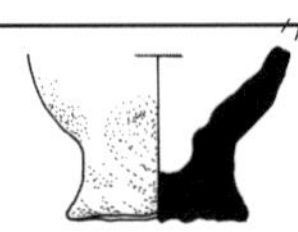

263 (1:2)

262

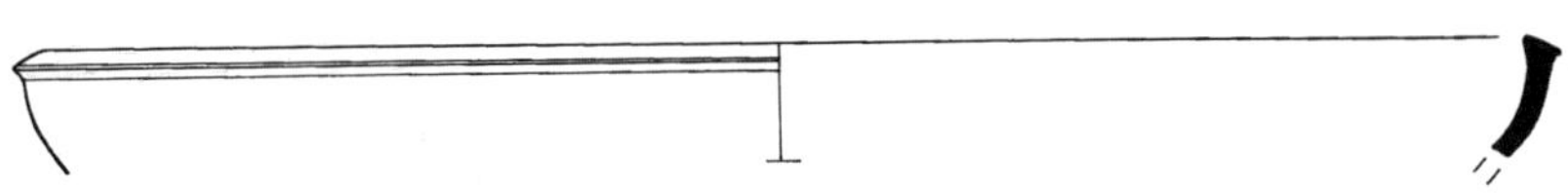

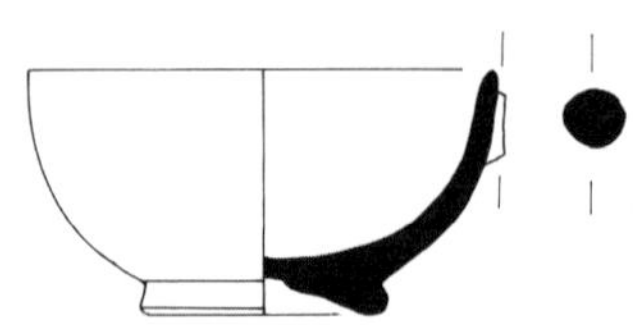

261

265

Plate 12 *Pottery from AREA III, room XI. 1:3.*

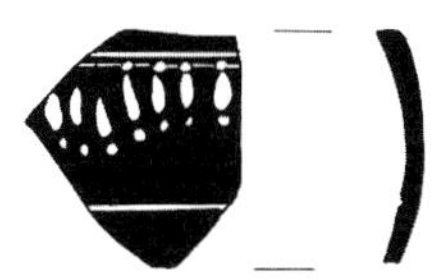

266 (1:2)

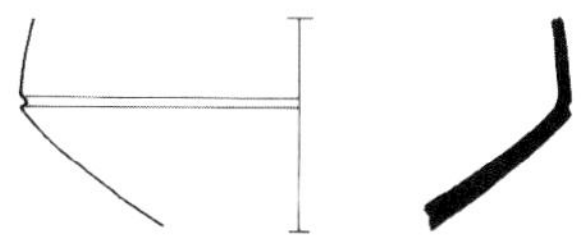

267

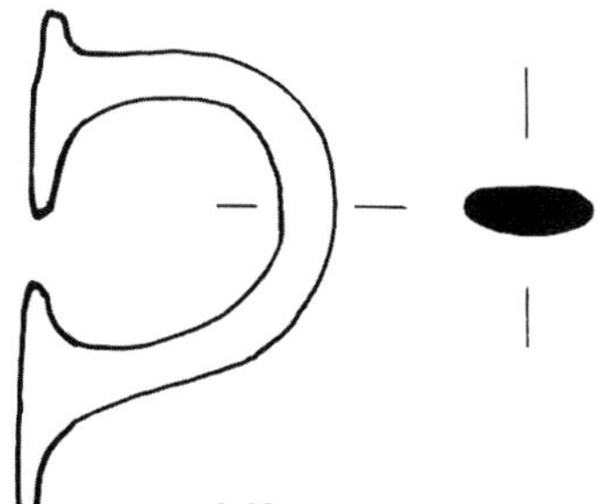

268

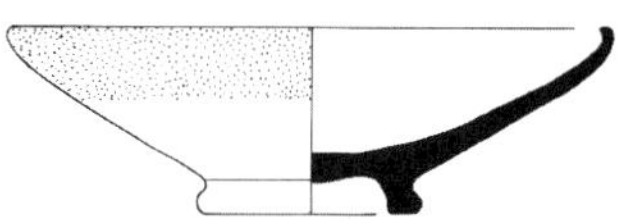

269

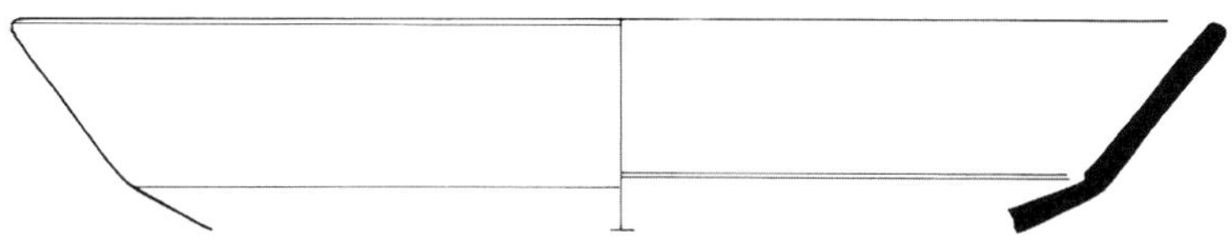

271

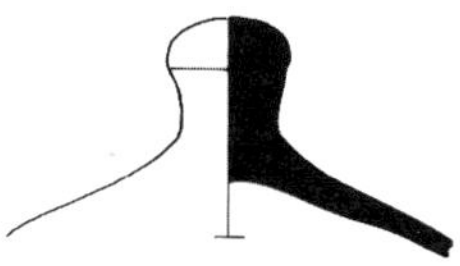

272 (1:2)

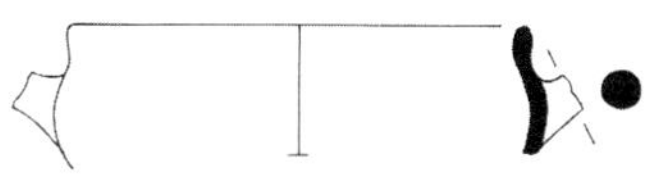

275

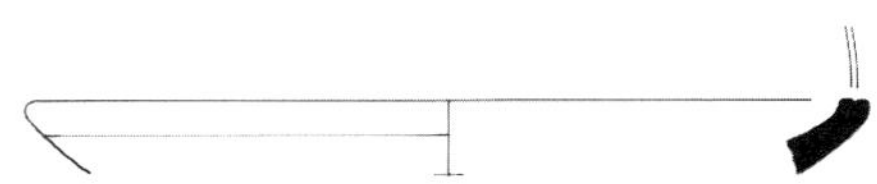

276

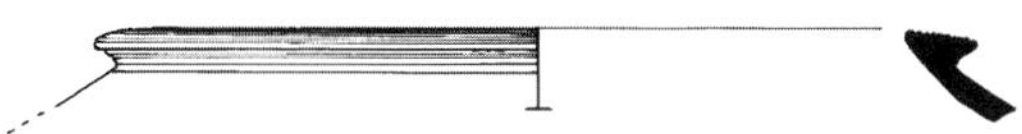

279

285

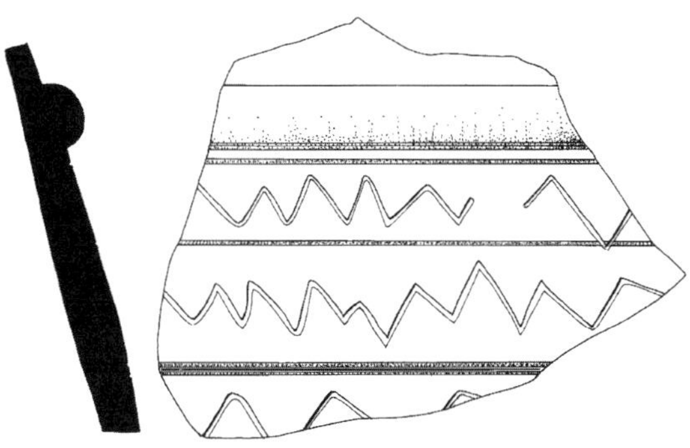

286

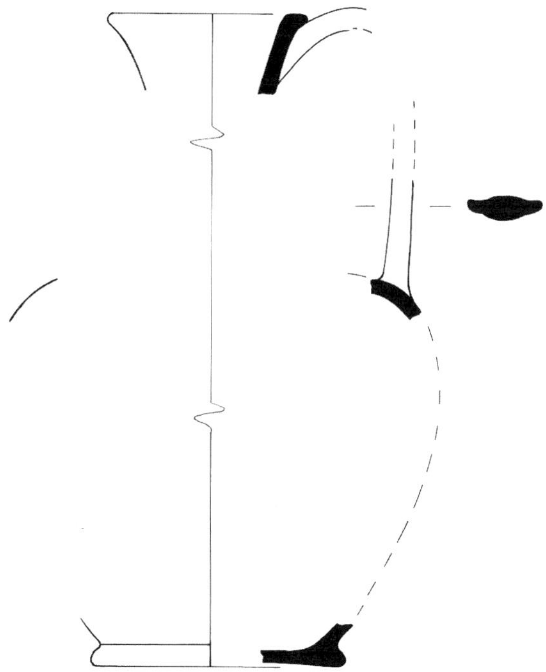

280

Plate 13 *Pottery from AREA III, unit XII and room XIV. 1:3.*

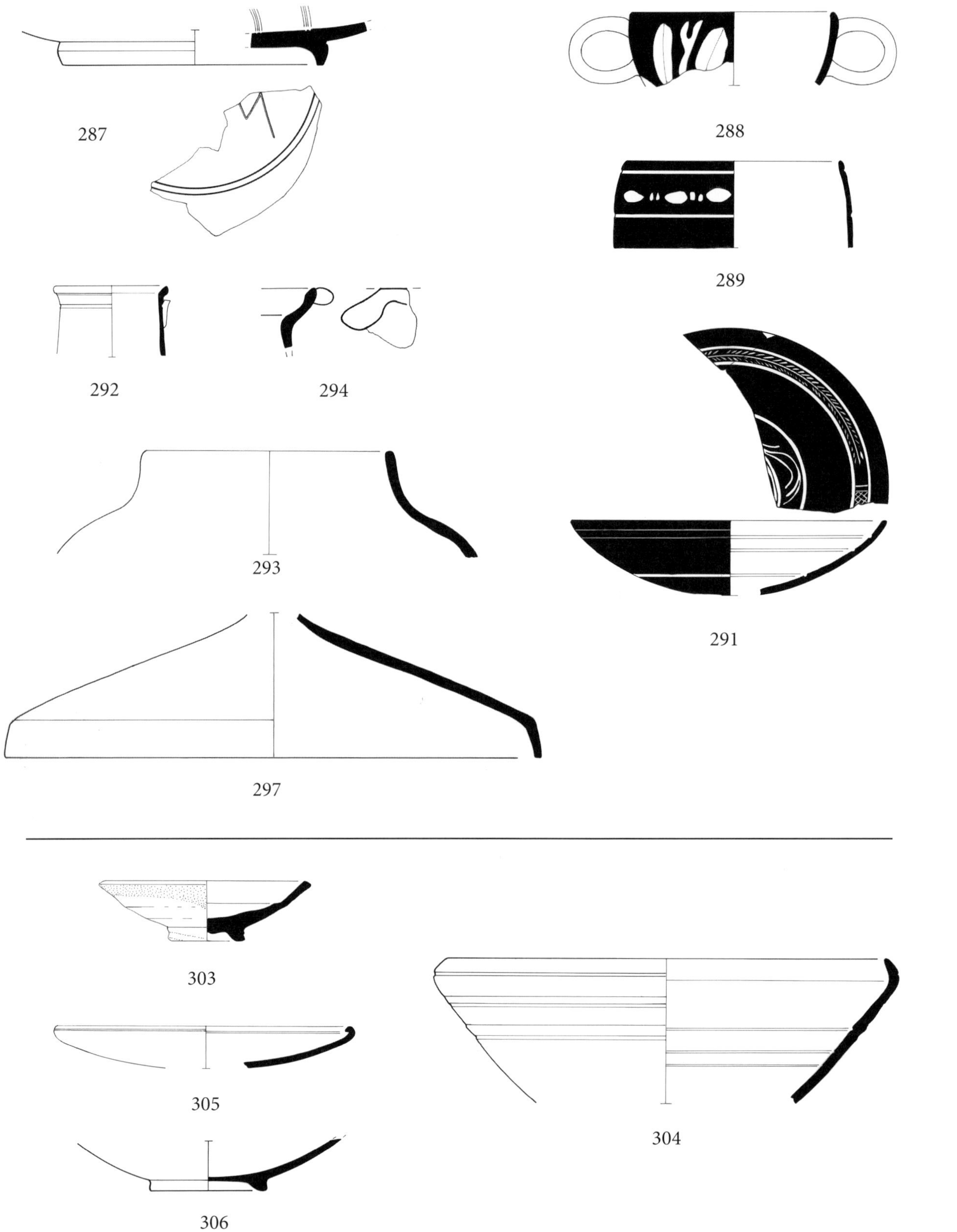

Plate 14 *Pottery from AREA III, room XIV and room XV. 1:3.*

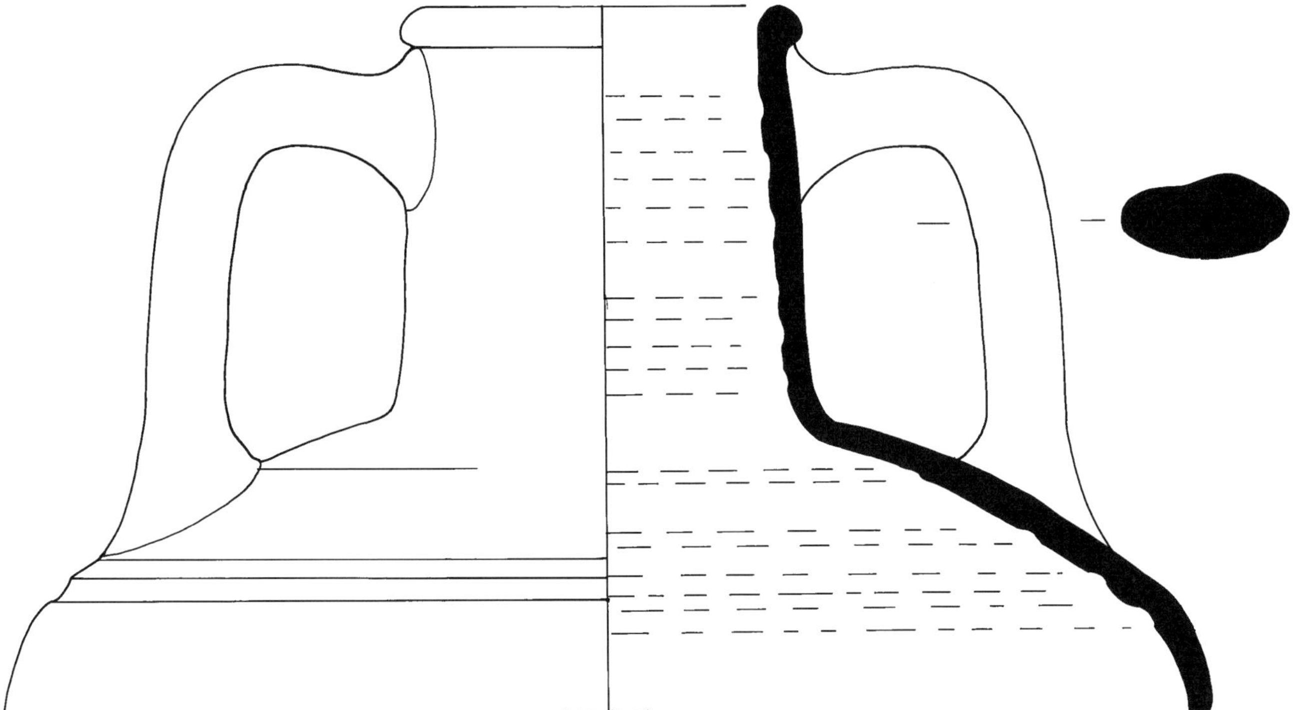

307 (1:5)

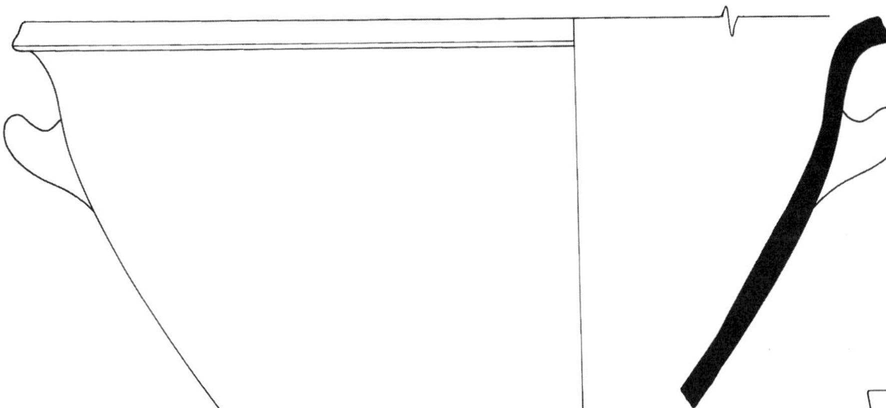

308

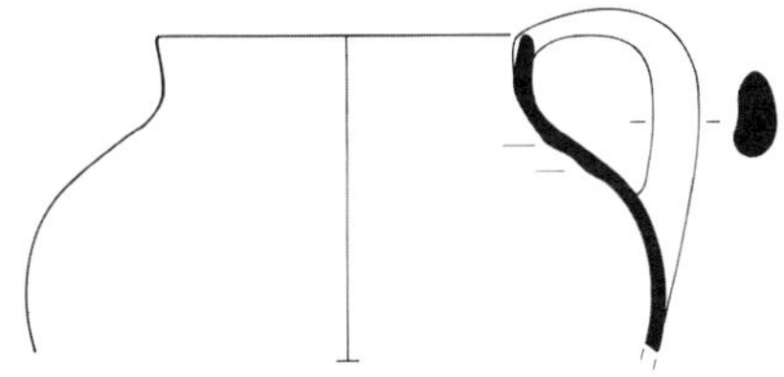

310

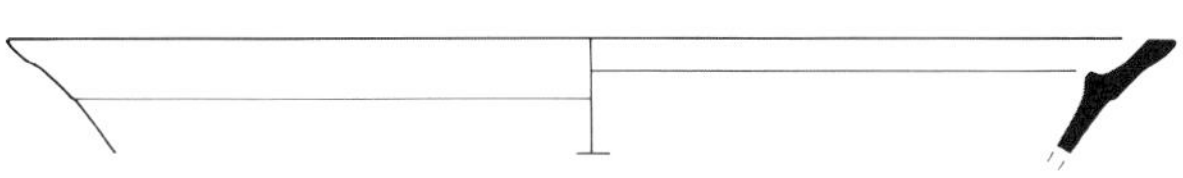

309

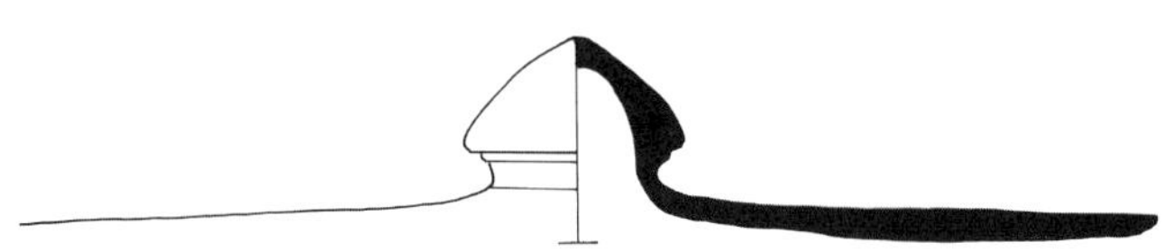

311

Plate 15 *Pottery from AREA III, room XV. 1:3.*

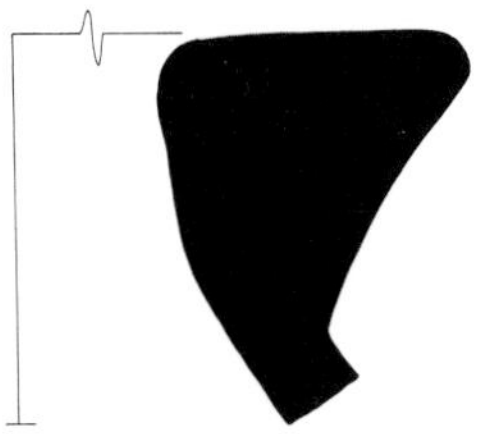

312

315

321

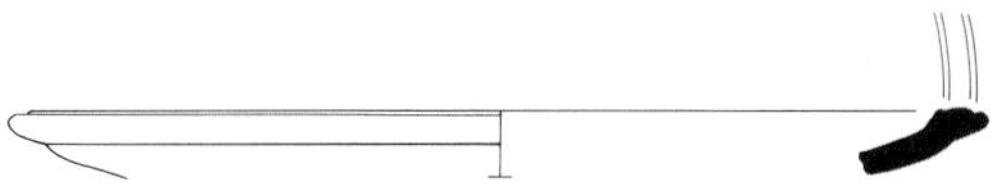

317

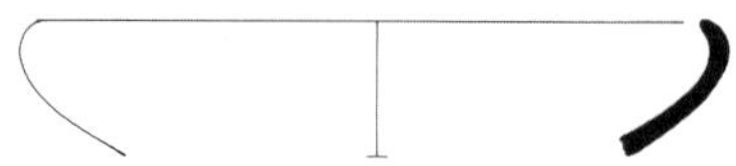

319

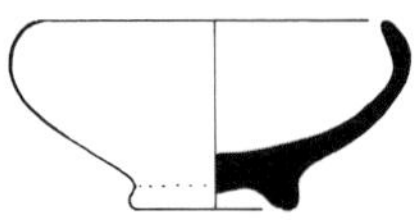

322

324 (1:2)

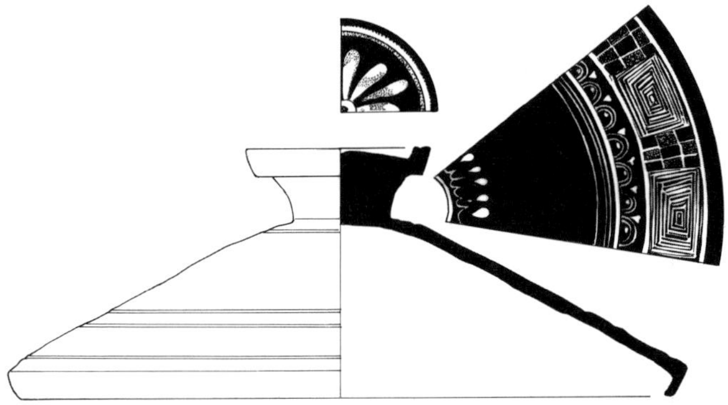

323

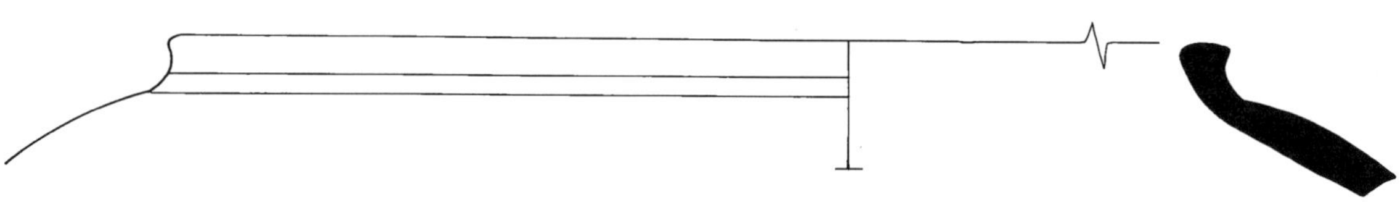

326

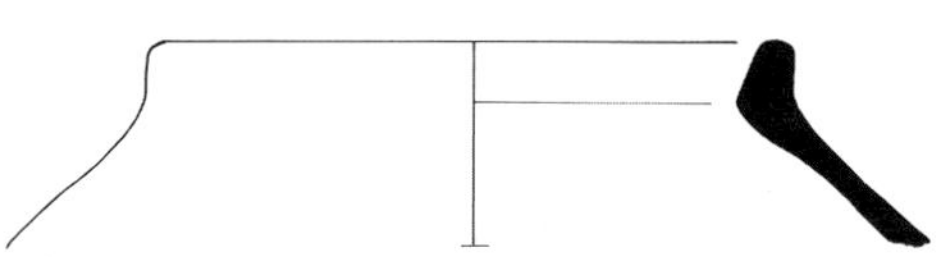

327

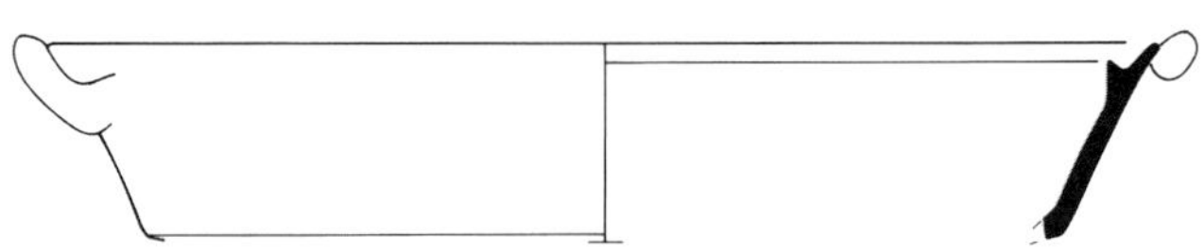

329

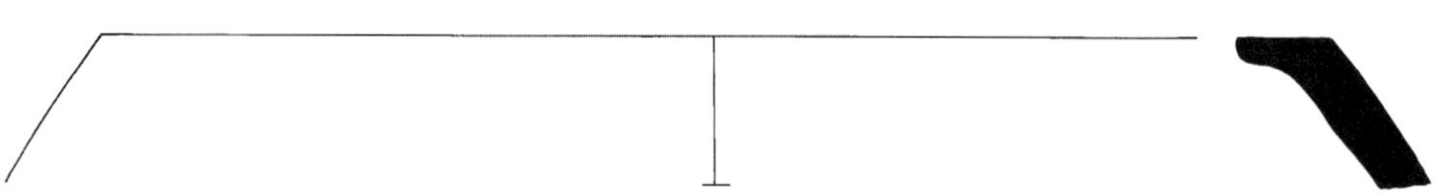

328

Plate 16 *Pottery from AREA III, room XV. 1:3.*

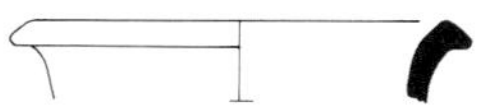

330

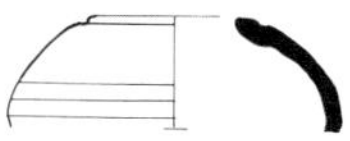

332 (1:2)

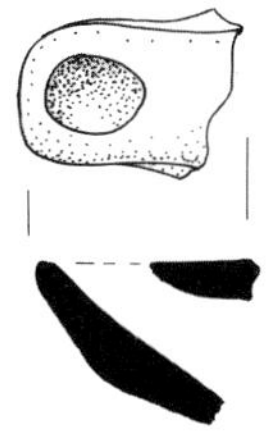

333 (1:2)

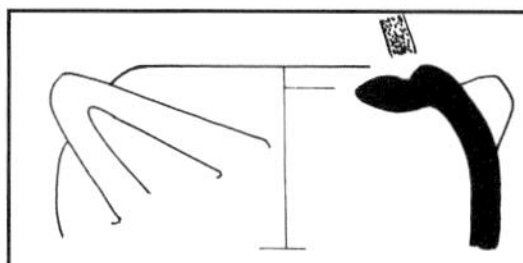

334 (1:2)

Plate 17 *Pottery from AREA III, room XV. 1:3.*

D. THE LATE CLASSICAL FORTIFICATION AT PANGALI

D. The Late Classical Fortification at Pangali*

*Mette Mouritzen, Lazaros Kolonas and Søren Dietz**

Introduction

Remains on the Pangali terrace are shown on Figs. 86 and 87. To the north, the terrace is defined by the huge fortification wall *PAA*, to the south by the wall *PAN*. The maximum distance between the two walls is around 560 metres – from gate to gate. The terrace with walls and architectural remains was surveyed in 1995 by Poul Erik Skovgaard Petersen while the curtains themselves were measured by Mette Mouritzen in the following years. On Fig. 86 the northern part of the terrace with the spread of buildings is depicted at a larger scale. The buildings are all constructed of large sandstone blocks of approximately the same size as the stones used in the fortification walls and prepared with the same technique (Fig. 87). The house walls were probably entirely stone built – with no mud bricks in the upper courses. The stones were quarried on the Varassova mountain, close to the site. It should be mentioned that a wall, parallel with the coastline, was found in the shallow water below the plateau, probably a fortification line or a quay (the wall was not measured)

Fig. 85 *Plan of Pangali terrace (measured by Poul Erik Skovgaard 2003).*

Architecture

The buildings are founded directly on the rugged, rocky surface of the terrace and oriented almost in the same direction – NNW-ESE (22^0 N of W). Only the building *PAL* is oriented N-S/E-W.

Of the nine architectural remains in the area we have selected and partly reconstructed three of the better preserved buildings on Fig. 88. The largest one is the long house *PAD*, preserved as a rectangular structure measuring approximately 32 × 16 metres or 512 m². An inner structure along the East wall, approximately 5 × 12 metres, is separated into two parts by a cross wall. The doorway was probably to the South and faint traces of other cross walls indicate that a narrow, ap-

* The authors are greatly indebted to Silke Müth for critical comments and many good suggestions.

** The fortification walls, Plans I-X were drawn by Mette Mouritzen, architect.

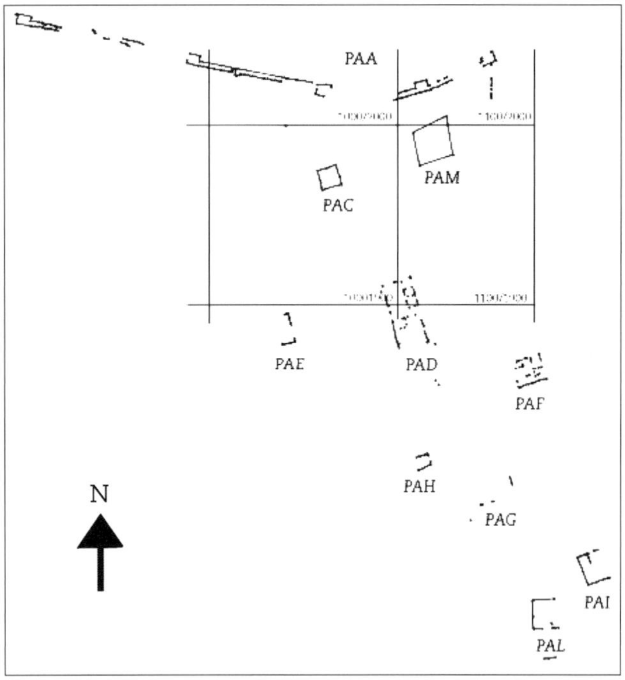

Fig. 86 *Plan of the northern part of the Pangali terrace showing the north fortification wall PAA and nearby buildings.*

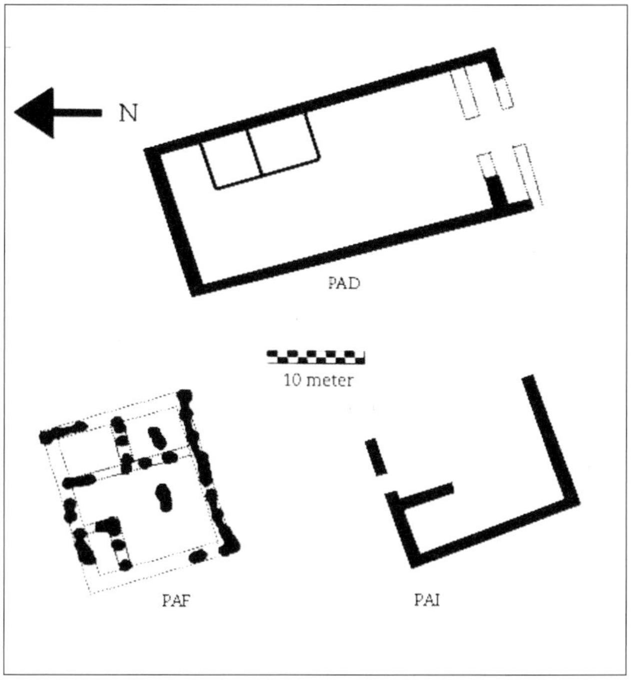

Fig. 88 *Sketches of three buildings at Pangali, PAD, PAF and PAI.*

Fig. 87 *Foundation PAL at Pangali.*

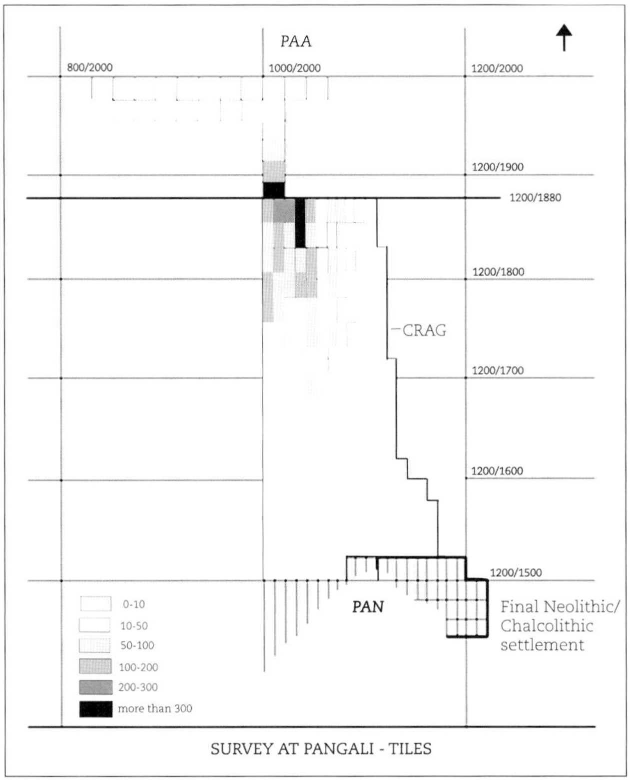

Fig. 89 *Survey 1995. Concentration of tiles at Pangali.*

proximately 2 metre broad entrance hall (or an anteroom?), could have been situated inside the door. Another entrance was perhaps situated on the East side and the central room could have been divided in a northern and a southern room by a cross wall.

A rather similar, but less well preserved, rectangular construction, *PAI,* was situated further south, closer to the eastern crag (the crag is seen on the plan Fig. 85). The structure might have been even bigger than *PAD* as the side is 18 m wide. A 5 m wide room seems to have been constructed along the southwestern short side and a doorway (?) might have been situated on the side to the northwest.[302] The third building *PAF* on Fig. 89, is smaller and more square, but still relatively large: 18 × 16 metres or 288 m^2. The construction seems to have been divided into several roughly square rooms.[303]

Survey 1995

In 1995 an intensive survey was conducted on the terrace.[304] On Fig. 89 the concentration of tiles found on the terrace is depicted (the large N-S oriented rectangles below the line 1200/1880 point measure 20 × 10 m). The concentration of tiles is by far greatest around the large square building *PAD*, less concentrated around the remaining structures. South of the 1700 N line only very dispersed tiles and sherds were found – the sherds dating up to the Final Neolithic/ Chalcolithic settlement in the Southern part of the plateau.[305] Only very few sherds were found during the survey (see below).

Finds

Tiles. The tiles were badly preserved and no samples were drawn or photographed. As seen on Fig. 89 many thousands of tile fragments were counted around buildings in the northern part of the terrace; most, however, were very worn and fragmentary. A selection of diagnostic pieces were collected which give, if not really a representative picture, at least an indication of the character of the Pangali tiles.

Of 115 diagnostic tile pieces, 104 were of Laconian type, while 11 were Corinthian. The relative high percentage of Corinthian tiles is surprising, if we compare with the many thousand pan-tiles from the Workshops at Aghia Triada, which are all Laconian – except one Corinthian tile used on the floor near the drain in room I.[306] Probably all tiles from the late 4th/3rd BC century from the workshops were mould made and most were red painted. In Kalydon the later tiles from the Peristyle building (late 3rd/2nd century BC) were all mould-made Laconian – without paint.

The reddish yellow-fabric Pangali tiles are all very coarse tempered, handmade and slightly thinner than the tiles from the workshops at Aghia Triada.

The most reasonable explanation for the differences between the three groups is that the Pangali group of handmade, coarse tempered tiles with more

302 A reconstruction is suggested by Portelanos 1998 (73).
303 Portelanos 1998 (73) reconstructs this building (ktirio b) with an approximately 60 m^2 large, square central room, surrounded by eight smaller rooms along the walls.
304 The survey logistics are described by Sanne Houby-Nielsen in *FPR*, 255 ff.
305 Mavridis and Sørensen in *Chalkis Aitolias I*, 2006.
306 Above Fig. 49a/b.

Fig. 90 *A well-preserved lamp from Pangali, found in 1999 as a stray find X-50.*

Corinthian tiles is older than the two other groups of tiles. The three groups thus evidently represent three stages in the development of tile production in the coastal area of Aitolia.

The sherds collected are few and usually coarse and un-diagnostic; only a few fine ware sherds were black-glazed. One coarse tempered jug/bowl with tall ring foot suggests a Classical/Hellenistic date.[307]

A well-preserved lamp from Pangali was found in 1999 as a stray find X-50/23.07 1999 (Fig. 90): BISCUIT: Pink (7.5YR 8/4), fine tempered. SURFACE: Covered with dark, reddish grey paint (5YR 3/4). SHAPE: ... ring foot, traces of the beginning of the spout. L: 8.6 cm. W: 5.7 cm. D (hole): 2.3 cm. D (ring-foot): 3.8 cm.

COMMENTS: Howland 1958, 61. Type 23d "Third quarter of 4th century BC down into latest years of the century". Broneer 1977, 15, type VIIB, Late 4th century BC.

THE FORTIFICATION WALLS (Plans I-X)

The architecture of the fortification walls of the Pangali terrace has been studied by several scholars since Woodhouse's first treatment.[308] Ferdinand Noack made the first real study, produced a topographical plan (still most valuable) and suggested reconstructions of details in the lay-out. Later on, the site was visited by A.W. Lawrence who made several comments on its constructions and chronology.[309] In addition, Winter[310] mentioned and commented on the site. More recently the site has been treated extensively by Anastasios K. Portelanos.[311]

The northern wall (PAA) is constructed with large limestone blocks quarried on the slope of Varassova to the west and above the wall (Fig. 92). Even if a large part of the curtain has fallen down the steep slope to the North, where dismantled blocks from the wall are spread around abundantly, larger parts of the curtain are still rather well preserved (Fig. 92). The total length of the northern wall is around 290 metres (this measurement involves a slight estimation as the lower part of the wall to the east is missing). The distance between the towers is larger on the steeper part of the wall to the west. Between tower 1 and tower 2, the distance thus measures 85 m, between tower 2 and tower 3-64 m, while the distance, as the crow flies, between tower 3 and 4 is 44 m. It has been suggested that there was a gate between towers 3 and 4 where the wall is not preserved (Pl. VII). More certain is the gate between tower 4 and 5 where the distance is only 32 m (see below). It is of significance that the wall in this section is of the double faced type and that the towers are fixed to the north side of the wall and not integrated in the curtain in combination with right-angled "jogs" as on the western run (see below).

The top of the western part of the north wall consists of a continuous, c. 50 cm wide, buttressed[312] parapet constructed from square or, often, trapezoidal blocks with the quarry face outwards, and an inside wall-walk with steps between horizontal stretches.

The buttresses are called traverses by Lawrence and are connected to the merlons.[313] Traverses are known on other crenellated parapeth for instance at Phyle, Messene, Caunus, and Dura and not at least at Lilaea, compared by Lawrence with those at Aetolian Chalkis.[314] The wall at Lilaea is stepped as in

307 Comp. *Kalydon* 2011, 445, no. 59.

308 Woodhouse 1897, 106-114. See also Houby-Nielsen in *FPR*, 255.

309 Lawrence 1979 passim.

310 1971, 141-142.

311 Portelanos 1998, 263-287.

312 See Plan V – and Noack 1916, Abb. 17.

313 Lawrence 1979, 360-361.

314 Lawrence 1979, 351, Fig. 80 and 359-360, Pls. 73-74. See also Typaldou-Fakiris 2004.

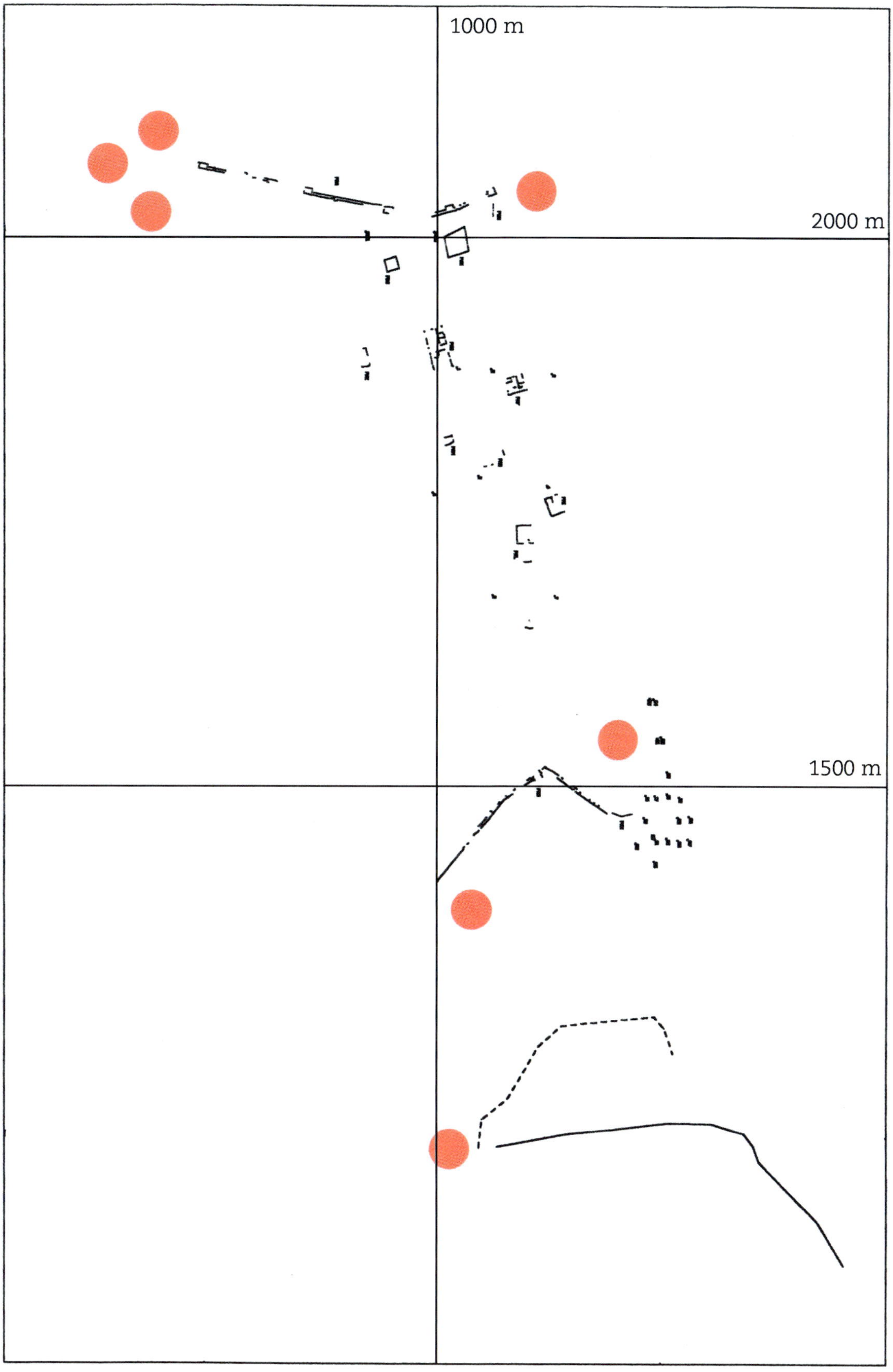

Fig. 91 *Plan of Pangali showing the location of the quarries (shown as red circles) (Mette Mouritzen del.)*

Fig. 92 *Pangali. The curtain of the North wall. From East.*

Pangali.[315] The fortification in Lilaea is dated to the time of Philip II, but the principle is known over large areas and from many earlier and later constructions.[316]

The curtain itself is constructed in the so-called emplekton technique with headers and stretchers and with a filling of broken stones derived from cutting the blocks (Fig. 93).[317] – between, the blocks are joined by angular or slanting joints.[318] Clamps are never used.[319] Drafted corners are found only at towers. The total width of the wall is between 2.0 and 2.5 metres (Plans II and V). The buttresses are placed at suitable intervals[320] and in between there are merlons with openings measuring: 1.02 m., 1.07 m., 1.08 m. and 1.12 m. (Plan V). The lower frame of the openings are formed by heavy ashlar which forms the window sill and in the upper surface of the under-lying block, square cuttings (13-14 cm wide) are pierced through the stone along its whole width (Plan IV-V. Fig. 93). A reconstruction as "closed epalxis" is suggested in Noack 1916, Abb. 17.[321] Lawrence 1979 and Winter 1971 are among the many prominent supporters of the idea of the "closed epalxis" in Chalkis.[322] There are several theories on these cuttings, the newest ones presented and older ones summarized in Kuhn 2008. In addition, these cuttings are often found under the gaps in between merlons.[323]

A **water drain** is found between tower 2 and tower 3.

315 Lawrence 1979, 217.

316 Lawrence 1979, 359.

317 Müth 2010, 67 and, in general, Karlsson 1992, 67-70.

318 Müth 2014, 112, Fig. 5 for Messene. Also in Hagia Triada, see above p 67-68.

319 See *Kalydon* 2011, 67, n. 49.

320 Between 3.25 and 3.83 meter on the Plan V. Woodhouse 1897, opposite p. 110 and Noack 1916, Abb. 15-16.

321 See also Adam 1982, 39 and Schwandner 1977. Silke Müth (personal communication) expressed the opinion that, as no lintels were found, the openings could quite easily have been intervals between merlons. This leaves us with the possibility, that the "closed epalxis" at Chalkis, generally accepted to have existed at *Pangali/Chalkis Aitolias* since the suggested reconstruction by Noack in 1916 – could be wrong (see also Ober 1992, 166-7.

322 See also Portelanos 1998 who reconstructs the parapet following Noack 1916, where sticks support the top suspended shutters when open (the principle is illustrated in Noack 1916, Abb. 12. For more details and a supplementary suggestion, see Lawrence 1979, 418, n. 10

323 Information kindly supplied by Silke Müth.

Up towards tower 1 (Plan I, East of the tower), ten courses of the wall (including the parapet) were preserved, measuring almost 6 m in height as is the case West of tower 2 (Plan IV). It is important to emphasize that the walls were not excavated and only in a very few cases we have been able to record a foundation. At towers 1 to 3, however, the socle of roughly dressed stones was visible, protruding approximately 10 cm further out than the wall itself. As the foundation of the wall must have been approximately at the same level as the tower socle itself, it seems reasonable to suggest, that the original curtain was at least 6 m high, including the parapet.

The upper part of the curtain followed the slope downwards at a 10^0 angle, in long level sections between vertical steps. If the wall is reconstructed with embrasures, the height would increase by around 1 metre and the total original height would be at least around 7 m on the North side – while the length of the level surfaces, between the steps, would be between 3.5 and 4.0 metres (based on measurements of the best preserved North side of the curtain (Plan IV)). If, however, the curtain is reconstructed with merlons, the total height of the original wall should have been around 6 metres (at least) and the level sections between 2.5 and 3.0 metres, interrupted by a vertical, rectangular embrasure before the vertical step. This means that the right side of the embrasure, as seen from the North, was higher than the left side.

Posterns. There are two posterns in the Northern wall (Fig. 94), one below tower 1 (Plan I) and another between tower 2 and tower 3 (Plan IX).[324] The upper (Western) postern is placed 8.80 m from the inner corner of tower 1 and measures: W: 1.10-1.20 m while the visible H is: 2.20 m (N). The postern below tower 2 is preserved to a height of 2.45 m W: 1.20 m, the width of the wall at this point is 2.30 m. Between tower 2 and the lower postern, is 36.5 m from tower 2 and 26.5 m from tower 3. The upper postern could thus rather easily be protected from tower 1 while the lower postern was more vulnerable. There are no traces of closing arrangements connected with the posterns.

324 Lawrence 1979, 248, counted only one postern.

The rectangular Towers (2+3) are included in the wall creating right-angled "jogs" in the curtain (see Fig. 94), the system called "semi-internal" by Lawrence.[325] As seen on the plans, the towers are adapted to the heavily sloping ground, and very different in size and height above surface. As on the long curtains, the walls in the towers are constructed by large blocks, often larger and more regular than the ones used for the curtain walls, placed in a "rather" isodomic order, with many trapezoidal components and some angular or slanting joints where the blocks join. Their width is approximately as on the walls curtain, 50 cm or larger. Drafted margins (D: 7-8 cm.) are clearly seen on all corners of the towers (Fig. 93, 3).

Tower 1, high up the slope, is the best preserved with two windows on the North side looking towards the valley and one with a view along the curtain wall to the east (Plans I-II and Fig. 95). Width of stones between 55 and 65 cm. The inside room of tower 1 measures L: 5.50 m. x W: 3.80 m. = 20.90 m^2 (outside measures at uppermost level: L: 6.64 m. x W: 5.02 m. = 33.33 m^2). A door is situated on the west side with an opening to the west, where the north curtain is prolonged 3.5 m towards the mountain of Varassova – thus protecting the door (Plan II). The door measures W: 1.00-1.20 m, H: 2.10 m. A huge block W: 2.50 m, H: 0.60 m, Th: 0.50 m forms the lintel above the opening. The north wall is preserved in 12 courses, measuring H: 7.80 m at the highest point, at the Northeast corner. One of the two triangular windows in the wall is pointed at the top, the other is arched. NW window (arched): W: 0.42 m (outside)-0.54 m (inside), H: 1.08 m and NE window (pointed): 0.42 m (outside)-0.54 m (inside), H: 1.11 m above floor level (Plan I and II). The windows narrow from inside to outside.[326] The pointed window in the Eastern facade measures W: 0.49 m (outside) – 0.52 m(inside). H: 1.10 m. The eastern door opening to the wall walk measures (towards W) W: 0.80 m. (base) – 1.00 m (top) and H: 1.95 m, surmounted by a huge, rectangular block, W: 2.15 m, H: 0.80 m. and T: 0.60 m.

The original height of the tower is difficult to estimate, as no blocks with cuttings for beams or other traces to indicate the existence of an upper floor were found in the neighborhood. Between 8 and 12 metres might be a qualified guess based on various other, contemporary fortifications (Eleutherai, Messene). The tower protrudes 3 metres from the curtain, thus with a good view to the North side of the wall down towards tower 2.

Tower 2 (Fig. 95, 2) is less well preserved, but is still in a rather good shape.[327] The construction of the north wall is more irregular than in tower 1 as the lower five courses measure: H:55-80 cm, followed by a course H:40 cm and three courses with H:60-95 cm and one H: 45 cm. The uppermost course preserved has a H of 60 cm. The inner dimensions are almost as tower 1, L: 5.20 m. x W: 4.00 m. or 20.8 m^2 (Plan V) (outside measures: L: 6.60 m x W: 5.35 m= 35.31 m^2. The height of the room is suggested to have been 2.65 m. The door opening to the east onto the wall walk measures: W: 0.70-1.05 m. Undoubtedly the tower also had a door in the NW corner, leading to the wall walk along the northern curtain which is only partly preserved between towers 1 and 2. The eastern wall is 3.12 m wide and rather well preserved with the drafted northeast corner (Plans V and VI. Fig. 95, 2). A triangular, pointed window to the east is placed 0.90 m above floor level and measures W: 0. 55 m. x H: 1.34 m. The north wall is preserved at the eastern end near the corner, where part of a pointed window is still to be seen. The trapezoidal block on the left side of the window (seen from n) with the one side of the triangular pointed window has a square cutting, like the drillings below the window sills in the curtain further north. We suggest that the trapezoidal block was originally designed for the parapet, but then used above the window – perhaps in connection with a repair to the tower.

The preserved height of the tower is 7.50 m (part of the protruding foundation is still visible). The original

325 1979, 381, Fig. 80 or "indented trace" see Müth & Ruppe (forthcoming, 8).

326 In Messene windows with curved triangular coverings (tower 8) could similarly be distinguished from straight triangular (towers 6 and 11). Information kindly supplied by Silke Müth. Müth 2010, 73 and n. 32)

327 The entrance seen on plan V, left has now collapsed (2015).

1.

2.

3.

Fig. 93 *Pangali. 1-2: Details of the North wall (PAA). 3: Tower 3.*

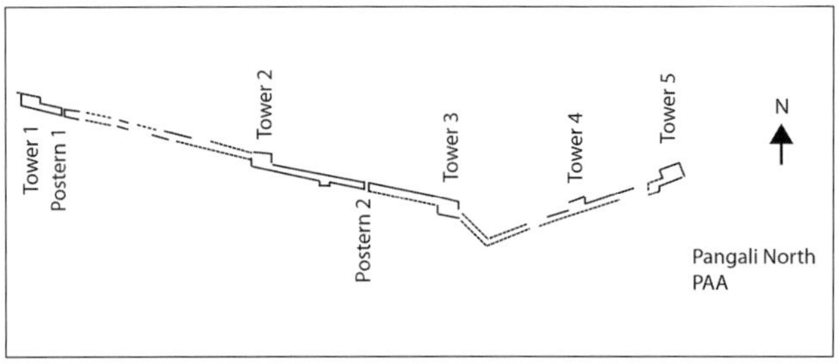

Fig. 94 *Pangali The curtain of the North wall (PAA). Showing tower numbers.*

height is thus at least 8 metres. There are no signs of an upper floor.

Tower 3 (Plan VII and Fig. 93, 3)(as only the lower part of the towers 3-5 are preserved they could have been platforms – it is far more likely, however, that they were towers). Only the two opposite drafted corners to the Southwest and Northeast are preserved. The inner dimensions must have been L: 7.00 m. x W: 5.30 m or around 37 m² and considerably larger than the two upper towers. (the outer dimensions (estimated): L: 8.20 m x W: 6.00 m= 49.20 m². The drafted Southwest corner is preserved with four courses and a protruding socle.[328]A cutting in a detached block (a bed for a roof beam) found inside the tower and pieces of pan tiles, indicate that tower 3 had an upper floor with a tile roof.

In contrast to the curtain West of the break, the badly preserved eastern part is of the canonical double faced type (no cross walls preserved) with stone rubble filling the space between the two faces. The best preserved part of this wall is the approximately six metres West of tower 4 (Plan VIII), around 2.7 m wide and thus considerably wider than the West curtain with parapet and wall walk.

Tower 4 only projects towards the N side of the wall, without the curtain performing a jog here, and measures L: 6.75 m x 5.80 m=39.15 m². As the wall itself measures 2.80 m. at this point, the tower protrudes 3.0 m. from the wall. Both tower 4 and the double faced wall are thus quite similar to the towers and walls of Kalydon[329] in position, construction and dimensions, but in contrast to Kalydon they are built of limestone and the corners are drafted.

Tower 5 is an end tower of the same size and dimensions as tower 4 measuring L: 6.75 m. x W: 5.54 m= 37.4 m². At this point the wall measures 2.52 m and the tower thus protrudes 3 meter from the wall as does tower 4. Approximately 4 metres West of tower 5, there is a square projection inside the wall: 4.52 × 1.22 m. It has been interpreted as a staircase connected with a corner probably indicating a narrow gate entrance, a plan rather similar to the central gate on the Southern wall. Approximately 3 metres of the northern front of tower 4 is visible with 5 courses of blocks, some trapezoidal, placed in a fine isodomic order.

The southern wall (PAN), 208 metres long, following the rugged sloping border of the rock against the steep hillside to the south and the sea, is less well preserved and more overgrown than the northern wall (Plan X). Only the western part of the wall closest to Varassova is preserved. The blocks with horizontal upper and lower surfaces are very different in height and form (many are trapezoidal). They are adapted to fit each other in many cases by a slanting or angular joint at the end, very much like the wall *ABY* at Hagia Triada (see above p 66-68). The best preserved part of the South wall is approximately 4 m high (Plan X) – from what is preserved, it is not possible to estimate the original height. Due to bad preservation and low visibility, it was not possible to measure the width of the wall or to get an impression of the construction. Window openings (or gaps between merlons) are attested in the wall, probably it has the same dimensions as in the northern wall. The windows are situated only 2.20 m above the outer, indicating that a closing arrangement must have been installed.

The gate tower is oriented at a slight angle to the curtain, a width of 7.25 m. Its ground level protrudes 3 m in front of the wall. It is suggested that a staircase was constructed behind the tower. Several blocks with

328 For similar drafted corners in Messene see Müth 2014, Fig. 7.

329 *Kalydon* 2011, 65-69.

1\.   2.

3\. 

Fig. 95 *Tower 1 from East. 2-3: Details of Tower 2 East side with pointed window.*

cut beds for beams indicate that the tower had an upper floor. The entrance is placed East of the tower, near where the Eastern and the Western sections of the wall meet almost at a right angle. Left of the gate, an angular indentation is created in the wall of the tower, which together with a square angle in the Eastern section of the wall, create an approximately 4 × 7 metres rectangular space in front of the 3 metre wide gate opening. A 15 × 25 cm square cutting in a stone on the Western side of the gate shows that the gate could have been blocked by a bar. It is suggested that the gate was approached via a track running from the coast up the Western flank of the ravine. The position of this could, however, not be confirmed because heavy scrub covered the area.

CONCLUSIONS [330]

Lawrence expresses the opinion that Chalkis Aitolias together with Eleftherai (founded 365 BC), Messene (369 BC), and Assos "... must belong to the same ill-

330 As for a general treatment of Ancient Chalkis including Pangali in ancient written sources and modern travel accounts see Sanne Houby-Nielsen in FPR, 238-254.

defined period when development of catapults had reached a stage at which they had become essential anti-personnel weapons, but so recently that the changes in design to receive them were still being made empirically". He also states that "the semi-internal towers of Chalkis[331], are obviously the most primitive and perhaps the earliest ...".[332] Müth 2010 reaches the same conclusion for Messene: "Die Türme der Stadtmauer Messenes reihen sich trotz ihrer Unterschiede alle aufgrund ihrer Dimensionen und der Größe und Anlage ihrer Öffnungen in die frühe Phase einer ersten Generation von Katapultgeschütztürmen ein, die im zweiten Viertel des 4. Jhs. v. Chr. anzusiedeln ist ...... "[333]. In general Lawrence uses Chalkis as a type site with many references to Messene ("perhaps slightly earlier" ... than Messene) ... p. 403: "The windows at Aetolian Chalkis[334] are roughly datable from their resemblance to some of better shape and construction in the western towers of Messene which was founded in 369". The windows protected by wooden shutters are identified as the *Epalxis* mentioned by ancient writers. According to Winter 1971, "The Hellenistic type of epalxis was certainly not common before the second half of the fourth century".[335] As has been emphasized above, however, the reconstruction with closed Epalxis is not generally agreed – the possibility that these "windows" were in fact open embrasures is quite possible.

As argued above, a dating in the 4th century BC seems reasonable. We would suggest a dating around the 370 to 360 or contemporary with the foundation of Messene. An interesting suggestion is put forward by Klaus Freitag[336] who writes about Pangali that: "Dieses Teichos würde möglicherweise von thebanischen Architekten während der Zeit der thebanischen Hegemonie (371-362/1) errichtet, z.Zt als die Boioten unter Epaminondas im Golf agierten und in Naupaktos und Kalydon achaïsche Garnisonen entfernten." The character of the wall and the close parallels to Messene and other fortifications of the 2nd quarter of the 4th c. BC influenced by the Thebans (especially Eleutherai and Siphai) makes it likely that the Chalkis walls date to this time. Only the closed epalxis proposed by some scholars could point to a later date, but not necessarily: firstly, it is not certain that it really was a closed epalxis with windows, and secondly, even if it was, the appearance of this feature cannot be precisely dated within the 4th c. Also the windows or catapult openings and the tower dimensions point to such a date – one has to be careful with such arguments, however, as sometimes and in some places, old fashioned types and techniques were also used later on.[337]

It has been argued, that the emplekton technique was introduced by Boeotian engineers during the Boeotian hegemony (371/2-362 BC) and was part of a comprehensive programme inspired by Epaminondas. The technique could, however, also have been slightly older.[338] We conclude, that the construction on the coastal site could be seen as a defence work created against the Achaians (see above Chapter A3) on the other side of the gulf of Kalydon. Another question is of course whether the fortifications were ever in use? ... the general lack of "habitation remains" suggests that they were probably not.

331 Lawrence 1979, fig. 80.

332 Lawrence 1979, 381.

333 2010, 81.

334 Lawrence 1979, Pl. 82.

335 Noack 1916 and Winter 1971, 140.

336 1999, 56.

337 The authors are grateful for this useful comment by Silke Müth.

338 As the emplekton technique and its use in Messene/ Megalopolis and Mantinea see Roy 2014 passim. Karlsson (1992) sees its origin around 400 BC in Sicily.

E. VARIOUS STUDIES

E.1 Millstones and an olive press from Chalkis Aitolias

Søren Dietz

Catalogue

1) Upper stone of a Mill (Fig. 96 a-c).
Bag.no. 4610/F00-1091/Trench T27B/20.10.00 (AREA III. Room XI)
Very hard sand stone (probably not local). DESCRIPTION: U*pper side* (Fig. 96a): Rectangular sandstone with a rectangular depression in the middle leading down to a slit, an irregularly pointed oval opening in the middle, running lengthwise. The rectangular depression is surrounded by a flat frame. In the middle of the short sides are grooved square slots, with a square hole at one end. At the same end, a further three square holes, two on one side, one on the other side of the slot are cut within the flat frame. The three holes are filled with folded bands of lead. LOWER SIDE (Fig. 96 b-c): The pointed oval opening divides the striation into two ornamental zones, of fishbone patterns. The ornament on the right side has a clear mid-rib from which the straight lines project out. On the left side of the pointed oval opening the lines join and project out from the middle, where no central rib is marked. The lines are straight except for the upper most on both sides which are slightly curved. The stone is broken in the middle and rather worn, but is otherwise, well preserved.
L: 44.0 cm. W: 39.0 cm. Th: 11.0 cm.

2) Lower stone of a Mill (Fig. 96 d-e).
Located close to the south wall in AREA III. Room XI (see Fig. 63).
Black volcanic stone (?) (imported, see below). DESCRIPTION: The striation pattern on the right side has up-curving, parallel lines around a central mid-rib. On the left side the lines are straight, parallel, joining a vertical mid-rib. The stone is broken on this side, but it is reasonable to suggest that the left, straight, parallel lines are only one half of a whole, perhaps centred around a vertical mid-rib. The back is undecorated (Fig. 96 e). Except for the missing section, the lower stone is well preserved.
Pres. L: 51.0 cm. W: 45.0 cm. Th: 10.0 cm.

3) Upper stone of a Mill (Fig. 97 a-b).
F97-2007/Trench T6NA/08.07.97 (AREA III).
Very hard, black volcanic stone (imported, see below). Fragmented long side of an upper stone of a Mill. UPPER SIDE (Fig. 97 a): Fragment of a rectangular groove sloping in a right line downwards toward a central oblong opening (not preserved) at the bottom. The rectangular groove is surrounded by a flat, rectangular frame. LOWER SIDE (Figs. 9 b): With striation pattern of parallel, slanting lines from the edge towards the central slot.
Pres. L: 43.0 cm. Pres. W: 14.0 cm. Th: 10.0 cm.

4) Fragment of a lower stone of a Mill (Fig. 97 c).
X-16/17.07.97 – Stray find from NE slope.
Hard sandstone (imported?). UPPER SIDE (Fig. 97 c): part of the lower part of a Millstone. No sides are preserved. Striation in a herring bone pattern with parallel, slanting lines around a central rib.
Pres. L: 32.0 cm. W: 28.0 cm. Th: 10.0 cm.

5) Oil/Wine press bed – probably square (Fig. 97 d)
Bag no. 4610/F00-1091
Hard sandstone
Pres. L: 50.0 cm. Pres. W: 37.5 cm. Th. 10.0 cm. D (outer circle): 57 cm.

COMMENTS

Millstones are reported in various locations from AREA III, but except for Catalogue nos. 1) and 2) from Room XI they are all out of (original) context. Thus in

Fig. 96 *a-c: Upper Millstone, upper side and under side + line drawing of pattern. d: Lower Millstone, upper side and under side + line drawing of pattern. e: under side of Lower Millstone.*

Fig. 97 *a-d: Upper millstone, upper side and under side + line drawing of pattern. d: Lower Millstone, upper side and under side + line drawing of pattern.*

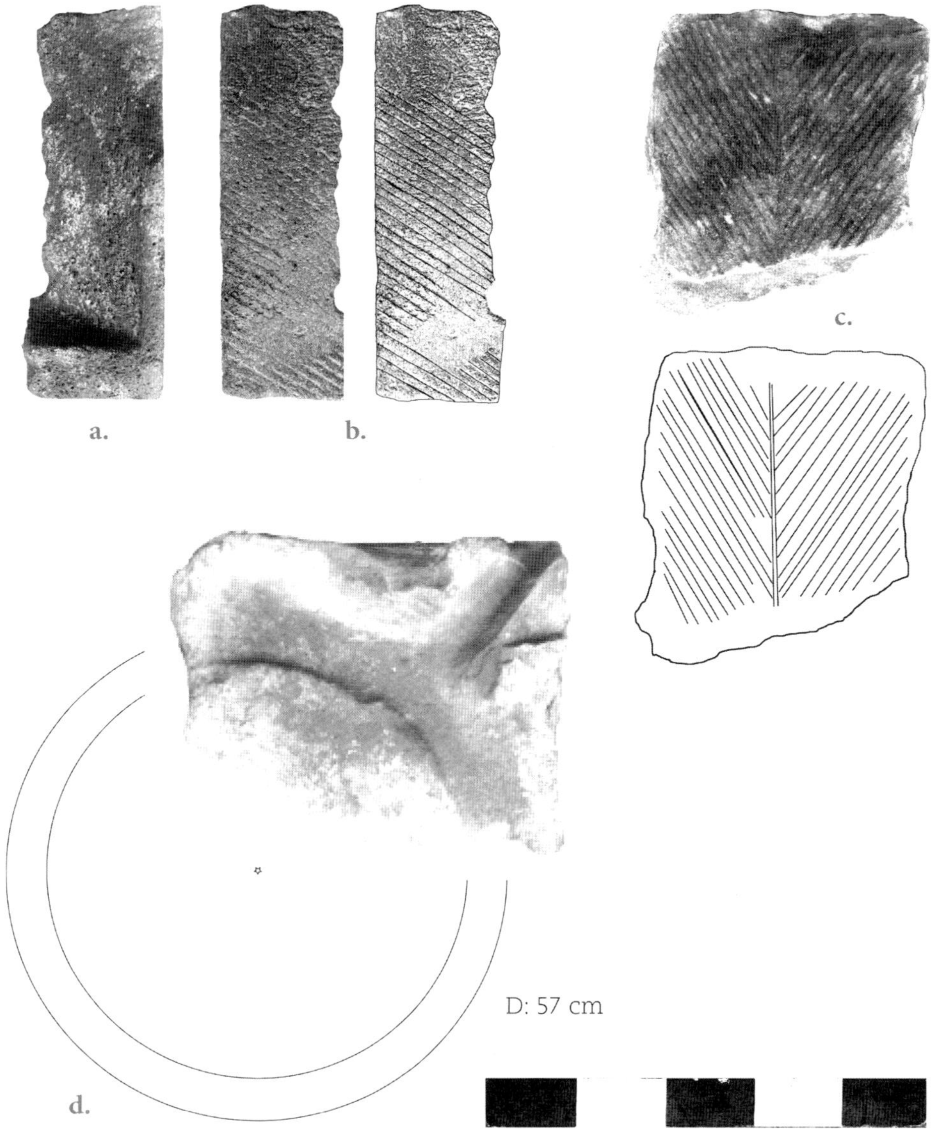

the drain *ADM* in AREA I, fragments of a millstone (F98-1143) were used as one of the vertical slabs lining the south eastern wall of the drain near the wall *ADO* (not registered). One more millstone (F98-3002) was recorded in the trial trench 5 (Tx60/1). The trench was located on the Western slope running towards the harbour, bedrock was found under a shallow cover of soil (a floating layer).[339] Thus, together with the three catalogued examples, five millstones were counted of which only number 1) is entirely preserved. In some cases round, flat stones were recorded as millstones, but a closer examination reveals that the identification was probably not correct, and they are rather whetstones or the like.

Catalogue numbers 1) and 2) make up the upper and lower part of a so-called "Olynthus Mill".[340] Frankel divides the upper stones ("the hoppers") (in a series of subtypes of which our no. 1) is the Lever Operate Olynthus Mill of standard type (I1) with the slots on the short sides.[341] Frankel reports that lead and iron is sometimes found in the small holes at the end of the short sides – but not on the rim as

339 *SPR*, 240. Not registered.

340 Frankel 2003. "of the classic form" (Peacock 2013, 38, Fig. 3.2).

341 Also William-Thorpe and Thorpe 1993, 269.

the Chalkis Aitolias sample.[342] As for the function of these holes see Peacock 2014.[343] The striation and the shape of the slit on the lower side of the hopper are astonishingly closely related to a quern from the Mahdia wreck found in the sea near the Tunisian coast in 1907. The ship is supposed to have been en route from Piraeus to Italy, when it was driven aground by a storm on the North African coast during the first half of the 1st century BC.[344] The striation pattern is unusual as pointed out by Frankel, and related to another piece from Demetrias in Thessaly, which "suggest a common origin"[345] – this should thus also be the case with the Chalkis Aitolias sample. The supposed place of origin is not stated by Frankel (somewhere in the Aegean might be a realistic guess). Use of the Chalkis piece is safely dated in the 3rd century BC and is thus almost 200 years earlier than the Mahdia shipwreck. The millstone from the Mahdia ship, however, was heavily worn before the ship was wrecked.[346]

The striation on the lower stone is not related to the lower stone from the Mahdia Mill.[347] The Chalkis striation is rather specific with its up-curving, parallel lines around the central mid-rib. It is somewhat related to the stones from Tamansky, Tell Halaf and Delos, respectively the Pontic region, North Syria and the Aegean. The combination of the up-curving lines around the mid-rib and the more traditional fishbone pattern on the left side is not found on Frankels Fig. 7. We suggest that there might have been a vertical mid-rib approximately where the stone is broken which means that the lower stone was probably 10 to 15 cm longer or some 60 cm. That makes sense considering that the somewhat shorter upper, rubber stone measured 44 cm in length.[348] The black volcanic stone could be a lava stone from Nisyros?[349]indicating an Aegean origin for this stone as well.[350]

It is interesting that the only saddle quern found in Chalkis Aitolias derives from a building on the Eastern Terrace, AREA I (N28) dating to the late 7th century BC, Archaic period.[351]

The press-bed[352] catalogue no. 5 was found in the same area as the Olynthus type mill, catalogue nos. 1 and 2, but not in context on the floor in room XI. A very similar press bed was found in Olynthus, house A.[353] The Olynthus bed measures 0.68 m. in diameter and is thus slightly larger than the one from Chalkis Aitolias. Several press-beds were found in Delos.[354] There seem to be no difference in principle between press-beds for wine and for olive oil.[355]

342 Also Peacock 2013, 43 and Moritz 1958, 456.
343 and Frankel 2003, 5-6. Reference to Runnels 1981, 296, with samples from Aegina, Isthmia, Halieis, Athens and Corinth.
344 Around 80 BC. See also Baatz 1994, Figs. 5, 6.
345 Frankel 2003, 13.
346 Also Baatz 1994, 99.
347 Frankel 2003, Fig. 7b.
348 Peacock 2013, 38.
349 See William-Thorpe and Thorpe 1993 and Peacock 2013, 46 ff.
350 The Olynthian ("hopper-rubber") lever-operated mill, development and importance of this early "machine" is discussed in detail by Moritz 1958, 42 ff and more recently by Peacock 2013, 39-43.
351 Houby-Nielsen in *Chalkis Aitolias II* (forthcoming). Peacock 2013, type 4, 15 Fig. 2.5.
352 See also Frankel 1999.
353 Robinson and Graham 1938, 342 and Pl. 83.1.
354 Deonna 1938, 97, 101. Pls. 273-276 – one is round, the rest are square.
355 Drachmann 1932, 50 based on Roman evidence. The process of oil extraction is carefully described by Lin Foxhall 2007, 131-217.

E.2 Fauna through the Ages, a view from the Aitolian Coastland

Pernille Bangsgaard

INTRODUCTION

This article represents a first attempt at creating an overview of the faunal history of the Aitolian coastland, based on excavated animal bone materials. The collections originate from three sites in the area, which collectively span the periods from the Final Neolithic to the Late Byzantine period. The Archaic through to the Hellenistic periods is represented by remains from two sites, whereas the remaining periods are solely represented by remains from a single site.

The faunal results raise several interesting points as to the nature of the observable variation between the three sites and variation in animal use patterns between periods. There are some clear shifts in the importance of key species across time and particularly so between the Late Neolithic and the later historic periods. For the later historic periods the faunal variation appears at first glance to be based on the specific site and context and not on a set period in time.

THE SITES AND FAUNAL COLLECTIONS

The three sites were excavated during the 1990's or later, as part of two separate excavation campaigns; the Chalkis Aitolia Project and the Kalydon Project.[356] As such all the faunal remains mentioned in this article were excavated in recent years, with modern excavations techniques and standards. It is, however, worth noting that all three collections are primarily the result of hand collection during excavation, as only minor and occasional sieving of sediments was carried out. It is therefore possible that some distortion of the distribution of fragments have occurred. Due to a lack of sieving bones of a small size, such as fish and bird bones, could have been overlooked. But this potential bias should be equal for all three sites with similar excavation and extraction techniques and similar soil consistency and type.

As the purpose of this article is to summarise the changing faunal use pattern, only material which could be positively identified to a specific period or periods has been included. This limits the total NISP (number-of-identified-specimens) to 3.563 fragments from among a total number of 11.398 bones from all three collections. The severe reduction in number of fragments is partly due to a lack of secure dating of some contexts and simply mixed contexts. Additionally, all unidentified fragments were excluded, as they contribute little knowledge to the analysis. Table 1-2 includes the full dataset for all three sites, according to period.

Pangali

The faunal sequence commences with the material from the Final Neolithic site of Pangali. The site was not extensively excavated, with just a single test trench of four square meters. But the excavation recovered a large amount of archaeological materials from the approximately 60 cm deep deposits, including animal bones. The faunal remains includes 1.371 fragments (1.801 grams) of which 298 fragments (925 grams) have been identified to species or family, leaving 1.073 fragments (876 grams) as unidentified, see table 1

The collection is characterized by an abundance of sheep (Ovis aries) and goat (Capra hircus), which

356 Both projects were collaborations between the Danish Institute at Athens and the Ephoria in Patras and Mesolonghi and were led by Dr. Søren Dietz.

Table 1 *Distribution of all fragments from the sites of Pangali and Chalkis, which could be identified to a specific period.*

	FN Pangali	Helladic Chalkis	Archaic Chalkis	Helladic-Archaic Chalkis	Archaic-Hellenistic Chalkis	Classical-Hellenistic Chalkis
Domesticates						
Pig, *Sus* sp.	35	43	21	10	18	60
Cattle, *Bos taurus*	12	32	65	22	51	46
Horse, *Equus caballus*	–	–	–	–	–	–
Donkey, *Equus asinus*	–	–	–	–	–	–
Horse/donkey, *Equus* sp.	–	–	2	4	–	6
Sheep, *Ovis aries*	15	4	8	4	6	20
Goat, *Capra hircus*	23	13	11	5	8	25
Goat/sheep, *Capra hircus/ Ovis aries*	140	43	62	30	47	75
Dog, *Canis familiaris*	–	4	3	1	15	13
Cat, *Felis domesticus*	–	–	–	–	–	–
Chicken, *Gallus gallus domesticus*	–	–	–	–	–	8
Wild mammalian species						
Wild pig, *Sus scofa*	6	–	–	–	–	–
Red deer, *Cervus elephus*	–	–	–	1	–	3
Roe deer, *Capreolus capreolus*	18	–	1	–	1	–
Fallow deer, *Dama dama*	–	–	–	–	–	–
Deer, *Cervid* sp.	2	–	–	–	–	–
Hare, *Lepus europaeus*	11	–	–	–	1	–
Wolf, *Canis lupus*	–	–	–	–	–	–
Red fox, *Vulpes vulpes*	4	–	–	–	–	3
Wildcat, *Felis silvestris*	9	–	–	–	–	–
Beech marten, *Martes foina*	–	–	1	–	–	–
Carnivore, *Carnivora* sp.	–	–	–	–	–	–
Avian species						
Great cormorant, *Phalacrocorax carbo*	–	–	–	–	–	–
Pheasant & Qails, *Phasanidae* sp.	–	–	–	–	–	–
Tern, *Sterna* sp.	–	–	–	–	–	–
Tawny oxl, *Strix aluco*	–	–	–	–	–	–

Trush, *Turdus* sp.	–	–	–	–	–	–
Mute swan, *Cygnus olor*	–	–	–	–	–	–
Pigeon, *Columba* sp.	4	–	–	–	–	–
Duck, *Anas* sp	–	–	–	–	–	–
Goose, *Anser* sp.	–	–	–	–	–	–
Crow, *Corvidae* sp.	1	–	–	–	–	–
Bird, *Avian* sp.	9	–	–	–	–	10
Marine species						
Mullet, *Mugillidae* sp.	–	–	–	–	–	–
Mackerel, *Scomber* sp.	–	–	–	–	–	–
Sea bass & grouper, *Serranidae* sp.	–	–	–	–	–	–
Blue fish, *Pomatomus saltator*	–	–	–	–	–	–
Bream & Porgy, *Sparidae* sp.	–	–	–	–	1	–
Fish, *Pisces* sp.	10	1	1	–	–	–
Other species						
Rodent, *Rodentia* sp.	–	–	–	–	–	1
Turtoise, *Testudae* sp.	–	2	7	3	1	–
Unspecified						
Ungulates large	1	8	11	1	2	5
Ungulates medium	96	27	36	4	18	48
Unspecified	976	227	209	76	257	247
Total	1371	404	438	161	426	570
Weight (in grams)	*1801*	*3021*	*4470*	*1614*	*2849*	*3452*

account for more than 59 % of the identified fragments and with three goats to every two sheep. The remaining two domesticates of pig (Sus sp.) and cattle (Bos taurus) only represent 12 % and less than 4 %, respectively. Instead wild animals account for the remaining approximately 25 %. This latter group consists mainly of roe deer (Capreolus capreolus), but also hare (Lepus europaeus), wild pig (Sus scofa), wild cat (Felis silvestris), red fox (Vulpes vulpes), fish and birds, including pigeons (Columbidae sp.) and crows (Corvidae sp.) were identified.[357, 358] Such a distribution with a high percentage of wild fauna is unusual for a Late/Final Neolithic site, where the domesticated

357 Bangsgaard 2006 a.

358 Marine molluscs were also collected, primarily species from the rocky coast habitats and in particular limpets. In total 64 shells were recovered during the excavation, thus representing a small supplement to the diet, see Strand Petersen 2006.

Table 2 *Distribution of all fragments from the site of Kalydon, which could be identified to a specific period.*

	Archaic Kalydon	Archaic-Hellenistic Kalydon	Classical-Hellenistic Kalydon	Classical-Roman Kalydon	Byzantine Kalydon
Domesticates					
Pig, *Sus* sp.	15	79	133	125	147
Cattle, *Bos taurus*	3	54	37	20	154
Horse, *Equus caballus*	–	–	–	1	4
Donkey, *Equus asinus*	–	–	1	–	7
Horse/donkey, *Equus* sp.	–	10	7	5	55
Sheep, *Ovis aries*	1	23	24	15	17
Goat, *Capra hircus*	4	19	16	3	65
Goat/sheep, *Capra hircus/ Ovis aries*	20	269	143	82	265
Dog, *Canis familiaris*	–	5	7	4	8
Cat, *Felis domesticus*	–	1	–	–	–
Chicken, *Gallus gallus domesticus*	2	8	13	13	23
Wild mammalian species					
Wild pig, *Sus scofa*	–	3	6	3	6
Red deer, *Cervus elephus*	–	5	2	8	9
Roe deer, *Capreolus capreolus*	–	3	3	1	1
Fallow deer, *Dama dama*	–	3	1	2	1
Deer, *Cervid* sp.	–	1	2	1	–
Hare, *Lepus europaeus*	–	4	12	9	2
Wolf, *Canis lupus*	–	–	1	–	–
Red fox, *Vulpes vulpes*	–	–	3	–	–
Wildcat, *Felis silvestris*	–	–	–	–	–
Beech marten, *Martes foina*	–	–	–	–	–
Carnivore, *Carnivora* sp.	1	–	2	–	–
Avian species					
Great cormorant, *Phalacrocorax carbo*	–	–	6	–	–
Pheasant & Qails, *Phasanidae* sp.	1	2	4	6	8
Tern, *Sterna* sp.	–	1	–	–	–
Tawny oxl, *Strix aluco*	–	–	–	–	–

Trush, *Turdus* sp.	1	–	1	–	–
Mute swan, *Cygnus olor*	–	–	2	1	–
Pigeon, *Columba* sp.	–	2	4	1	–
Duck, *Anas* sp	–	3	17	3	–
Goose, *Anser* sp.	–	1	–	–	–
Crow, *Corvidae* sp.	–	–	–	–	–
Bird, *Avian* sp.	4	7	22	17	2
Marine species					
Mullet, *Mugillidae* sp.	–	2	4	1	–
Mackerel, *Scomber* sp.	–	–	–	–	1
Sea bass & grouper, *Serranidae* sp.	–	1	–	–	7
Blue fish, *Pomatomus saltator*	–	–	–	–	1
Bream & Porgy, *Sparidae* sp.	–	2	6	7	–
Fish, *Pisces* sp.	1	12	15	3	6
Other species					
Rodent, *Rodentia* sp.	–	1	3	7	–
Turtoise, *Testudae* sp.	1	2	2	4	16
Unspecified					
Ungulates large	4	21	38	27	138
Ungulates medium	8	40	89	42	51
Unspecified	133	743	808	258	916
Total	199	1346	1434	858	1921
Weight (in grams)	*551*	*6731*	*5498*	*3457*	*16364*

species are normally clearly in majority.[359] In total a minimum of 12 species were identified in the faunal material.

The Late Neolithic data testifies to a pastoral community, which took advantage of the local environment they lived within, supplementing the domesticated economy by collecting, hunting and fishing in the valley, in the mountainous hinterland and in the nearby sea. Although the faunal collection cannot definitively establish the seasonality of the habitation, nor establish or rule out the presence of a year round occupation at Pangali, the presence of foetal and pullus bones from pig as well as sheep and goat, suggest that the site was settled during the first half of the year, January through to June, as a minimum.[360]

Chalkis

The mound of Haghia Triadha is a multi-period site and the faunal collection includes material from the

359 See e.g. Rivals et al 2011; Halstead 2011.

360 Bangsgaard 2006 a; seasons based on Halstead 2005.

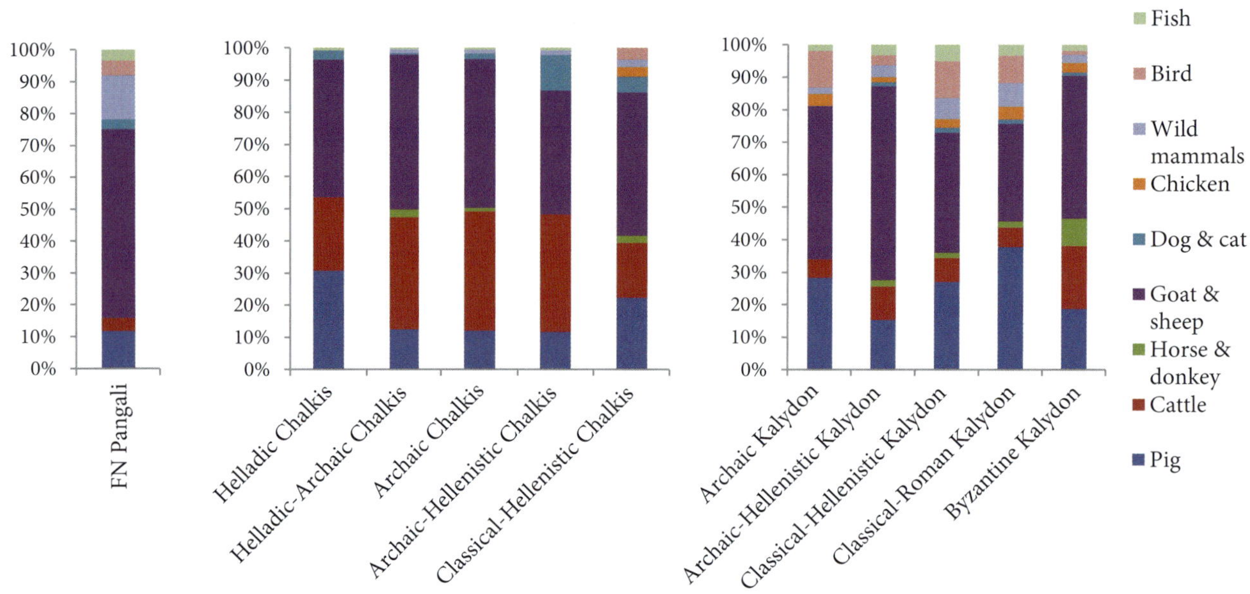

Fig. 98 *Distribution of main species distributed according to period and site.*

Helladic (EHI, MH/LH and LHIIIB/C) through to the Hellenistic Periods. In total the entire collection includes 3.694 fragments (28.155 grams) of which 1.718 fragments (21, 648 grams) have been identified to family or species. But the remains that could be dated amount to 1.999 fragments (15.406 grams) of which 823 could be identified; see table 1 and Fig. 98. The bone material originates from several different areas of the site; these include excavation AREAS I and II, located on the eastern terrace of Aghia Triada and west of Aghia Triada respectively. Two additional excavation areas are also represented, one on the northern terrace of Aghia Triada (AREA IV), the other on the eastern terrace of Aghia Triada, SE of AREA I (AREA III) (see table 3 for a full overview of the areas). The excavation of these contexts have revealed architecture and other evidence from a number of small workshops, as well as a substantial building complex with multiple room functions, probably ritual provision of meals and eating as well as weaving or actual weaving workshops.[361]

At least 15 species are represented in the collection, but the domesticated animals are clearly much more abundant than the wild animals. Sheep (*Ovis aries*) and goat (*Capra hircus*), are again the most common species with 45 %, although pig (18 %) and cattle (29 %) also played an important role (Sus sp. and *Bos taurus*). Additionally, dog (*Canis familiaris*), horse or donkey (*Equus sp.*) and chicken (*Gallus domesticus*) are also present at the site (6 % in total). A number of wild species were identified, although in small numbers (2 %), these include red deer (*Cervus elaphus*), roe deer (*Capreolus capreolus*), wild pig (*Sus scofa*), red fox (*Vulpes vulpes*), hare (*Lepus europaeus*), turtle and a few fish. The distribution of wild animals does not indicate any major environmental shifts compared to the present, as all species are all found in the general area today.[362]

Despite the varied origin and dating of the faunal collection from Chalkis there are clear similarities in the distribution of species across time, with sheep and goat as the major contributors to the diet. But they are closely followed by cattle and with some pig. The evidence from the earliest and latest evidence does, however, vary from the norm at Chalkis, see Fig. 98.

361 See above General Introduction and Dietz & Kolonas 1998, *Chalkis Aitolias II.*

362 Bangsgaard 2006c.

Table 3: *Distribution of contexts from the three Aitolian sites, according to each period.*

Chronology	Pangali	Chalkis	Kalydon
Neolithic	A single test trench	–	–
Helladic	–	Tx20, 43 – AREA I, the eastern terrace of Aghia Triada K27& Tx70-72 – AREA II, west of Aghia Triada F15 – the northern terrace of Aghia Triada	–
Helladic-Archaic	–	N26 – AREA I, the eastern terrace of Aghia Triada	–
Archaic	–	N26-28 AREA I, the eastern terrace of Aghia Triada K2729 – AREA II, west of Aghia Triada	Well DS36, Section D some loci, Acropolis Section H
Archaic-Hellenistic	–	K27-28 & Tx70-71 – AREA II, west of Aghia Triada	AREA X, Acropolis, Section H
Classical-Hellenistic	–	O26-27 & T26-31, T6 – the eastern terrace of Aghia Triada, SE of AREA I	Acropolis, Section H D12a under Peristyle build. Section D Lower kiln, Section D
Hellenistic	–	K26 – AREA II, west of Aghia Triada	Same as below
Hellenistic-Roman	–	–	Peristyle build., Section D Kiln fill, Section D Acropolis, Section H
Byzantine	–	–	Pits on the Acropolis, Section H

The evidence from the Helladic Period indicates a significantly higher frequency of pig during this time balanced primarily by a lower amount of cattle. At the other end of the time scale the chicken makes an appearance during the Classical to Hellenistic Periods, although only as a small component of the total diet. Additionally, the amount of wild game, deer, red fox and bird increases in this latter phase and the amount of cattle drops to be replaced partly by more pig and partly by more sheep and goat. Despite these changes in the beginning and the end of the sequence of faunal material the overall impression at Chalkis is one of a stable faunal use pattern across time.

Kalydon

Within its city walls, Kalydon comprises an area of approximately 35 ha. Investigations and excavations have revealed the urban layout of the town in Antiquity and attested to the function of various quarters, however only a small area has been excavated so far.[363] The complete faunal collection comprises some 6.333 fragments (36.173 grams), but the remains included in this study amounts to 5.788 fragments (32.599 grams), of which 2.472 fragments could be identified to family or species, see table 2 and Fig. 98.

363 *Kalydon* 2011.

Table 4: *Distribution of species as percentages from the three Aitolian sites, according to each period.*

	Final Neolithic Pangali	Helladic Chalkis	Helladic-Archaic Chalkis	Archaic Chalkis	Archaic-Hellenistic Chalkis	Classical-Hellenistic Chalkis	Archaic Kalydon	Archaic-Hellenistic Kalydon	Classical-Hellenistic Kalydon	Classical-Roman Kalydon	Byzantine Kalydon
Pig	12	31	13	12	12	22	28	15	27	38	19
Cattle	4	23	35	37	36	17	6	10	8	6	20
Horse & donkey	0	0	3	1	0	2	0	2	2	2	8
Goat & sheep	59	43	48	46	39	45	47	60	37	30	44
Dog & cat	0	3	0	2	11	5	0	1	1	1	1
Chicken	0	0	0	0	0	3	4	2	3	4	3
Wild mammals	17	0	1	1	1	2	2	4	6	7	2
Bird	5	0	0	0	0	4	11	3	11	9	1
Fish	3	0	0	1	1	0	2	3	5	3	2

The faunal collection originates from several different contexts across the site, and covers the timespan from the Archaic until the Late Byzantine Period, see table 3 for an overview of the contexts. Although most periods are represented by more than one context, it is worth noticing that the Archaic-Hellenistic remains are dominated by layers on the Acropolis, whereas the Hellenistic remains primarily originate from within the Peristyle building. This building, with its colonnaded courtyard and a *Matroon* room, probably dedicated to the Anatolian goddess Cybele, was an important building in the Lower Town.[364] The marble sculpture, incense burners, clay figurines and lamps were found almost, as they were left when the roof collapsed during the middle of the 1st century AD. On the Acropolis the objects and sporadic architectural remains suggest that a shrine was established by Late Archaic times, sometime in the late 6th century BC.[365] Additionally, the faunal remains from the Late Byzantine Period come exclusively from a series of pits found on the Acropolis (12th century AD). Without any architectural or other remains, their exact function and context is not entirely clear at present.[366]

The faunal collection includes at least 18 species of mammal, bird, fish and reptile, see table 1. Once more the domesticated species make up the bulk of the assemblage, with sheep (*Ovis aries*) and goat (*Capra hircus*) taking up 44 %, then pig (*Sus sp.*) with 23 % and cattle (*Bos taurus*) with 12 %. Other domesticated species include horse (*Equus caballus*) and donkey (*Equus asinus*) with 4 %, chicken (*Gallus domesticus*) with 3 % and dog (*Canis familiaris*) and cat (*Felis domesticus*) with 1 %. Additionally, there are a number of wild species, including mammals, birds and fish. In total the wild species contribute 13 % of the collection. These include a substantial number of species; the mammals include wild pig (*Sus scofa*), red deer

364 *Kalydon* 2011.
365 *Kalydon* 2011.
366 Ibid.

Table 5 *Distribution of goat (Capra hircus) remains, which contain information regarding time-of-death and distributed according to period.*

Fusion[370]	**Bones**	**Final Neolithic, unfused**	**Final Neolithic, fused**	**Helladic-Archaic, unfused**	**Helladic-Archaic, fused**	**Archaic-Hellenistic, unfused**	**Archaic-Hellenistic, fused**	**Classical-Hellenistic unfused**	**Classical-Hellenistic fused**	**Late Byzantine, unfused**	**Late Byzantine, fused**
0-6 months	P Metapodium, R Radius	-	2	-	6	-	3	1	8	1	12
0-12 months	D Humerus, Pelvis, Scapula	-	2	1	1	-	4	1	4	4	7
12-18 months	2. Phalanger, 1. Phalanger	2	3	1	1	1	2	2	7	1	5
18-30 months	D Metapodium, D Tibia	1	1	1	2	-	3		4	5	2
30-48 months	Calcaneus, Femur, P Ulna, D Radius, P Tibia	1	-	1	1	-	1	1	2	9	9
48+ months	P Humerus	-	-	-		-	-	-	-	2	1

Table 6 *Distribution of sheep (Ovis aries) remains which contain information regarding time-of-death and distributed according to period.*

Fusion[371]	Bones	Final Neolithic, unfused	Final Neolithic, fused	Helladic-Archaic, unfused	Helladic-Archaic, fused	Archaic-Hellenistic, unfused	Archaic-Hellenistic, fused	Classical-Hellenistic unfused	Classical-Hellenistic fused	Late Byzantine, unfused	Late Byzantine, fused
0-6 months	P Metapodium, P Radius	-	1	-	1	-	4	-	3	-	-
6-12 months	Pelvis, Scapula, D Humerus	-	-	1	4	-	2	-	7	-	1
12-18 months	2 Phalanger, 1 Phalanger	3	4	-	1	-	3	1	10	2	4
18-30 months	D Tibia, D Metapodium	-	-	1	2	1	1	-	2	-	3
30-48 months	Calcaneus, D Radius	-	-	-	1	1	4	-	3	1	-

(*Cervus elaphus*), roe deer (*Capreolus capreolus*), fallow deer (*Dama dama*), hare (*Lepus europaeus*), wolf (*Canis lupus*) and red fox (*Vulpes vulpes*). The birds and fish were to a large extent only identified to family, these include: phasant and qail (*Phasanidae sp.*), tern (*Sterna sp.*), trush (*Turdus sp.*), pigeon (*Columba sp.*), duck (*Anas sp.*), goose (*Anser sp.*), crow (*Corvidae sp.*), mullet (*Mugillidae sp.*), mackerel (*Scomber sp.*) and bream and porgy (*Sparidae sp.*). The fragments that could be identified to species included: great cormorant (*Phalacrocorax carbo*), tawny owl (*Strix aluco*), mute swan (*Cygnus olor*) and blue fish (*Pomatomus saltator*). The list of wild species is diverse and also fairly impressive for a historic period site, where game often represents a negligible small contribution to the diet.

Generally the intra site variation is noticeable

Period	Wear stage Payne[372]	Wear stage Zeder[373]	Number	Age
Helladic -Archaic	C-D	III-IV	1	6-24 months
	F	VI	1	3-4 years
Archaic-Classical	C-D	III-IV	1	6-24 months
	D-F	IV-VI	1	1-4 years
Classical-Hellenistic	B-C	II-III	2	2-12 months
	C	III	2	6-12 months
Byzantine	C	III	2	6-12 months
	E-F	V-VI	1	2-4 years
	G	VII	2	4-6 years

Table 7 *Distribution of goat (Capra hircus) mandibles with time-of-death data, according to period*

Period	Wear stage Payne[374]	Wear stage Zeder[375]	Number	Age
Archaic	F	VI	1	3-4 years
Archaic-Classical	B-C	II-III	1	2-12 months
	C	III	1	6-12 months
	F	VI	1	3-4 years
	E-G	V-VII	1	2-6 years
Classical-Hellenistic	E-G	V-VII	1	2-6 years
	G	VII	1	4-6 years
	G-H	VII-VIII	1	4-8 years
Byzantine	G	VII	1	4-6 years
	H-I	VIII-IX	2	6-10+ years

Table 8 *Distribution of sheep (Ovis aries) mandibles with time-of-death data, according to period*

with several species varying significantly according to period, see Fig. 98. The Late Byzantine material displays a substantial variation in the abundance of cattle as well as horse/donkey compared to the rest, the Archaic-Hellenistic assemblage has significantly more sheep and goat than any other period, whereas the Classical-Roman remains hve the highest number of pigs. In the Classical-Hellenistic Period and to some extent also the Hellenistic-Roman period the amount of game species is high.

As this shows, the Kalydon faunal use pattern appears less stable compared to Chalkis. Part of this variation can be due to the different places of origin, with the Classical-Hellenistic and Hellenistic Roman periods being mainly represented by the Peristyle Building. It is therefore possible that the high amount of game animals during these phases could be related to the probable cult of Cybele. The Archaic and Archaic-Hellenistic material on the other hand mainly represents the probable Shrine on the Acropolis, but little else is known about the daily activities there due to later disturbances. Finally the Late Byzantine material comes from the pits on the Acropolis, but no other finds could indicate their precise function. Thus there may be a substantial variation in the function of each area included in the study, with some specialised

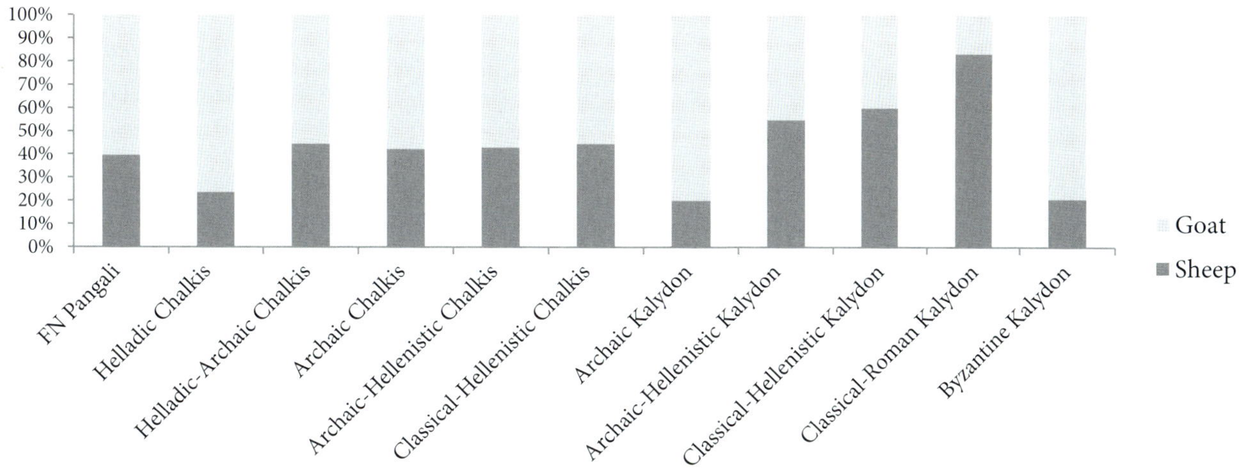

Fig. 99 *Distribution of goat (Capra hircus) and sheep (Ovis aries) distributed according to period and site.*

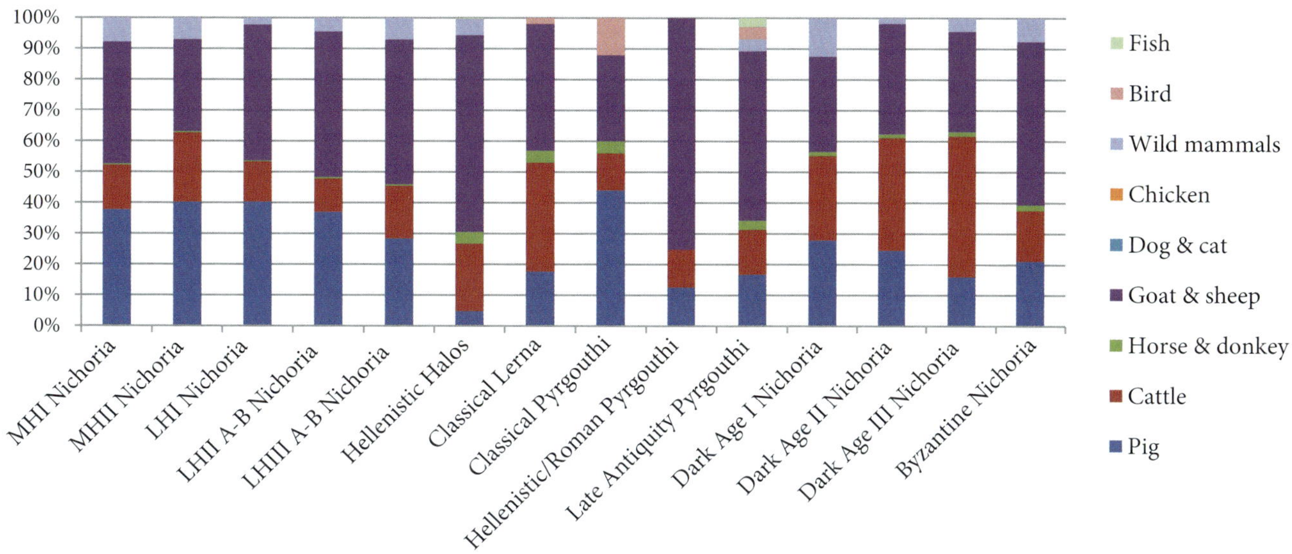

Fig. 100 *Distribution of main species distributed according to period and site from other mainland and Peloponnesian sites*[376]

functions of a religious or cultic nature and as such this may at least in some parts influence the species distribution.

SUMMARY OF PERIODS AND SITES

The varied species distribution between the three sites is visually clear from Fig. 98 and at first glance the site based variation also appears to be more pronounced than any variation seen over time.

The inhabitants of Pangali appears to have been primarily pastoralists with sheep and goat (59 %) clearly supplying the majority of the nutrition and more so than at any of the other sites. The unusually large amount of wild animals (22 %) also characterises the assemblage and testifies to the importance of hunting, supplemented by fishing and the collection of marine molluscs.[367]

At Kalydon cattle appear to play a limited role in most periods, as their presence varies from 6 to 10 %, see table 4 and Fig. 98. The only exception is the Late Byzantine Period, where cattle represent 20 % of the entire NISP collection. Opposing this distribution is the much higher amount of cattle during most periods

367 Bangsgaard 2006a and Strand Petersen 2006

at Chalkis, particularly from the Archaic – Helladic until the Hellenistic -Roman, where cattle make up between 35 to 37 % of the NISP collection. The reverse is to a large extent visible for the pig remains; they are consistently more common in the Kalydon assemblages (from 15 to 38 %) compared to contemporary Chalkis assemblages (from 12 to 2 %). The Helladic material sticks out from the rest of the Chalkis material with 31 % pigs. Interestingly, there is also a consistent higher component of wild species in the Kalydon material (with 10, 15, 21 and 22 %) compared to contemporary Chalkis material (with 0 to 6 %). The only exception to the rule at Kalydon is the Late Byzantine assemblage, where only 5 % of the collection is from wild species.

The slight difference in location is not likely to be the main cause, as the distance between the two sites is less than 10 km as the crow flies. Variation in bone recovery may have influenced recovery of smaller bones from bird and fish negatively however, this is not likely to be the only cause, as larger mammal species such as red deer are also lacking in the Chalkis assemblages compared to Kalydon. Apart from the likely cultic context at Kalydon, it is also possible that the inhabitants of Kalydon actually had a more diverse meat diet. Perhaps there was a better access to wild game, birds and fish through the market of such a larger urban site, which pulled resources into the centre from a substantial hinterland. An increased interest in game species could also be fuelled by the complex social positioning in an urban setting, meaning that there was more focus on the consumption or display of non-domesticated animals as part of the daily power struggle and social positioning. Additionally, the introduction of chicken appears to happen earlier at Kalydon that at Chalkis, chicken remains are found from the Archaic Period onwards at the former and only make an appearance at the latter during the Classical-Hellenistic Period.

Horse and donkey is never a major component in any of the assemblages, but the Late Byzantine pits at Kalydon do contain substantially more equid bones than any other period, with 8 % compare to 0-3 % at all other periods and sites. The group of dogs and cats consists almost exclusively of remains from the former species, as cat is only represented by a single fragment from Archaic-Hellenistic Chalkis. The choice was made to include these in the various tables and figures displaying the distribution of species. There is ample evidence from Greece, that particularly dogs were utilised for both food and skins, along with a likely function as hunting and guarding dogs. The evidence comes from multiple periods and sites and consists mainly of cut-marks related to dismembering and skinning,[368] as is also the case at Chalkis.[369]

Sheep and goat are consistently the most abundant species during all periods and at all three sites, with the single exception of Hellenistic -Roman Kalydon where pig (38 %) is more abundant than sheep and goat (30 %). But the importance of sheep and goat varies significantly from 60 to 37 % of the total NISP collections. Also the internal distribution of the two species varies somewhat, see Fig. 99. Again Hellenistic -Roman Kalydon stands out with significantly more sheep to goat. At Chalkis the distribution is fairly consistent with slightly more goat than sheep, whereas at Kalydon the distribution varies significantly from one period to another. Due to the substantial amount of sheep and goat remains, it was possible to include age profiling based on both fusion of long bones and on teeth eruption and wear, see tables 5-8. But neither species include enough remains for a full division according to period and site and therefore it was only possible to divide the material according to period and not to site. There is a tendency for the sheep remains to indicate a higher age profile than the goat remains, and this overall pattern is fairly consistent for both long-bones and dental profiling data. Such a difference could indicate that sheep were used more than goat for products other than meat, a likely candidate would be wool production. A closer look at the very limited amount of goat data reveals a more ambiguous distribution, with variation between both period and type of evidence.

368 See Snyder et al, 2003
369 Bangsgaard 2006c
370 Based on Zeder, 2006
371 Based on Zeder, 2006
372 Based on Payne, 1973
373 Based on Zeder, 2006
374 Based on Payne, 1973
375 Based on Zeder, 2006

CONCLUDING REMARKS

Overall the faunal collections from the three Aitolian sites are mainly consistent with material generated from everyday household consumption, but with a component of material, which potentially may come from more specialised cultic or religious activities. The domesticated animals were probably kept primarily for their meat, but with the utilization of some additional products, such as skin, milk, wool and traction. The consistently high age of the sheep could indicate that either wool or milk was important for the keeping of this species. Cattle and horse or donkey was probably also utilised as beasts of burden. The wild mammals represent a supplement to the diet, although for most historic periods they probably only played a minor economic role in the overall consumption pattern of meat.

In order to contextualise the Chalkis and Kalydon data within a wider regional scope, a couple of sites with available faunal data are included here, see Fig. 100. As the Pangali assemblage has previously been analysed and contextualised in much detail it will not be fully treated here. But the previously analysed comparative material includes a significant number of sites covering eastern and southern Mainland Greece, the Peloponnese and with two nearby islands. These sites include material from periods immediately before and after the period 4.500 to 4.200 BC. In the article two points were made: Firstly, the importance of sheep and goat in the Neolithic has been pointed out by several scholars.[377] However, at Pangali there is an even more pronounced focus on these two species. Secondly, although domesticates are the main meat supplier from the beginning of the Neolithic onwards, the evidence from Pangali indicates that to a greater extend than seen elsewhere the group chose to utilise local wild animals as an extra food source. Together these two trends could point to a subsistence strategy of diversification.[378]

The faunal collections included here originate from four sites, which cover the southeastern Mainland and the Peloponnese as well as the Periods from the Helladic to the Byzantine. The majority of the material originates from Nichoria, which apart from a large corpus of Helladic remains also includes Dark Age and Byzantine layers. Due to a very large assemblage only a selection of the Helladic fauna has been studied, including all datable loci, which amount to 14 % of the total bulk. But the later remains include the entire collection recovered during excavation. Between the Helladic and the Dark Ages a shift occur in the husbandry pattern. Shifting from sheep (and goat) and some pig to a majority of cattle with a smaller component of the other species.[379] Other comparative material includes material from the sites of Lerna (Classical Period),[380] New Halos (Hellenistic Period)[381] and Pyrgouthi (Classical Period to Late Antiquity).[382] All these collections are of a limited size and as such have similar statistical challenges as the collections from Aitolia, but the faunal materials do represent several different types of contexts including several houses.[383]

It is worth noting that none of these four additional historic sites displays such a high component of wild game as Kalydon. The game component is particularly high at Kalydon in the Classical-Hellenistic and Hellenistic l-Roman Periods, but the other periods also include reasonably high amount of game species. The question remains whether this pattern is a result of a specific focus on such species at the site. Even though game may not be the main supplier of meat in the diet, perhaps the activity itself (hunting), or perhaps the game as a consumption object or symbol of were of particular importance at Kalydon.

A general comparison of all sites does not reveal any clear patterns of compatible distribution of species across the period. This is perhaps not surprising, as there is not otherwise any evidence for clear shifts in species importance and in household practices from one period to another. Instead the variation in contexts from house to shrine to workshop as well as variation in status and accessibility to resources is more likely to be the cause. What should be taken

376 Gejval 1969, Hjohlman 205, Mancz 1989, Prummel 203
377 See e.g. Halstead & Isaakidou 2011; Cherry 1988.
378 See Dietz and Bangsgaard (forthcoming).

379 Sloan & Duncan 1978.
380 Gejvall 1969.
381 Prummel 2003.
382 Hjohlman 2005
383 Prummel 2003, 153…

away from this overview of the three Aitolian sites, Pangali, Chalkis and Kalydon, is that there is clearly no single unambiguously historic development in the faunal use pattern, even within such a geographically limited area. Instead the faunal evidence should give evidence in more detailed analysis of the specific use pattern for separate contexts and areas of these sites, and so they may assist in interpretation and analysis there and at other archaeological sites.

PLANS I-X (1:200)

A digital version of the Plans I-X is accessible
at the website of the Danish Institute at Athens:

www.diathens.gr (Chalkis Aitolias III – Plans I-X).

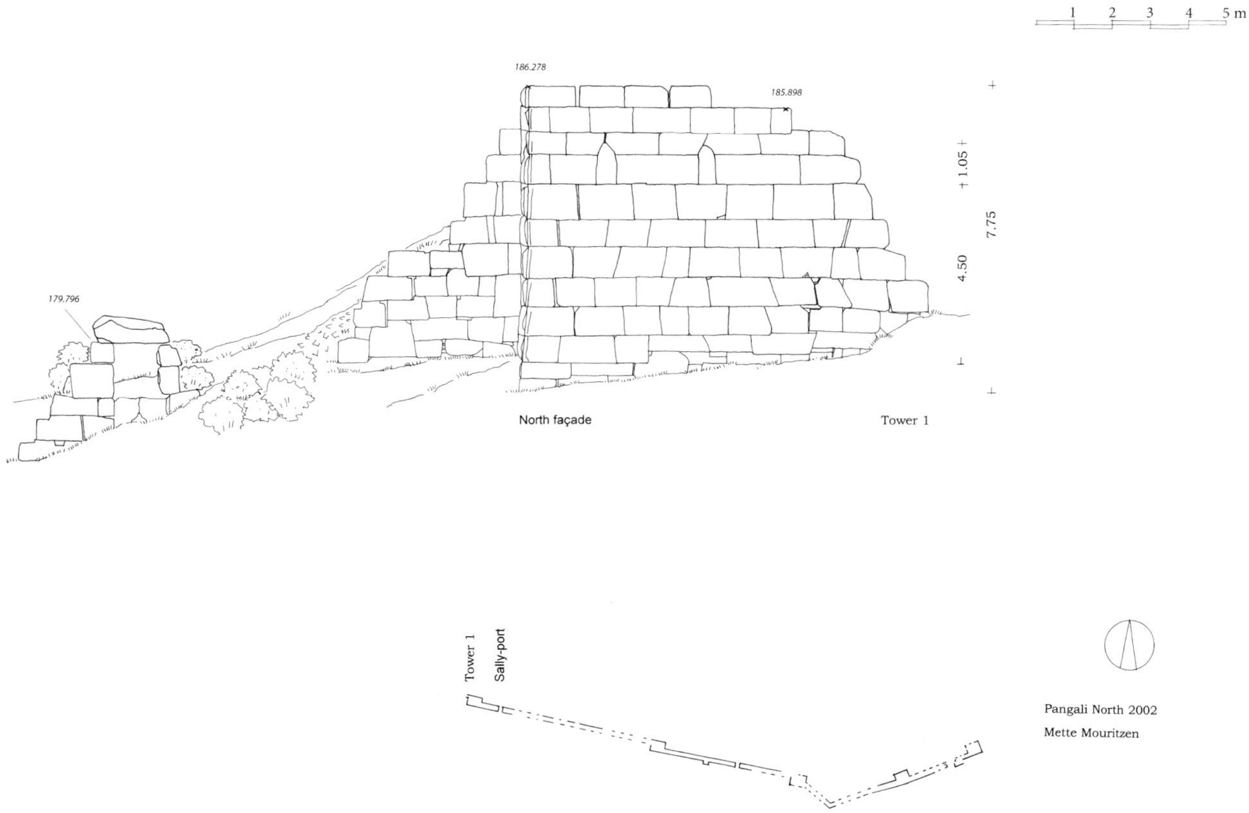

Plan I *Pangali fortifications. North wall PAA, tower 1. North elevation.*

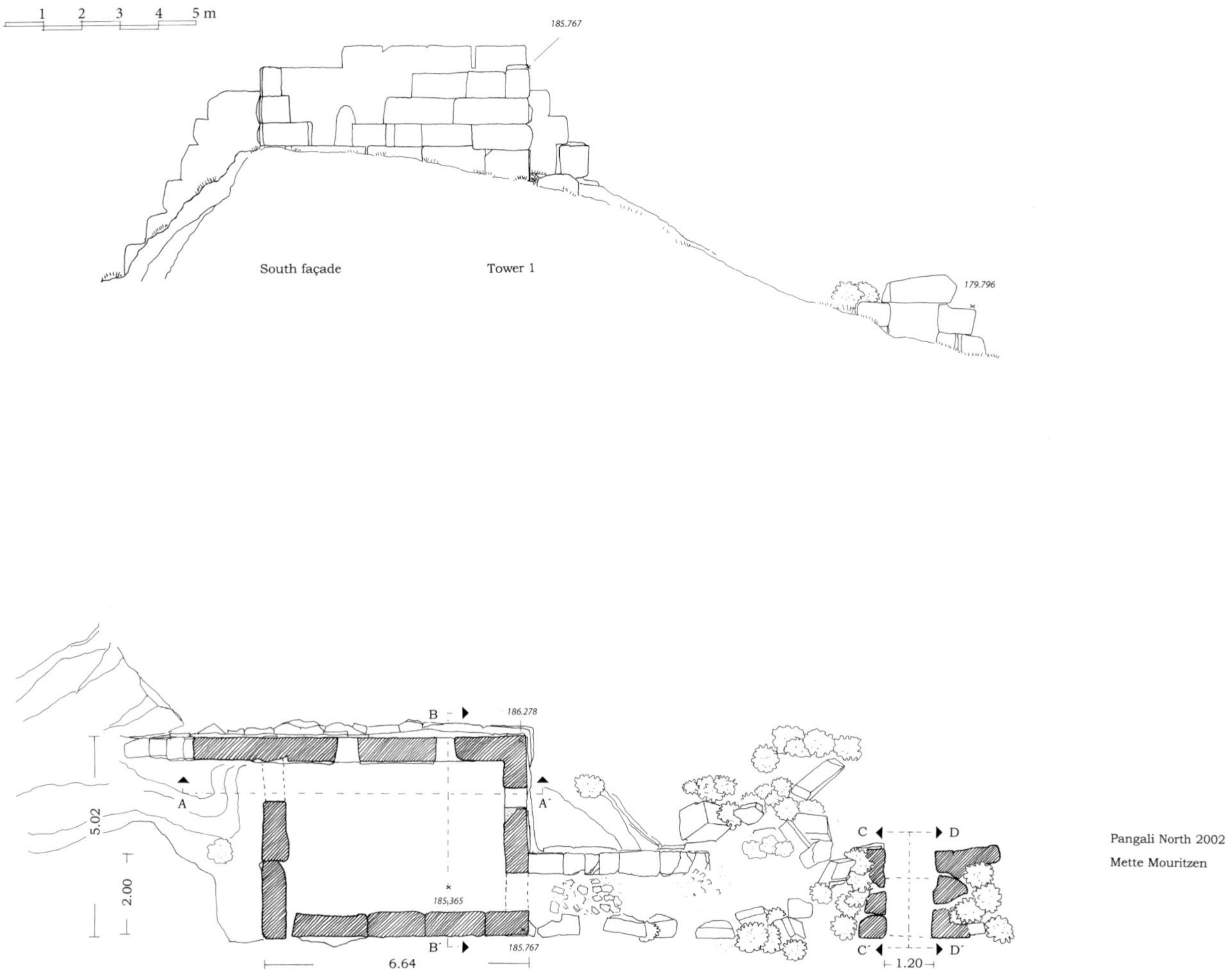

Plan II *Pangali fortifications. North wall, tower 1 and postern 1. Ground plan and South elevation.*

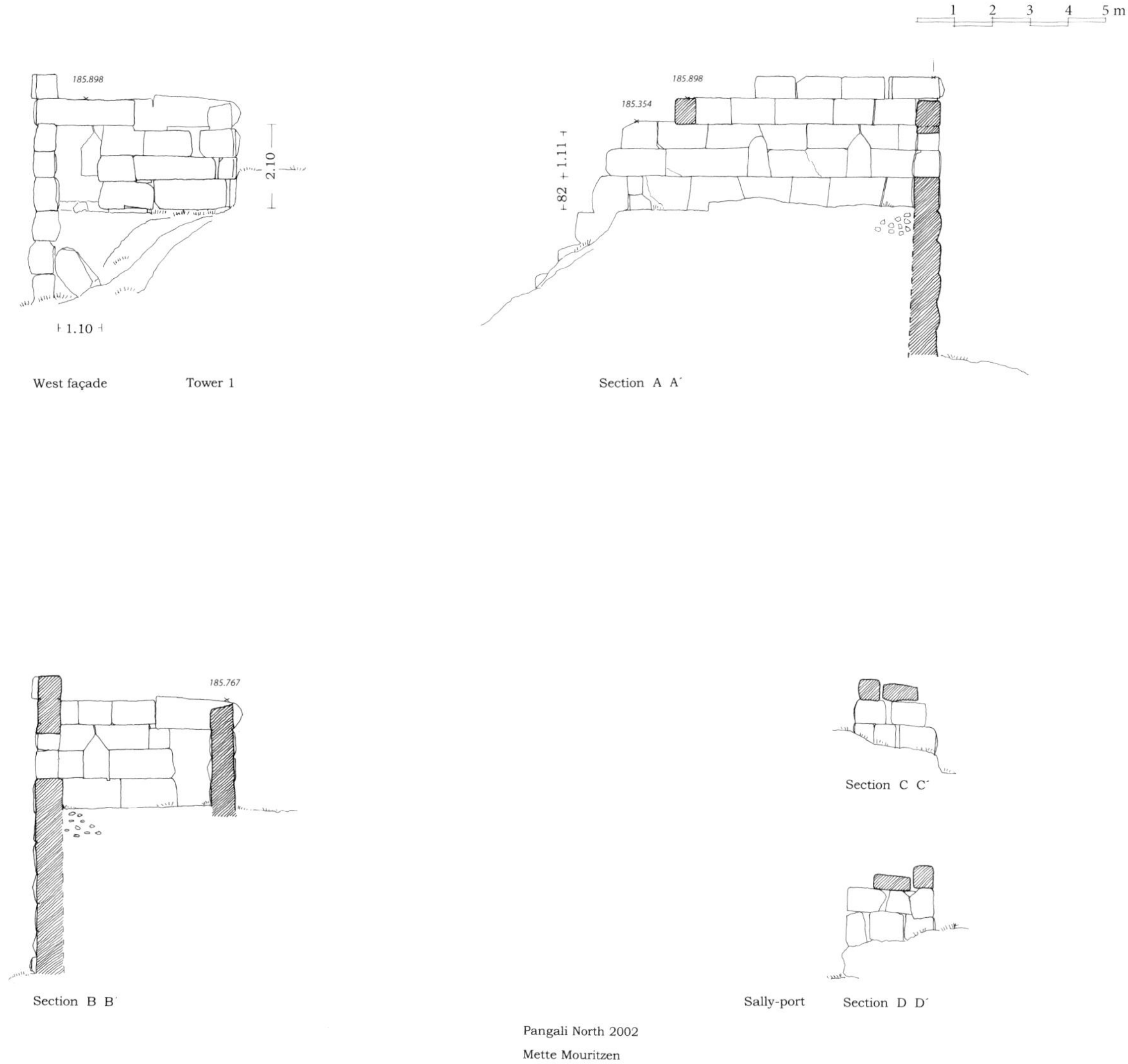

Plan III *Pangali fortifications. North wall. Sections of tower 1 and postern 1.*

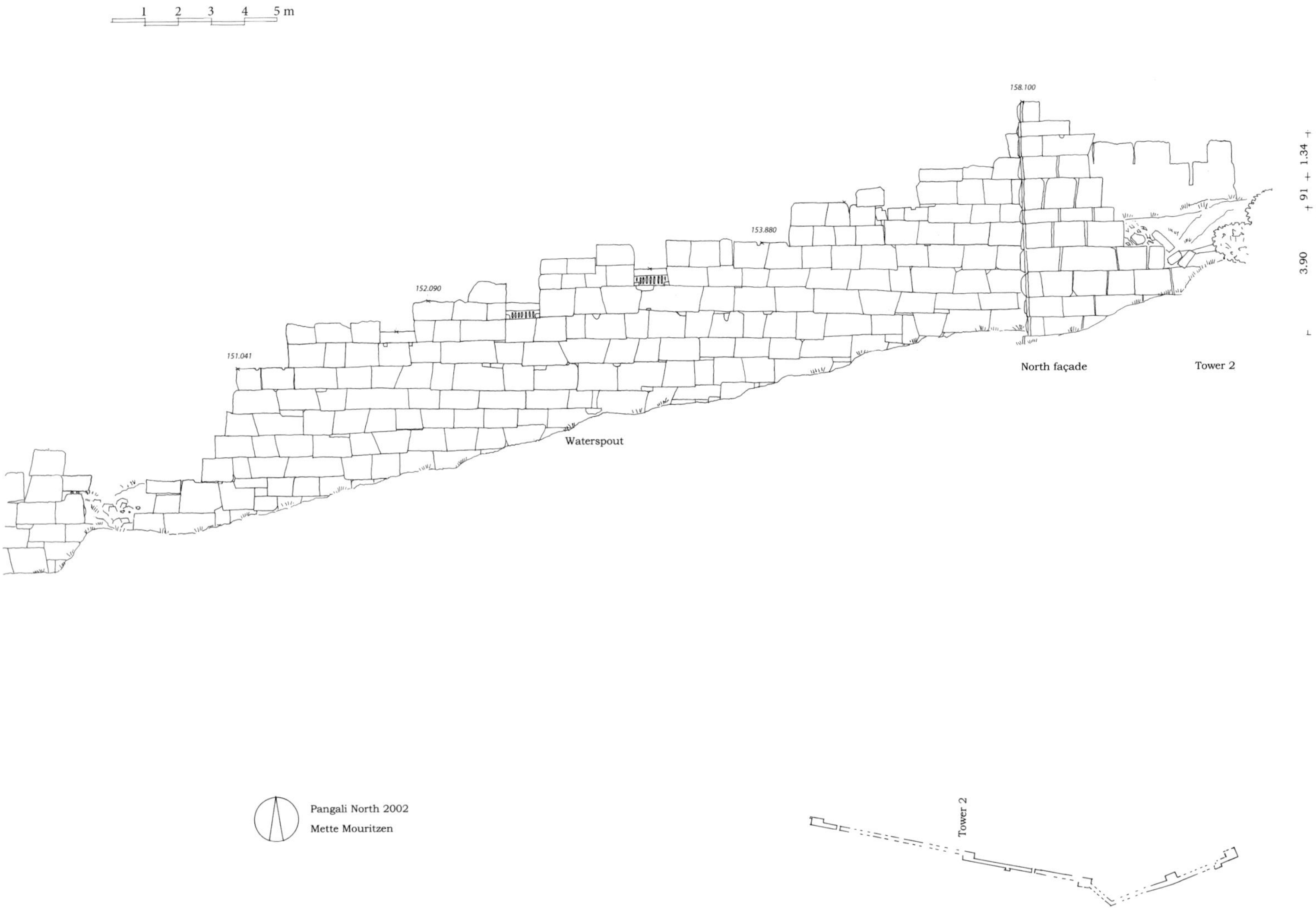

Plan IV *Pangali fortifications. North wall, North elevation of tower 2 and curtain wall.*

Plan V *Pangali fortifications. North wall, tower 2, South elevation and curtain wall plan.*

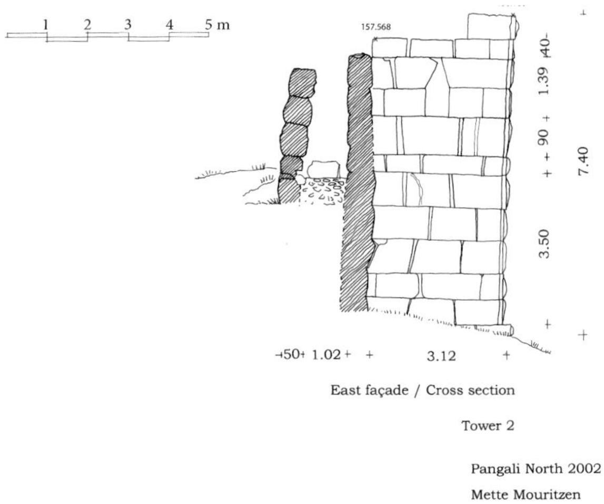

Plan VI *Pangali fortifications. North wall, east elevation of tower 2 and cross section through wall.*

Plan VII *Pangali fortifications. North wall, ground plan and north and south elevations of postern 2 and adjacent curtain wall; sections through postern 2.*

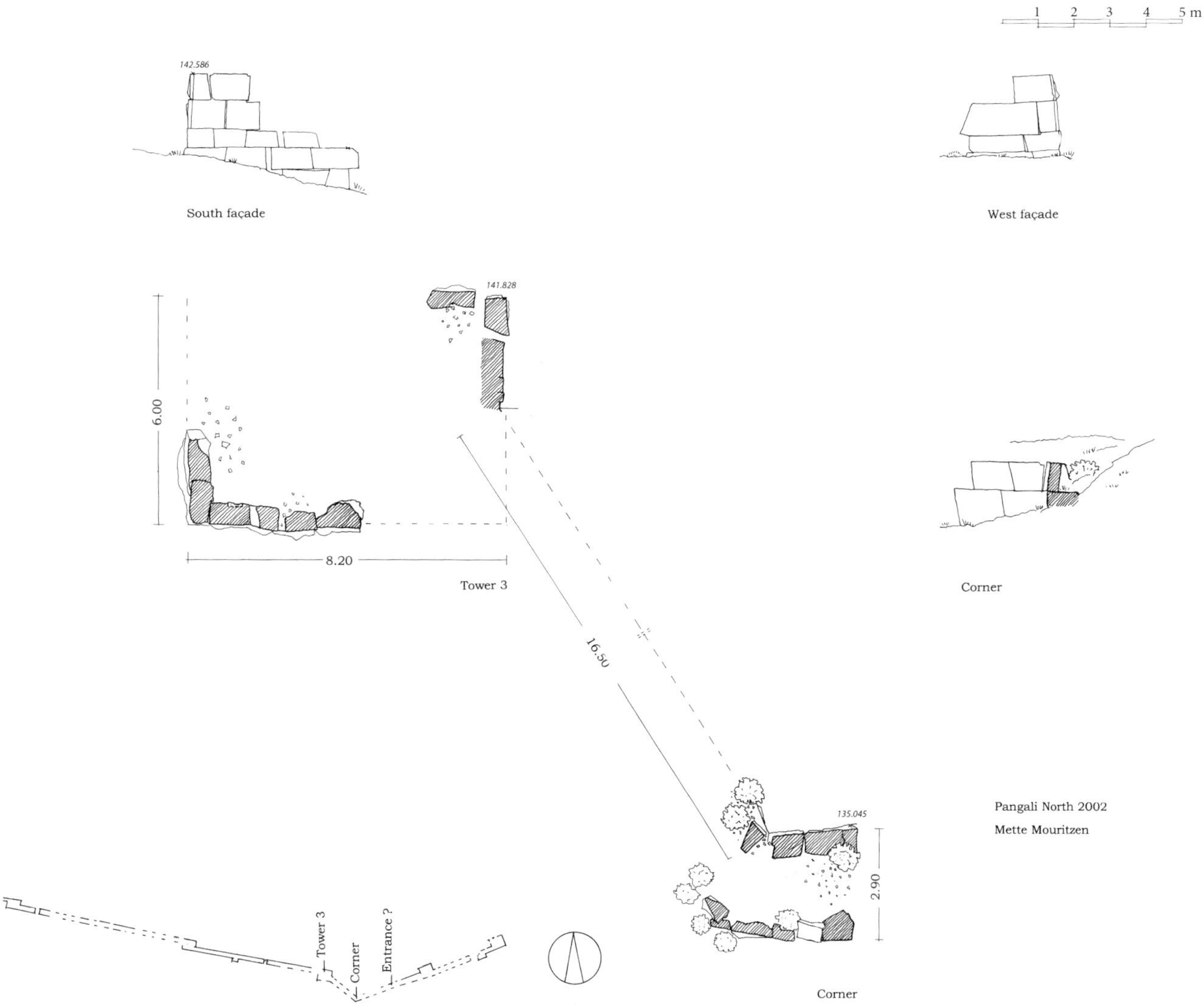

Plan VIII *Pangali fortifications. North wall, ground plan and south and west elevations of tower 3 and adjacent curtain wall.*

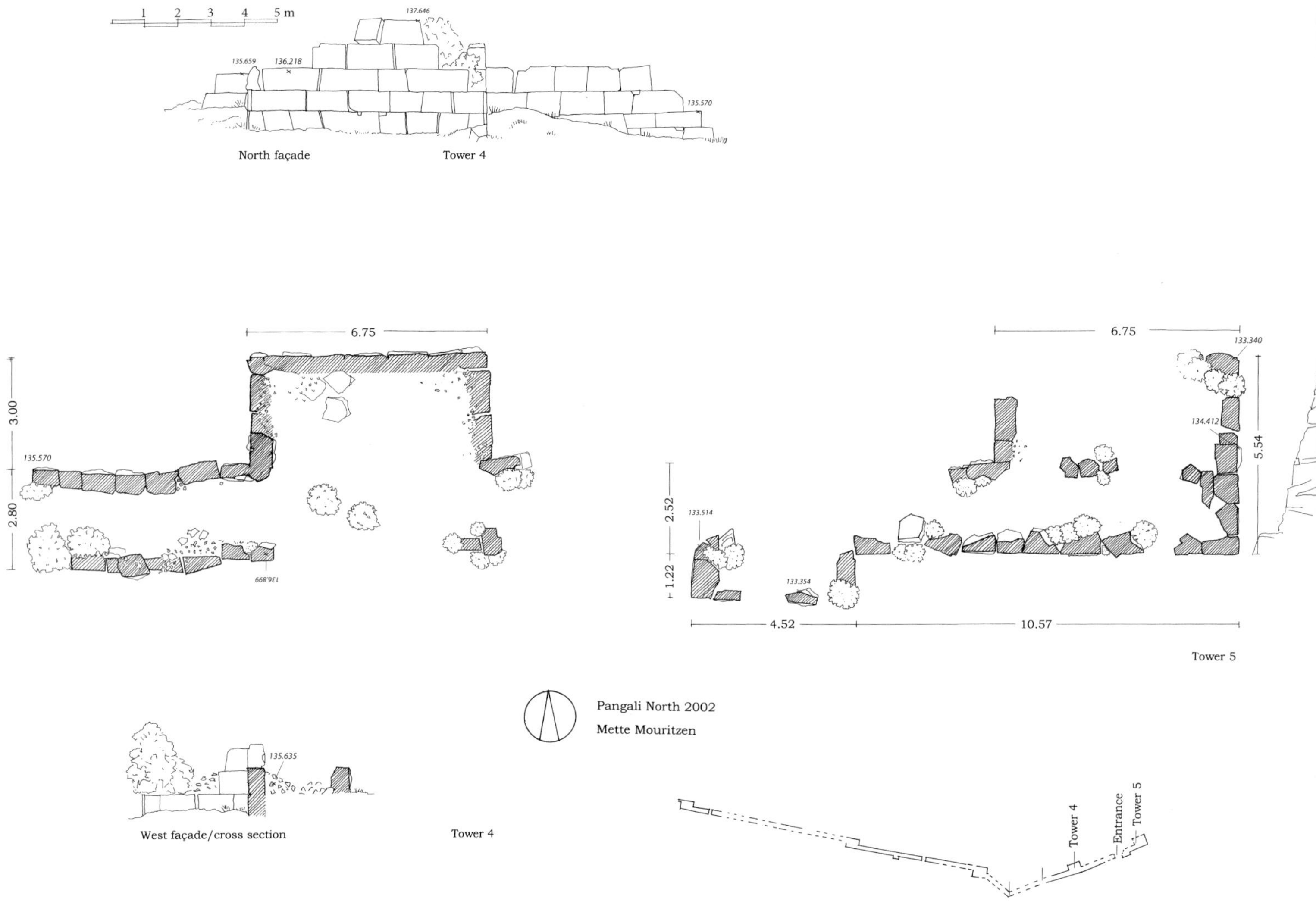

Plan IX *Pangali fortifications. North wall, ground plans of towers 4 and 5; north and west elevations of tower 4 plans.*

Plan X *Pangali fortifications. South wall, ground plan, elevation and section of south curtain wall, ground plan of main gate.* →

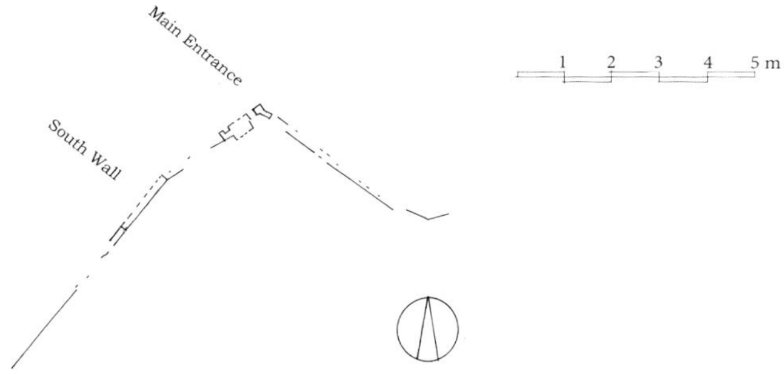

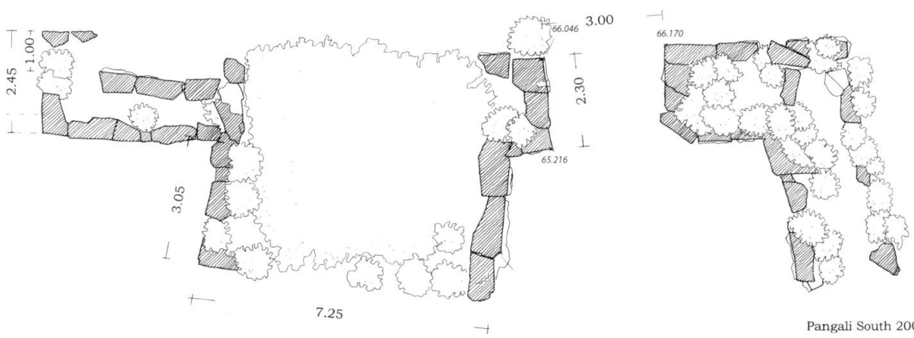

Main Entrance

Pangali South 2002
Mette Mouritzen

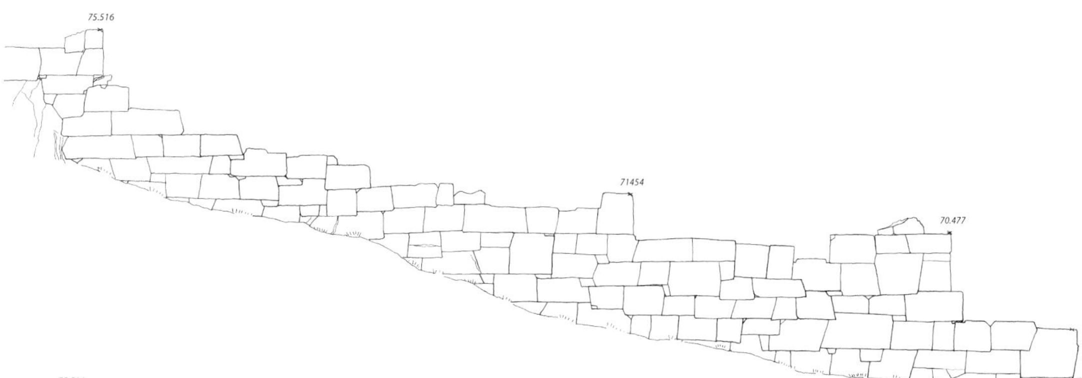

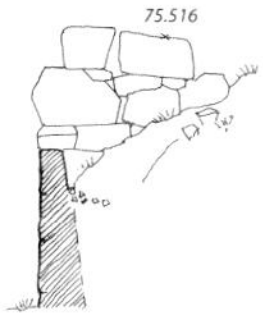

Section A A

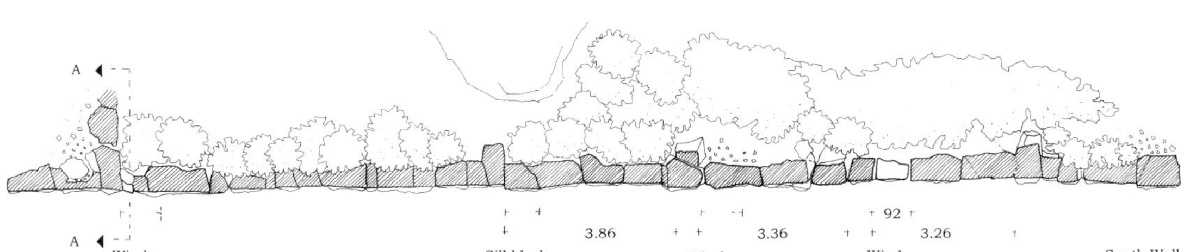